ENDANGERED and THREATENED WILDLIFE of NEW JERSEY

ENDANGERED and THREATENED WILDLIFE of NEW JERSEY

Edited by Bruce E. Beans and Larry Niles

RUTGERS UNIVERSITY PRESS
New Brunswick, New Jersey, and London

Library of Congress Cataloging-in-Publication Data
Endangered and threatened wildlife of New Jersey / edited by Bruce E. Beans
and Larry Niles.
    p.   cm.
    Includes bibliographical references (p.).
    ISBN 0-8135-3208-6 (alk. paper) — ISBN 0-8135-3209-4 (pbk. : alk. paper)
    1. Endangered species—New Jersey.   I. Beans, Bruce E.   II. Niles, Larry.
QL84.22.N5 E55 2003
591.68′09749—dc21

                                                                    2002031726

British Cataloguing-in-Publication information is available from the British Library.

Manufactured in China

Contents

Foreword, *by Robert L. McDowell*   ix

Acknowledgments   xi

Introduction   xiii

One   MAMMALS

Indiana Bat, *by Beth Hartmaier and Bruce E. Beans*   1
Allegheny Woodrat, *by Michael Valent*   7
Whales, *by Bruce E. Beans*   13
 Sperm Whale / Fin Whale / Sei Whale / Blue Whale / Humpback
 Whale / North Atlantic Northern Right Whale (or Black Right
 Whale)
Bobcat, *by Kris Schantz and Michael Valent*   23

Two   BIRDS
(All by Sherry Liguori unless otherwise indicated)

Pied-Billed Grebe   30
Black-Crowned Night-Heron   35
Yellow-Crowned Night-Heron   40
American Bittern   45
Northern Goshawk   50
Cooper's Hawk   56
Red-Shouldered Hawk   61
Bald Eagle, *by Steve Paturzo and Kathleen Clark*   67
Northern Harrier   73
Osprey   80
Peregrine Falcon   86
Black Rail   92
Piping Plover, *by Sherry Liguori and Dave Jenkins*   97
Upland Sandpiper   102

Red Knot, *by Larry Niles*   108

Roseate Tern   116

Least Tern, *by Dave Jenkins*   120

Black Skimmer   124

Barred Owl   129

Long-Eared Owl   133

Short-Eared Owl   137

Red-Headed Woodpecker   143

Sedge Wren   148

Loggerhead Shrike   151

Bobolink   156

Savannah Sparrow   160

Grasshopper Sparrow   164

Henslow's Sparrow   167

Vesper Sparrow   171

Three   REPTILES

Bog Turtle, *by Sherry Liguori and Jason Tesauro*   176

Wood Turtle, *by Sherry Liguori*   181

Marine Turtles, *by Bruce E. Beans*   185
Loggerhead Turtle / Leatherback Turtle / Kemp's Ridley Turtle /
Green Sea Turtle / Hawksbill Turtle

Corn Snake, *by Sherry Liguori*   193

Northern Pine Snake, *by David M. Golden and Dave Jenkins*   193

Queen Snake, *by David M. Golden*   201

Timber Rattlesnake, *by Kris Schantz and Michael Valent*   203

Four   AMPHIBIANS
(All by Sherry Liguori unless otherwise indicated)

Blue-Spotted Salamander, *by Sherry Liguori and Jason Tesauro*   210

Tremblay's Salamander   210

Eastern Tiger Salamander, *by Sherry Liguori and Kathleen Clark*   214

Long-Tailed Salamander   218

Eastern Mud Salamander   222

Pine Barrens Treefrog   224

Southern Gray Treefrog   228

Five   FISH

Shortnose Sturgeon, *by Jeanette Bowers-Altman*   232

Six   *INSECTS*

Northeastern Beach Tiger Beetle, *by Jeanette Bowers-Altman*   235
American Burying Beetle, *by Bruce E. Beans*   237
Lepidoptera *(all by David M. Golden unless otherwise indicated)*   241
Appalachian Grizzled Skipper   241
Arogos Skipper, *by David M. Golden and Jason Tesauro*   243
Bronze Copper   246
Mitchell's Satyr, *by Jason Tesauro*   248
Checkered White   250
Frosted Elfin   252
Silver-Bordered Fritillary   254

Seven   *BIVALVES: Freshwater Mussels*
by Jeanette Bowers-Altman   257

Dwarf Wedgemussel / Brook Floater / Green Floater / Yellow
Lampmussel / Eastern Lampmussel / Eastern Pondmussel / Tidewater
Mucket / Triangle Floater

Bibliography   267

Index   295

Foreword

Our Real Job Is to Keep New Jersey's Wildlife Off Our Endangered and Threatened Lists

I'm often asked why endangered and threatened species matter. In a state where ecotourism is a rapidly growing, multimillion-dollar industry, there are some extremely strong economic arguments that can be made on wildlife's behalf.

In the nation's most densely populated state, however, wildlife species serve an even more critical role: as front-line indicators of the condition of our environment. To cite just one example, the crash of certain bird populations, such as bald eagles, ospreys, and peregrine falcons, after the post–World War II introduction of DDT ultimately sounded alarms that led to the ban of the harmful pesticide.

Conversely, if you find a bog turtle, chances are good you've stumbled upon a wetland with extremely high water quality. That's also true of many species of freshwater mussels. In fact, Division of Fish and Wildlife biologists have identified a suite of wildlife species that function as key environmental indicators. The point is, every New Jersey citizen—whether or not he or she can identify an eastern tiger salamander, or would even care to do so—is interested in good water, clean air, and a healthy environment.

That's why the efforts of the Division's Endangered and Nongame Species Program (ENSP), which was established as part of the 1973 New Jersey Endangered and Nongame Species Act, are so critical. The species detailed in this book, and listed under the act, were only granted such protection after significant, demonstrable declines.

But, belying the impression and oft-heard criticism that being listed as an endangered or threatened species is a one-way ticket to oblivion, some of these species represent great success stories. For example, of the aforementioned raptors, bald eagles and osprey have rebounded magnificently, and since a pair of reintroduced peregrines established the first post-DDT nest east of the Mississippi River in New Jersey in 1980, the state's population has grown to 17 nesting pairs.

Other species, such as the Cooper's hawk, have also been upgraded from endangered to threatened, and several years ago great blue herons, little blue herons, and cliff swallows were removed from the threatened list.

But as development continues to alter and fragment wildlife habitat, the task continues to be quite difficult. Recently the ENSP documented declines in glossy ibis and the already threatened barred owls. And the list of endangered and threatened species continues to grow. The red knot, a migrating shorebird, was added to the threatened list in 2000, and during 2001 new groups of mussels and butterfly species, which never before had been listed, were added.

Indeed, as this book indicates, today many species face formidable challenges—challenges that can only be met by a partnership of our staff, working together with New Jersey's communities and citizens such as yourselves, to conserve our state's wildlife diversity.

In fact, our ultimate goal must be to prevent native species from ever becoming threatened or endangered. That can only be achieved by integrating the protection and management of *all* wildlife species and habitats, and maintaining the healthy and viable ecosystems critical to wildlife—and to our own well-being.

Robert L. McDowell
Former Director, New Jersey Division of Fish
and Wildlife

Acknowledgments

The editors would like to thank and acknowledge the contributions of the Department of Environmental Protection and the Division of Fish and Wildlife, especially the Endangered and Nongame Species Program staff, as well as all the consultants with whom the ENSP has contracted. The program also could not have accomplished all that it has without the volunteers, businesses, and corporations—including members of the Wildlife Conservation Corps' Citizen Scientist Program—who over the years have devoted so much time and effort on behalf of the state's endangered, threatened, and rare wildlife.

We'd also like to thank the citizens of New Jersey who, through their purchase of Conserve Wildlife license plates and state income tax check-offs, have provided the majority of financial support for the Endangered and Nongame Species Program. Kudos as well to the Conserve Wildlife Foundation (CWF); Linda Tesauro, CWF executive director; Keara Giannotti, CWF staff member; the CWF board of trustees and executive council; and to all the citizens, corporations, and foundations who have contributed to the CWF in order to provide the ENSP with critical funding.

In addition, for their longtime scientific guidance and sage counsel, we wish to thank the ENSP Advisory Committee: Chairperson Jane Morton-Galetto, James Applegate, Ph.D., Joanna Burger, Ph.D., Michael Catania, Emile DeVito, Janet Larson, Rick Lathrop, Ph.D., Dale Schweitzer, Ph.D., Jim Shissias, Clay Sutton, and all of the committee's former members, including recently retired Rich Kane and the late Robert Shomer, V.M.D.

For their help with the book itself, we wish to thank Michael Amaral of the U.S. Fish and Wildlife Service; Phil Clapham, George Liles, and Cheryl Ryder of the National Marine Fisheries Service; Bob Schoelkopf and Vikki Socha of the Marine Mammal Stranding Center; Sue Barco of the Virginia Marine Science Museum; as well as Sue Canale, Jim Dowdell, Vince Elia, Beth Hartmaier, Dave Iftner, Jerry Liguori, Kate McGuire, John C. O'Herron II, Steve Paturzo, Sharon Paul, Dale Schweitzer, Jim Sciascia, Eric Stiles, Pat and Clay Sutton, and Joan Walsh.

Proving, indeed, that an image can speak volumes, we are grateful for all the photographers who contributed their fine images to this book, including

Michael Amaral, Rudolf G. Arndt, R. and N. Bowers, Anja G. Burns, Rick Cech, H. Cruickshank, Chris Davidson, R. and S. Day, Saul Friess, Jane Morton-Galetto, Ryan Hagerty, C. E. Harold, D. R. Herr, Eugene Hester, Al Hicks, Robin Hunter, Joshua D. Ingram, G. M. Jett, Breck P. Kent, Richard Kuzminski, S. Maslowski, Dave Menke, A. Morris, Clay Myers, J. P. Myers, M. Patrikeev, Mark Payne, Blaine Rothauser, F. K. Schleicher, Brian E. Small, Jim Springer, Gary M. Stolz, Merlin D. Tuttle, T. J. Ulrich, T. Vezo, David Vogel, Wade Wander, Doug Wechsler, B. K. Wheeler, Chris Williams, James D. Young, and Robert Zappalorti.

For their invaluable help in gathering photographs, we would also like to thank Doug Wechsler of the Academy of Natural Science's VIREO project, Gene Nieminen and LaVonda Walton of the U.S. Fish and Wildlife Service, Kristin Hay of Bat Conservation International, John Alderman of the North Carolina Wildlife Resources Commission, and John O'Herron II.

We also wish to thank all the authors of these species accounts, in particular former ENSP staffer Sherry Liguori, who profiled a plurality of the state's endangered and threatened species, as well as Jeff Tash and Pete Winkler, who skillfully transformed species' breeding data into the statewide maps that accompany the accounts.

With deep gratitude we also wish to thank Lucent Technologies and the New Jersey Education Association for their strong financial underwriting of this book.

Finally, we are indebted to the Rutgers University Press and its staff, particularly Helen Hsu, Nicole Lokach Manganaro, Audra Wolfe, and copy editor Alice Calaprice, for their fine work in publishing this volume.

Introduction

New Jersey's Outstanding Natural Diversity

As citizens of New Jersey, we often endure the insults of visitors whose sole experience of the state comes from trips on the New Jersey Turnpike or a glimpse from the skyscrapers of New York. Is it deserved? We do have the highest population density and the most Superfund sites in the country. And despite all the jokes, we do measure our own travels by turnpike exits and highway interchanges more than residents of any other state.

But if only our detractors could see the New Jersey that our wildlife sees, they would know such attitudes are undeserved. Every corner of the state harbors a natural heritage of such value that it attracts birders and other naturalists from around the world. Because the state is situated at a biological crossroads unique to our geographic region, its wildlife varies tremendously across a small land area. Species such as the Allegheny woodrat, eastern tiger

High on the Ben Franklin Bridge between Camden and Philadelphia, ENSP principal zoologist Kathy Clark bands a peregrine falcon chick. © Doug Wechsler/VIREO

salamander, Pine Barrens treefrog, southern gray treefrog, and arogos skipper are at or near the northern limit of their range in New Jersey, while species as diverse as the northern goshawk and the blue-spotted salamander are at or near the southern limit of their range in the state. Few people realize that our waters and marshes are among the last in the winter to freeze and the first in the spring to thaw, attracting a range of birds from bald eagles to woodcocks looking for an easy winter.

Although less rural than many states, New Jersey harbors a wide variety of habitats. From the barrier beaches and coastal marshes of the ocean edge, through the floodplain forests and barrens of pine, across the fertile rolling hills of the piedmont, to the highlands, ridges, and valleys of northwestern New Jersey, the state is a cornucopia of wildlife. With over five hundred species, New Jersey ranks as one of the most diverse wildlife habitats in the country.

Our natural heritage doesn't stop at our borders, either. New Jersey is crucial to the lives of species that fly the breadth of the globe. Red knots and other shorebird populations that winter as far south as Tierra del Fuego rely on horseshoe crab eggs on the Delaware Bay to fuel their flights to their Arctic breeding grounds. Without the eel grass and sea lettuce of the Atlantic Coast, wintering Atlantic brant would starve. Without the food and shelter the forests and fields of the lower Cape May peninsula provide, the migration of primarily juvenile hawks and owls across the broad and sometimes treacherous Delaware Bay might be jeopardized. This is to say nothing about the several hundred passerine, butterfly, and dragonfly species that use our ocean coast and mountain ridges as a migratory highway.

An Unparalleled Conservation Challenge

Our wildlife diversity is equally matched by a rich cultural history. Each significant habitat sprouts a unique and diverse community of wildlife that has endured centuries of settlement and use. From the American Revolution and the industrial revolution of past centuries to the technological and informational revolutions of today, human history and natural history have been inextricably intertwined in New Jersey. While ecological purists who seek "untamed" nature might be put off by this history, most of us appreciate the enviable and interesting environment created by the contrast of human culture and natural history. It heightens our outdoor experience and increases the inherent natural value of the land. Unfortunately, it also makes the job of stewardship all the more important and difficult.

We now race to protect our rich cultural and natural history. Our major opponent: sprawl. Tentacles of development spread across the state in all directions from the New York and Philadelphia metropolitan areas, following I-80, I-55, the Garden State Parkway, the New Jersey Turnpike, the Atlantic City Expressway, and all the smaller roads in between. We've lost a bewildering amount of land in the last 20 years, at least 20,000 acres every year, and the end of sprawl is nowhere in sight.

ENSP principal zoologist Mike Valent prepares to release a live-trapped Allegheny woodrat at the base of the N.J. Palisades.
© Blaine Rothauser

Making matters worse, the damage is far greater than the sum of the developed area. Have you ever wondered what happens to wildlife when we destroy a valuable habitat? Some die outright, crushed by a bulldozer or as easy prey to a hungry dog or hawk. Most flee like war refugees. When they can, they squeeze into adjacent, often suboptimal habitat, sometimes squeezing out weaker or younger wildlife in the process. When they do move into more densely developed areas, they are more at risk from speeding autos or predators. Those that can escape, do so, sometimes just flying away and never coming back.

Over time, the damage from development continues to grow worse. Each new house or business is accompanied by a suite of animals—raccoons, crows, blue jays, feral cats to name a few—that tolerates or even prospers from development. They thrive on open trash cans or food at the back door and then fan out, destroying nests, taking the best breeding sites, or killing inexperienced young. Sometimes the effect is obvious. For example, a single house cat can depopulate ground- or shrub-nesting birds from acres of otherwise suitable habitat; with densities of more than one hundred cats per square mile in some areas of New Jersey, the effect is pervasive.

But sometimes the effect is less obvious. In the wake of development, great horned owls will out-compete barred owls, which rely solely on prey found in unbroken forest. If we break up a forest into 10-acre housing lots, 10 years later—even if most of the woods remain—the barred owls will be gone and the night will only be filled with the *hoo, hoo, hoo* calls of great horned owls.

Conservation Initiatives Renowned Nationwide

We face a bewildering array of problems that could make any biologist or nature lover want to move to Maine. Fortunately, however, New Jersey has become a leader in land stewardship and protection measures. The Governor's Million-Acre Acquisition Program will create more public land in New Jersey than in most eastern states. Our Land Use Regulatory Program strictly protects wetlands and surrounding uplands. After 30 years, the Pinelands Commission still impresses conservationists around the world for its strength and diligence in protecting the Pinelands National Reserve. The Department of Environmental Protection's Watershed Management and Indicators programs surpass federal mandates and offer hope for transferring protection authority for water and watersheds to community governments, which could help promote local conservation and stewardship.

In this tradition of strong protection, the New Jersey Endangered and Nongame Species Program (ENSP), which was established in 1973, has distinguished itself among wildlife programs across the country and throughout the world. Our biologists are widely known for their expertise and innovative projects on ospreys, peregrine falcons, bald eagles, migrant passerines and shorebirds, piping plovers, beach-nesting birds, rattlesnakes, and bog turtles. Our database includes more animal sightings than that of most states, even those states many times our size. We have 17 years of shorebird data, 27 years of colonial waterbird data, 19 years of piping plover data, even 19 years of Allegheny woodrat data. We have conducted a management program for bald eagles for 27 years, osprey for 30, beach-nesting birds for 22, eastern tiger salamanders for 25, and bog turtles for 21 years.

This experience gives our program a distinctive depth that has led to tangible success. Our bald eagle population has grown from one nesting pair in 1980 to 28 active pairs in 2002. Peregrine falcons have increased from 0 to 17 pairs, ospreys from 68 to 340 pairs, and ospreys went off the state endangered list to that of threatened status. Despite New Jersey's population density and relatively small size, we have the third most peregrine falcons and fourth

ENSP principal zoologist Dave Jenkins (right) leads a crew constructing a predator exclosure around a piping plover nest. © Clay Myers

most bald eagles among northeastern states. We stemmed the decline of piping plovers and now support 120 pairs.

Some of our success comes from simply locating unknown populations. We now know of far more bog turtle breeding sites than we did a decade ago. Nine years ago, scientists assumed the dwarf wedgemussel had vanished from New Jersey, but since then biologists from the ENSP, the state's Natural Heritage Program, and the U.S. Geological Survey discovered three new populations.

Even so, the loss of habitat is relentless. It takes more than innovative species protection to overcome the tightening grip of development. Our experience has taught us that plans for short-term piecemeal protection, developed without the help of citizens and local communities, could never succeed. We needed a long-term, large-scale protection strategy.

The Landscape Project: A Guidepost for the Future

The Landscape Project, the ENSP's most ambitious and challenging conservation project, grew from this realization. After years of fine-tuning, peer review, and data collection, our biologists have created a groundbreaking map of critical habitat for all of New Jersey's endangered and threatened species. The computer-generated map uses the Department of Environmental Protection's (DEP's) state-of-the-art Geographic Information System and combines it with all we know about New Jersey wildlife and wildlife habitats. We started with a habitat map based on satellite imagery interpreted by Rutgers University's Center for Remote Sensing and Spatial Analysis. We next methodically defined every important patch of forest, field, and wetland in the state, and finally applied a new system that ranks the value of these habitats based on the suitability for, and presence of, rare species.

The result: for the first time, thanks to the Landscape Project, the citizens of New Jersey can see where the most important areas for wildlife occur. Local and state agencies can now use these maps to avoid development conflicts, or can make scientifically informed decisions about acquiring public lands. These maps will truly make a difference as local, state, and federal agencies develop regulatory, planning, and acquisition strategies.

When first viewed, the Landscape Project mapping is startling. Compared to the statewide land-use map, with its gaping wounds from sprawl splashed nearly everywhere, the landscape map presents us with a remarkable view of all that remains. The amount of critical habitat still in existence surprised even us, because we know it represents only the best patches, those that satisfied minimum size or species-presence criteria. Many of these most special habitats still remain. Clearly, there is room for hope for the state's rare species.

We hope that you'll use this volume to get to know every endangered and threatened species in the state. You'll learn what each species needs and how those needs can be met. You will also learn that much work needs to be done if we are to preserve our rich wildlife legacy for future New Jersey generations.

And we cannot stress *we* enough. The task before us is far greater than what the ENSP, the Division of Fish and Wildlife, and the DEP can accomplish alone. But with your help, involvement, and interest, it can be done. We must succeed because these species are windows that provide a unique view of the New Jersey you can't see from the turnpike—the state that mostly exists for us, its residents. All those colored patches in the Landscape Project maps represent more than just habitat for endangered and threatened species. These patches are the stream corridor that a child uses to explore or understand nature, or the tranquil woodlot treasured by local citizens who don't want it developed. They represent the array of open spaces that a community folds into its master plan to create an atmosphere that suggests Europe—where the demarcations between town and country are more sharply defined—than Coney Island.

As we all try to plan a New Jersey that our children will be proud to call home, these species and their habitats—some of the most fascinating, interesting animals and natural places on the face of the earth—are our dual guideposts.

Written primarily by ENSP staff biologists, this book contains information about each of the state's endangered and threatened species, arranged in taxonomic order within the following classes: mammals, birds, reptiles, amphibians, fish (currently only one species, the shortnosed sturgeon), insects, and bivalves (freshwater mussels). Each entry discusses the species' current state and federal status; its identification characteristics, distribution, habitat, diet, and breeding biology; conservation measures that have been undertaken; limiting factors and threats to the species' recovery; and recommendations to speed recovery. The accounts are accompanied by photographs of each species and, in some cases, its habitat. Maps illustrate the current and/or historic in-state ranges (breeding ranges unless otherwise

Larry Niles, ENSP's chief, prepares to capture an eaglet for banding at the Stow Creek nest near the Delaware Bay in Cumberland County. © Clay Myers

noted) of all the listed species. For all the accounts, reference sources are listed at the back of the book.

Finally, a brief word about the meaning of "threatened" and "endangered" species. For New Jersey, endangered species are those whose prospects for survival in the state are in immediate danger because of a loss or change in habitat, overexploitation, predation, competition, disease, or contamination. Assistance is needed to prevent future extinction in New Jersey. Threatened species are those that may become endangered if conditions surrounding them begin or continue to deteriorate.

Any species found in the state that is listed as endangered or threatened by the federal government automatically is listed on the state endangered or threatened lists. However, species listed as endangered or threatened by New Jersey might not also be listed by the federal government because—either regionally or nationally—the species is doing better outside of New Jersey. For example, several years ago the federal government declared the peregrine falcon recovered in the East and removed it from the federal threatened list. But it is still considered endangered in New Jersey. The state recently also added another category, "species of special concern," which indicates that, while it is not endangered or threatened, the species bears watching. The federal government also maintains some similar categories, such as Migratory Nongame Bird of Management Concern, which on occasion you will find listed in this book.

How You Can Help Keep Wildlife in New Jersey's Future

- *"Check-Off for Wildlife" on your state income tax form.* These tax-deductible contributions are one of the Endangered and Nongame Species Program's primary funding sources and are dedicated by law to the protection of endangered and nongame wildlife.

- *Make a direct donation.* Your tax-deductible contribution made out to the Conserve Wildlife Foundation helps ENSP meet the challenges of wildlife preservation. Send your check to the Conserve Wildlife Foundation of New Jersey, P.O. Box 1641, Toms River, NJ 08753-1641.

- *Purchase a Wildlife Conservation license plate.* Eighty percent of the $50 goes directly to preserving New Jersey's endangered wildlife. License plates can be purchased at all DMV agencies, from any New Jersey automobile dealer, or through the mail by calling (609) 292-6500.

- *Become a Wildlife Conservation Corps Citizen Scientist.* The time and talents of these volunteers are crucial to many ENSP projects. To be a part of the WCC Citizen Scientist Program, contact us at the phone, website, or address listed below for an application.

- *Join our Speaker's Bureau.* Help us spread the word about the ENSP by giving slide presentations to interested groups.

- *Support the Marine Mammal Stranding Center.* The center, which cares for marine mammals and sea turtles stranded along the state's beaches, is located in Brigantine. For information, call (609) 266-0538 or visit the center's website at *www.mmsc.org.*

- *Report sightings of endangered and threatened species.* For a reporting form, go to *www.njfishandwildlife.com* and click on "endangered and threatened species."

- *Visit the New Jersey Division of Fish and Wildlife's website* at *www.njfishandwildlife.com* for more information about the Endangered and Nongame Species Program.

- *Write to us* at ENSP, Division of Fish and Wildlife, P.O. Box 400, Trenton, NJ 08625 or *call us* at (609) 292-9400.

One MAMMALS

Indiana Bat, *Myotis sodalis*
Status: State: Endangered   Federal: Endangered

Identification

The Indiana bat is a medium-sized member of the genus *Myotis*. The head and body length ranges from 41 to 49 mm (1.6–1.8 in.), while the forearm length ranges from 35 to 41 mm (1.3–1.6 in.) (U.S. Fish and Wildlife Service 1999). The species closely resembles the little brown bat (*Myotis lucifugus*) and the northern long-eared bat (*Myotis septentrionalis*). The Indiana bat has a strongly keeled calcar, a foot spur of cartilage that supports the membrane between the foot and tail. Its hind feet tend to be small and delicate with fewer, shorter hairs (that do not extend beyond the toenails) than those of the little brown and northern long-eared bats. The fur lacks luster, and the ears and wing membranes have a dull appearance and flat coloration that do not contrast

Indiana bats hibernate in dense clusters.
© Merlin D. Tuttle/ Bat Conservation International

with the fur. The chest and belly fur is lighter than the dull, pinkish brown fur on the back, but does not contrast as strongly as does that of the little brown bat or northern long-eared bat. The skull is marked lengthwise by a small sagital crest, and the brain case tends to be smaller, lower, and narrower than that of the little brown bat. The little brown's fur is bronze, and, on average, it has a longer body and weighs more than the Indiana.

Distribution

Indiana bats are found over most of the eastern half of the United States, from Michigan, New York, and Connecticut in the north, southward to Florida and Alabama. Its range stretches westward to Iowa, Missouri, Arkansas, and Oklahoma. In New Jersey, it is one of eight species of bats considered to be regular residents.

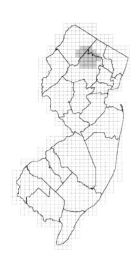

Historically, caves provided hibernating habitat for bats. In the 1800s, more than 10 million Indiana bats hibernated in Kentucky's Mammoth Cave alone (Tuttle 1999). But today, most caves are subject to human disturbance and therefore are not suitable for use by bats. In many parts of the country, including New Jersey, abandoned mines and tunnels have replaced natural caves as the primary winter habitat for bats because they are often unsafe to enter or inaccessible to people. In New Jersey, the largest known bat hibernaculum—and the only one in which Indiana bats are known to hibernate—is the Hibernia Mine in Rockaway Township, Morris County. More than 30,000 bats, including an estimated two to three dozen Indiana bats, were counted clinging to the walls during a February 1999 survey.

Indiana bats have also been captured in mist nets outside the Mt. Hope Mine, a deep, vertical-shaft mine near the Hibernia Mine in Morris County. A postlactating female was also captured at the Picatinny Arsenal, which is also located in Morris County. Recently, wintering populations of Indiana bats were found in New York State mines. However, the only large hibernating populations of Indiana bats are found in Indiana, Missouri, and Kentucky.

Habitat

Indiana bats hibernate in limestone caves and open, abandoned mine shafts (hibernaculum) from October to April. *M. sodalis* is highly selective of hibernation sites. Medium-sized caves with large, shallow passageways are preferred. During midwinter, ideal conditions inside caves include an average temperature of 3°–6°C (37°–43°F) (Evans et al. 1992) and a relative humidity of 87% (Barbour and Davis 1969). Throughout hibernation, bats periodically move to the coldest parts of the cave. Some individuals also remain active, awakening approximately every eight to ten days. These bats may return to any of the hibernating clusters (Barbour and Davis 1969).

When Indiana bats hibernate together, their densities can range from 300 to 484 bats per square foot (Tuttle 1999). They often hibernate with other species. At the Hibernia Mine in New Jersey, Indiana bats hibernate primarily with little brown bats, as well as big brown (*Eptesicus fuscus*), northern long-eared, and eastern pipistrel (*Pipistrellus subflavus*) bats.

During the summer, females occupy maternity roosts of up to 100 females in riparian and floodplain forests under the loose bark of dead or dying trees. They have also been found under the loose bark of living trees and in cavities of dead trees. The use of upland habitats is also becoming more common for some populations. A study by Garner and Gardner (1992) indicated that 75% of roost trees were upland species, while the other 25% were floodplain species. Species used as roost sites include, but are not exclusive to, American elm (*Ulmus americana*), slippery elm (*Ulmus rubra*), bitternut hickory (*Carya cordiformis*), shagbark hickory (*Carya ovata*), sweet pignut hickory (*Carya ovalis*), northern red oak (*Quercus rubra*), post oak (*Quercus stellata*), white oak (*Quercus alba*), silver maple (*Acer saccharinum*), sugar maple (*Acer saccharum*), cottonwood (*Populus deltoides*), green ash (*Fraxinus pennsylvanica*), and sassafras (*Sassafras albidum*) (Evans et al. 1992). One colony was also found roosting in the cavity of a dead sycamore (*Platanus occidentalis*) (Kurta et al. 1993).

Maternity colonies may establish both primary and alternate roost sites, which differ in location and in the number of bats using the roost site. Since the temperature of the roost site is important, primary roosts are located in areas that can be heated by the sun, such as in openings or at the edges of forests. Alternate roost sites are also located in forest interiors and are used when temperatures are above normal or when it is raining (USFWS 1999). During the summer, males roost alone or in small groups, usually near female roosts. However, some adult males occupy caves during the summer as well (USFWS 1999; Harvey 1992).

Trees located within the floodplain and along the sides of streams are particularly important in providing areas in which to forage for insects. Open bodies of water, such as lakes and reservoirs, are also used as foraging areas. During the summer, females and juveniles forage in riparian and floodplain areas. Pregnant and lactating females also prefer open bodies of water and have been known to fly up to 2.4 km (1.5 mi.) from upland roosts. Foraging also occurs in the canopy of upland trees and over clearings with early successional vegetation (USFWS 1999).

Diet

Indiana bats eat a variety of flying aquatic and terrestrial insects found along rivers or lakes and in upland areas. Foraging ranges differ slightly for males and females, and also depend on reproduction and age (Garner and Gardner 1992). Postlactating adult females exhibit the largest foraging range and prefer floodplain areas with closed (greater than 80%) canopies. In general, all bats, regardless of sex or age, prefer floodplain forests with closed canopies (Garner and Gardner 1992). Males are known to travel up to 4.2 km (2.6 mi.) while foraging (USFWS 1999).

Breeding Biology

Caves provide important locations for mating and hibernation. Bats mate at night from September to mid-October during autumn swarming, with most mating occurring during the first ten days of October. Mating takes place on

Indiana bat in flight.
© Merlin D. Tuttle/
Bat Conservation
International

the ceilings of large rooms near the entrances to hibernation caves. Females begin hibernation almost immediately after mating, while most males stay active into November and even December (Evans et al. 1992).

Indiana bats reproduce through an interesting feature called "delayed fertilization." After mating, females store the sperm through the winter and become pregnant in spring soon after they come out of hibernation. Beginning in April, bats move to summer roosts, with the females leaving first. Females can travel long distances to establish roost trees and forage for food. A study by Garner and Gardner (1992) indicates that bats return to the same roost sites each year, with females using the same trees to give birth. Research in the Midwest also indicates that bats travel north to summer roosts, although they may move in other directions as well (USFWS 1999). The females, which have a relatively low birthrate, generally produce one or sometimes two young pups per year after reaching their nursing colonies.

Migration back to hibernacula begins in August, with bats arriving in late August to early September (Barbour and Davis 1969). During autumn swarming, males establish roosts during the day. Research in Kentucky indicates that bats roost within 2.4 km (1.5 mi.) of their hibernaculum, while a study done in West Virginia found bats within 5.6 km (3.5 mi.) of hibernaculum. In both cases, roosts were located on ridge tops, in areas exposed to direct sunlight (USFWS 1999).

Status and Conservation

The Indiana bat was listed as endangered by the federal government in 1967 because of declines in their numbers that were documented at their seven major hibernacula in the Midwest. It was automatically added to the New Jersey endangered species list following passage of the state's Endangered and Nongame Species Act in 1973. At the time of the federal listing, about 85% of the entire population hibernated at only seven sites, and fully half of the entire population hibernated in only two caves.

Human disturbance at these sites was considered to be a major factor in the bats' population decline. Since then, steps have been taken to protect most of the major hibernating sites, as well as minor sites such as Hibernia Mine. In Indiana, bat numbers in 2001 appeared to be stable to slightly increasing. In Kentucky, their numbers appeared to be declining, but not so rapidly as in Missouri. There, the USFWS termed the situation "catastrophic." Between 1975 and 1995, the number of Indiana bats at the major hibernating sites declined from more than 120,000 to nearly 20,000. In the wake of such declines, some researchers believe the Indiana bat might be extirpated from Missouri— and possibly Iowa, where most of the bats hibernating in Missouri spend their summers—within the next 10 to 20 years (USFWS 2001).

Throughout the range of the Indiana bat, most of the major caves and abandoned mines that are used for hibernation have been gated or protected in other ways to guard against human disturbance during winter.

Limiting Factors and Threats

Indiana bats are considered extremely vulnerable to human disturbance, in part because of their habit of living in large numbers in only a few caves. In the Midwest, the density of hibernating bats can range from 300 to 484 bats per square foot (.09 m), with some of the most important caves supporting over 80,000 Indiana bats. Thus a significant portion of the total population can be affected by just one event. Episodes of large numbers of deaths of Indiana bats have occurred due to human disturbance at hibernacula.

Cave commercialization drives bats away, and any gating that prevents access or alters the airflow temperature, humidity, and amount of light is harmful. In some areas, trees that can be used as roost sites during the summer are

Portrait of an Indiana bat. © Merlin D. Tuttle/Bat Conservation International

no longer plentiful, and the habitat that Indiana bats use during the summer has been degraded and eliminated due to forest fragmentation. This may have caused declines in local situations.

Pesticide usage can also limit the supply of insects and affect the quality of that food source. According to the USFWS, the population declines that continue today may be due to pesticide use. It is possible that the bats may be eating contaminated insects, drinking contaminated water, or absorbing chemicals when feeding in areas that have been recently treated with pesticides.

The bats' low birthrate of one to two young per year, combined with the large number of adult deaths, is also a limiting factor. Since so few young are born each year, it takes a long time to replace lost individuals.

Recommendations

In 1994, the ENSP successfully negotiated an agreement with the owners of the Hibernia Mine that permitted the installation of a special bat conservation gate. Soon afterward, the site was acquired by the state's Green Acres program and became part of the Division of Fish and Wildlife's Wildcat Ridge Wildlife Management Area. In addition to conducting biennial surveys there, the ENSP continues to search for and protect additional mines and tunnels that support wintering bat populations.

The state's Freshwater Wetland Protection Act can also play a vital role in protecting the Indiana bats' summer habitat, since streamside forests are used for roosting during the summer foraging season. The act requires that wetlands that provide habitat for endangered species be given a classification of "exceptional resource value wetlands." The U.S. Fish and Wildlife Service has determined that bats are present within an 8 km (5 mi.) radius of hibernacula sites from April 1 through November 15. Therefore, the USFWS recommends that all wetlands within an 8 km (5 mi.) radius of hibernacula be given an exceptional resource value. An exceptional resource value classification provides a 45.7 m (150 ft.) buffer adjacent to wetlands. Thus, it is possible to protect vital Indiana bat habitat on both public and private lands that can be used for roost sites.

Overall, ideal summer habitat is characterized by deciduous forest with at least 30% canopy closure, with permanent water available within a 1.0 km (0.63 mi.) radius and suitable roost trees located within a 0.4 km (0.25 mi.) radius. However, deciduous forest with at least 5% cover can also provide suitable habitat. Optimal densities of roost trees (greater than 9 in. dbh, or diameter at breast height, 4.5 ft. [1.37 m] aboveground) are 27 trees per acre in upland habitats and 17 trees per acre in floodplain habitats. However, lower densities of potential roost trees can also provide suitable habitat (Garner and Gardner 1992).

Certain conditions must also be considered in determining which trees are appropriate roost sites. These include whether the tree is dead or alive, the quantity of loose or peeling bark, the amount of direct sunlight the tree receives and its proximity to other trees, water sources, and foraging areas

(USFWS 1999). Ideally, at least 25% of the tree's bark should be loose and/or peeling (Garner and Gardner 1992). Trees exposed on their east-southeast and south-southwest sides receive adequate sunlight to warm maternity roosts, which is important for the development of the young. Maternity roosts are generally close together (within a few meters of each other), although some are several kilometers apart.

Since *M. sodalis* is known to return to the same roost sites each year, preserving this habitat is critical to the species' survival. Although *M. sodalis* has exhibited the ability to adapt when roost sites are lost, it is still important to preserve several roost sites in an area to maintain their success (USFWS 1999). Bats prefer mature forests with mostly closed canopies for primary roost sites and insect foraging. They also prefer trees that are close to intermittent streams.

In addition, *M. sodalis* tends to avoid noncontiguous forest fragments, forested areas with open canopies, open pastures, and areas close to paved roads as roost sites. In particular, reproductively active females avoid paved roads, with roost sites averaging 1,500 m (4,921 ft.) from paved roads. Adult males averaged 930 m (3,051 ft.) from paved roads (Garner and Gardner 1992). Therefore, it is important not only to preserve roost sites, but also to provide a buffer from highways and other paved roads. *M. sodalis* also uses areas of interior forest for alternate roost sites and riparian forest and stream corridors for travel and foraging. More research is needed to determine the specific summer roost requirements of both males and females, their migration and foraging habits, and reasons for their decline.

Beth Hartmaier and Bruce E. Beans

Allegheny Woodrat, *Neotoma floridana magister*
Status: State: Endangered   Federal: Candidate species

Identification

The Allegheny woodrat is a medium-sized rodent that superficially resembles the Norway rat, *Rattus norvegicus,* an introduced species that is common in urban areas and around farms. The Allegheny woodrat is most easily distinguished from the Norway rat by its larger, naked ears and its hairy, bicolor tail that is dark gray above and white below. Norway rats have scaly tails that are very sparsely haired. The woodrat's new winter pelage is a buffy gray color heavily overlaid with black. The hair along the midline is darker than that on the sides. The throat, belly, and feet are white with creamy buff armpits (Hamilton 1963). During the winter months the pelage is slightly darker and longer, fading to dull gray and brownish by March. Woodrats have four toes on the front feet and five on the rear. The sexes are identical in pelage color. Females have four mammae.

A longitudinal strip having little hair runs the length of the ventral side. Glands located along this strip exude a strong-smelling oily pheromone during the breeding season (Poole 1940).

The head and body length in adults ranges from 20 to 23 cm (8–9 in.). The tails are shorter than the total head and body length and range from 15 to 20.3 cm (6–8 in.). Adult woodrats range in body weight from 200 to 385 gm (7–13.5 oz.). Adult males typically attain weights greater than 300 gm (10.5 oz.) whereas adult females rarely exceed 250 gm (8.8 oz.).

Distribution

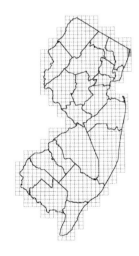

Allegheny woodrats occur primarily along the Appalachian Mountains from the Tennessee River north through most of Tennessee and Kentucky, extreme southern Indiana and Ohio, western North Carolina and Virginia, all of West Virginia, portions of western Maryland, most of the central and northeastern portions of Pennsylvania, northern New Jersey, and formerly southeastern New York.

Woodrats have been declining and disappearing from areas in the northern part of their range. Woodrat populations have been extirpated in New York since the 1980s. In Pennsylvania, woodrats have disappeared from about a third of their former range. Isolated populations now occur in New Jersey, Ohio, and Maryland (LoGiudice 2000).

Habitat

Allegheny woodrats typically occur in rocky areas associated with mountain ridges such as cliffs, caves, talus slopes, and rocky fissures. The rocky barrens where they den are generally devoid of vegetation with the exception of the occasional tree that manages to survive among the rocks. Active primarily at night, woodrats leave the security of their rocky dens to visit adjacent areas to feed on the available vegetation. In general, food is less important in habitat selection than is cover. Rock outcrops must have numerous deep fissures and overhanging rocks and ledges.

In New Jersey, Allegheny woodrats occur in extensive talus fields at the base of rock outcrops. They are typically found in talus fields having large-sized boulders (greater than 4 ft., or 1.25 m, in diameter). Vegetative associations include birch (*Betula* spp.)/chestnut oak (*Quercus prinus*) forests, scattered birch, oaks, and shrubs with herbaceous plants at the base of slopes. The exotic paulownia (*Paulownia tomentosa*) tree is one of the dominant trees found growing among the talus slopes of the Palisades, the site of New Jersey's last remaining woodrat population.

Diet

The diet of the Allegheny woodrat is a varied one that is based on observations of food caches. It has been reported to consist mainly of various parts of most of the plant species found in its domain (Poole 1940). Researchers have reported the woodrats' food as various fruits and berries, including dogwood (*Cornus* spp.), blackberry (*Rubus* spp.), American mountain ash (*Sorbus americana*), wild cherries (*Prunus* spp.), wild grape (*Vitis* spp.), and shadberry (*Amelanchier* spp.). Others have observed the fruits and stalks of pokeweed and sassafras (*Sassafras* spp.), fungi, ferns, nuts, rhododendron (*Rhododendron* spp.), and a host of other plants. These are often left in green condition on the rocks, which suggests a hay-making practice similar to that of the pika (*Ochotona princeps*) (Hamilton and Whitaker 1979).

Stomach contents of a few individuals contained hemlock (*Tsuga canadensis*), black birch (*Betula lenta*), chestnut (*Castanea dentata*), scrub oak (*Quercus ilicifolia*), flowering dogwood (*Cornus florida*), and apple (*Pyrus malus*). Laboratory experiments have suggested that woodrats discriminate between food items based on perishability and make decisions about what to eat and what to store accordingly (Reichman 1988).

Woodrats are well known for their propensity to collect many different kinds of objects from their environment. This has earned the species the nickname of packrat. They have been observed to collect such items as bones, feathers, foil, coins, nails, rubber bands, shotgun shells, and dung of various animals (Poole 1940). Several researchers have reported finding the dung of other species in and around woodrat nests. However, it is not known whether these items are collected as potential food items.

Breeding Biology

Allegheny woodrats are primarily nocturnal and are active all year long except during extremely cold or wet weather. They construct somewhat bulky nests deep in the fissures of talus, on rock shelves, or in caves. They always occur in areas that are well protected from the elements. They are open at the top and consist of sticks and twigs lined with fine materials. The use of shredded bark of cedar (*Juniperus virginiana*) and grapevines has been reported. Middens that contain only potential food items are located close to the nest and are usually depleted by spring.

In experiments with captive individuals, it was found that dominant individuals defended their nests, but that subordinates lived in communal groups

Allegheny woodrats inhabit the large-bouldered talus slope at the base of the Palisades. © Blaine Rothauser

and avoided the dominants. The number of dominant individuals appeared to be dictated by the number of available nest sites. Woodrats are generally intolerant of other woodrats and have been observed to fight when their paths cross. Fighting consists of jabs of the head and front feet.

Allegheny woodrats breed from early spring to late summer and early fall. Lactating females have been caught in October and November in New Jersey (James Sciascia, pers. comm. 1997). Woodrats frequently have two litters per year but may have up to four in some parts of their range when winters have been mild and good mast crops were available. Litters range from two to six, with two being most common. The gestation period is 33 to 38 days, with an average of 35.

Young woodrats weigh approximately 15 gm (0.5 oz.) at birth. They are born naked and acquire hair at about 5 days of age. They have a full coat by the end of the second week (Rainey 1956). The eyes open at three weeks and they are weaned by the fourth week. By the third month they acquire the typical adult pelage coloration. Young born early in spring may breed in their first year of life but most do not breed until their second year (Godin 1977).

Woodrats have a number of potential enemies, including snakes, bobcats, foxes, weasels, hawks, and owls. Great horned owls are believed to be one of the chief predators of woodrats.

Status and Conservation

Allegheny woodrat populations have experienced declines over the past 30 years, especially in the northern part of its range. Woodrats were considered extirpated in New York State by 1987 (Hicks 1989). Extensive surveys in Pennsylvania have revealed that woodrats declined in the northeastern portion of the state and have disappeared from approximately one-third of their former range there. Similar declines have been noted in Maryland and Ohio.

In 1984 and 1985, the New Jersey Division of Fish and Wildlife's Endangered and Nongame Species Program conducted surveys of three historic sites and 16 sites that had suitable habitat. No animals were captured, although old sign was discovered at several sites.

In 1982, two new populations of Allegheny woodrat were discovered at Picatinny Arsenal in Morris County and at the Palisades in Bergen County. The Picatinny Arsenal site has been considered extirpated since 1984, leaving the population at the Palisades the last remaining one in the state. The Allegheny woodrat was afforded protection under the New Jersey Endangered Species Act when it was added to the list as endangered in 1991.

The Palisades population has been monitored by live trapping since the mid-1980s. Trapping results indicate that the population has remained stable over the past several years.

The rapid decline of Allegheny woodrat populations throughout the northern portion of its range has caused much concern about the species' future. The declines have prompted researchers to begin examining the possible causative factors that have led to the declines. Much of this research has focused on the parasite *Baylisascaris procyonis* (raccoon roundworm), a nematode that can be fatal to woodrats.

In the early 1990s, the New Jersey Division of Fish and Wildlife's Endangered and Nongame Species Program supported research by Kathleen LoGiudice that attempted to develop an effective protocol for reducing contamination of the environment with *B. procyonis* eggs. The technique involved treating infected raccoons with anthelminthic drugs delivered via baits. Although results of the study were inconclusive due to a lack of recaptured animals treated with the drug, a strong deductive argument was presented for the effectiveness of the technique. First, the baits containing the anthelminthic drug were constructed in a way that a raccoon could not consume the bait without getting a dose of the drug (piperazine). Second, it was shown in the laboratory that the ingestion of the drug reduced *B. procyonis* burdens and completely interrupted egg shedding for a period of about three weeks. Third, captive raccoons showed no preference between untreated (cornmeal) and treated (piperazine) baits. This technique may provide an effective means of reducing raccoon roundworm egg deposition at woodrat sites during periods of peak egg shedding (Sept.–Nov.), thus reducing the threat of this parasite in woodrat populations.

The ENSP conducts annual monitoring of the Palisade population via live-trapping during the early fall. Trapping results between 1999 and 2001 indicate that this population has remained stable and may be increasing slightly. Annual monitoring of this population has become a priority due to the rapid decline and extirpation of the species from their former range in New York and portions of eastern Pennsylvania.

Limiting Factors and Threats

The rapid decline and extirpation of populations of the Allegheny woodrat in the northern parts of its range have given rise to several hypotheses. The food decline hypothesis was proposed by Dr. John Hall based on his observation that the disappearance of woodrats in parts of Pennsylvania occurred at about the same time that gypsy moth infestations were at a peak. Repeated defoliation of oak trees caused widespread mast failures and tree mortality. His hypothesis was that woodrat populations were responding to this decline in mast production.

A second hypothesis proposes that fragmentation of the forests that surround woodrat habitat has contributed to their decline by affecting food supplies and dispersal routes. Woodrats are habitat specialists that inhabit rocky areas. While there is little evidence of widespread destruction of these habitats, the forests surrounding them have experienced varying degrees of disturbance. Due to the patchy distribution of woodrat populations, forest fragmentation could have an adverse effect by blocking major dispersal routes (LoGiudice 2000).

A third hypothesis suggests that *B. procyonis* is causing significant mortality in woodrat populations and may be the primary factor in population extirpations. The eggs of this parasitic nematode are passed to the intermediate hosts through the direct ingestion of raccoon (*Procyon lotor*) feces or by incidental ingestion during grooming. Ingested larvae hatch in the small intestine of the intermediate host and then migrate into the circulatory system. The larval migrants can end up in the brain and cause direct death due to central nervous system damage or indirectly by making the host more susceptible to predation.

Although none of these hypotheses clearly explain the decline of woodrat populations, many researchers have suggested that each has contributed to the woodrat's demise. These factors may have an additive or, in some cases, a synergistic effect on woodrat populations (LoGiudice 2000).

Recommendations

The rocky habitats occupied by Allegheny woodrats are generally not subjected to the alteration, disturbance, and destruction that threaten other habitat types that are more suitable for housing development. However, surrounding forest habitat should be protected from development and other disturbances that could negatively impact woodrat populations. Woodrats are dependent on these forested habitats for food and as routes for dispersal into new habitat. Development and increased human use of areas near woodrat habitat can also result in increased raccoon densities, thus increasing the threat of *B. procyonis* contamination.

Vigilant monitoring of woodrat populations will provide early detection of population declines or increases in raccoon densities. Monitoring raccoon feces for the presence of *B. procyonis* can help alert biologists to the need for treating raccoons with anthelminthic drugs to minimize woodrat exposures to this deadly parasite.

Michael Valent

WHALES

Sperm Whale, *Physeter macrocephalus*
Status: State: Endangered   Federal: Endangered

Fin Whale, *Balaenoptera physalus*
Status: State: Endangered   Federal: Endangered

Sei Whale, *Balaenoptera physalusborealis*
Status: State: Endangered   Federal: Endangered

Blue Whale, *Balaenoptera musculus*
Status: State: Endangered   Federal: Endangered

Humpback Whale, *Megaptera novaeangliae*
Status: State: Endangered   Federal: Endangered

North Atlantic Northern Right Whale (or Black Right Whale), *Eubalaena glacialis*
Status: State: Endangered   Federal: Endangered

Identification

As is the case the first time one sees a bald eagle, few people fail to vividly remember their first encounter with a whale surfacing from the depths of the Atlantic. Given their great size and—in some cases—great mystery, it's hard not to be fascinated with these marine mammals that, for centuries, were the object of storied hunting.

Cetaceans, an order that includes whales, dolphins, and porpoises, are divided into two suborders: Odontoceti and Mysticeti. Odontoceti have teeth and a single blowhole, or nostril, at the top of the head. Of this suborder, the sperm whale is the only one that regularly produces a visible spout or blow. The Mysticetes, or baleen whales—which includes the other five species listed here—have no teeth and two blowholes. Instead of teeth, great plates of horny baleen, which extend from the upper jaw, are used to strain food from large mouthfuls of water (Audubon Society 1983).

Sperm whales (Family Physeteridae): These whales have a distinctive jaw that both recedes and is located directly under the head's center.

Sperm whale. The sperm whale's huge head extends a quarter to a third of its entire length, which can be as much as 21 m (69 ft.). Its single blowhole, well left of the center and far forward on the head, emits a distinctive spout: small, bushy, and angled sharply forward. The sperm whale's skin, a dark brownish gray, looks corrugated. Occasionally its belly and front of the head

Sperm whales. Photo courtesy NOAA Central Library

Fin whale. Photo courtesy NOAA Central Library

Blue whale. Photo courtesy NOAA Central Library

are grayish, and the mouth area is white. The blunt, square snout extends far beyond the tip of the lower jaw, which has a row of large teeth on either side; smaller teeth are embedded in the upper jaw. Two-thirds of the way back from the snout the whale has a distinguishing dorsal hump; behind that are a number of bumps.

The sperm whale has a keel on its belly, and the flukes, or sides of the flat tail, are broad, triangular, and heavily notched at their back edges (Audubon Society 1983).

Rorquals (Family Balaenopteridae): Long, slender streamlined whales with grooves on the throat and/or chest.

Fin whale. The fin whale, which in the North Atlantic can reach lengths of 24.1 m (79 ft.), has a blue-black body and a white underside. There is a distinctive grayish white chevron on the back behind the head, and its V-shaped snout has a single dorsal ridge running down its middle. Its mouth is also quite distinctive, with the right lower jaw lip white, in contrast to the black left lower jaw; this asymmetry is unique among cetaceans. The mouth cavity is yellowish white and the upper right lip at times is also white. Meanwhile, the left lips are dark. The baleen plates are also white on the right side; the rest are alternately striped yellowish white and bluish gray to grayish white. The fin whale's head is flat. Far back is situated a steeply angled dorsal fin, and behind that runs a tell-tale ridge. Underneath, ventral grooves line the belly at least to the navel (Audubon Society 1983). The blow is tall and columnar in shape (Phil Clapham, pers. comm. 2001).

Sei whale. Reaching lengths of 18.9 m (62 ft.), the sei whale's dark steel-gray body frequently looks galvanized. The body is frequently covered with small pitlike circular scars, originating from the bites of cookie-cutter sharks. Underneath, the belly is grayish white around the ventral grooves, which stretch only midway between the base of the flippers and the navel. The right lower lip is gray, and the baleen plates are primarily grayish black. The whale's snout is barely arched, while its slightly pointed rostrum—the forward extension of the upper jaw—sports a single median dorsal ridge. Located two-thirds of the body length at the back of the head, the tall dorsal fin is very falcate, or curved like a sickle. Finally, the leading edges of the flukes are occasionally white (Audubon Society 1983). The blow, either bushy or columnar, is usually quite tall (Clapham, pers. comm. 2001).

Blue whale. The largest animal alive and probably the largest animal that has ever existed, the blue whale has reached lengths greater than 30.5 m (100 ft.) and has reached weights of about 178,000 kg (196 tons), although it averages 23 to 27 m (70–90 ft.) with weights of 90,000 to 135,000 kg (100–150 tons). The blue whale's skin is light bluish gray and mottled with gray or grayish white; it appears distinctly blue when seen through the water. Underneath, the belly sometimes has a yellowish tinge as a result of diatoms that have attached themselves in cold water, hence the nickname "sulphur bottom whale." The belly's ventral grooves also extend to or just beyond the navel. Almost U-shaped, the broad, flat rostrum has a single median dorsal

Humpback whale.
Photo by Robin Hunter,
courtesy USFWS

ridge. The pectoral flippers are long and thin, while the dorsal fin is very small and far back (Audubon Society 1983). The blow is high and columnar. Like the fin whale (and unlike the sei), the blowholes appear before (not with) the dorsal fin as the whale surfaces (Clapham, pers. comm. 2001).

Humpback whale. These whales, which reach lengths of 16.2 m (53 ft.), have broad, rapidly tapering bodies that are primarily black. Their bellies are sometimes white, and in the North Atlantic the flippers are usually white both ventrally and dorsally (top and bottom). Their baleen plates are black, with black or olive-black bristles. Both the top of their heads and lower jaws are dotted with randomly placed fleshy knobs. The lower jaw also has a rounded projection on its tip. The long flippers are the most distinctive feature of this whale, since at one-third the body length they exceed those of any other species; they have scalloped leading edges. The dorsal fin is highly variable in shape and size, from almost absent to high and falcate; it is located on a small hump a little more than two-thirds of the way back. Finally, their concave, deeply notched flukes have scalloped rear edges. The pattern on the underside of the tail varies from all white to all black; each pattern is individually distinctive, allowing researchers to identify and track individual whales. The humpback's blow is often wide and balloon shaped, although it can be tall and columnar in larger animals (Audubon Society 1983; Clapham, pers. comm. 2001).

North Atlantic Northern right whale off the New England Coast. Photo courtesy NOAA Central Library

Right whales (Family Balaenidae): Large-headed, robust whales. Besides bowhead whales, which frequent the edge of the Arctic ice, in North America this family includes the following.

North Atlantic Right whale. As long as 16.2 m (53 ft.), the right whale is large and rotund, with mottled brown to nearly black coloring. Both chin and belly show some white, while the dark brownish to dark gray or black baleen plates are long (up to 2.4 m, or 8 ft.) and black—although they might look pale yellowish gray far offshore. The highly arched jaw curves upward. The head and sometimes the lips are characterized by a series of bumps called "callosities"; these are naturally gray but appear yellow or white because of massive infestation by whale-lice (cyamids). The pattern of callosities can be used to identify individuals; the bonnet, the biggest of these bumps, is located just in front of two large blowholes. The right whale has no dorsal ridge or fin. Broad flukes, which are dark underneath, have pointed tips that are very concave toward a deep notch. Its blow is V-shaped when seen from ahead or behind (Audubon Society 1983).

Distribution

Historically, whales were frequently seen, captured, and stranded along the New Jersey coastline and estuaries. Right whales, for example, were common in New York's Bight and in Delaware Bay and were hunted from the mid-seventeenth century until they were no longer found early in the twentieth century (Van Gelder 1984).

In a 1683 letter, William Penn wrote that 11 right whales were taken that year at the mouth of the Delaware. In a description of New Netherlands (New York), Vanderdonck wrote: "Whales are numerous in winter on the coast and in the bay, where they frequently ground on the shoals and bars." By 1691, the whaling industry in Cape May was so profitable that the business of a cooper for oil barrels "made the demand and pay for casks certain." Right whales were taken in the Delaware in 1814 and 1862, the former reaching the

Migration range

falls at Trenton, where a rorqual or right whale was also reported in 1688 (Rhoads 1903).

In 1833, 75-year-old Stephen Inman, one of 12 Long Beach islanders, said that during his entire life his family had caught whales, usually two or three each year during February and March, along the coast. Large whalebones frequently were seen bleaching on the sand (Rhoads 1903). In 1874, a right whale, whose skeleton for awhile was displayed in the Rutgers University Geology Museum, swam up the Raritan River nearly to South Amboy, where it was "shot with a rifle, hacked with an axe, and at last killed with a harpoon!" Egg Harbor whalers also captured one off the coast in 1882 (N.J. State Museum 1907).

There are also historical records of fin and sperm whales along the New Jersey coast, and a 67-foot-long blue whale was stranded at Ocean City in 1891. However, blue whales are extremely rare off the eastern coast of the United States; their normal range extends no farther south than the shelf waters of Nova Scotia.

Today, during the winter, sperm whales concentrate off Cape Hatteras. In the spring the concentration moves off the Virginia and Delaware coasts, and the whales are widespread throughout the mid-Atlantic and southern portion of Georges Bank. During the summer, that distribution also includes areas east and north of Georges Bank, as well as the continental shelf south of New England. The fall finds them concentrated on the continental shelf south of New England and on the edge of the mid-Atlantic continental shelf (Waring et al. 2000).

While male sperm whales occur in the highest latitudes of this range, females rarely migrate north of the Canadian border, and they and juveniles concentrate more in tropical and subtropical waters. Off the northeastern United States, mixed schools of adult females, calves, and juveniles of both sexes averaging from 20 to 40 individuals have been sighted along the continental shelf and in deeper waters (Waring et al. 2000).

Fin whales are common in U.S. waters from Cape Hatteras northward to New England and beyond; New England's waters are a major feeding ground. In all seasons, between Cape Hatteras and Nova Scotia, fin whales are the dominant large cetacean species (Waring et al. 2000).

A deep-water, continental shelf-edge species that rarely ventures into more shallow and inshore waters, the sei whale during the spring and summer ranges from the Gulf of Maine to the Scotian Shelf off Nova Scotia (Waring et al. 2000).

In the Atlantic, the blue whale ranges from the Arctic Circle to at least mid-Atlantic waters, where occasional incursions into U.S. waters may represent the southern limit of its feeding range. Though some records suggest blue whales range as far south as Florida and the Gulf of Mexico, the actual southern limit of its range is unknown (Waring et al. 2000).

During spring, summer, and fall, humpback whales feed over a range that encompasses the eastern coast of the United States. In addition to a Gulf of Maine feeding stock, there are five other distinct subpopulations keyed to feeding areas that are determined matrilineally (depending on where a whale's mother has fed). These feeding stocks range through Canadian waters to Greenland, Iceland, and Norway. In the winter, all six subpopulations mate and calve primarily in the West Indies, where spatial and genetic mixing of feeding area subpopulations occur. However, not all whales migrate annually to the West Indies; significant numbers remain in mid- to high-latitude waters. During 1992, for example, an increased number of young humpbacks were sighted in the vicinity of the Delaware and Chesapeake Bays; 38 humpback whale strandings occurred between 1985 and 1992 in mid-Atlantic and southeastern states. Some of the whales found off the mid-Atlantic in winter are known to have come from the Gulf of Maine as well as from Canadian waters (Waring et al. 2000).

The western North Atlantic right whale population ranges from wintering and calving grounds in the coastal waters off Georgia and Florida to summer feeding and nursery grounds in New England waters northward to the Bay of Fundy and Nova Scotia. Migrating whales from southern waters are thought to remain close to shore, entering New Jersey waters in late winter and early spring (Waring et al. 2000).

Between 1929 and 1961, 14 fin whales stranded themselves in New Jersey and since then have continued to strand themselves the length of the state's coast. In 1978 a sperm whale stranded itself at Monmouth and Ocean Counties, and after being towed out to sea, stranded itself again in Cape May County. The first confirmed stranding of a humpback whale in New Jersey occurred in 1972 at Island Beach State Park (Van Gelder 1984). Between its founding in 1978 and 2001, the Marine Mammal Stranding Center based in Brigantine responded to stranding reports of 18 fin whales, 12 humpback whales, 5 sperm whales, and 3 northern right whales (Vikki Socha, pers. comm. 2001).

Whale watching excursions out of Cape May, which operate generally between the last weekend in March and the first weekend in December, report seeing humpback whales as close as a mile offshore and as far up the Delaware Bay as the mouth of the Cohansey River. Fin whale sightings most frequently occur between 5 and 13 miles offshore. One whale-watch boat usually encounters two to three right whales per year, in either the spring or the fall (Jeff Stewart, pers. comm. 2001).

Habitat

The waters of the Atlantic Ocean and, depending on the species, estuaries and shallow coastal areas.

Diet

Sperm whales feed primarily on squid, including giant squid, but also eat a variety of fish.

Most baleen whales depend heavily on krill, shrimplike invertebrates that are a type of zooplankton (animal plankton). However, off the U.S. coast, small schooling fish are often the primary prey. To enable them to feed on krill and related species, the rorqual members of the baleen whales—the fin, sei, blue, minke, Bryde's whale, and humpback—have pleated throat or ventral grooves that expand when the whales gulp large quantities of prey-containing water.

Fin whales eat small fish, marine crustaceans, and squids. Sei whales (named for the sei fish, the Norwegian name for pollock (*Pollachius virens*), one of its prey species, primarily eats plankton, as well as small schooling fish and squids. Blue whales primarily feed on krill during their polar feeding season in the summer. Humpbacks feed on krill and small schooling fish, often concentrating their prey by trapping them within a wall of air bubbles they release while swimming in a circle underneath the water surface. In New England waters, humpbacks often feed on herring (*Clupea harengus*), sand lance (*Ammodytes* spp), and other small fish. On their New England feeding grounds, right whales feed primarily on copepods, minute marine crustaceans.

Breeding Biology

All the baleen whales listed here have gestation periods of about 11 to 12 months. The rorquals—fin, humpback, blue, and sei—calve at intervals ranging from two to three years, while right whales calve once every three to five years (Clapham, pers. comm. 2001). After a gestation period of about 16 months, sperm whales produce young about once every four years (Audubon Society 1983).

Fin whales apparently calve in the mid-Atlantic Ocean between October and January, but it is unknown where most of the population calves, mates, or winters. Humpback whales mate and calve primarily in the waters of the Dominican Republic, particularly on the Silver Bank northwest of Puerto Rico and northeast of the D.R., but they are also found from Puerto Rico to the Venezuela coast (Waring et al. 2001; Robert Schoelkopf, pers. comm. 2001). Right whales calve off the coasts of Georgia and Florida (Sue Barco, 2001); New England waters serve as a nursery for the right whales, and perhaps also as a mating ground (Waring et al. 2001).

Sperm whales calve in the tropical and subtropical waters of the mid-Atlantic, where blue whales also probably calve. Sei whales also calve somewhere in the mid-Atlantic.

To prevent calves from drowning at birth, whales—like all cetaceans—are usually born tail first. At birth, the calf of the blue whale, for example, is about 7 m (23 ft.) long and weighs between 2,250 and 2,700 kg (5,000–6,000 lb.). Feeding on milk that contains about 35% to 50% milk fat, the calves gain up to 9 pounds an hour or more than 91 kg (200 lb.) a day (Marine Mammal Center 2001).

Currently, only Japan and Norway are still engaged in commercial whaling. The only species affected in the North Atlantic is the Barents Sea minke whale, which is hunted primarily for its meat (Clapham, pers. comm. 2001).

Whaling in North America was reported as early as A.D. 890 (Grzimek 1979). The principal attraction of whaling was the whale's subcutaneous blubber, which yielded oil ideal for lamp oil and, much later, was used in the production of margarine. Baleen and, in the case of the sperm whale, whale teeth, were also of value. Whalebones were also used in the manufacture of glue, gelatin, and manure. Besides being eaten by humans, the meat has also been used in dog food and, when dried and crushed, cattle feed.

By the time Plymouth colonists began shaling in the 1600s, the stock of right whales may have already been substantially reduced during the previous century by Basques who captured the leviathans in waters between Labrador and Newfoundland. The right whale is so-named because it was considered the "right" whale for whaling ships: it swam slowly, was easy to approach and kill, and it didn't sink after death. It was sought for both its oil and baleen, the latter of which was used for corset stays among other things.

Also widely hunted, the sperm whale was prized for the spermaceti and the fine grade of oil contained in its forehead. Sailors and artisans also favored its ivorylike teeth for scrimshaw carvings. A sperm whale that rammed and sunk the New England whaling ship *Essex* in 1820 in the Pacific was the inspiration for Herman Melville's classic novel, *Moby Dick*.

In reaction to the decline of various whale species, the first international agreement to halt whale hunting was reached in the mid-1930s. All six species discussed here were listed by the federal government as endangered in 1970 and, as a result of that federal status, were automatically added to the New Jersey endangered species list following enactment of the New Jersey Endangered and Nongame Species Conservation Act in 1973.

Although not terribly reliable, the best available abundance estimates for sperm whales indicate there are about 4,700 individuals in U.S. Atlantic waters. For western North Atlantic fin whales, the best available population estimate, admittedly conservative, is 2,200.

The total number of sei whales in U.S. waters is unknown. A very dated tag-recapture study from 1977 estimated the stock ranged between nearly 1,400 and 2,250 sei whales. Little is known about blue whale populations outside of the Gulf of St. Lawrence, where a 1987 report cataloged 308 individuals. Although this is considered a minimum population estimate for the entire western North Atlantic stock, no evidence exists to refute one estimate that the entire western North Atlantic population is in the low hundreds (Waring et al. 2000). Humpback whales in the North Atlantic are estimated at more than 11,000 (Clapham, pers. comm. 2001).

The northern right whale is among the most critically endangered large whales in the world. Once thought to number at least 1,000 whales during the early to mid-1600s, its greatest declines were suffered during the 1700s. By the time international protection for right whales was initiated in 1935, they may have numbered fewer than 100. In 1998, the total population was estimated to be just 291 individuals. Between 1986 and 1992, there were suggestions that the stock was showing signs of slow recovery. However, a 1999 study concluded that between the early 1980s and late 1990s the northern right whale had suffered a decline in survival rates, a decline that was particularly marked in adult females (Waring et al. 2000).

Limiting Factors and Threats

Though hunting caused a major decline in these whale species, they are no longer endangered by that activity. However, some of these whales occur adjacent to human population centers, and all are affected by human activities throughout their range. Both habitat and prey are affected by human-induced factors that could impede their recovery. These factors include subsistence hunting, incidental entrapment or entanglement in fishing gear, collision with ships and disturbance or displacement caused by noise and other factors associated with shipping, recreational boating, high-speed thrill craft, whale watching, and air traffic. Introduction and/or persistence of pollutants and pathogens from waste disposal; disturbance and/or pollution from oil, gas, or other mineral exploration and production; habitat degradation or loss associated with coastal development; and competition with fisheries for prey species may also impact the whales. These factors could affect individual reproductive success, alter survival, and/or limit availability of needed habitat (National Marine Fisheries Service 1991).

In the case of the right whale, the greatest cause of human-induced mortality is ship collisions; entanglement with fishing gear is also a source of serious injury and mortality.

Recommendations

More information is needed concerning the occurrences of these whales along the New Jersey coast. That's particularly true of northern right, fin, and humpback whales, the most common of these whales found near the coast. Proximity of whales to shipping traffic, distance from coastline, feeding and other critical areas, swimming speed, interaction with commercial fishing gear, and other relevant details concerning whale behavior remain unknown. More important, there is no system in place allowing notification to mariners that whales are in a particular location at any given time. Establishing an early warning system off New Jersey coastal waters and other mid-Atlantic states would provide additional protection to migrating female whales and their calves.

Given the particularly precarious status of northern right whales, the Endangered and Nongame Species Program (ENSP) plans to propose a project under Section 6 of the Endangered Species Act to the National Marine Fisheries Service. Its objectives would be as follows:

- Determine migration routes and critical areas for right whales in shipping lane vicinities and along the New Jersey coast.
- Identify individual migrating right whales and supplement the existing New England Aquarium photo-identification catalog database.
- Establish an Early Warning System network between NMFS, the U.S. Coast Guard, and the ENSP and form a mid-Atlantic EWS consortium.
- Investigate right whale interactions with commercial fishing gear off the New Jersey coast and participate in a mid-Atlantic disentanglement team.
- Develop a right whale management plan based on annual surveillance and monitoring.

The project would involve aerial surveillance of areas with heavy shipping activity (i.e., Delaware Bay and Raritan/New York Bay) during the March–April spring migration period. In addition to right whales, all marine mammals and sea turtles sighted would be recorded.

Working with the National Marine Fisheries Service and the U.S. Coast Guard, the ENSP will establish a right whale Early Warning System for the New Jersey coast. Upon a right whale sighting, the ENSP will immediately transmit location information to NMFS so that vessels in the vicinity can be warned about the whale's presence and projected course. If successful, the ENSP would like to work with state biologists in Maryland, Delaware, and Virginia to expand the system and establish a mid-Atlantic consortium EWS network that would include monitoring of heavily used shipping lanes in the Chesapeake Bay area.

As part of the Large Whale Take Reduction plan, the ENSP will participate in a mid-Atlantic disentanglement team and associated activities. Although there are no reported right whale entanglements off the New Jersey coast, at least one-half of all North Atlantic right whales show visible scars from interactions with commercial fishing gear. Through aerial surveillance, the ENSP will investigate right whale interactions with various gear types off the coast, determine if potential hazards exist, and, if necessary, work with NMFS and the Bureau of Marine Fisheries to explore the feasibility of modifying particular gear types during migration periods.

Finally, the ENSP will develop a right whale management plan that focuses on protecting critical migration routes off the New Jersey coast. Through aerial surveillance and monitoring efforts, a protection strategy will be developed that identifies crucial migration areas via GIS technology and ensures safe passage for right whales through the Early Warning System, gear modifications and disentanglement efforts, and possible critical-areas designations.

Ultimately, the ENSP would also like to conduct similar research with other whale species, particularly those that frequent New Jersey waters.

Bruce E. Beans

Bobcat, *Felis refus*
Status: State: Endangered Federal: Not listed

Identification

Taxonomically, bobcats belong to the order Carnivora, or carnivores, meaning that they are primarily flesh eaters. They are members of the Felidae family and are commonly known as felines. All members of this family look somewhat similar in appearance. Bobcats have retractable claws and five digits on each foot. Their pelt color varies throughout different parts of their range within the continental United States. In this part of the country, bobcats generally have a tawny to grayish-brown fur with spots and streaks and a whitish colored underside that is also spotted and streaked. The fur around their lips, chin, and underside of the neck are also light colored. Bobcats have ruffs of fur on both sides of their face and small tufts on the ears. The top of their short tails is tipped black.

Like all other felines, bobcats have vertically shaped pupils that widen to

maximize light reception for nocturnal activity. In addition, they have relatively long legs in relation to their bodies, with the hind legs being longer than the front. This posture accentuates the bobbed tail, which ranges in length from 12.7 to 17.8 cm (5–7 in.). A mature bobcat is approximately 89 cm (35 in.) in length and 51 cm (20 in.) high at the shoulders. Their weight ranges from about 6.75 to 11.25 kg (15–25 lb.) for adult females and 9 to 15.75 kg (20–35 lb.) for adult males. However, large males can weigh up to 18 kg (40 lb.).

Distribution

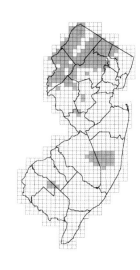

Bobcats are native only to North America. Their historic range extends from southern Canada through the United States and into central Mexico (Godin 1977). They are found from the Pacific Coast to the Atlantic Coast.

At one time bobcats were found throughout New Jersey. Today, they are found primarily in the northern counties of Morris, Passaic, Sussex, and Warren (James Sciascia, pers. comm. 1977). However, unconfirmed but reliable sources have reported bobcats in parts of Mercer, Somerset, and Bergen Counties in the north and in Burlington, Ocean, Atlantic, Salem, Cumberland, and Cape May Counties in the south.

Habitat

Bobcats are extremely adaptable animals that can survive in a variety of habitats. In our western states they are found in deserts and mountains. In the South they inhabit swamps, river bottoms, and forests. In the Northeast they can be found in forests, areas of mixed forest and agriculture, and even in rural areas near cities and small towns. In general, bobcats use rough, broken habitat that has a mix of early and late successional stages. They do not prosper in highly suburbanized areas or in areas that have been severely altered by intense agriculture. This explains their absence from many Midwest states.

However, bobcats can survive in agricultural areas that are interspersed with natural cover if they support adequate prey populations (Godin 1977; Mc-Cord 1977).

Bobcats prefer habitats that provide dense cover in the form of understory vines, briars, shrubs, and saplings (Leopold et al. 1995). These cover types provide areas for resting, and protection from both weather and predators (Leopold et al. 1995; Godin 1977). In northern New Jersey, typical bobcat habitat consists of large areas of contiguous forest and fragmented forests interspersed with agricultural areas or early succession vegetation. Bobcats often use areas with rock outcrops, caves, and ledges that provide shelter and cover for hunting, resting, and rearing young. Where rocky areas are not available, swamps, bogs, conifer stands, and rhododendron and mountain laurel thickets provide good cover and excellent hunting grounds (N.J. Division of Fish, Game, and Wildlife 1995). In southern New Jersey, dense thickets of briars and conifers serve as resting and escape cover (N.J. Division of Fish, Game, and Wildlife 1995). Clearly, bobcats are extremely versatile creatures that have the ability to adapt to a wide variety of habitat types and prey species.

Diet

Bobcats are opportunistic feeders that eat whatever prey is readily available. Mammalian prey is their mainstay, and cottontail rabbits (*Sylvilagus floridanus*), when available, make up the bulk of their diets. Bobcats will also eat squirrels, chipmunks (*Tamias striatus*), mice, voles (*Microtus* spp), woodrats (*Neotoma floridana*), and porcupines (*Erethizon dorsatum*) (Pollack 1951; Leopold et al. 1995). When their preferred prey is scarce, they may feed on fresh white-tailed deer (*Odocoileus virginianus*) carrion or deer wounded or killed by hunters (Pollack 1951; Koehler 1987; Leopold et al. 1995). Bobcats have been reported to take adult deer during the winter when snow and the deer's physical condition interfere with their escape (Marston 1942; McCord 1974). Bobcats seldom attack livestock (Koehler 1987). Like other felids, their typical hunting strategy includes ambush as well as sitting, watching, listening, and stalking and then pouncing (Marshall and Jenkins 1966; Godin 1977).

Breeding Biology

Bobcats are active throughout the entire year. They do not hibernate. Breeding begins as early as February and continues into April (Koehler 1987; N.J. Division of Fish, Game, and Wildlife 1995). Females are reproductively mature at one and a half years of age and males after two years (Crowe 1975). They are polygamous creatures, and during the breeding season toms (males) will travel to tabbies (females) in heat. A tabby may breed with several toms in a single season.

The gestation period for bobcats is about 60 days. They have litters of between one and five kittens, with three being the average. The kittens are typically born in a den under logs, among brush piles, or within small natural recesses found in rocky terrain (N.J. Division of Fish, Game, and Wildlife 1980). The kittens are born with fur, and their eyes open in about 9 to 11 days.

A bobcat kitten.
© Blaine Rothauser

They are weaned from their mother in between 60 and 70 days (N.J. Division of Fish, Game, and Wildlife 1980). Although bobcats are solitary animals, the female is very protective of her young and will stay with them and teach them to hunt through the summer and into early fall. The family groups begin to disperse in late fall and early winter. If the kittens are born late they may remain with the female through winter (McCord 1977). The male takes no part in rearing the young.

At about seven months of age, juveniles become slightly more independent. They begin to move away from their mother and may choose resting sites up to a third of a mile away (Wassmer et al. 1988). At about 9 to 10 months, juveniles disperse to areas at the edges of the adult's range (Wassmer et al. 1988; N.J. Division of Fish, Game, and Wildlife 1995). At about 13 to 14 months, they move away from the adult female's range (Wassmer et al. 1988).

In the wild, bobcats can live up to 14 years, although 10 to 11 years is a more typical life expectancy (N.J. Division of Fish, Game, and Wildlife 1995). A captive bobcat in New Jersey lived to 25 years of age. They have a high reproductive potential and females are capable of reproducing until they die (McCord 1977). Mortality can be quite high for kittens and juveniles (Crowe 1975) and may be linked to the availability of prey.

Although they are generally considered nocturnal animals, researchers have found that bobcats have peak periods of activity that occur around dawn and dusk, indicating that they may be more accurately described as crepuscular creatures (Leopold et al. 1995). Occasionally, they are active during the daytime (Wassmer et al. 1988). Their daily activity is influenced by their prey's activity and by seasonal changes. In the fall and winter, when the days are warmer than the nights, they become more diurnal. However, during spring and summer, when the days are hot, they become more nocturnal (Leopold et al. 1995).

The bobcat's home range and habitat selection appear to be influenced greatly by food availability (Crowe 1973). However, more recent research suggests that female home range size may depend on prey diversity and abundance, while male home range size depends on mating opportunities (Leopold et al. 1995). Home range varies in size from 0.5 sq. km (0.2 sq. mi.) to more than 208 sq. km (80 sq. mi.) (Koehler 1987). In northern New Jersey, radio telemetry data from two adult male bobcats revealed home ranges of approximately 18 sq. km (7 sq. mi.) (James Sciascia, pers. comm. 1997).

Female bobcats tend to be more territorial than males and therefore their territories seldom overlap. Female ranges may overlap with male territories at times. Males have well-defined territories, but the ranges of several males may overlap with portions of the other's (McCord 1987). This generally holds true except when prey is scarce (Koehler 1987; Wassmer et al. 1988). During the breeding season, there may be some overlap of home ranges among adult males when they are seeking the same female (Sciascia, pers. comm. 1997).

Juveniles are not territorial. When they disperse they usually wander about on the fringes of adult bobcat territories. Some occupy a small portion of an existing territory and remain there for an extended period of time. They may establish a territory after an adult moves or dies (Koehler 1987). Others travel extended distances to occupy new habitat. This nomadic behavior may be beneficial to the population since it guarantees that there are surplus animals ready to occupy vacated territories and move into new habitat (McCord 1977).

Bobcats typically mark the boundaries of their territories by olfactory and visual signs (Wassmer et al. 1988). They will mark their territories using scat, urine, or exudate, a substance from anal scent glands. They will also make "scrapes" in the soil using their front feet. The scrapes are often marked with urine or scat (Bailey 1972).

Status and Conservation

The bobcat has been extirpated from much of the Midwest due to habitat changes resulting from modern agricultural practices. It is considered endangered in Iowa, Indiana, and Ohio. However, Illinois removed the bobcat from its threatened list in 1999, and Pennsylvania, which had permitted no legal hunting between 1970 and 1999, reinstituted a limited hunting and trapping season beginning in 2000.

In New Jersey, the bobcat population experienced severe declines near the turn of the nineteenth century as most forests were cleared for lumber, fuel, charcoal, and agricultural use. As the remaining habitat became highly fragmented, bobcat numbers plummeted. During the 1950s and 1960s, reports of bobcat sightings and killings persisted, but by the early 1970s it was thought that the feline had been extirpated from the Garden State. The bobcat gained full legal protection under New Jersey regulations in 1972 when it was classified as a game species with a closed season.

In 1977, the N.J. Division of Fish, Game, and Wildlife initiated a project to restore the species to suitable habitat within the state. Between 1978 and

1982, 24 bobcats were captured in Maine and released in northern New Jersey (Sciascia, pers. comm. 1997). In the years that followed, reports of bobcat sightings increased, suggesting that the project had been a success. In 1991 the status of the bobcat was changed again to endangered under New Jersey's Endangered and Nongame Species Conservation Act.

The N.J. Division of Fish, Game and Wildlife's Endangered and Nongame Species Program conducted a scent-post survey in 1995 and confirmed bobcat presence in Sussex, Warren, Morris, and Passaic Counties. In addition, reliable bobcat sightings have been reported from Mercer, Somerset, Bergen, Burlington, Ocean, Atlantic, Cape May, Cumberland, and Salem Counties (Sciascia, pers. comm. 1997).

In 1996, the ENSP began a pilot project using radio telemetry to monitor the movements of bobcats in northern New Jersey. The objective was to determine the bobcats' home range and habitat preferences in that part of the state. The work is continuing, although technological advances now allow biologists to fit bobcats with satellite transmitters. Bobcat locations can now be monitored on a continual basis using satellites.

Limiting Factors and Threats

Although past efforts to restore bobcats in New Jersey have been successful, the population has maintained its endangered status. Bobcats are still at risk of being extirpated within the state due to the continued loss and alteration of habitat. Habitat destruction and alteration resulting from agricultural practices and urban sprawl are now the greatest threats to New Jersey's bobcat populations. Even with New Jersey's aggressive open-space acquisition efforts and its already large acreage of land in public ownership, habitat availability is the most significant limiting factor to bobcat survival in our state. Bobcats are wide-ranging animals that require large, contiguous patches of suitable habitat to survive. Suitable travel corridors must exist to allow for movement between patches. The loss or fragmentation of large, interconnected parcels of habitat could isolate individuals and result in population declines. Research suggests that bobcat habitat use may be dictated by factors of diversity, abundance, and stability of prey species. This explains why intensively farmed areas provide little in the way of habitat for bobcats.

Feline distemper is a deadly viral disease that is transmitted to bobcats by domestic and feral house cats, whose numbers are greatest in areas inhabited by people and in the vicinity of farms. Bobcats can contract the virus when they are exposed to the feces of infected cats. The virus is extremely hardy and can persist in the environment for up to six months. Bobcats may be especially susceptible to the disease since olfactory signs or "scent marking" appears to play a major role in territory recognition in bobcat populations. When bobcats exist in areas void of feral and domestic house cats, their population densities are low enough for the disease not to be a major cause of mortality. In areas where feral cat populations are high, bobcats can suffer significant mortality from feline distemper.

Recommendations

Bobcats use a wide variety of habitat types and occupy relatively large home ranges. Conservation efforts must include the protection of large contiguous parcels of habitat that are relatively free from human habitation and alteration. Large blocks of habitat in rugged areas that contain a wide variety of cover types provide excellent habitat for bobcats. A mix of habitats in early and late succession stages should be protected. Areas that provide suitable den sites, such as dense rhododendron and mountain laurel thickets as well as rock outcrops, should be protected. Networks that connect existing tracts of suitable habitat should be protected to enable movement between populations.

Bobcat conservation should be incorporated into forest management plans for state and federal lands. Management practices such as prescribed burning, thinning, and small-scale clear-cuts can provide habitat conditions that support healthy populations of prey species. Prescribed burns on a three-year cycle in the pinelands create early succession stages, increasing prey species and possibly increasing bobcat use.

Kris Schantz and Michael Valent

Two BIRDS

Pied-Billed Grebe, *Podilymbus podiceps*
Status: State: Endangered   Federal: Not listed

Identification

The pied-billed grebe is a small, brown, ducklike diving bird with a stocky body, thin neck, and relatively large head. The undertail coverts are white and the tail feathers are short and brown, making the grebe appear stubby and tail-less. The legs and lobed toes, which are situated far back on the body, are gray. The bill is thick and stout, enabling the grebe to crack open hard shells of mollusks and crustaceans. In breeding plumage, the ivory-colored bill is encircled with a black ring and the throat is black. In nonbreeding plumage, the throat is white and the bill is unmarked. The iris is dark reddish brown with a thin white ring encircling the eye. Although males are slightly larger than females, the sexes are alike in appearance.

Pied-billed grebe.
Photo by Dave Menke,
courtesy USFWS

Young pied-billed grebes are downy and vividly marked with brown and white stripes on the head, neck, and body and with rufous (reddish brown) patches on the back of the head and behind the eye. The young have grayish green legs and dark brown eyes. Juveniles resemble adults but may retain some brown and white streaking on the head and neck until October.

As denizens of aquatic habitats, pied-billed grebes spend nearly all their time on water. Leaping forward during head-first dives, the grebe has been nicknamed "hell diver." If threatened, a grebe may quickly dive or sink slowly into the water, emerging with only its head visible. The brown plumage of pied-billed grebes camouflages them among marsh vegetation.

Pied-billed grebes are well adapted for swimming underwater. Grebes are able to waterproof their feathers by preening them with secretions from the oil gland located at the base of the tail. Their eyes possess cone-dense retinas, an adaptation for locating prey underwater. Relatively solid bones and the ability to compress their feathers, releasing trapped air to reduce buoyancy, enables grebes to remain underwater longer. Their short, narrow wings aid in maneuverability when swimming, and the location of the legs far back on the body facilitates underwater propulsion. Although the location of their legs makes them strong swimmers, it also renders grebes awkward on land. Before taking off in flight, grebes run along the water to gain speed.

The call of the pied-billed grebe, which is given primarily during the breeding season, is a *ko-ko-cow-cow-cow-cowp-cowp,* reminiscent of a yellow-billed cuckoo (*Coccyzus americanus*). Pied-billed grebes are extremely secretive during the breeding season and are much more likely to be heard than seen.

Distribution

The pied-billed grebe breeds throughout North America from southern British Columbia, Ontario, southwestern Quebec, and Alaska through the United States, Central America, and South America to Argentina and Chile. Wintering grebes occur throughout the Americas, ranging from Massachusetts, Kansas, and Washington State south to southern Argentina and Chile.

In New Jersey, the pied-billed grebe is a rare breeder, nesting in scattered wetlands throughout the state. Breeding has been documented or suspected in northern New Jersey within the past few decades at Vernon, Hardwick, Rockaway Valley, the Pequannock Watershed, Wayne, Great Meadows, Raritan Center, Kearny Marsh in the Hackensack Meadowlands, Kingsland Marsh, Bound Brook, Edison, Linden, Trenton Marsh, and Assunpink Wildlife Management Area. In southern New Jersey, breeding has been reported at Pedricktown Marsh, Mannington Marsh, Whitesbog, Manchester, Edwin B. Forsythe National Wildlife Refuge, Fishing Creek, and Cape May Point State Park.

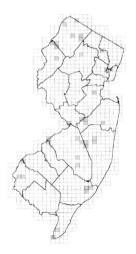

The pied-billed grebe is a fairly common migrant and winter resident throughout New Jersey. Fall migrants occur from early September to mid-November. Wintering grebes may remain in New Jersey until water freezes over, forcing them to move south. Spring migrants occur from mid-March to early May.

Habitat

Pied-billed grebes nest in freshwater marshes associated with ponds, bogs, lakes, reservoirs, or slow-moving rivers. Breeding sites typically contain fairly deep open water at depths of 0.25 to 2.0 m (0.8–6.6 ft.) interspersed with submerged or floating aquatic vegetation and dense emergent vegetation. Vegetative species found at breeding sites include cattails (*Typha* spp.), bulrushes (*Scirpus* spp.), arrow arum (*Peltandra virginica*), and phragmites (*Phragmites australis*). Marshes created by impoundments or through the industrious actions of beavers (*Castor canadensis*) may serve as nesting locales. Infrequently, pied-billed grebes nest in coastal estuaries that receive minimal tidal fluctuations.

Pied-billed grebes occupy a greater diversity of habitats during the non-breeding season. Inland freshwater ponds, impoundments, lakes, rivers, brackish marshes, estuaries, inlets, and coastal bays may be inhabited. When fresh-water freezes over, pied-billed grebes can be found in brackish marshes or tidal creeks.

Diet

The diet of the pied-billed grebe consists of a variety of aquatic organisms, including fish, crustaceans, insects, mollusks, amphibians, seeds, and aquatic vegetation. During the breeding season, invertebrates, such as leeches and odonate (dragonfly) eggs and larvae, constitute a large portion of the diet. During winter, grebes primarily eat fish. Grebes exhibit the curious habit of consuming feathers or feeding them to their young. This may protect the digestive tract from sharp fish bones or aid in the regurgitation of pellets.

Breeding Biology

Pied-billed grebes arrive on their breeding grounds by late March to mid-April, when waters are free of ice. During the breeding season, these grebes are highly territorial, requiring 0.2 to 4 hectares (0.5–10 acres) of habitat. However, several pairs may occur within large wetland complexes containing suitable habitat.

Both the males and females construct a floating nest consisting of live and dead vegetation and sealed with mud. Located within vegetative cover, the nest is anchored to live emergent plants. By virtue of its organic composition, the nest rots while it is in use, requiring the adults to repair it throughout the season. Heat generated from the rotting nest incubates the eggs while the adults are away foraging.

As early as mid-April, the female pied-billed grebe lays a clutch of six to eight eggs. The eggs, although white when laid, are often stained buff or brown by the muddy nest. Incubation, which spans about 23 days, is shared by both adults. Soon after hatching, the chicks leave the nest, naturally adept at swimming and diving underwater. Vulnerable to predation from large fish and frogs, snapping turtles (*Chelydra serpentina*), crows (*Corvus* spp.), and raccoons (*Procyon lotor*), the young closely follow the adults and ride on their parents' backs, even during underwater hunting excursions. The chicks are

Pied-billed grebe
tending its nest.
© H. Cruickshank/
VIREO

initially fed insects, particularly dragonfly larvae, but receive fish as they grow older. They are able to fly at about 35 days old and fledge during late July or early August. Young pied-billed grebes may breed the following year.

Status and Conservation

During the 1800s, the pied-billed grebe was a fairly common breeding species within suitable habitat in New Jersey. Market hunters harvested grebes as food and for their feathers, which were used to make earmuffs and hats. Consequently, by the late 1800s and early 1900s, grebe populations were greatly reduced. By 1940, there were only 12 known nesting sites in northern New Jersey. The large amount of land preserved and managed for waterfowl from the 1940s to the 1960s facilitated an increase in grebe populations. Despite the protection of wildlife refuges, many marshes continued to be drained and filled, resulting in a decline of nesting grebes in New Jersey since the 1970s.

Due to population declines resulting from habitat loss, the pied-billed grebe was listed as a threatened breeding species in New Jersey in 1979. Despite the grebe's protected status, its habitat continued to be destroyed and degraded, resulting in a further reduction in the number of breeding pied-billed grebes. In 1981, there were only two known breeding sites in the state: Kearny Marsh, which contained 16 pairs, and Pedricktown, which held one pair. Due to its dire status in the state, the pied-billed grebe was reclassified as an endangered species in 1984. The New Jersey Natural Heritage Program considers the pied-billed grebe to be "demonstrably secure globally," yet "critically imperiled in New Jersey" (Office of Natural Lands Management 1992). Due to declines in New Jersey, the pied-billed grebe was included on the National Audubon Society's Blue List of Imperiled Species as a local problem species in 1982. Concern for the pied-billed grebe is evident in other northeastern states, including New Hampshire, Massachusetts, and Connecticut, where it is listed as endangered.

Limiting Factors and Threats

Habitat degradation and destruction resulting from the draining, dredging, filling, pollution, and siltation of wetlands are the greatest threats facing the pied-billed grebe population in New Jersey. The breeding habitat of these grebes—palustrine emergent wetlands, inland wetlands such as marshes and swamps without flowing water and less than 0.5% ocean-derived salinity—is one of the most threatened wetland types in the United States. Changes in hydrology may render breeding sites unsuitable or may destroy nests through flooding. Contamination from roadway runoff, pesticides, and herbicides threaten pied-billed grebes and the aquatic organisms upon which they feed. Carbamates, agricultural pesticides that can be lethal to pied-billed grebes, may leach from farmlands into aquatic environments. Grebes are susceptible to oil toxicosis and may die if impacted by an oil spill.

Pied-billed grebes are sensitive to human disturbance, particularly during incubation. Intruders can cause the adults to spend a prolonged duration away from the nest, leaving the eggs vulnerable to weather and predators. Boating activity near nest sites can disturb breeding grebes and destroy nests through increased wave action.

Recommendations

Habitat preservation and management are essential to support a stable population of breeding pied-billed grebes. Existing wetlands, particularly those that exceed 10 hectares (25 acres) and contain a mix of emergent vegetation, submergent vegetation, and open water should be protected from habitat degradation, destruction, and human disturbance. Although large marshes containing suitable habitat are required to support numerous breeding pairs, smaller wetlands of 5 hectares (12.5 acres) or less can provide habitat for single pairs. Buffers surrounding breeding habitats should be preserved to minimize disturbance and protect from runoff. Additional habitat, such as man-made wetlands or impoundments, can be created to bolster low populations. Pied-billed grebes should be included in waterfowl management plans for state and federal wildlife refuges.

When managing habitats for pied-billed grebes, the successional stage of wetland vegetation must be maintained by periodic cutting of tracts on a rotational basis. Breeding ponds should contain floating and submerged aquatic vegetation as well as emergent vegetation. During the nesting season, water levels must remain stable. If draw-downs are conducted during the nonbreeding season, the marsh should not be completely dried, as this may kill prey such as overwintering odonates and small fish. During the nonbreeding season, flooding within a shallow-water marsh with medium vegetative density can create a slough of deeper water. Wetlands must be protected from pollution, runoff, and siltation, and water quality should be regularly monitored.

Human activity should be seasonally prohibited at sites containing breeding pied-billed grebes.

Sherry Liguori

Black-Crowned Night-Heron, *Nycticorax nycticorax*
Status: State: Threatened   Federal: Not listed

Identification

The black-crowned night-heron is a stocky, medium-sized, black, gray, and white wading bird. In comparison to other egrets and herons, the legs and neck of the night-heron are relatively short. Adult black-crowned night-herons are distinct, with a black back and crown, gray hind neck and wings, and a white cheek and underparts. In breeding plumage, long white streamers extend from the crown down the back beyond the neck. The bill, which is black in adults, is thick, stout, and spear-shaped. The legs are greenish yellow but turn pink in breeding adults. Eye color changes from yellow in juveniles to red in adults. In flight, the toes extend beyond the tail. The call of the black-crowned night-heron is a loud, guttural *woc*!

Although their body shape is similar, juvenile black-crowned night-herons have a plumage quite different from that of adults. Juveniles are buff below with brown streaking and brown above with buff-white markings. The bill is grayish yellow at the base with a dark tip. Adult plumage is acquired by two years of age.

Black-crowned night-herons are similar in appearance to yellow-crowned night-herons (*Nyctanassa violacea*), especially in juvenile plumage. The yellow-crowned has a longer neck and more slender body than the stocky black-crowned night-heron. The adult yellow-crowned lacks the black back of the

Black-crowned night-heron. Photo by Gary M. Stolz, courtesy USFWS

black-crowned and has a black head with a white cap and cheek patch. The juvenile yellow-crowned is darker brown above, with smaller buffy markings on the back and more brown below. The bill of the yellow-crowned is shorter, yet heavier, than that of the black-crowned, and does not have a light base in juveniles. In flight, the legs and feet extend beyond the tail in the yellow-crowned, while only the toes extend beyond the tail in the black-crowned night-heron.

Juvenile black-crowned night-herons may also be confused with American bitterns (*Botaurus lentiginosus*). In flight, the night heron shows a solid brown upperwing, while that of the bittern is two toned. The bill of the bittern is also longer, thinner, and lighter colored. The back of the bittern is chestnut brown and lacks buffy spotting.

Distribution

Breeding black-crowned night-herons occur throughout the United States and southern Canada, ranging from Washington, Alberta, southern Quebec, and the southeastern Canadian coast through the Atlantic and Pacific Coasts and the interior United States. In addition, breeding populations occur in Central and South America. Black-crowned night-herons winter from southern New England along the Atlantic Coast, along the Gulf and Pacific Coasts, in the West Indies, and in Central and South America. The Atlantic Coast breeding population winters largely in the Bahamas and the Greater Antilles, including Cuba, Jamaica, and the Dominican Republic.

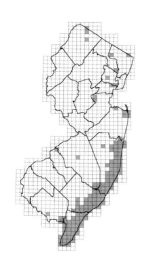

In New Jersey, black-crowned night-herons nest primarily along the Atlantic Coast, occurring from Cape May to the Hackensack Meadowlands. In addition, the species infrequently nests along the coast of the Delaware Bay and River and rarely nests inland. Nonbreeding individuals may reside in the state during the summer months. Some black-crowned night-herons arrive at breeding sites as early as the beginning of March, although most arrive during mid- to late March. Spring migrants occur in the state during April and May. Fall migration of black-crowned night-herons, which peaks from mid- or late September to mid-October, may extend through mid-November. Small numbers overwinter in New Jersey but are forced south during harsh winters.

Black-crowned night-herons undergo a postbreeding dispersal. Some young-of-the-year birds move north after fledging, traveling as far north as Quebec and Newfoundland, only to migrate south during the fall. Similarly, dispersing young from southern nests appears in New Jersey and other northeastern states. During this dispersal, juveniles banded in Massachusetts have been recovered far from their natal colonies, in Ontario, Texas, and the Florida Keys (Byrd 1978). Despite far postfledging movements, young nightherons traditionally exhibit fidelity to natal sites, returning to their colony of birth when they are able to breed. However, exceptions occur, as evidenced by an individual banded from a nest in Saskatchewan that was recovered as a breeding adult along the Atlantic Coast (Byrd 1978).

Habitat

Forests, scrub/shrub, marshes, and ponds serve as nesting, roosting, and for-aging habitats for black-crowned night-herons. Heronries may be located in wooded swamps, coastal dune forests, vegetated dredge spoil islands, scrub thickets, or mixed phragmite (*Phragmites communis*) marshes that are in close proximity to water. Black-crowned night-herons avoid nesting at exposed sites that offer little cover. Mixed hardwood forests containing red maple (*Acer rubrum*), sweetgum (*Liquidambar styraciflua*), black gum (*Nyssa sylvatica*), and blueberry (*Vaccinium* spp.) may be used by nesting or roosting birds. Dense thickets containing red cedar (*Juniperus virginiana*), holly (*Ilex opaca*), greenbrier (*Smilax* spp.), and poison ivy (*Toxicodendron radicans*) may also serve as nesting and roosting habitats. In addition, colonies have been docu-mented in stands of cherry (*Prunus* spp.) as well as in marshes containing phragmites and marsh elder (*Iva frutescens*). Islands created through the de-position of dredged material may provide nesting and roosting habitat when revegetated.

Black-crowned night-herons nest in forested or scrubby habitats contain-ing vegetation of various heights. Maximum heights of vegetation at local colonies range from 1.5 to 12 m (4.9–39.4 ft.) (Burger 1978). Within these habitats, nests are located, on average, 0.19 to 3.95 m (0.6–13 ft.) above the ground (Burger 1978). When nesting in mixed-species colonies with low veg-etation height, black-crowned night-herons tend to nest closer to the ground than other species. Similarly, when in mixed-species colonies, black-crowned night-herons tend to nest nearby other black-crowned night-herons due to their similar habitat preferences.

Black-crowned night-herons forage in marshes and along the edges of ponds and creeks. Within coastal salt marshes, shallow tide pools, tidal chan-nels, mudflats, and vegetated marsh provide foraging habitat.

Diet

Black-crowned night-herons are generalist predators whose diet ranges from insects to other birds. Fish and crustaceans, including shrimp, crabs, and crayfish, constitute much of the birds' diets while foraging in coastal marshes. However, they also pursue aquatic and terrestrial insects, earthworms, leeches, mollusks, frogs, toads, tadpoles, salamanders, snakes, lizards, eggs, and young of other birds, small mammals, and carrion. Infrequently, algae and fruit, such as beach plums, are consumed.

Black-crowned night-herons hunt along the shores of tidal creeks and ponds within marshes and estuaries. Although largely nocturnal, night-herons may also hunt during the day, especially when prey is abundant or when a clutch of hungry chicks demands food. Foraging activity is strongly influenced by tidal cycles, as prey availability varies with the tides. Black-crowned night-herons often sit and wait for prey or slowly stalk prey before lunging at it with their daggerlike bills.

Breeding Biology

Arriving during March and April, black-crowned night-herons are one of the first species to appear at wading bird breeding colonies. They nest in single- or mixed-species colonies that typically include other herons, egrets, and the glossy ibis. Although nesting pairs often occupy the same rookery in successive years, previous nest failures, predation, or disturbance may cause birds to abandon and relocate. In addition, accumulations of excrement from a large heronry may kill or defoliate trees, also causing relocation.

Nests are located within dense cover in trees, shrubs, or thickets and may infrequently be placed on the ground. The platform nest, which is built by both the male and female, is constructed of sticks, twigs, and reeds and lined with thinner twigs, roots, grasses, and pine needles. During early May, the female lays a clutch of three to four greenish blue eggs. Both adults incubate the eggs for 24 to 26 days. By early to mid-June, the eggs hatch and the chicks are cared for by both adults. At two to three weeks of age, the young branch out from the nest, climbing and hopping about in the surrounding vegetation. Chicks that fall to the ground during this time are vulnerable to ground predators such as dogs, cats, raccoons, and foxes. Until they are about four weeks old, young night-herons return to the nest to receive food, in the form of regurgitant, from their parents. At four weeks of age, the young, now feathered, are fed away from the nest. They are capable of flight at about six weeks old (usually by late July).

Following fledging, some young may disperse far from their natal colonies (see Distribution). They are able to breed at two to three years of age, although some individuals may breed when only one year old. Black-crowned night-herons exhibit strong fidelity to natal sites, often returning to these areas as adults.

Status and Conservation

The black-crowned night-heron was historically a common breeding species along the New Jersey coast. During the late 1880s, the species was frequently shot at nesting and roosting sites for its plumes and as food. Following the 1910 ban of plume sales in New York markets, populations began to recover quickly. By the 1930s, the species was once again common along the Atlantic Coast, with colonies in excess of 300 pairs. A peak migration count included 1,050 individuals at Cape May on October 23, 1935 (Stone 1965a). In recent years, a peak migration count of 400 individuals was tallied at Cape May Point on October 2, 1994 (Sibley 1997).

The destruction of coastal maritime dune forests to accommodate the growing number of summer cottages along the Atlantic shore greatly reduced habitat for black-crowned night-herons. Consequently, their populations declined during the 1940s and 1950s. Habitat loss also contributed to the decline of inland breeding populations during this period. Contaminants, including PCBs and DDT, caused further reductions of black-crowned night-herons in the Northeast during the 1950s and 1960s. PCBs affected growth, metabolism, reproduction, and behavior. The pesticide DDT caused reduced clutch size and lower productivity due to the breakage of thinned-shelled eggs. Eggshells collected in 1952 exhibited significant thinning in comparison to those collected prior to 1947 (Ohlendorf et al. 1978). With the ban of DDT in the United States in 1972, night-heron populations began gradually to recover during the 1970s. Although Breeding Bird Surveys showed an increase in black-crowned night-heron numbers in the Northeast from 1966 to 1979, the population declined from 1980 to 1999 (Sauer et al. 2000).

The black-crowned night-heron population in New Jersey has declined from about 1,500 individuals in the late 1970s to only 200 in the late 1990s, nearly a 90% loss. This reduction, attributed to habitat destruction, disturbance to nesting colonies, and contaminants, led to the inclusion of the black-crowned night-heron on the New Jersey list of threatened species in 1999. The New Jersey Natural Heritage Program considers the breeding population of the black-crowned night-heron to be "demonstrably secure globally," yet "rare in New Jersey" (Office of Natural Lands Management 2000).

Limiting Factors and Threats

Habitat loss, human disturbance, environmental contaminants, and predation threaten black-crowned night-heron populations. The development of New Jersey's barrier islands has greatly reduced the amount of habitat available for breeding colonies. In addition, the loss and contamination of wetlands have decreased and degraded foraging habitat. Due to heavy levels of human recreational activity along the coast, night herons frequently encounter people at nesting and foraging sites. Frequent or repetitive disturbance by people encroaching upon rookeries may discourage nesting or result in nest abandonment or intensified predation levels. Night-herons are especially vulnerable to disturbance during nest building and egg laying. Human intruders within nesting colonies may flush adults or cause chicks to fall to the ground, rendering them vulnerable to predation. Predators of night-heron eggs and young include crows, raccoons, foxes, dogs, cats, and great horned owls (*Bubo virginianus*). Pesticides may continue to impact black-crowned night-herons that acquire contaminants on their wintering, breeding, or migratory grounds. Pesticides banned in the United States, such as DDT, may be used in countries in which night-herons reside during the winter.

Recommendations

The conservation of nesting habitat is imperative to the long-term survival of black-crowned and yellow-crowned night-herons in New Jersey. Existing nesting colonies or areas of potentially suitable habitat should be safeguarded from development, degradation, or human activity. In addition, predator control may be necessary at some sites.

Dredged material islands can be used to create nesting and roosting habitat for night-herons. Such islands, consisting of materials dredged from inlets and bays, should be 2 to 20 hectares (5–50 acres) in size and 1 to 3 m

(3.3–9.9 ft.) above the high-water line (Jenkins and Gelvin-Innvaer 1995). Sediment can be deposited onto established low-water islands, but should not cover existing nest sites or areas of suitable habitat. The impacts of exposing and disturbing contaminants from within the sediment should be considered when dredging.

Heronries should be afforded buffers from human activity. Erwin (1989) recommended set-back distances of 100 to 200 m (328–656 ft.) to protect breeding wading bird colonies from human disturbance. Similarly, Rodgers and Smith (1995) recommended set-back distances of 100 m (328 ft) from wading bird colonies to minimize disturbance from approaching pedestrians and motor boats. Burger et al. (1995) found that ecotourists who viewed heronries from a distance of 50 to 100 m (164–328 ft.) or more did not have any discernible effect on the birds. DeMauro (1993) used a buffer of 229 m (751 ft.) to protect heronries from disturbance. The use of boats and personal watercraft should be prohibited within 100 to 200 m (328–656 ft.) of nesting colonies located near water (Erwin 1989; Rodgers and Smith 1995). Rookeries should be fenced prior to the arrival of nesting birds, and human activity should be prohibited within nesting colonies. Telescopes can be provided at frequently visited heronries to allow observers to view the birds without disturbing them. Educational signs, designated viewing sites, heronry stewards, and local community support can be used to encourage low-impact ecotourism of rookeries.

Sherry Liguori

Yellow-Crowned Night-Heron, *Nyctanassa violacea*
Status: State: Threatened   Federal: Not listed

Identification

The yellow-crowned night-heron is a medium sized, short-legged wading bird. Adults are blue-gray with a black-and-white patterned head. The head of the adult is black with a yellow-white crown and a white cheek patch. In breeding plumage, long white streamers extend from the crown. Eye color is red in adults. The legs are yellow and turn pinkish red on breeding adults. The bill is short, stout, and black on both adults and juveniles. The yellow-crowned night-heron flies with slow wing beats, trailing the legs behind the body. The call is a guttural *whoc,* often emitted when the bird is disturbed.

Juvenile yellow-crowned night-herons differ in plumage from adults. The juvenile is grayish brown overall with thin, buffy spotting on the back and upperwings. The throat and body are buff-white with heavy amounts of fine, grayish brown streaking. The legs of juveniles are greenish yellow and eye color is yellow or orange. Yellow-crowned night-herons acquire adult plumage by two years of age.

Yellow-crowned night-herons are similar in appearance to black-crowned night-herons (*Nycticorax nycticorax*) and American bitterns (*Botaurus lentiginosus*). The adult black-crowned night-heron lacks streaking on the head, and

Yellow-crowned night-heron. Photo by Eugene Hester, courtesy USFWS

instead has a black cap and white cheeks. The adult black-crowned also has a black back, while that of the yellow-crowned is solid gray. In comparison to the immature black-crowned night-heron, the yellow-crowned is darker brown above with smaller and rounder buff-white markings. Although the underparts can vary, those of the yellow-crowned tend to be darker with a greater amount of brown streaking. The bill of the yellow-crowned is shorter and heavier without a light-colored base. In addition to plumage, body shape can be used to differentiate the two night-herons. The yellow-crowned is slimmer-bodied with an elongated neck and posture, contrasting with the stocky-bodied and shorter-necked black-crowned, which often appears hunched over. In flight, the legs and feet extend beyond the tail of the yellow-crowned, while only the toes of the black-crowned extend beyond the tail. In contrast to the American bittern, which has a two-toned upperwing, the immature yellow-crowned night-heron shows a solid upperwing in flight. The bittern lacks buffy-spotting on the upperparts and has a much longer, thinner, and lighter-colored bill than the night-heron.

Distribution

The breeding range of the yellow-crowned night-heron extends from Massachusetts and Connecticut south along the Atlantic and Gulf Coasts to Central

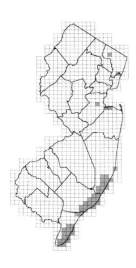

and South America. Northern breeding populations winter in southern Florida, the Gulf Coast, and Central America. Wintering birds occur, although in lesser numbers, along the Atlantic Coast north to southern North Carolina.

Although nesting pairs may have been previously overlooked, the yellow-crowned night-heron was not officially documented as a breeding species in New Jersey until 1927. During the 1940s and 1950s, the species expanded its range northward along the Atlantic Coast, increasing in numbers in the Northeast. Currently, yellow-crowneds occur along the New Jersey coast from the Hackensack Meadowlands to Cape May, with most colonies located in coastal Cape May and Atlantic counties. Because New Jersey is near the northern limit of the species' range, migrants are uncommon. Fall migration peaks from late August to mid-October, yet extends into mid-November. Spring migrants occur from late March through April.

Habitat

Yellow-crowned night-herons nest on barrier islands, dredge spoil islands, and bay islands that contain forested wetlands or scrub/shrub thickets. Colonies may be located in dense shrubby thickets, forests with an open understory, or suburban parks and yards that offer suitable habitat. Yellow-crowned night-herons use similar habitat types for both nesting and roosting, avoiding areas with insufficient cover. When nesting in mixed-species colonies in habitats with low vegetation height, yellow-crowneds tend to nest closer to the ground and group with other yellow-crowned night-herons. At one New Jersey colony, nests were located 2.5 m (8 ft.) above the ground in cherry trees (*Prunus* spp.) that reached a maximum height of 8 m (26 ft.) (Burger 1978).

Yellow-crowned night-herons hunt along the shores of tidal creeks and tide pools within salt and brackish marshes dominated by salt marsh cordgrass (*Spartina alterniflora*). They also wade in shallow water and mudflats in search of prey and seek food along the wrack line during low tides. Similar foraging and roosting habitats are used throughout the year.

In recent years the ENSP has received reports and has documented yellow-crowned night-herons nesting in residential neighborhoods, parks, campgrounds, and other areas in close association with humans. This is similar to trends observed in the Virginia Tidewater area where more than 80% of the known population nests in residential areas (Watts 1991). In these areas they prefer an open understory and park-like appearance (Watts 1989).

Diet

Yellow-crowned night-herons are specialist feeders, preying almost exclusively on crustaceans, such as fiddler crabs (*Uca* spp.), marsh crabs (*Sesarma reticulatum*), and blue crabs (*Callinectes sapidus*) in marine habitats, and on crayfish in freshwater habitats. The large, heavy bill of the night-heron is well adapted for crushing the shells of crustacean prey. Other items comprising minor amounts of the diet include leeches, polychaete (marine) worms, aquatic insects, prawns, snails, fish, eels, frogs, toads, tadpoles, newts, snakes, lizards, turtles, rodents, and birds.

Yellow-crowned night-herons forage primarily during the evening but are also active around dawn and dusk. Foraging activity is dictated by the tidal availability of prey, driving birds to forage during daytime hours as well. Foraging often peaks within three hours of low tide. Solitary hunters, the birds either stand still and wait for prey or slowly stalk prey. Once prey is sighted, the night-heron lunges at it with its bill. Upon capture, the night-heron shakes a crab to detach its pincers before swallowing the animal whole.

Breeding Biology

By mid-April, yellow-crowned night-herons arrive on their breeding grounds and begin to form pairs and establish territories. Because breeding activity depends upon prey availability, nesting may be delayed due to cold weather that prohibits the emergence of crabs.

Yellow-crowned night-herons nest in pairs or in small-to-large, single- or mixed-species colonies. Colonies often occupy the same sites in successive years, although they may abandon an area due to disturbance, predation, or poor nesting success. Pairs may use the same nest in subsequent years, adding to its size each year.

Both the male and female construct the stick nest within trees or shrubs. Often, only one pair nests in each tree, possibly to reduce the risk of predation. The male gathers nesting materials and transfers them to the female, which intertwines them into the nest. The male may also fit sticks into the nest while the female watches. The pair lines the nest with grasses, twigs, leaves, and rootlets.

Approximately three weeks after their arrival at breeding territories, yellow-crowned night-heron females lay a clutch of three to six pale blue-green eggs that are incubated by both adults for 21 to 27 days. Each parent may incubate the eggs for 14 to 18 hours before being relieved by its mate. Although they produce one clutch of eggs each year, yellow-crowned night-herons may replace lost clutches.

Both the male and female care for the young, sharing brooding and feeding duties. The chicks are fed regurgitant at the nest. The adults brood the chicks for about two weeks after hatching. At 30 to 44 days old, the young fledge, seeking cover in vegetation near the nest site. They return to the nest to roost and receive food for an additional two to three weeks, spending more time away from the nest as they grow older. Once independent, the juveniles disperse and do not return to their breeding grounds until they are able to breed, at two years of age.

Status and Conservation

Killed for the plumes that adorned breeding birds, the yellow-crowned night-heron was pursued by gunners who sold the birds' feathers and meat in city markets during the late 1800s and early 1900s. The year 1910 marked the end of the millinery trade and the start of the birds' population recovery.

In the northeastern United States, the yellow-crowned night-heron was rare prior to the 1900s. Although the species may have nested in small numbers in New Jersey during this time, breeding was not officially documented in the state until 1927. Over the next several decades, populations in New Jersey began to build, leveling during the mid-1950s and 1960s.

The surge in coastal development in the latter half of the twentieth century destroyed much of the suitable habitat for nesting yellow-crowned night-herons in New Jersey. The number of breeding birds in the state dropped from the late 1970s throughout the 1980s. In 1984, the yellow-crowned night-heron was listed as a threatened species in New Jersey due to population declines and habitat loss. Because it is located near the northern extent of the species' range, the effects of habitat loss and other threats to the New Jersey population are intensified by low recruitment from neighboring populations. The New Jersey Natural Heritage Program considers the yellow-crowned night-heron to be "demonstrably secure globally," yet "imperiled in New Jersey because of rarity" (Office of Natural Lands Management 1992). Declines of this species have occurred in other states, resulting in its listing as endangered (Indiana), threatened (Pennsylvania, Illinois, Kentucky), or of special concern (Connecticut, Virginia). Recent changes in nesting habitat selection may help yellow-crowned night-heron populations begin to recover.

Limiting Factors and Threats

Habitat loss, human disturbance, nest predation, and environmental contamination limit yellow-crowned night-heron populations. The loss of coastal forests and scrub has greatly diminished the amount of available breeding and roosting habitat for this species. The destruction, degradation, and pollution of wetlands reduce foraging habitat and expose birds to harmful contaminants that can affect their growth, metabolism, reproduction, and behavior. As habitat loss continues, night-herons are increasingly vulnerable to collisions with electrical wires and vehicles. In addition, nest predation is often elevated in fragmented habitats. Predators of eggs and young include crows, raccoons, opossums, foxes, dogs, cats, hawks, and owls. Human activity, particularly during nest building and egg laying, may result in nest abandonment or elevated predation levels. Young from disturbed nests may fall to the ground, where they are vulnerable to mammalian predators. The recent shift in nesting habitat to include residential neighborhoods may indicate an increased tolerance to human disturbance and may actually begin to lead to more direct conflicts with humans.

Recommendations

The conservation of nesting habitat is imperative to the long-term survival of the black-crowned and yellow-crowned night-herons in New Jersey. Existing nesting colonies or areas of potentially suitable habitat should be safeguarded from development, degradation, or human activity. In addition, predator control may be necessary at some sites.

Dredged material islands can be used to create nesting and roosting habitat for night-herons. Such islands, consisting of materials dredged from inlets and bays, should be 2 to 20 hectares (5–50 acres) in size and 1 to 3 m (3.3–9.9 ft.) above the high-water line (Jenkins and Gelvin-Innvaer 1995). Sediment can be deposited onto established low-water islands but should not cover existing nest sites or areas of suitable habitat. The impacts of resurfacing contaminants from within the sediment should be considered when dredging.

Heronries should be afforded buffers from human activity. Erwin (1989) recommended set-back distances of 100 to 200 m (328–656 ft.) to protect breeding wading bird colonies from human disturbance. Similarly, Rodgers and Smith (1995) recommended set-back distances of 100 m (328 ft.) from wading bird colonies to minimize disturbance from approaching pedestrians and motor boats. Burger et al. (1995) found that ecotourists who viewed heronries from a distance of 50 to 100 m (164–328 ft.) or more did not have any discernible effect on the birds. DeMauro (1993) used a buffer of 229 m (751 ft.) to protect heronries from disturbance. The use of boats and personal watercraft should be prohibited within 100 to 200 m (328–656 ft.) of nesting colonies located near water (Erwin 1989; Rodgers and Smith 1995). Rookeries should be fenced prior to the arrival of nesting birds, and human activity should be prohibited within nesting colonies. Telescopes can be provided at frequently visited heronries to allow observers to view the birds without disturbing them. Educational signs, designated viewing sites, heronry stewards, and local community support can be used to encourage low-impact ecotourism of rookeries.

Sherry Liguori

American Bittern, *Botaurus lentiginosus*
Status: State: Threatened   Federal: Migratory Nongame Bird of Management Concern

Identification

A booming *pump-er-lunk* echoes throughout an otherwise still marsh. This resounding call, the hallmark of the American bittern, has earned the species its alias, "thunder pumper." Although bitterns may call throughout the night, vocal activity is greatest at dawn and dusk. Infrequently, they may call during the day, particularly when skies are overcast.

The cryptic plumage and elusive behavior of American bitterns enable them to dwell, often undetected, within densely vegetated marshes. Laterally compressed bodies allow bitterns to maneuver through thick reeds and grasses. When disturbed, bitterns assume a reedlike position in which the

head points skyward and the body sways back and forth as if it were a blade of grass blowing gently in the breeze. When flushed, bitterns often emit a harsh, croaking *kok-kok-kok* call.

The American bittern is a stocky, medium-sized wading bird. The neck and body are buffy white with brown vertical streaking, and the upperparts are rich brown. Black flight feathers contrast with brown upperwing coverts, giving the wing a two-toned appearance in flight. Adult bitterns have a black patch extending down both sides of the white throat. The heavy, spearlike bill is yellow with a dark wash on the upper mandible and a dark tip. Adult bitterns have yellow eyes that turn orange during courtship. The legs of the American bittern are long and yellowish green. Sexes are similar, although males are slightly larger than females.

Juvenile American bitterns closely resemble adult birds. However, juveniles do not acquire the black patches that border the throat until their first fall, usually by late October. In addition, the eye color changes from light olive in nestlings to yellow in adults.

American bitterns resemble young black-crowned and yellow-crowned night-herons (*Nycticorax nycticorax* and *Nyctanassa violacea*) but can be distinguished by wing pattern, bill shape, plumage, and flight style. While American bitterns show a two-toned wing in flight, young night-herons have solid brown wings. Night-herons also have shorter, stouter bills than bitterns. In addition, bitterns have a richer, more reddish brown color than young night-herons, which are grayish brown. Appearing awkward in flight, the American bittern flies with stiff, laboring wingbeats that are quicker than those of other herons. Bitterns fly characteristically low over marshes with their legs trailing behind the body.

Distribution

The breeding range of the American bittern extends from northern Canada south to the mid-United States, east to the Atlantic Coast, and west to California. During the winter months, bitterns occur in Mexico and along the Atlantic, Gulf, and Pacific Coasts of the United States.

In New Jersey, the American bittern is a rare breeding species, occurring in scattered areas of suitable habitat throughout the state. Recently, breeding has been confirmed or suspected at Allendale Celery Farm, Troy Meadows, Kearny Marsh, Hackensack Meadowlands, Great Swamp National Wildlife Refuge, Trenton Marsh, Whitesbog, Edwin B. Forsythe National Wildlife Refuge, Mad Horse Creek, and along the Wallkill and Pochuk Rivers. Historically, American bitterns nested in inland wetlands and in coastal marshes along the Delaware Bay and Atlantic Coasts.

The American bittern is an uncommon migrant and rare winter resident in New Jersey. Its protracted fall migration occurs from mid-August to late November and peaks from mid-September to late October. Although most bitterns have departed by late November, some individuals may remain and overwinter in New Jersey. During the nonbreeding season, bitterns can be found at inland marshes, such as Allendale Celery Farm, Great Swamp National Wildlife Refuge, and Assunpink Wildlife Management Area, and at marshes along the Delaware Bay and Atlantic Coasts. Spring migrants occur from early March to mid-May.

Habitat

During the breeding season, American bitterns inhabit emergent wetlands, such as cattail ponds, sedge marshes, and marshes created by impoundments or beaver dams. Nesting habitats typically contain shallow water, often at depths less than 10 cm (4 in.), and dense vegetation, which may be 1 m (3 ft.) high. Cattails (*Typha* spp.), bulrushes (*Scirpus* spp.), wild rice (*Zizania aquatica*), sedges (*Carex* spp.), and arrow arum (*Peltandra virginica*) often dominate breeding sites. Bitterns infrequently nest in coastal brackish marshes that contain reed grass (*Phragmites communis*), salt-hay grass (*Spartina patens*), and saltmarsh cordgrass (*S. alterniflora*). Occasionally, wet fields or grasslands containing tall vegetation serve as nesting habitats.

Although American bitterns occupy similar sites throughout the year, habitat use is less restrictive during the nonbreeding season. Bitterns may be found in freshwater wetlands, coastal salt or brackish marshes, phragmites marshes, grassy fields, and marsh edges during migration or winter.

Diet

The American bittern is an opportunistic feeder, consuming small mammals, amphibians, reptiles, crustaceans, crayfish, mollusks, eels, fish, dragonflies, damselflies, grasshoppers, and other insects. Concealed by its cryptic plumage, the bittern may stalk prey or stand motionless waiting for prey before

American bittern with young. © James D. Young/VIREO

lunging its spearlike bill at its next meal. Bitterns are solitary hunters that forage within marshes, at vegetational edges, or along the shorelines of creeks during the day or at night.

Breeding Biology

From late April to May, the booming calls of American bitterns echo throughout their breeding marshes. Bitterns form limited pair bonds and may exhibit polygyny, in which several females nest within the territory of one male.

The female bittern constructs a platform nest either on the ground or atop a clump of vegetation several inches over water or mud. Bittern nests, which average 15 to 25 cm (6–10 in.) high and 30 to 40 cm (12–16 in.) wide, are constructed of reeds, sedges, and other emergent vegetation and lined with thin grasses. Dense vegetative cover conceals the nest, and pathways of trampled vegetation lead to and from the nest. To disguise the nest's actual location, bitterns land a distance away from the nest and cautiously follow a path leading to it. Likewise, when departing from the nest, bitterns walk away from the nesting area before flying.

During May to mid-June, female bitterns lay three to five buff-brown-colored eggs. The eggs of the American bittern are readily distinguished from those of other North American herons and bitterns, which have blue-green colored eggs. The female bittern incubates the eggs for 24 to 29 days. After they hatch, the female broods the chicks and feeds them regurgitant. The young, although not yet independent, leave the nest at about two weeks of age and remain in the area for an additional two weeks. The exact age at fledging remains unknown.

Status and Conservation

Before the early 1900s, the American bittern was a fairly common breeding species within suitable habitat in New Jersey. By the 1920s, market hunting and the destruction of wetlands had caused initial declines in bittern populations. However, bitterns remained within suitable habitat throughout the state during the first half of the century. Since the 1950s, habitat loss has occurred at an alarming rate in New Jersey, destroying wetlands critical to breeding American bitterns. The Breeding Bird Survey detected annual decreases in American bittern populations survey wide from 1966 to 1999 (Sauer et al. 2000). Likewise, the number of bitterns detected on Christmas Bird Counts in New Jersey had declined by 68% from the early 1970s to the mid-1980s (Vince Elia, Cape May Bird Observatory, pers. comm. 1999).

Due to population declines and habitat loss, the breeding population of the American bittern was listed as threatened in New Jersey in 1987. The New Jersey Natural Heritage Program considers the American bittern to be "apparently secure globally," yet "rare in New Jersey" (Office of Natural Lands Management 1992). The American bittern was included on the National Audubon Society's Blue List of Imperiled Species from 1976 to 1986, the final year of the list. Due to its patchy distribution and dependence on declining wetlands, this bittern was also designated as a Migratory Nongame Bird of Management Concern by the U.S. Fish and Wildlife Service in 1982. Elsewhere in the Northeast, it is listed as endangered (Massachusetts, Rhode Island, and Connecticut), threatened (Pennsylvania), or of special concern (Maryland).

Limiting Factors and Threats

Dependent on wetlands throughout their annual cycle, American bitterns are limited primarily by the loss and degradation of habitat. Freshwater emergent wetlands, which are among the most threatened habitat types in the United States, have been greatly reduced in New Jersey. Eutrophication, siltation, and pollution jeopardize existing wetlands. Exotic plants such as phragmites and purple loosestrife (*Lythrum salicaria*) have invaded marshes and outcompeted native vegetation, degrading habitat quality for many wildlife species. Human activity at breeding sites may deter bitterns from nesting or cause nest abandonment.

Recommendations

Protection and restoration of American bittern populations is mostly a matter of protecting and restoring their sensitive wetland habitats. Strong enforcement of existing land use and other environmental regulations is needed to protect emergent wetlands from development, filling, draining, illegal dumping, pollution, and other forms of human encroachment. Habitat acquisition must consider adequate buffer areas to guard wetland habitats against secondary impacts of adjacent development. During the breeding season, human activity should be prohibited near known nesting areas.

Habitat management or restoration practices can be implemented to create or improve additional habitat for American bitterns and other wetland species. A mix of dense emergent vegetation, submerged and floating aquatic vegetation, and open water should be provided with water depths maintained at a maximum of 10 cm (4 in.). A minimum marsh area of 2.5 to 5 hectares (5–12.5 acres) is recommended to support nesting bitterns with a buffer of dense, woody vegetation surrounding the marsh to protect it from human disturbance and runoff. Vegetative succession within the marsh should be suppressed either through cutting or controlled burning during the non-breeding season. In addition, programs for controlling invasive plant species such as phragmites and purple loosestrife need to be developed and implemented. Managing vegetative plots on a rotational scheme can provide habitat while management is underway.

Because of the secretive nature and patchy distribution of American bitterns, much of their biology and population status remains unknown. Surveys are needed to locate additional breeding sites, monitor existing nesting areas, and determine population trends. Research is also required to determine the impacts of phragmites, purple loosestrife, and wetland degradation on habitat use and breeding activity. Specific habitat management guidelines for bitterns should be developed and implemented on state and federal conservation lands.

Sherry Liguori

Northern Goshawk, *Accipiter gentilis*
Status: State: Endangered   Federal: Not listed

Identification

The northern goshawk is the largest of the three North American accipiters, or forest hawks. Female goshawks are similar in size to the common red-tailed hawk (*Buteo jamaicensis*), whereas male goshawks are somewhat smaller. Like all accipiters, goshawks exhibit short, rounded wings and a long tail compared to those of buteos such as the red-tailed hawk. The goshawk's wings are more tapered or falconlike, and its tail is broader than that of its closest relative, the Cooper's hawk (*A. cooperii*). The wingbeats of the northern goshawk are heavy and deep like those of some of the larger species of buteo. The call of the northern goshawk is a series of loud, piercing *cacks* that can be heard from nearly a mile away.

Adult northern goshawks are pale blue-gray on the back and whitish underneath with fine charcoal-colored barring. Juveniles are brown above with a narrow, tawny bar across the upperwing and buff-colored below, with broad,

Northern goshawk.
© R. & S. Day/VIREO

dark vertical streaking on the breast and belly. Juvenile goshawks obtain adult plumage during their first molt, which occurs in their second year of age. All ages show a diagnostic broad, white superciliary (eyebrow) line. Eye color changes from yellow in juveniles to blood red in adults. The sexes are nearly identical in plumage.

Distribution

The breeding range of the northern goshawk extends from Alaska and Canada south to California in the west and southern New England and the Appalachian Mountains in the east. In the past several decades, the goshawk has expanded its range southward along the East Coast, nesting in New York, Pennsylvania, Connecticut, and New Jersey, and in the Appalachian ridges of Maryland and West Virginia. Goshawks may either remain at breeding areas throughout the year or migrate to southern wintering grounds. Wintering goshawks occur throughout their breeding range and may infrequently winter as far south as the southeastern United States, northern areas of the Gulf Coast states, and, rarely, Florida. Wintering goshawks are irruptive, their numbers increasing abruptly in certain areas depending on prey availability. When prey is scarce in the northern part of their range, they occur in greater numbers to the south. Although most migrants are typically immatures, adults may also move south during irruptive years.

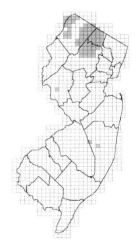

Northern goshawk breeding was not confirmed in New Jersey until the later half of the twentieth century, when nests were discovered in the northwestern portion of the state. Since then, goshawk nesting has been confirmed or suspected at Sunrise Mountain, High Point, the Delaware Water Gap, the Kittatinny Mountains, Mashipacong Bogs Preserve, Vernon, Wawayanda State Park, Greenwood Lake, Bearfort Mountain, West Milford, Mahlon Dickerson Reservation, Green Pond Mountain, the Pequannock Watershed, Rockaway, Boonton, Hampton Township, and Kingwood. In 1995, the first nesting goshawks were discovered in the coastal plain of southern New Jersey in Lacey Township.

Goshawks occur throughout New Jersey during the nonbreeding season. Fall migrants can be observed along inland ridges and coastal sites from mid-October to mid-December. Spring migrants can be seen from mid-March to mid-April. Wintering goshawks may occur in suitable forested habitat throughout the state.

Habitat

The northern goshawk nests in mature, contiguous forests that are safeguarded from human activity and development. Characteristics of goshawk breeding forests include large-sized trees, a closed canopy, and an open understory. Northern goshawks may nest in wooded swamps, lower gentle slopes, or flat areas at elevation. Goshawk nesting territories may contain small, unfrequented roads or trails within the forest, which the birds may use for foraging or as landmarks. In the Highlands region of New Jersey and New York, goshawk nests were located, on average, more than 1,000 m (3,280 ft.) from paved roads or areas of human habitation (Bosakowski and Speiser 1994).

Northern goshawks may occupy coniferous, deciduous, or mixed forests. In northern New Jersey, territories have been located in northern hardwood/hemlock stands, oak-dominated stands, maple forests, mixed-conifer (hemlock, pine, cedar)/northern hardwood stands, or groves of white (*Pinus strobus*) and red pine (*P. resinosa*). The southern New Jersey nest was located in a dense Atlantic white cedar (*Chamaecyparis thyoides*) swamp surrounded by mature mixed forest. Nests may be located in either deciduous or coniferous trees, although deciduous trees are used more frequently by goshawks nesting in New Jersey. The nest is constructed in a crotch in the lower canopy layer of a large, canopy-sized tree, such as an American beech (*Fagus grandifolia*), black birch (*Betula lenta*), oak (*Quercus* spp.), maple (*Acer* spp.), white pine, red pine, or hemlock (*Tsuga candensis*). Within their nesting territory, goshawks maintain plucking posts, favored sites such as trees, stumps, fallen logs, or old nests, where the birds consume their prey.

Goshawk habitat use is much less restrictive during the nonbreeding season. During migration and winter, goshawks may forage in mature as well as young woods, scrubby areas, and treelines along marshes or open fields. Forested stands are favored for roosting, as they provide shelter against harsh weather.

Diet

The northern goshawk is a formidable predator, capable of capturing birds as large as grouse. Goshawks are well adapted for pursuing prey within dense forests. Short, rounded wings and a long, narrow, rudderlike tail enable a goshawk to maneuver among thickets and branches in pursuit of prey. Goshawks ambush their prey, flying concealed through dense vegetation or along forest edges and openings to surprise and flush their quarry. Then, persistently giving chase, they quickly kill their prey with a strong blow to the body and a fatal bite to the spinal column.

The goshawk is an opportunistic predator, exhibiting both sexual and seasonal differences in diet. The male goshawk, which is smaller and more agile, is adept at capturing passerines, such as jays, thrushes, songbirds, and woodpeckers. During the breeding season, nestling birds, as well as adults, may be pursued. The larger female goshawk is capable of capturing more sizable prey, including gallinaceous birds such as grouse and pheasants, rabbits, squirrels, pigeons, and crows. Chipmunks, squirrels, mice, shrews, and, infrequently, snakes and insects may also fall prey to the goshawk.

The diet of the northern goshawk varies seasonally with prey availability.

Northern goshawk.
© D. R. Herr / VIREO

Northern populations of goshawks exhibit cyclical fluctuations in productivity, reflective of relative population cycles of dominant prey species such as ruffed grouse (*Bonasa umbellus*) or snowshoe hare (*Lepus americanus*).

Breeding Biology

Depending on prey availability during the winter months, northern goshawks that breed in New Jersey may remain near their nesting territories year-round. Regardless, by February or March, pairs return to their breeding territories. Both the male and female perform aerial courtship displays as well as interpair and territorial vocalizations. Courting goshawks soar in circles high above their territory while calling and fanning out their white undertail coverts. Displaying birds may also perform a slow flapping and undulating flight in which the goshawk quickly descends, then rebounds upward. Although goshawks typically do not breed until their third year, some females breed during their second year.

A goshawk pair may build a new nest or repair an existing nest. Goshawk nesting territories often contain several nests that are constructed over the years. A pair may use the same nest in consecutive years or alternate among the different nests within their territory. The female constructs the nest, with limited assistance from the male. Goshawk nests are located on sturdy horizontal limbs at the crotch of a tall, canopy-sized tree. Goshawks utilize a variety of tree species, usually deciduous, for nesting. A tree that provides a suitable crotch for nest placement may be more important than specific tree species when selecting a nest location. The goshawk's nest is constructed of sticks and lined with bark, leafy twigs, or conifer sprigs. A plucking post where prey is consumed is located near the nest. Feathers and fur littering the ground and branches marked with whitewash are telltale evidence of a plucking post.

During mid- to late April, the female lays a clutch of two to three eggs, each interspersed by two- to three-day intervals. The female begins incubation with the first egg, resulting in young of staggered ages and sizes. This strategy of asynchronous hatching, employed by many birds of prey, ensures that during lean years there will be an older, larger, and dominant chick. This oldest chick will be more aggressive at securing food than its smaller and younger siblings. By having young of different sizes, most of the food will be seized by the one dominant chick, rather than dividing limited food resources among three young of equal size, in which case none may survive.

Incubation and brooding are done largely by the female, which is fed by the male. The female incubates the eggs for 36 to 41 days and broods the altricial (dependent) young for 8 to 14 days. At 34 to 40 days old, the young, not yet capable of flight, vacate the nest and perch in nearby branches. As the young grow older, the female begins to leave the nest and aid the male in securing food.

At about 45 days old, the young goshawks begin to fly. Within the following week, they start to hunt, although they are still dependent upon their parents for food. As their flying ability improves, they venture farther away from the nest for longer periods of time. By 70 to 80 days of age, the young gain independence. However, they may remain near their nest site until they disperse in late summer. Male goshawks, which are smaller, fledge earlier than the larger females.

Status and Conservation

Historically, northern goshawks were shot in large numbers by farmers and hunters who regarded the goshawk as a pest because it consumed chickens and game birds. In 1929, Pennsylvania passed a law entitling gunners a $5 bounty for each dead goshawk. Fortunately, conservation has accomplished a great deal and laws now exist to protect rather than harm birds such as the goshawk.

The northern goshawk was not discovered as a breeding species in New Jersey until the second half of the twentieth century. Although possible breeding was suspected in the 1950s, the first goshawk nest in New Jersey was not confirmed until 1964. During the 1960s and 1970s, the goshawk expanded its breeding range in the Northeast, nesting in northwestern New Jersey, Pennsylvania, New York, and Connecticut. The maturation of eastern forests may have facilitated the surge in nesting goshawks. In 1982, there were nine confirmed pairs of goshawks in New Jersey (Speiser and Bosakowski 1984). The Breeding Bird Atlas confirmed breeding goshawks in 13 atlas blocks from 1993 to 1997 (Walsh et al. 1999).

Due to its need for large contiguous old-growth forest, a habitat type of limited availability in the state, and its rarity as a breeder, the northern goshawk was listed as a threatened species in New Jersey in 1987. Breeding Bird Surveys revealed a decline in goshawk populations in the Northeast from 1980 to 1999 (Sauer et al. 2000). Due to the increasing threats facing forested habitats and the scarcity of nesting goshawks, the status of the goshawk was reclassified as endangered in 1999. The New Jersey Natural Heritage Program considers the goshawk to be "apparently secure globally," yet "critically imperiled in New Jersey because of extreme rarity" (Office of Natural Lands Management 1992).

In 1995, the first goshawk nest was discovered in the Pinelands of southern New Jersey. Perhaps in the future, contiguous, mature forests protected in the Pinelands Preserve will provide additional sanctuary for nesting goshawks, enabling them to expand their range and increase their population in the state.

Limiting Factors and Threats

Habitat loss and human disturbance are the major threats facing the nesting goshawk population in New Jersey. Large tracts of contiguous forests are rare in the state and, if under private ownership, are vulnerable to destruction and development. The construction of housing developments, roads, and highways is expanding from northeastern New Jersey into the more forested and rural northwestern corner of the state, where forests are threatened by the encroaching suburban sprawl. Timber harvesting may also degrade or destroy nesting habitat by removing large trees, decreasing canopy coverage, and promoting dense understory growth.

Human disturbance can have profound impacts on nesting birds, resulting in nest abandonment or mortality. Human activity near nest sites may cause adult goshawks to flush or mob the intruder(s), alerting predators and leaving the eggs or young vulnerable. Repeated or prolonged human activity near nest sites, resulting from campers, hikers, or off-road vehicles, can cause nest abandonment.

Recommendations

Suitable nesting habitat for northern goshawks must be protected from development and intrusive levels of human activity. Blocks of mature, contiguous forests containing large canopy trees and an open understory should be targeted for protection and/or acquisition. Such areas that are adjacent to already protected sites should receive high priority. Areas of high-quality habitat should be surrounded by buffers where development and timber harvesting are restricted.

Human activity must be restricted at known goshawk nesting sites. During the breeding season, hiking and ATV trails, as well as campsites, that are within or adjacent to goshawk territories should be temporarily closed.

Sherry Liguori

Cooper's Hawk, *Accipiter cooperii*
Status: State: Endangered   Federal: Not listed

Identification

On a cool fall day at Cape May Point, observers scan the skies as streams of accipiters zip past at tree level. Darting through the cedars in pursuit of a

Cooper's hawk preying
upon a herring gull.
© Blaine Rothauser

yellow-rumped warbler is a Cooper's hawk, one of the three species of North American accipiters—woodland hawks that prey chiefly on birds. The Cooper's hawk, as well as its accipiter cousins, the sharp-shinned hawk (*Accipiter striatus*) and the northern goshawk (*A. gentilis*), are forest-nesting raptors that are able to quickly maneuver through dense cover while chasing prey.

About the size of a crow, the Cooper's hawk has short, rounded wings and a long, narrow tail. When soaring, the head extends beyond the wrist, making it appear large-headed. In flight, the silhouette of a Cooper's hawk appears cross-shaped, whereas the similarly plumaged sharp-shinned hawk looks small-headed and T-shaped. Sharp-shinned hawks usually exhibit a shorter, more squared-off tail. In addition, the wingbeats of the Cooper's hawk are stiffer and more powerful than the fluttery wingbeats of the sharp-shinned hawk.

The adult Cooper's hawk has a dark cap, blue-gray back, and rusty, barred underparts. The juvenile's back is brown with rufous (reddish brown) feather edges and sparse white spotting, and the underparts are light colored with brown vertical streaking on the breast. In all ages, the tail is usually rounded and has a white edge along the tip. Juveniles molt into adult plumage during their second year. Eye color changes from yellow-green in immature birds to dark orange or red in adults. Females are significantly larger than males. The call of the Cooper's hawk, which is often given during the breeding season, is a loud and nasal *cak-cak-cak*.

Distribution

The breeding range of the Cooper's hawk encompasses southern Canada, the contiguous United States, and northern Mexico. During the winter months, Cooper's hawks occur primarily in the United States as well as Mexico and occur casually south to northern South America.

In New Jersey, breeding Cooper's hawks have been confirmed or suspected in most counties throughout the state. The fall migration of Cooper's hawks occurs in the state from September to November, with an early October peak. Migrants can be observed both along the coast and inland ridges. Cape May Point boasts the highest daily and seasonal counts of Cooper's hawks in eastern North America, with 456 tallied on October 3, 1994, and a total of 5,009 in the autumn of 1995 (Walsh et al. 1999). Cooper's hawks can be observed throughout the state during the winter. Spring migration occurs from mid-March through mid-May.

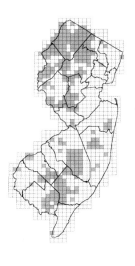

Habitat

During the breeding season, Cooper's hawks inhabit deciduous, coniferous, and mixed riparian or wetland forests. In southern New Jersey, breeding habitats include large, remote red maple (*Acer rubrum*) or black gum (*Nyssa sylvatica*) swamps and, on occasion, Atlantic white cedar (*Chamaecyparis thyoides*) swamps. Within these sites, high-bush blueberry (*Vaccinium corymbosum*) and greenbrier (*Smilax rotundifolia*) typically dominate the shrub layer. Adjacent

Cooper's hawk in flight.
© B. K. Wheeler/VIREO

upland pine or mixed pine/oak forests provide an additional habitat buffer for nesting Cooper's hawks. In northern New Jersey, Cooper's hawks inhabit mixed riparian woodlands, eastern hemlock (*Tsuga canadensis*)/white pine (*Pinus strobus*) forests, and conifer plantations. Dominant tree species within such habitats may include red maple, sugar maple (*Acer saccharum*), eastern hemlock, white pine, black birch (*Betula lenta*), white oak (*Quercus alba*), Scotch pine (*Pinus sylvestris*), and Norway spruce (*Picea abies*).

Cooper's hawk nest sites are often located within subclimax forests that provide a closed canopy, moderate to heavy shrub cover, and trees more than 30 years old. Territories often contain forest edges and small openings along streams or roads, which may be used for hunting. In northern New Jersey, Cooper's hawk territories contained over 70% forested habitat within 0.3 km (0.2 mi.) of nest sites and were, on average, 0.5 km (0.3 mi.) away from the nearest house (Bosakowski et al. 1993). Home ranges of breeding Cooper's hawks in the United States may comprise 105 to 1,800 hectares (260–4,450 acres) (Johnsgard 1990; Rosenfield and Bielefeldt 1993).

During the 1970s, when the Cooper's hawk was first listed as an endangered species in New Jersey (1974), breeding was documented only within large, contiguous forests. As the Cooper's hawk population increased, pairs have nested in smaller woodlots containing mature trees and fragmented woods within agricultural, suburban, or urban landscapes. This may be attributed to both a larger breeding population and increased fragmentation of forested habitats. Cooper's hawks may exhibit limited tolerance for human disturbance and habitat fragmentation.

Cooper's hawks, which occur year-round in New Jersey, use many of the same habitats in winter as during the breeding season. However, because of limited prey availability during the winter months, habitat use during this season is less restrictive than during the breeding season. Consequently, Cooper's hawks forage within a variety of forest types as well as woodland edges. Wintering hawks may also frequent residential areas, where they hunt songbirds and doves at bird feeders. Cedar forests, conifer groves, and other dense woods that provide protection from harsh weather are favored for roosting.

Diet

The diet of the Cooper's hawk is largely comprised of small- to medium-sized birds such as thrushes, jays, woodpeckers, blackbirds, doves, sparrows, and European starlings (*Sturnus vulgaris*). Given the opportunity, these hawks will pursue almost any bird species within an appropriate-sized range. Cooper's hawks exhibit sexual size dimorphism, as do many raptor species, with larger females able to secure larger prey items. Infrequently, small mammals, reptiles, or amphibians may be included in the diet.

These hawks are woodland raptors adapted for hunting within forests. They possess short, rounded wings and long tails that enable them to maneuver through dense vegetation while pursuing avian prey. In addition, their long legs and toes help them to grasp birds in flight. Cooper's hawks may fly low along forest openings and edges or swoop from high altitudes to surprise prey. They then employ swiftness and agility to overcome their targets.

Breeding Biology

In New Jersey, the breeding season for Cooper's hawks extends from April through July. Pairs mate for life and typically return to the same nesting area in successive years. A breeding area may contain several nests that have been used by a pair over the years.

From late March to late April, mated pairs perform courtship flights over their nesting territories. Typically initiated by the male, this display consists of deep, slow flaps with wing tips nearly touching on the upstroke. The courting birds also shake their bodies and pump their tails up and down. Occasionally, Cooper's hawks exhibit courtship flight during spring migration.

The stick nest, located within the canopy of a deciduous or coniferous tree, is typically situated in a crotch off the main trunk. An old hawk or crow nest may serve as a foundation. The nest, which is constructed by the male, is lined with pieces of bark or green twigs. The height of the nest tree may range from 12 to 36 m (39–118 ft.) high, with the nest usually located 8 to 15 m (26–49 ft.) above the ground (Jones 1979; Rosenfield and Bielefeldt 1993). A nearby log, stump, old nest, or large branch is established as a plucking post where prey is consumed.

Four to five white eggs are laid by the female at two-day intervals, resulting in young of staggered ages and sizes. Incubation commences with the third egg and spans from 30 to 36 days. During incubation and brooding, the male delivers food to the female, which leaves the nest only to eat. If prey availability is low, only the older and larger chicks may survive. When the young are about three weeks old, the female leaves the nest to hunt. Young Cooper's hawks vacate the nest and perch in nearby branches at 30 to 34 days old. In New Jersey, young typically fledge during mid- to late July, with the smaller males fledging a few days earlier than the larger females. Independence is gained at eight or more weeks of age. Cooper's hawks reach sexual maturity at two years of age, although females may sometimes breed when one year old.

Status and Conservation

Until the mid-1930s, many raptor species, including the Cooper's hawk, were shot in large numbers during migration and on their breeding grounds because of suspected poultry and game-bird predation. Regardless, the Cooper's hawk remained a fairly common breeding species in New Jersey's forests until the 1950s, when habitat loss caused population declines. In addition, the pesticide DDT impaired reproduction and contributed to population declines observed from the 1950s to 1970s. Due to the reduction in the state's breeding population and the loss of habitat, the Cooper's hawk was listed as an endangered species in New Jersey in 1974. The New Jersey Natural Heritage Program considers the Cooper's hawk to be "apparently secure globally," yet "rare in the State (breeding)" (Office of Natural Lands Management 1998). Concern for this species is evident in nearby states, such as New Hampshire, Rhode Island, and Connecticut, where it is listed as threatened, and Massachusetts and New York, where it is considered a species of Special Concern. The National Audubon Society also included the Cooper's hawk on its Blue List of Imperiled Species from 1971 to 1982 and in 1986, the final year of the list.

Following the nationwide ban of DDT in 1972 and the reforestation of fallow lands throughout the state, Cooper's hawk populations began to recover. Cooper's hawks experienced increases in New Jersey Christmas Bird Counts from 1959 to 1988 and Breeding Bird Surveys from 1980 to 1999 (Sauer et al. 1996; Sauer et al. 2001). Other recent surveys have also shown a substantial increase in the breeding population of Cooper's hawks in New Jersey. As a result, the status of the Cooper's hawk was reclassified from endangered to threatened in New Jersey in 1999. The loss of large, contiguous forests remains a threat to this species and warrants the continued protection of Cooper's hawk nesting habitats.

Limiting Factors and Threats

Habitat loss and fragmentation continue to threaten the Cooper's hawk population in New Jersey. Currently, upland forests receive inadequate regulatory protection from development pressure. Of 18 Cooper's hawk nests located in the Highlands region of northern New Jersey between 1979 and 1990, one-third were encroached upon by development (Bosakowski et al. 1993). Residential development within 100 to 500 m (328–1,640 ft.) of nests resulted in immediate abandonment or absence of birds the following year, evidence of this species' intolerance of nearby development (Bosakowski et al. 1993). In addition, expanded residential development increases the threats of road mortality and window collisions of Cooper's hawks. Human activity near nest sites may result in nest abandonment or nest predation.

Although Cooper's hawks have expanded their range in New Jersey to include fragmented woodlots, such forests are key habitats for competitors such as great horned owls (*Bubo virginianus*) and red-tailed hawks (*Buteo jamaicensis*). Further, residential development and fragmented habitats favor predators such as raccoons (*Procyon lotor*), opossums (*Didelphis marsupialis*), and great horned owls, which prey upon eggs, chicks, and adults. In small habitat patches, human activity may result in elevated disturbance levels, causing nest abandonment. Because of these threats, Cooper's hawk populations located in small fragmented woodlots may be increasingly susceptible to localized extirpation.

Recommendations

The protection of large, contiguous forests, both wetland and upland, is integral to sustain a healthy breeding population of Cooper's hawks in New Jersey. Innovative strategies for land conservation, such as the Endangered and Nongame Species Program's Landscape Project, must be implemented to safeguard otherwise vulnerable habitats. Wooded tracts surrounding known Cooper's hawk nesting sites, particularly those already located within large forests, should be targeted for protection. Human activity should be restricted within a quarter-mile of Cooper's hawk nest sites during the breeding season, from early April to late July. Planting groves of conifers and offering a mosaic of wooded, edge, and field habitats can provide habitat for wintering and migrant Cooper's hawks.

Sherry Liguori

Red-Shouldered Hawk, *Buteo lineatus*
Status: State: Endangered (breeding population), Threatened (nonbreeding population)   Federal: Migratory Nongame Bird of Management Concern

Identification

The red-shouldered hawk is a crow-sized buteo, or soaring hawk. The adults are strikingly plumed, with rufous (brownish red) shoulder patches and a rufous barred breast. Rufous lesser and median upperwing coverts form the "red shoulders" evident on this species. The flight feathers of adults are barred black and white and show a white crescent-shaped window across the primaries, which is visible in flight. The underparts, which are rufous with white barring, often exhibit thin, dark streaks on the chest. The head and back are dark brown. The black tail is bisected by several narrow white bands. Although females average slightly larger than males, plumage is similar for both sexes. The call of the red-shouldered hawk is a series of nasal drawn-out *aahhh* cries.

Juvenile red-shouldered hawks can be distinguished from adults by their overall browner, less brilliant plumage. The shoulder patches of juveniles are paler rufous and the crescents across the primaries are tawny. The underparts

Red-shouldered hawk with prey. © G. M. Jett/ VIREO

are whitish with variable amounts of brown streaking. The tail is brown with several thin, pale bands. Adult plumage appears in the second year.

The red-shouldered hawk is a long-tailed buteo with squared-off wings and a protruding head. Characterized by quick choppy wingbeats interspersed with short glides, the flight style of this hawk is similar to that of an accipiter. When soaring, most buteos hold their wings straight out, whereas the red-shouldered hawk bows its wings forward.

Distribution

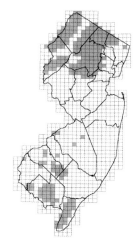

The red-shouldered hawk breeds throughout the eastern United States from the Gulf Coast north to southern Canada, with an isolated western breeding population in California. Northern breeding populations are migratory, traveling as far south as Mexico and the Gulf Coast states for the winter. The eastern breeding population winters east of the Mississippi River as far north as southern New England.

In New Jersey, the red-shouldered hawk is a rare breeder in secluded wet woods throughout the state. Nesting strongholds in southern New Jersey include Bear Swamp, Cumberland County, and Fishing Creek, Cape May County. In northern New Jersey, breeding strongholds occur in the Pequannock Watershed and along the Delaware River in Stokes State Forest, High Point, and the Delaware Water Gap National Recreation Area. The Pequannock Watershed contains possibly the largest red-shouldered hawk population in New Jersey, an estimated 12 pairs (Benzinger et al. 1988). The New Jersey Breeding Bird Atlas confirmed nesting pairs in 32 blocks statewide (Walsh et al. 1999). Other breeding areas include Cape May, Belleplain State Forest, Great Swamp National Wildlife Refuge, Wawayanda State Park, and the Kittatinny Mountains. Because they are sensitive to disturbance, red-shouldered hawks typically nest in remote areas of contiguous forest. However, nests have been documented near developed areas such as Floodgates, along the Delaware River, and Wenonah, Gloucester County (Clay Sutton, pers. comm. 1999).

The autumn migration of red-shouldered hawks in New Jersey occurs from mid-October through late November and peaks during the first two weeks of November. Record fall migration counts at Cape May Point include 165 on November 10, 1994, and a seasonal total of 872 in 1994 (Walsh et al. 1999). During spring migration, red-shouldered hawks are dispersed throughout the state with small concentrations along the ridges and the coast. Spring migration occurs from mid-March through mid-April and peaks during late March. The red-shouldered hawk is an uncommon winter resident throughout the state.

Habitat

Mature wet woods such as hardwood swamps and riparian forests typify red-shouldered hawk breeding habitat. Nesting territories, which occur in deciduous, coniferous, or mixed woodlands, are typically located within remote and extensive old-growth forests containing standing water. Consequently, breeding barred owls (*Strix varia*) and Cooper's hawks (*Accipiter cooperii*) are often found in habitats containing red-shouldered hawks.

Red-shouldered hawks select large, deciduous, and, to a lesser extent, coniferous trees for nesting. Nests have been documented in oak (*Quercus* spp.), pine (*Pinus* spp.), maple (*Acer* spp.), ash (*Fraxinus* spp.), beech (*Fagus grandifolia*), birch (*Betula* spp.), basswood (*Tilia americana*), chestnut (*Castanea dentata*), hemlock (*Tsuga canadensis*), elm (*Ulmus* spp.), cherry (*Prunus* spp.), hickory (*Carya* spp.), and tulip poplar (*Liriodendron tulipifera*). Forest characteristics include a closed canopy of tall trees, an open subcanopy, and variable amounts of understory cover.

Red-shouldered hawks inhabit wetland forest types unique to the different physiographic regions throughout northern and southern New Jersey. In north Jersey, they occupy riparian forests, wooded wetlands, beaver meadows, and mesic (slightly moist) lowland forests. Within the Pequannock Watershed, red-shouldered hawks are found in stream bottomlands and coniferous or mixed forests containing eastern hemlock or white pine (*Pinus strobus*). Nests are predominantly located in wilderness areas where there are abundant wetlands, small forest openings, and limited areas of large open water such as lakes. In the Pequannock Watershed, red-shouldered hawks avoid areas of human habitation, steep uplands, dry slopes, open water, areas with limited conifers, and areas with too many or too few forest openings. Although red-shouldered hawks require extensive tracts of forested habitat for nesting, territories may also contain edges where the birds forage.

The majority of red-shouldered hawk nests in southern New Jersey are contained within vast contiguous freshwater wetlands. Hardwood or mixed hardwood/cedar swamps containing red maple (*Acer rubrum*), black gum (*Nyssa sylvatica*), sassafrass (*Sassafras albidum*), sweetbay magnolia (*Magnolia virginiana*), and Atlantic white cedar (*Chamaecyparis thyoides*) are occupied by red-shouldered hawks. Often, such large forested tracts are surrounded by oak/pine forests or agricultural fields. Although red-shouldered hawks nest in large contiguous tracts of wet old-growth forests in Cumberland County, they occupy younger wet woods, often on private property safeguarded from high levels of human activity, in Cape May County.

An area-sensitive species, the red-shouldered hawk typically nests away from residences, roads, and development. In the Pequannock Watershed, red-shouldered hawk nests were located an average of 1,013 m (3,323 ft.) and a standard deviation of plus or minus 614 m (3,324 ± 2,014 ft.) from the nearest building; and an average of 812 m and a standard deviation of plus or minus 634 m (2,664 ± 2,080 ft.) from the nearest road. Red-shouldered hawks avoid small, fragmented woodlots and forests that do not contain trees large enough for nesting.

Red-shouldered hawks require large, contiguous wooded tracts of 100 to 250 hectares (250–620 acres) (Johnsgard 1990). Eastern populations occupy breeding home ranges of 109 to 339 hectares (270–838 acres) (Crocoll 1994). In the Pequannock Watershed, red-shouldered hawk breeding densities were estimated at one nest per 450 hectares (1,112 acres) with an average distance of 1.2 to 1.6 km (0.75–1.0 mi.) between nests in areas containing the highest breeding concentrations (Bosakowski et al. 1991). Home-range sizes of males exceed those of females, during both the breeding and nonbreeding seasons. Individuals of either sex may expand their home ranges while rearing young or throughout the winter months.

During the nonbreeding season, red-shouldered hawks are less restrictive in their habitat use. They inhabit the traditional wetland forests occupied during the breeding season as well as uplands, fragmented woods, smaller forests, open areas, and edges.

Diet

The diet of the red-shouldered hawk varies throughout the year due to seasonal changes in prey availability. During the breeding season, red-shouldered hawks prey upon frogs, snakes, lizards, insects, salamanders, spiders, crayfish, snails, beetles, grasshoppers, small turtles, and, to a lesser extent, birds and mammals. During migration, they are opportunistic, consuming available birds, mammals, reptiles, and amphibians. In the winter months when reptiles and amphibians are inactive, the diet shifts to songbirds, doves, and small mammals, such as mice, voles, shrews, rabbits, and chipmunks. Red-shouldered hawks either perch and wait for prey or actively search within the forest understory, openings, meadows, or marshes. They may secure small mammals from the ground at burrow entrances.

Breeding Biology

During late March and April, courting red-shouldered hawks call and circle above nesting territories with wings spread and tails fanned. Prior to copulation, the displaying male conducts aerial acrobatics, ascending and descending in a series of steep, rapid dives. Exhibiting strong site fidelity, a pair often occupies the same territory for life and may use the same nest in several consecutive years. Red-shouldered hawks mate for life and maintain pair bonds throughout the year.

Nests are typically located 5 to 25 m (15–75 ft.) high within dense cover in a crotch off the main trunk of a midcanopy-level tree. Red-shouldered hawks may build their own stick nests or use an old hawk, owl, crow, or squirrel nest as a foundation. Both the male and female construct the nest and line it with conifer sprigs, green leaves, bark, lichens, or dried tent caterpillar webs.

Egg dates for the red-shouldered hawk in New Jersey span from late March to May. In northeastern populations, red-shouldered hawks lay an average of two to four and, on rare occasions, five eggs. The eggs are buff colored with variable amounts of reddish brown speckling. Incubation is conducted primarily by the female, with some assistance from the male. Incubation is initiated with the first egg and spans five weeks. Consequently, the eggs hatch asynchronously, resulting in young of staggered ages and sizes. During years when food resources are scarce, only the older and larger chicks may survive. Both adults care for the young, which leave the nest at five to seven weeks of age. The parents continue to guard and feed the young until they leave the nesting area.

Both young and adult red-shouldered hawks may suffer high levels of predation by great-horned owls (*Bubo virginianus*), particularly in areas of New Jersey, such as Cumberland County, with dense owl populations. On average, successful red-shouldered hawk nests fledge two young, which, in turn, will be able to breed at two years of age.

Status and Conservation

The red-shouldered hawk was once considered a common resident of wet lowland forests in New Jersey. Only a century ago, bounties were placed on birds of prey, which were accused of poultry and game predation. This unfortunate practice, coupled with egg collecting and the placement of wild red-shouldered hawks in captivity, may have caused initial population declines. The clearing of forests and filling of wetlands exacerbated red-shouldered hawk declines, which were noted as early as the mid-1920s. Reduced numbers of red-shouldered hawks wintering in New Jersey were documented from the early 1950s to the 1970s, as development increased and forest contiguity and patch size decreased. As a result, the red-shouldered hawk, with an estimated 100 breeding pairs in the state, was listed as a threatened species in New Jersey in 1979. In 1982, the U.S. Fish and Wildlife Service listed the red-shouldered hawk as a Migratory Nongame Bird of Management Concern due to population declines and restricted habitat requirements. In addition, the red-shouldered hawk was included on the National Audubon Society's Blue List of Imperiled Species from 1972 to 1986, the final year of the list.

During the 1980s, habitat loss continued to pose an increasing threat, causing red-shouldered hawk populations to decline even further. By the late

1980s and early 1990s, the state's breeding population was estimated at only 36 pairs, nearly one-third the population size at the time of original listing. As a result, the breeding population of the red-shouldered hawk was reclassified as endangered in 1991. The nonbreeding population remained listed as threatened. The New Jersey Natural Heritage Program considers the red-shouldered hawk to be "demonstrably secure globally," yet "imperiled in New Jersey because of rarity" (Office of Natural Lands Management 1992). Habitat loss and declines of red-shouldered hawks in the Northeast have resulted in the listing of this species as threatened in New York and of special concern in Connecticut.

Limiting Factors and Threats

Habitat loss and degradation, human disturbance, and predation are the primary factors limiting red-shouldered hawk breeding populations in New Jersey. The red-shouldered hawk typically only nests in large contiguous forests. Forest fragmentation results in decreased habitat suitability and may cause displacement due to increased disturbance, competition, or predation. Likewise, degradation of habitats, either through stand thinning, tree topping, or water quality reduction, may render areas unfavorable for breeding red-shouldered hawks. As fewer and fewer large forested tracts remain, red-shouldered hawks may be forced to utilize suboptimal habitats and may therefore suffer decreased reproductive success.

Encounters with humans also increase as development expands. Off-road vehicles, hikers, and campers can disturb nesting red-shouldered hawks, which are extremely sensitive during the breeding season. In the Pequannock Watershed, at least 25% of red-shouldered hawk nest failures were directly or indirectly attributed to off-road vehicle use (Bosakowski et al. 1991). Human activity and disturbance limits red-shouldered hawk nesting to the most remote areas of forests and may preclude their use of otherwise suitable locations.

Forest fragmentation favors the great horned owl, a voracious predator of both adult and young red-shouldered hawks. Red-shouldered hawks may seasonally or permanently abandon sites where they have experienced predation by these owls. Christmas Bird Counts have revealed that Cumberland County, New Jersey, contains the greatest concentration of great horned owls in the United States. In such areas of high owl density, red-shouldered hawk territories invariably overlap with those of owls, often with ominous results.

Recommendations

The most critical measure that must be undertaken to ensure the future of red-shouldered hawk populations in New Jersey is the preservation and protection of forested habitats. Large contiguous forests should be set aside as "no cutting" wilderness preserves that are safeguarded from development and offer limited access. On private property, cooperation with landowners and incentive programs are imperative to ensure the protection of forests. Within large wooded blocks, managers should refrain from implementing forestry practices that may adversely affect red-shouldered hawks, such as clear-cutting, selective logging, and tree topping. Activities that would jeopardize water quality within wetland forests should be prohibited. Likewise, the integrity of wetland complexes must be maintained. Nest sites, buffer zones, and the surrounding forest area should be safeguarded from development and disturbance.

Human activity must be restricted near red-shouldered hawk nesting areas. During the breeding season, off-road vehicle use should be restricted and hiking trails should be closed or rerouted if they occur within nesting territories. Population monitoring of breeding red-shouldered hawks should be conducted every three to five years.

Sherry Liguori

Bald Eagle, *Haliaeetus leucocephalus*
Status: State: Endangered   Federal: Threatened (proposed for delisting)

Identification

Adult bald eagles are distinguished by their large size (2.1 to 2.4 m [7–8 ft.] wingspan), full white heads and tails, and a dark brown, almost black body. They reach their adult size by the time they can fly. Their adult plumage, however, develops in their fifth year. Prior to that, their juvenile appearance varies from year to year. In their first year, their wings are slightly broader and entirely dark brown. The next year, they begin to molt their flight feathers, and the trailing edge of their wings appears symmetrically serrated as shorter adult feathers replace the longer juvenile ones. Their plumage is usually mottled, brown and white, and is widely variable with a considerable amount of white on the breast and belly. Bald eagles are even more mottled in their third year

Bald eagle fishing.
© T. Vezo/VIREO

and begin to show signs of change from dark brown to light yellow in their eye and bill color, and may have some lighter plumage appearing on their heads and tails.

During their fourth year, bald eagles begin to appear unmistakably as our national symbol. This is when they are transitioning from juvenile to adult and appear for the first time with a white head and tail. At this age, they retain some brown in the white plumage, giving them a dirty appearance. They also retain some white flecking in the brown of their bodies. In their next molt, they attain the clean white head and tail and solid brown body plumage of a full adult bald eagle.

Distribution

Bald eagles occur across most of Canada, Alaska, all of the lower forty-eight United States, and remote parts of Mexico. In New Jersey, we have scant records of nesting locations prior to the late 1960s (Brown and Amadon 1968). Gleaned from anecdotal records, a map of their historical range in the state reflects their occurrence throughout the southern Atlantic coastal region and the habitat adjacent to Delaware Bay.

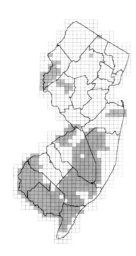

Currently, the greatest number of bald eagles occurs in the southern part of the state, with concentrations in the Delaware Bay and lower Delaware River areas. Eagle pairs now also nest in the central and northern parts of the state near lakes and reservoirs, and on the upper Delaware River. In winter, New Jersey breeding adult eagles are joined in the state by eagles from northeastern states and eastern Canada. Bald eagles can be found near open waters statewide, especially near the Delaware Water Gap on the upper Delaware and Delaware Bay tributaries such as the Maurice and Cohansey Rivers. In January 1997, a record 176 eagles were counted in New Jersey during the national midwinter eagle survey; in January 2001, 140 were tallied.

Habitat

Bald eagle habitat consists of areas of forest that are associated with bodies of water. With fish as their primary diet, bald eagles in New Jersey have historically been associated with the forests near the Delaware River and Bay as well as all the rivers that empty into the Atlantic Ocean and Delaware Bay (Niles 1995). In northern and central New Jersey, bald eagles are resident on inland reservoirs and on the Delaware River. Throughout the state, these large birds require a nesting location that is safe from the threat of human disturbance, and they usually choose their nest tree accordingly. Typically, the tree they choose for building their large nests is a "supercanopy" tree that is taller than the trees immediately surrounding it. By nesting in such a tree, eagles can place their nest within the shelter of the crown and still be above the surrounding trees, enabling them to arrive and depart from the nest with ease.

In the northern part of the state, where the topography is hilly or mountainous, eagles can nest in trees that are on a slope and therefore have one side that is higher than its neighboring trees on the slope below it. Occasionally, bald eagles will choose a lone tree in an open field.

In addition to nesting habitat, eagles also have habitat requirements for foraging and wintering, which might overlap their nesting habitat, but not necessarily. Foraging habitat for bald eagles consists of large perch trees near a body of water. Both of these elements are critical due to the "sit and watch" foraging behavior of eagles. Wintering habitat consists of the same, with the added condition of open, ice-free water. Parts of the Delaware River, such as the Delaware Water Gap, where the current is swift and the river remains open, or deep reservoirs with enough current or a dam to keep part of the water ice free, serve as good wintering habitat for eagles. The tidal areas of southern New Jersey marshes are also ideal locations for winter foraging.

Diet

Bald eagles are primarily fish eaters. They are extremely opportunistic, however, and will eat almost anything that presents itself as a meal. As majestic a bird as it is, the bald eagle will happily dine on carrion. It will harass cormorants and mergansers into regurgitating their last meal and snatch the largest parts as a meal for themselves. Bald eagles regularly pirate, or steal away, the catch of ospreys or other eagles. Winter usually poses the greatest problem for eagles, as it does for other wildlife, and they will seek out dead deer and dead or injured waterfowl for food.

Evidence of their diet, in the form of prey remains near their nests, has revealed that bald eagles in New Jersey eat a wide variety of animal species. In addition to fish and waterfowl remains, biologists have found turtle shells, muskrat skulls, egret remains, and gull wings.

Breeding Biology

In New Jersey, bald eagles begin their breeding season in late December and early January. During this period, the pair demonstrates its bond with aerial courtship displays. Together, they will fly high, chasing each other and touching talons. One of their more spectacular displays involves the pair locking talons and tumbling toward the ground.

During this period, the pair will also work diligently to build or repair its nest. The typical first-year nest measures 0.6 m (2 ft.) high and 1.5 m (5 ft.) across, with a slight grass-lined depression in the middle for the eggs (Beans 1996). Eagles use the same nest from one year to the next, adding sticks and making it larger and larger, in some cases until the tree can no longer support the weight. Copulation also occurs during this period; frequently, the pair will do this on the nest-in-progress.

By the middle of February, most of New Jersey's eagles have begun to lay their clutch of one to three eggs. Incubation commences when the first egg is laid, with both adults sharing the responsibility, making several quick exchanges throughout the course of a day. Eagle eggs require approximately 36 days to hatch, and because incubation begins at the arrival of the first egg,

Two bald eagle chicks
(about 10 days old).
Photo courtesy NJ ENSP

the chicks hatch asynchronously. Eagles will rarely lay a second clutch of eggs, but may do so only if the first clutch is lost early in incubation.

From the time of hatching until well beyond fledging, the adults spend all of their time caring for the chicks by brooding (to keep them warm), feeding, and defending them. Eagle nestlings are altricial, requiring constant care in the first few weeks; at the age of five weeks they can sit up and begin to tear their own food. Young eagles fledge at 11 to 12 weeks of age. For as long as three months after the young fledge, the adults continue to provide food for them. During this period, the fledglings learn to fly proficiently and also begin to hunt for themselves prior to dispersal.

While adults in New Jersey remain in the vicinity of their nesting territory year-round, once they disperse, juveniles—though they may return to the area annually—embark on what can be very long seasonal wanderings. Young eagles banded and/or equipped with radio transmitters at Florida nests have appeared in Canada within months of fledging. One New Jersey juvenile was quickly traced to Chesapeake Bay, where many New Jersey young spend the winter.

Once they reach adulthood, however, bald eagles tend to return to the region where they were fledged to seek a mate and begin breeding.

Status and Conservation

Long before the introduction of the pesticide DDT after World War II, habitat destruction, shootings, and poisonings had greatly reduced the population of bald eagles in the lower 48 contiguous states. But the widespread use of DDT, which caused eagles to lay thin-shelled eggs that were often crushed during incubation, pushed the bird to the brink of extinction. New Jersey, where DDT was heavily used, in part for mosquito control, was no exception. By 1970, only one eagle nest remained in the state. Consequently, the bald eagle was listed as endangered under New Jersey's new Endangered Species Conservation Act in 1974, and listed as federally endangered throughout the lower 48 states in 1978.

Management of the state's only nest began in 1982, when biologists began climbing the nest tree to retrieve the thin-shelled eggs. They were then incubated in the lab underneath chickens before being returned to the nest as 10-day-old chicks, which were quickly cared for by the nest's adults. Shortly thereafter, the state launched a "hacking" program through which 60 eaglets, primarily from Canada, were released into the heart of New Jersey's bald eagle habitat between 1983 and 1989. Those efforts, combined with the 1972 federal ban on DDT, paid off rather quickly, with the appearance of the state's second eagle nest in 1988.

Since then, biologists have also been successful in encouraging eagles to nest in certain areas by building "starter nests," which eagles complete once they adopt them for nesting (Clark and Niles 1998). Building nests for eagles works best when a pair has already claimed a territory, and the birds may be drawn to a sturdy nest in a supercanopy tree.

Since the appearance of the second nest, the number of eagle nests has increased steadily. In 2002, a record 28 bald eagle nests were active statewide, mostly in southern New Jersey. A record 36 young fledged that year.

Three 7-week-old eaglets in a nest that's typically situated, in a supercanopy tree near foraging waters, here a tidal creek near Delaware Bay. Photo courtesy NJ ENSP

Limiting Factors and Threats

Three primary threats currently face bald eagles in New Jersey: habitat loss and degradation, human disturbance, and contaminants in the environment. All can contribute to nest abandonment or failure.

Habitat can be degraded by changes such as deforestation and forest fragmentation, encroaching development, and pollution. Development often brings a level of human activity that eagles cannot tolerate and can cause outright loss of perch trees and changes in prey populations. Their sizable habitat requirements have made it difficult to maintain eagles in the face of ever-expanding development; to be viable for a nesting pair, the habitat must support both nesting and open-water feeding areas. While a small percentage of eagle pairs have nested in close proximity to man, eagles generally require large trees in relatively undisturbed settings in which to rear their offspring successfully. Development and land use practices are frequently in conflict with the needs of bald eagles.

Human disturbance can cause abandonment of nests and eggs, especially during the most sensitive period of egg laying and incubation. Recreational activities, such as boating and off-road vehicles, often cause eagles to leave prime hunting areas. In winter, exclusion of eagles from good feeding areas can affect the birds' survival.

Environmental contaminants are thought to be the cause of nesting failures each year by at least three New Jersey eagle pairs. High levels of polychlorinated biphenyls (PCBs), DDE, and certain heavy metals have been recorded in the contents of eggs collected from failed nests in the lower Delaware River region (Clark et al. 1998). Certain nests in that region have failed for many consecutive years. While the habitat outwardly appears suitable, pollution has caused a chronic problem in the aquatic ecosystem.

Recommendations

The Endangered and Nongame Species Program (ENSP) relies on volunteers to regularly monitor active nests to determine nesting chronology and nest success in addition to monitoring and minimizing human disturbance near nests. Cooperation and support by landowners and neighbors is essential for the long-term protection and survival of eagle nesting; volunteer observers assist biologists with on-site management.

ENSP biologists also draw blood samples from young eagles at the age of six to eight weeks during nest visits to band nestlings; unhatched, addled eggs are also collected where possible. The blood and egg contents are tested to monitor contaminant levels and gauge their possible impact on the eagle population. Determining the sources of organochlorine contamination in eagle nest areas should be followed by pollution clean-up or containment to prevent further infiltration into the food web.

Habitat conservation is essential, and the ENSP's landscape critical habitat mapping can help identify potential eagle nesting habitat for proactive protection. Habitat near nest sites and in recognized wintering areas, such as along the major southern New Jersey rivers, along the upper Delaware River, and at inland reservoirs, must be protected through acquisition and landowner agreements. Continued enforcement of coastal and forest wetland regulations will be important to maintain and support the state's bald eagle population.

Steve Paturzo and Kathleen Clark

Northern Harrier, *Circus cyaneus*

Status: State: Endangered   Federal: Migratory Nongame Bird of Management Concern

Identification

Often seen conspicuously hunting low over the open coastal marshes of New Jersey, the northern harrier is a medium- to large-sized hawk. A white "rump patch," low buoyant flight, and the position of its wings in a shallow "V" dihedral characterize the airborne northern harrier. This bird has an owl-like facial disk that aids it in detecting prey in tall grass or low-light conditions by concentrating sound toward the ears.

Adult northern harriers are sexually dimorphic in both plumage and size. The smaller males are slate gray above and white below, with contrasting black wingtips and a black trailing edge to the wing. The male's white breast has varying amounts of light rufous (rusty) spotting. The larger female harriers are brown above and buff colored below, with brown vertical streaking on the chest and belly. Unlike that of the male, the underwing of the female is dark and the black wingtips are obscured. On all harriers, white uppertail coverts that form the white rump patch are a key in-flight field mark. Adult harriers of both sexes have lemon-yellow eyes. On all ages, the legs are long

The northern harrier's owl-like facial disk aids in detecting prey.
© Blaine Rothauser

and yellow, the cere—the fleshy area behind the base of the bill—is yellow, and the bill is black.

Juvenile northern harriers are extremely similar in appearance to adult females. Juveniles are brown above, although slightly darker than adult females, and have a cinnamon wash to the underside that is faintly streaked. As this reddish hue fades during their first winter, juveniles tend to appear much more like adult females. Juvenile males are born with grayish eyes that turn to an adultlike lemon yellow by their first winter. Juvenile females have dark brown eyes that take at least two years to appear yellow.

Northern harriers employ several different calls. A chirplike call between male and female is given during food exchange or on the ground during copulation. This call is also exchanged between females and nestlings. Harriers reiterate an alarm call consisting of a series of *kak*s when a predator or intruder disturbs the nesting area. A high-pitched, gull-like whine is emitted, most often by the male, during courtship and territorial display flights.

A northern harrier hunting low over a marsh is one of the most distinctive raptors in flight. Reminiscent of a turkey vulture (*Cathartes aura*), the harrier holds its wings in a dihedral and rocks from side to side. The harrier is a slim, buoyant hawk with narrow wings and a long, slender tail, providing it with maneuverability and agility. On migration, harriers can appear significantly different in flight. When soaring, the harrier looks slender bodied and cross shaped and soars on flat wings. In a glide posture, the wings are pulled up into a modified dihedral as the hands are leveled out for maximum lift. The northern harrier flaps with deep, floppy wingbeats, whereas most other hawks' wingbeats appear stiff and shallow.

Distribution

The northern harrier breeds throughout much of North America, ranging from Canada and Alaska south to California and Texas in the West and through the mid-Atlantic states south to Virginia in the East. Northern harriers winter throughout the contiguous United States south to Mexico, Central America, the Caribbean Islands, and, less frequently, northern South America.

In New Jersey, the northern harrier is an uncommon breeding species in marshes along the Atlantic and Delaware Bay coasts and in inland fields and grasslands. Historically, the northern harrier was a locally common breeding species with nesting documented at numerous sites, including Hackensack Meadows, Overpeck Creek, Newark Bay, Troy Meadows, Great Swamp, Long Beach Island, Cape May, and in marshes along the Delaware Bay and Atlantic coasts. Marshes along the Delaware Bay shore in Cape May, Cumberland, and Salem Counties are the stronghold of breeding harriers in the state. Nesting has also been suspected or confirmed in recent years at Black River, Troy Meadows, Lyndhurst, Carlstadt, Hackensack, Berry's Creek, Piles Creek, Readington, East Amwell, Edison, Sayerville, Barnegat Bay, Little Egg Harbor, Long Beach Island, Atlantic City International Airport, Tuckahoe/Corbin City, Elmer, Canton, and Bridgeport.

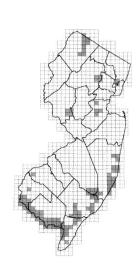

The northern harrier is a common migrant and winter resident in New Jersey. Although harriers may occur at inland marshes or fields, both the Atlantic Coast and Delaware Bay estuary act as strongholds for wintering harriers. Harriers that breed in New Jersey may remain in the state throughout the winter months.

Fall migration of northern harriers in New Jersey spans from early August to late December with a peak of juveniles during late September to early October and a peak of adults three to four weeks later. Record high daily migration counts within the state include 278 on November 12, 1980, and an autumn seasonal total of 3,115 in 1994, both at Cape May Point (Walsh et al. 1999). Migrant harriers occur both at inland ridge sites and along the coast, where they readily cross large expanses of water such as Delaware Bay. Communal roosts of harriers are often established during the fall and occupied throughout the winter. Spring migration occurs from March to May, with a peak during the first 2 weeks of April.

Habitat

Formerly known as the "marsh hawk," the northern harrier inhabits open country such as tidal marshes, emergent wetlands, fallow fields, grasslands, meadows, airports, and agricultural areas. Many nests in the state occur in brackish or saline marshes, particularly along the Delaware Bay shore. Within these areas, harriers nest in the drier areas of high marsh that are dominated by salt hay (*Spartina patens*), marsh elder (*Iva frutescens*), or reed grass (*Phragmites communis*). Harriers may also nest in freshwater tidal marshes that contain *Phragmites,* sedges (*Carex* spp.), or other emergent wetland plants. Inland breeding sites may be located in managed, fallow, or low-intensity agricultural fields that contain tall grasses and herbaceous vegetation.

Northern harriers forage over marshes, fields, bushes, and edges that contain low vegetation, often only 1 to 2 m (3–6 ft.) high. Although phragmites may be used for nesting, it offers poor foraging habitat for harriers because it forms dense, impenetrable stands.

Because they differ in size, male and female harriers exhibit sexual variation in diet and foraging habitat. During the nesting season, females typically hunt within the marsh itself, while males, in addition to foraging in the marsh, often seek prey along upland edges or fields. Males may fly considerable distances during hunting excursions and consequently have larger home ranges than females. In New Brunswick, Canada, breeding male harriers maintained territories ten times greater in size than those of females (Simmons 1983). Territory size also varies depending on the season and prey availability, with individuals occupying larger territories during the nonbreeding season and when food is scarce.

Northern harriers occupy similar habitats throughout the year. Communal winter roosts of harriers are located on the ground within drier portions of marshes or in grasslands. Roost sites can be readily recognized, as they are littered with pellets, feathers, and excrement.

Northern harrier in flight. © B. K. Wheeler / VIREO

Diet

Northern harriers are opportunistic feeders, consuming seasonally abundant prey such as small mammals, birds, reptiles, amphibians, and insects. Harrier densities are regulated by prey availability, accounting for low reproductive output during lean years.

During the breeding season, the abundance of fledging songbirds and mammals provides food for harriers. Frogs, snakes, and insects may also supplement the diet during this period. In the winter months, when reptiles, amphibians, and insects are no longer available, the diet shifts to small mammals such as voles, mice, shrews, rats, and rabbits, in addition to birds and carrion.

Northern harriers exhibit sexual dimorphism in prey selection, an adaptation to reduce competition between males and females while enabling a pair to broaden the range of prey species they can exploit. The more robust females are able to secure larger prey items, such as rails and waterfowl, while males rely on their agility to capture smaller avian and mammalian prey.

Foraging harriers quarter low over marshes, following creek banks and bisecting vegetative edges to flush prey. They rely on their acute sense of hearing and keen vision to locate their quarry. After spotting a potential meal, a harrier hovers and then pounces upon the intended prey.

Breeding Biology

In New Jersey, northern harrier courtship activity begins in late February and peaks during April. Courting male harriers perform elaborate aerial displays to reinforce their territory boundaries and establish and maintain pair bonds. The displaying male rises over the marsh, pausing for a moment in midair before descending in a series of steep, rapid dives. The female may fly below the male or perch on the ground. Additional aerial displays include leg lowering, talon grappling, and escorting intruders from nesting territories.

Although they are often monogamous, when resources are abundant harriers may exhibit polygyny, in which one male mates with two or more females. In such cases, the male attends to a primary female that receives a greater deal of male parental care, and a secondary female that receives a reduced amount of male assistance. Secondary females often experience lower productivity resulting from reduced clutch size or decreased nest attendance due to extended periods of time spent foraging away from the nest.

Nesting dates for the northern harrier span from mid-April to mid-June, varying annually with prey abundance and water levels. Spring flooding can reduce prey populations and obscure habitat, resulting in delayed nesting. Harriers exhibit limited fidelity to specific nest sites, although they may return to nest in the same general area in successive years. Elevated densities of breeding harriers may occur at high-quality sites.

Both the male and female harrier gather nesting material from which the female constructs a nest. Frequently located at a vegetational edge, the ground nest is fabricated of reeds, grasses, and sticks and is lined with thin grasses. In flood-prone areas, thicker nests may be built to avoid inundation. Also, if water levels rise during the nesting season, a pair may respond by adding material to the nest.

The female harrier lays a clutch of four to six white eggs and incubates them for 28 to 39 days. The eggs, which are laid at approximately two-day intervals, hatch asynchronously, resulting in young of staggered size. During lean years, only the larger, more aggressive chicks may survive.

Throughout incubation and brooding, the male delivers prey to the female via aerial transfers in which the male flies over the nesting area and drops prey to the female, who either captures it in midair or retrieves it at the nest. Initially, the female feeds the chicks pieces of flesh but later presents them with whole prey items. At about two weeks of age, the young, although still dependent upon the parents for food, wander from the nest, seeking shelter within nearby vegetation. At approximately five weeks old, the chicks begin to fly and they become independent several weeks later. Fledging dates range from late June to mid-August, depending on the initial date of nesting.

Status and Conservation

Before the early 1900s, the northern harrier was a common breeding species and winter resident within suitable habitat in the northeastern United States. Historic winter roosts in Hunterdon County, New Jersey, contained over 100 harriers. In the early twentieth century, northern harriers, as well as most other raptors, were commonly shot because of suspected predation on chickens, game birds, and waterfowl. Declines of breeding harriers in New Jersey were noted as early as the 1920s and continued into the 1940s. The loss of open areas resulting from reforestation and draining and filling of coastal marshes greatly reduced habitat for harriers. Harrier declines detected on

Christmas Bird Counts from 1952 to 1971 coincide with the extensive dredging and filling of coastal wetlands in New Jersey from the mid-1950s to the mid-1970s. The Breeding Bird Survey has also detected a declining trend of northern harriers in the Northeast from 1966 to 1999 (Sauer et al. 2000).

During the 1950s and 1960s, harriers exhibited reproductive failure resulting from contamination with the pesticide DDT. DDT, which biomagnifies at each trophic (food chain) level, accumulates in top-level carnivores, such as raptors. DDT contamination inhibits calcium metabolism, resulting in eggs with abnormally thin shells. During incubation, these weakened eggshells break under the weight of the adult. Following the federal ban of DDT in 1972, harrier populations began gradually to recover. However, DDE, a residual component of DDT, may continue to impact this species. Although current contaminant levels in northern harriers remain unknown, elevated levels of DDE have been documented in other raptors, including peregrine falcons and ospreys, nesting in marshes along the Delaware Bay coast.

Due to population declines and habitat loss, the northern harrier was listed as a threatened breeding species in New Jersey in 1979. In 1984, the harrier was reclassified as an endangered species because of limited population size, restricted range, sensitivity to disturbance, and continued loss of suitable nesting habitat. The New Jersey Natural Heritage Program considers the northern harrier to be "demonstrably secure globally," yet "imperiled in New Jersey because of rarity" (Office of Natural Lands Management 1992). This species has suffered a similar fate in other northeastern states and is consequently listed as endangered in Rhode Island and Connecticut and threatened in New Hampshire, Massachusetts, and New York. Due to population declines and reliance on threatened wetland habitats, the northern harrier has been listed as a Migratory Nongame Bird of Management Concern by the U.S. Fish and Wildlife Service's Office of Migratory Bird Management since 1982. In addition, the northern harrier was included on the National Audubon Society's Blue List of Imperiled Species from 1972 to 1986, the final year of the list.

In New Jersey, wintering populations of harriers are stable and the breeding population, although endangered, appears stable, provided that suitable habitat remains. During the 1980s, the breeding population in New Jersey was estimated at 40 to 50 pairs statewide, with 20 to 30 pairs in the Delaware Bay estuary (Dunne 1995). The New Jersey Breeding Bird Atlas documented confirmed or probable breeding pairs in 34 blocks within the state, over 50 percent of which occurred in the outer coastal plain (Walsh et al. 1999).

Limiting Factors and Threats

Habitat loss and alteration have reduced harrier numbers and continue to limit the breeding population in the state. The disturbance of wetland habitats has enabled phragmites to dominate coastal marshes, forming dense stands of this reed. Although harriers may nest in phragmites, it serves as suboptimal habitat, particularly for foraging. Tidal restoration activities may result in the flooding of harrier breeding habitat. The development and vegetative succession of fallow fields, grasslands, pastures, and agricultural lands has also reduced available nesting habitat.

Throughout the breeding season, especially during egg laying and incubation, northern harriers are extremely sensitive to human disturbance and may readily abandon nesting attempts in areas of high human activity. Coastal sites that contain otherwise suitable habitat may not be occupied due to high levels of human recreational activity.

As ground nesting birds, harriers are vulnerable to both flooding and nest predation by feral dogs, raccoons, fox, or owls. Prolonged periods of rain in the spring can delay nesting or result in the destruction or abandonment of nests.

Northern harrier populations are highly regulated by prey availability. Consequently, harriers may experience declines in reproductive success during times of reduced prey density.

Organochlorine residues, which persist in coastal and wetland habitats, may result in eggshell thinning, reproductive failure, or mortality of predatory birds. Elevated levels of DDE have been documented in peregrine falcon and osprey eggs in the Delaware Bay estuary, although contaminant concentrations in harrier eggs remains unknown.

Recommendations

The protection of known breeding sites and other suitable habitat is critical to maintain and increase nesting harrier populations in New Jersey. Existing breeding and roosting locations should be identified and protected from disturbance, development, or habitat alteration. To minimize disturbance during the breeding season, harrier nesting sites should be protected by 300 m (1,000 ft.) buffers in which human activity is prohibited.

Although a large fraction of marsh within the Delaware Bay estuary is in public ownership and consequently protected from development, coastal erosion threatens this habitat. Efforts must be made to maintain, protect, or create high-marsh habitats as erosion continues to engulf bay-shore marshes. Upland fields adjacent to coastal marshes, which are under heavy development pressure, should be acquired and managed to provide foraging and nesting habitat for harriers. Dense stands of phragmites should be converted to high marsh containing a mosaic of *Spartina patens, Distichylis, Juncus,* and *Iva* with only scattered patches of phragmites.

Large grasslands, including airports, can be managed to create habitat for northern harriers. Tall grassy vegetation should be encouraged, and woody growth resulting from vegetative succession must be controlled. Annual or biennial mowing or controlled burns can be used to maintain the successional stage but should only be implemented after all young have fledged. Habitat management should be conducted on a rotating schedule, ensuring that suitable habitat is available for harriers during the breeding season. Human activity, both recreational and agricultural, should be restricted in nesting areas during the breeding season.

Sherry Liguori

Osprey, *Pandion haliaetus*

Status: State: Threatened Federal: Not listed

Identification

The osprey is a large raptor with a wingspan of 1.4 to 1.8 m (4.5–6 ft.). When gliding, the osprey's long, narrow wings are pulled toward the body and its silhouette is analogous to an "M" shape, closely resembling a gull in flight. In a shallow glide or full soar, the wings are bowed downward. Ospreys fly with stiff and shallow wingbeats, pumping the head and body up and down while flapping.

The adult osprey is dark brown above and light below. The underside is white with contrasting dark carpal ("wrist") patches and barred flight feathers. The head is white with a broad, black eye stripe that extends to the back of the neck. The tail and flight feathers are dark brown with faint white bands. Adult females and juveniles of both sexes exhibit a "necklace" of dark feathers that contrast with the white feathers of the upper breast. The intensity of this necklace varies among individuals, with some adult males also displaying this trait. Females are only slightly larger than males and, excluding the necklace, the plumage of both sexes is identical. Juvenile ospreys closely resemble adults. However, juveniles exhibit buff-colored tips to the upperwing coverts, a more heavily streaked crown, mottled carpal patches, and a tawny wash to the underwing that fades by the following spring.

On all ages, the osprey has a pale blue-gray cere (fleshy area behind the base of the bill) and legs. Its toes are equipped with tiny spines, or spicules, that enable them to grasp slippery fish. The bill is black and strongly hooked with a sharp tip for piercing the skin of fish. The osprey's eye color changes from blood red in nestlings to orange-yellow in juveniles to yellow in adults.

The osprey's call is a high-pitched, down-slurred whistle that is often repeated in a short series.

Distribution

Ospreys breed in temperate regions worldwide. In North America, the breeding range of the osprey spans from Alaska and Canada through the northern United States, with populations extending throughout the Great Lakes and along the Atlantic, Gulf, and Pacific Coasts to Florida, Texas, and California. The North American breeding population winters in Florida and the Gulf Coast states, southern California, southern Texas, Mexico, the West Indies, Central America, and northern South America.

In New Jersey, breeding ospreys occur along the Atlantic and Delaware Bay coasts, as well as at inland lakes, reservoirs, and rivers. The largest concentrations of nesting ospreys in the state can be found along the Atlantic Coast, particularly at Island Beach State Park and Avalon/Stone Harbor. Fitted with satellite-tracked radio transmitters, osprey from New Jersey nests have wintered from Venezuela and Colombia to Brazil's Amazon River basin. The osprey is a common migrant in New Jersey, especially at coastal migration sites such as Cape May Point and Sandy Hook. Fall migrants can be seen as early as mid-August and may occur as late as early November. However, most migrant ospreys pass through from mid-September to mid-October, with a peak during late September and early October. Record fall migration counts include a season total of 6,734 in 1996 and a daily maximum of 1,023 on October 3, 1989, both at Cape May Point (Walsh et al. 1999). Spring migrants occur from mid-March to May, with a peak during mid- to late April.

Habitat

As a piscivorous species, the osprey is strictly associated with bodies of water that support adequate fish populations. Consequently, ospreys inhabit coastal rivers, marshes, bays, and inlets as well as inland rivers, lakes, and reservoirs. Ospreys nest on live or dead trees, artificial nesting platforms, light poles, channel markers, abandoned duck blinds, or other artificial structures that are in close proximity to fishing areas and offer an unobstructed view of the surrounding landscape. Infrequently, ospreys nest on the ground within coastal marshes. Territories typically contain poles, snags, or structures near the nest on which the ospreys perch.

Diet

As its former name, "fish hawk," implies, the osprey is a raptor that feeds exclusively on fish. Ospreys are opportunistic and will pursue most fish that are within one meter of the surface. However, in some areas, particular species may dominate the diet. Ospreys along the Atlantic Coast feed largely on menhaden (*Brevoortia tyrannus*) and summer flounder (*Paralichthys dentatus*), while ospreys along Delaware Bay consume menhaden, channel catfish (*Ictalurus punctatus*), and white perch (*Morone americana*).

A young osprey on its
Maurice River nest.
© Jane Morton-Galetto

Osprey productivity is strongly associated with fish availability. Consequently, ospreys may experience delayed breeding or reproductive failure in
years when fish populations are low. A nesting pair of ospreys with young
may require six to eight fish per day.

Breeding Biology

From mid- to late March, adult ospreys return to their nesting territories
throughout New Jersey. Mated pairs court and build or repair nests from late
March to mid-April. Ospreys construct large, bulky stick nests atop trees or
man-made structures near bodies of water. About 85% of New Jersey's osprey
nests are located on man-made nesting platforms or poles. Osprey nests often
are one meter in diameter and expand each year as breeding birds build upon
existing nests. Ospreys line their stick nests with marsh grasses and eelgrass
(*Zostera marina*) and often adorn nests with assorted rubbish such as fishing
line, plastic bottles, tin cans, and feathers.

Osprey pairs may nest in close proximity to one another and at some locations, such as Stone Harbor/Avalon and Island Beach State Park, they occur
in dense concentrations of more than 20 nesting pairs. Under these conditions, the ospreys respond to intruders much like a colonial-nesting species,
with individuals from neighboring nests joining together to mob a predator
or trespasser.

During mid-April to mid-May, the female osprey lays three to four tan-
colored eggs that are blotched and streaked with reddish brown markings.
Although the male may assist, the female typically incubates the eggs over
a 32- to 33-day period. Throughout this time, the male hunts and delivers
food to his mate. The female begins incubation with the first egg, resulting in
young of staggered ages and sizes. This strategy of asynchronous hatching,

employed by many birds of prey, ensures that there will be one chick that is larger and stronger than the others. During lean food years, the parents can invest their effort in this chick, which will have an increased probability of survival. If scarce resources were divided among several young, none may survive.

For their first few weeks, osprey chicks hunker down low in the nest, blending in with their surroundings. After about four weeks, they begin to sit up in the nest and stretch their wings. At seven to eight weeks old, the young ospreys, now capable of flight, may venture outside the nesting area, but continue to receive food from their parents. Ospreys are especially vulnerable to mortality from collisions with automobiles or electrical wires during this fledging period. Families may remain near their nesting territories until August, when they disperse or migrate.

First-year ospreys typically remain on their tropical wintering grounds throughout the spring and summer. Two-year-old ospreys may migrate north to nesting grounds, but often only establish "housekeeping," or practice, nests and do not produce any young. It is not until they are three years old that ospreys return to their breeding grounds as adults.

Status and Conservation

In the 1800s, the osprey was an abundant breeding species along the New Jersey coast. In 1884, there were 100 nests at Seven Mile Beach, currently Avalon/Stone Harbor, alone. However, by 1890, the number of ospreys nesting at Seven Mile Beach shrank to only 25 pairs, and similar declines were evident throughout the state. These early population declines are attributed to habitat loss, eradication of nest trees, egg collecting, and shooting. Further declines in the osprey population continued through the turn of the century

A pair of ospreys at the nest they built atop a man-made platform in the marshes near Stone Harbor. Photo courtesy NJ ENSP

and into the 1930s and 1940s. As human settlement along the coast increased during this time, trees that were used by ospreys as nesting sites were destroyed.

The pesticide DDT was first used to control mosquitoes in Cape May County marshes in 1946 and was applied at increasing rates until 1964. When introduced into the environment, DDT enters the food chain and bioaccumulates at each trophic level, contaminating top-level predators such as the osprey with high doses of this biologically harmful pesticide. DDT contamination inhibits calcium metabolism in birds, reducing the thickness of the eggshell. When an adult bird attempts to incubate an egg with a thinned shell, the egg will break under the weight of the bird. Because DDT contamination may remain within an adult osprey's body for years, pairs can continue to experience reproductive failure over a long period of time.

Following the use of DDT, osprey populations in New Jersey plummeted due to several decades of poor productivity. Prior to the 1950s, the osprey population in New Jersey was estimated at 500 pairs (Leck 1984). In 1950, there were 253 nesting pairs along the Atlantic Coast of New Jersey south of Barnegat Light. By 1975, only 53 pairs remained in this area and a total of only 68 pairs remained statewide.

Due to its disastrous environmental impacts, the use of DDT was banned in New Jersey in 1968 and in the United States in 1972. However, because of its persistence in biological systems, contamination from DDT and its metabolite, DDE, continued to impair osprey productivity. Ospreys in areas that experienced the most severe population declines and the lowest productivity in the state were also found to contain the highest DDT levels in their eggs. Osprey eggs collected in New Jersey during the early 1970s yielded much higher DDT and DDE concentrations than those from other states. In addition, analysis of eggs from New Jersey ospreys also revealed contamination from PCBs.

Pesticide contamination and habitat loss had reduced New Jersey's osprey population to a tiny fraction of its former level. Consequently, the osprey was one of the first species to be included on the New Jersey Endangered Species List when the New Jersey Endangered Species Conservation Act passed in 1973. With this legislation came the establishment of the New Jersey Endangered and Nongame Species Program (ENSP), a team of biologists dedicated to the conservation of New Jersey's imperiled wildlife. In 1979, the ENSP began an osprey reintroduction program in which biologists transplanted eggs from healthy nests in the Chesapeake Bay area into active, but unsuccessful, New Jersey nests. In addition, biologists erected nesting platforms to support a growing population and began annual surveys to monitor osprey productivity.

Slowly, the osprey population began to recover, as nesting success improved and the number of nesting pairs increased each year. The state population grew from a low of 68 pairs in 1975 to 87 pairs in 1981. Productivity had improved from 0.42 young per active nest in 1968–72 to 0.97 in 1979 and 1.18 in 1982–84. Due to its improved reproductive success, its acceptance of artificial nesting structures, and the decline of persistent pesticides, the status of the osprey was changed from endangered to threatened in New Jersey in 1985. The osprey, brought back from the brink, was the first to be removed from the endangered species list in New Jersey. The New Jersey Natural Heritage Program considers the osprey to be "demonstrably secure globally" yet "rare in New Jersey" (Office of Natural Lands Management 1992).

After 1985, New Jersey's osprey population grew beyond 200 pairs and productivity was stable at around 1.3 to 1.5 young per active nest. The ban of DDT, the reintroduction of healthy eggs, and the ospreys' acceptance of artificial nest sites are largely responsible for this species' recovery.

However, despite increases in productivity along the Atlantic Coast, osprey production along the Delaware Bay Coast, particularly in Salem County, remained low throughout the 1980s. Productivity in Salem County, which averaged 0.63 young per active nest from 1974 to 1984, was well below productivity in other areas of the state, which often exceeded one young per active nest. In addition, the number of active nests in Salem County declined from 1984 to 1987. In 1987, ENSP biologists initiated an investigation into the poor productivity of this population. Contaminant analysis revealed that Delaware Bay ospreys experienced more severe eggshell thinning and higher levels of contaminants such as DDE, DDD, PCBs, and dieldrin heptachlor epoxide than Atlantic Coast ospreys. In addition, fish samples collected from Delaware Bay in 1990 contained higher contaminant levels than those from the Atlantic Coast. Osprey eggs and blood collected from Salem County nests from 1991 to 1994 were compared to samples taken from declining populations around the Great Lakes. The analysis revealed that ospreys nesting along Delaware Bay had higher organochlorine and PCB levels than Great Lakes osprey populations. However, by the late 1990s, organochlorine pesticide levels had declined in osprey eggs and fish collected along the Delaware Bay, allowing for improved nesting productivity in this area. Productivity among Delaware Bay nests averaged a very healthy 1.78 young per nest in 2001.

Ospreys nesting along the Atlantic Coast of New Jersey experienced a dramatic reduction in productivity in 1997 and 1998, possibly due to a scarcity of prey. But productivity, which averaged only 0.6 young per nest along the Atlantic Coast during these years, returned to a normal average of 1.3 young per nest in 1999 and 2000, and was nearly 1.6 in 2001 and 1.4 in 2002. The biennial aerial osprey survey in 2001 tallied 340 pairs in the state, the majority of which were located along the Atlantic Coast.

Limiting Factors and Threats

Although pesticide contamination in ospreys is not as severe as it was several decades ago, water pollution and contamination of aquatic life may still jeopardize New Jersey's osprey population. Consequently, the ENSP continues to monitor osprey productivity annually to ensure that if such a problem arises again, it will be detected and addressed immediately. In addition, biologists continue to measure annual nest productivity, as well as prey fish abundance, as indicators of population and ecosystem health.

A lack of suitable nesting sites can be a limiting factor to a growing osprey population, such as New Jersey's. With the aid of generous donations and dedicated volunteers, the ENSP has been able to erect new nesting platforms each year. For example, in 1999 the ENSP initiated an "Adopt an Osprey Nest Project," in which volunteers donated the funds necessary to erect an osprey nest. This project was highly successful and was responsible for the creation of more than 20 new nests in 1999.

In addition to threats such as habitat loss and pesticide contamination, ospreys now face a growing threat resulting from increased recreational activity along New Jersey's coast. Each summer, the state's barrier islands swell with an expanding number of tourists that recreate within marshes and waterways. The use of personal watercraft (PWC) within coastal marshes and tidal creeks during the breeding season may negatively affect ospreys as well as other nesting species. PWCs enable people to enter otherwise inaccessible areas of the marsh, where human activity and noise can disturb sensitive wildlife species. Frequent or prolonged human activity near a nesting area can flush the adults from a nest, leaving their eggs and/or young vulnerable to predators and the elements. Repeated disturbance may also cause nest abandonment. Harassing ospreys and other threatened and endangered wildlife is illegal and punishable by state and federal laws.

Recommendations

As an indicator of environmental health that can be used to identify hazards to water quality and aquatic ecosystems, the osprey should continue to be closely monitored. New nesting platforms should be erected and existing platforms should be maintained. Human activity, especially the use of personal watercraft, should be prohibited in marshes, creeks, rivers, lakes, and reservoirs containing nesting ospreys.

Sherry Liguori

Peregrine Falcon, *Falco peregrinus*
Status: State: Endangered   Federal: Not listed

Identification

Peregrine falcons, like all falcon species, are designed for speed. With long, pointed wings, a long, tapered tail, and flat head, peregrines can attain rapid speeds in powered flight or stoops. Attaining dive speeds of up to 300 kmp or 200 mph, the peregrine falcon is the planet's fastest bird. Its wingbeats are stiffer and deeper than those of other falcon species. In a soar, they exhibit a soft-angled silhouette resembling that of a cocked bow and arrow. Significant sexual size dimorphism is displayed by peregrine falcons, the females of which can be as much as one-third larger than males. In addition, the crow-sized males are considerably slighter and more narrow winged than females. The peregrine falcon's call is a series of quick, loud *kee* notes.

Adult peregrines are blue-gray above, with a dark head and flight feathers and a paler rump. From below, adults are whitish with dark barring on the

Tall urban buildings are among the peregrine falcons' favorite nesting sites. Photo courtesy NJ ENSP

chest and underwing. Like most falcon species, peregrines show a distinct sideburn or "mustache" mark on each side of the face. The cere—the fleshy area behind the base of the bill that contains the nostrils—and legs are yellow, the bill is black, and the eyes are dark brown.

Juvenile peregrine falcons are dark slate brown on the upperside and often show a contrasting blonde crown. The underside is buff colored with dark brown checker-marked underwings and vertical streaks on the chest. The cere and legs are pale blue and the bill is black. Adult plumage is acquired the summer after fledging.

Distribution

The peregrine falcon is a cosmopolitan species, occurring throughout much of the world. Several races of peregrines nest in North America, ranging throughout the Canadian and Alaskan arctic and at scattered locations within Canada, the contiguous United States, and Mexico. Peregrines winter throughout the Americas, occurring along the Atlantic, Pacific, and Gulf Coasts of the United States south to Chile and Argentina.

Historically, peregrine falcons nested on cliffs in New Jersey along the Hudson and Delaware Rivers. Currently, peregrines nest atop city buildings, bridges, and man-made nesting towers. Most large bridges between New Jersey and New York or Philadelphia contain nesting pairs. Peregrines nest atop tall buildings in cities, and one pair even resides atop an Atlantic City casino. Man-made nesting towers are home to peregrines along both the Atlantic and Delaware Bay coasts.

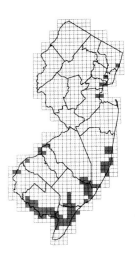

Peregrines that nest in New Jersey typically occupy their territories year-round. Migrant peregrines from northern nests occur in greatest numbers at coastal sites, such as Cape May Point, during the fall. Fall migration occurs from late August to mid-November and peaks during late September and early

October. A record number of 1,791 peregrines was counted at Cape May Point during the fall of 1997 (Walsh et al. 1999). Small numbers of peregrines occur in New Jersey throughout the winter. Spring migration, which sees much fewer peregrines than fall, spans from mid-April to mid-May and peaks during early May.

Habitat

Traditionally, peregrine falcon nest sites were restricted to cliffs and rock outcrops. As people began to inhabit areas occupied by peregrines, the birds took to nesting on buildings and bridges. Today, peregrines continue to nest on these structures, and there are no remaining cliff nests in New Jersey. During the peregrine's population recovery two decades ago, artificial nesting platforms were erected in coastal marshes. Peregrines continue to nest on these platforms today. Peregrine falcons favor open areas for foraging and often hunt over marshes, beaches, or open water.

Diet

The peregrine falcon specializes in pursuing avian prey, relying on speed and agility to capture other birds. A hunting peregrine dives with amazing speed toward its prey, striking the bird with such force that it is often killed upon impact. Peregrines feed on an array of birds, including songbirds, pigeons and doves, corvids (crows and jays), shorebirds, and waterfowl. Female peregrines, which are more robust, are capable of securing larger prey than males. The diet of the peregrine varies with its nesting habitat. City-nesting pairs often feed chiefly on pigeons (*Columba livia*) and starlings (*Sturnus vulgaris*). Peregrines nesting in marshes feed on migratory birds, such as shorebirds and passerines, during the spring and fall and prey upon locally nesting species, such as willets (*Catoptrophorus semipalmatus*) and clapper rails (*Rallus longirostris*), during the breeding season.

Breeding Biology

Peregrine falcons that breed in New Jersey typically remain near their nesting area year-round. Courtship activity among nesting pairs commences during March. The displaying birds circle high in the air, then dive at each other in a stoop toward the ground, sometimes while locking talons. Pairs also exchange food in midair.

From late March to late April, the peregrine falcon lays a clutch of three to four eggs. Peregrines do not construct nests, but lay their eggs either directly on the surface of the nesting structure or in a shallow, unlined scrape within small rocks or dirt. The eggs are cream colored and heavily marked with reddish brown spotting. The female lays eggs at two- to three-day intervals, but does not begin incubation until the clutch is complete, so eggs hatch around the same day. Still, sometimes the smallest chick may not survive if food is limited. If food is plentiful, all of the chicks may fledge.

Incubation, which spans 32 to 34 days, is conducted primarily by the female. The female also broods the altricial (dependent) chicks, while the male delivers food. For about two weeks after hatching, the male transfers prey to the female, which feeds it to the chicks. At about three weeks old, the chicks begin to walk and jump about in the nest. As the chicks grow, the female also hunts and both adults present the young with prey. At 40 to 48 days old, the chicks are able to fly but stay close to the nest site. They remain dependent on the adults for an additional two months. Peregrine falcons exhibit strong fidelity to their natal sites, and young birds may return to the area of their birth when they are able to breed. Juvenile males may breed the following year, but females do not breed until they are two to three years old.

Status and Conservation

The peregrine falcon historically bred in New Jersey on cliffs along the Hudson River (the Palisades) and along the Delaware River. During the 1930s and

A trio of just-banded peregrine falcon chicks in an ENSP-built nesting box. Photo courtesy NJ ENSP

1940s, there were about 350 pairs of peregrines nesting east of the Mississippi. Well into the 1940s and 1950s, egg collectors and falconers looted peregrine nests, while gunners, game wardens, and pigeon fanciers shot adult falcons, which were viewed as vermin. Human activity at nest sites, coupled with expanding development and road construction near peregrine nests, caused local nest abandonment.

While persecution and nest disturbances resulted in declines, it was the introduction of DDT that wiped out the species from much of its former range. The pesticide was regularly used for mosquito control from the mid-1940s to the mid-1960s. Initially thought to be harmless, DDT was later linked to devastating population declines in several bird species, including the peregrine falcon, osprey (*Pandion haliaetus*), and bald eagle (*Haliaeetus leucocephalus*). Once introduced into the environment, the concentration of DDT increased at each trophic, or food chain, level—a phenomenon termed "biomagnification." In top-level predators such as raptors, DDT had accumulated at levels high enough to impair reproduction. DDT, which inhibits calcium metabolism, caused eggshell thinning in contaminated birds. Consequently, the thin-shelled eggs cracked under the weight of the incubating adult. A reduction in eggshell thickness of nearly 23% was documented in peregrine eggs from the pre-DDT era to the 1950s.

The 1950s and 1960s saw a devastating crash in peregrine falcon populations. By the 1960s, there were no known nesting peregrines in the East. The extirpation of the peregrine alarmed the scientific community, which joined forces in the species recovery effort. The use of DDT was banned in New Jersey in 1968 and in the United States in 1972. The peregrine falcon was classified as a federally endangered species in 1970 and as a New Jersey endangered species in 1974. The following year (1975), a peregrine falcon recovery plan was initiated in the East. The goal of the plan was to restore the breeding population to at least half of pre-DDT levels. This resulted in an eastern goal of 175 to 200 pairs, a mid-Atlantic regional goal of 20 to 25 pairs, and a New Jersey goal of 8 to 10 pairs.

During the late 1970s, biologists released young peregrines into the wild throughout their former range. This process, known as hacking, was hoped to reestablish nesting populations, as peregrines often return to their natal sites to breed. Peregrines released at cliff sites experienced high mortality due to great horned owl (*Bubo virginianus*) predation, causing biologists to erect man-made nesting structures in coastal marshes, where owl numbers were lower and prey was abundant. In 1980, peregrine falcons nested at Edwin B. Forsythe National Wildlife Refuge in Atlantic County, the first nesting attempt in the state, and the eastern United States, in nearly a quarter century. Eggshells from New Jersey nests contained residual contaminants during the early 1980s, but not at levels high enough to impair reproduction. By 1986, the peregrine had reached its local recovery goal, with 10 pairs in New Jersey and 21 pairs in the mid-Atlantic region.

The peregrine falcon population in New Jersey had stabilized at approximately 10 pairs during the late 1980s and early 1990s. Productivity was high at Atlantic Coast nests, yet many nests along the Delaware Bay and Delaware River failed due to owl predation, abandonment, or unhatched eggs, possibly resulting from PCB contamination. Peregrines from Barnegat and Manahawkin Bays also showed elevated levels of PCBs as well as DDE, chlordane, and dieldrin in the early 1990s. Although the use of DDT was banned in the United States, migratory prey, such as shorebirds and passerines, may encounter this pesticide on their wintering grounds and pass the contaminant on to peregrine falcons.

Currently, the state's peregrine population remains stable at about 15 pairs. Although PCBs levels remain elevated in peregrine eggs, pairs are exhibiting good productivity, averaging 1.7 young per nest on buildings and towers since 1986. In 2002, a total of 17 pairs statewide produced 1.54 young per nest on buildings and towers and about 1.25 per nest on bridges.

Because national recovery goals were met, the peregrine falcon was removed from the federal endangered species list in 1999. Despite the fact that the peregrines have met state numerical recovery goals, their continued listing as endangered in New Jersey is warranted. They remain threatened by environmental contaminants and human disturbance and rely on active management of their nesting sites.

Limiting Factors and Threats

Pesticide contamination, nest predation, and disturbance to nest sites threaten peregrine falcons in New Jersey. Peregrines acquire contaminants through their prey, much of which includes migratory species that are exposed to environmental contaminants on their breeding, wintering, and migratory grounds. Great horned owls are both predators and nest competitors of the peregrine falcon. Owls prey upon peregrine young and usurp nesting structures from resident peregrines. Along the Delaware Bay shore, where great horned owl numbers are extremely high, peregrines frequently experience nest failure due to owl predation and competition.

Because peregrines nest in remote or inaccessible locations, they are often safe from human disturbance. However, nests in coastal marshes may be disturbed by boats, jet skis, or curious people. Construction near falcon nests located on buildings or bridges during the breeding season may cause abandonment.

Recommendations

The New Jersey Endangered and Nongame Species Program (ENSP) has managed peregrine falcon nesting sites in the state since the 1970s. Man-made nesting towers, consisting of a large nest box supported by telephone poles, are erected in coastal marshes. Predator guards are attached to the poles to prevent raccoons (*Procyon lotor*) from climbing up to the nest. Gravel is placed in the nest box to provide the birds with a nesting substrate. Each year, all known nests are monitored and the chicks are banded. During nest checks, prey remains are collected in an ongoing study of peregrine diet. In addition, eggshells and unhatched eggs are collected and analyzed for contaminants.

Dead peregrines that are recovered may also be analyzed for contaminants. By keeping close tabs on the health of New Jersey's peregrines, the ENSP is able to quickly react should a problem arise. In addition, as biological monitors of environmental health, peregrine falcons can act as an early warning system for contaminants that can also affect entire ecosystems as well as human health.

Peregrine falcon nest locations must be taken into consideration when conducting maintenance or construction on buildings or bridges. Construction, or other activities that may disturb nesting birds, should be conducted outside of the March 1 to July 31 breeding season.

Sherry Liguori

Black Rail, *Laterallus jamaicensis*
Status: State: Threatened   Federal: Migratory Nongame Bird of Management Concern

Identification

Measuring only about the size of a sparrow, the diminutive black rail is the smallest North American rail. Adult black rails are dark gray or nearly black overall with a variable amount of scattered white spotting on the back that may also extend onto the wing coverts and secondaries. The nape and upper back are deep chestnut colored. The dark gray undertail coverts and flanks are streaked with white or light gray. The tail is short and grayish brown. The bill is short and black and the legs and feet are grayish brown. Although the sexes are similar in size, they differ slightly in plumage. The throat of the female may be pale gray or white, while that of the male may be pale to medium gray.

Black rail.
© C. E. Harold/VIREO

Juvenile black rails resemble adults but are duller gray overall with less spotting above and thinner streaking on the flanks. Eye color, which changes with age, is red in adults and may range from brown to orange in juveniles.

The black rail is an elusive species that typically walks or runs rather than flies. Due to its secretive nature and nocturnal habits, this rail is more often heard than seen. The black rail's call, a repeated *kic-kee-doo* or *kic-kic-kerr,* may be given throughout the night but is most frequently voiced during the first few hours after sunset or before sunrise. Rarely, black rails may vocalize during the day. Vocal activity is greatest during the early breeding season, from late April to mid-May. Adults and young may communicate using *kik* or *yip* calls.

Distribution

The black rail is a widely distributed but locally occurring species in North America. It is found along the Atlantic Coast and coastal California, as well as very rarely in the north central United States. The breeding range of the Atlantic Coast race (*L. j. jamaicensis*) extends from Florida to Connecticut, with the northernmost breeding stronghold in southern New Jersey. Black rails winter along the Gulf Coast and the coasts of Florida, Mexico, and Central America.

In New Jersey, the black rail is a rare and local breeding species along the Atlantic and Delaware Bay coasts. Atlantic Coast nests were much more common in the early to mid-1900s, when black rails were documented at Seven Mile Beach (Avalon/Stone Harbor), Sea Isle City, Ludlam's Beach, Beesley's Point, the Great Egg Harbor River, Longport, Brigantine, Tuckerton, Holgate, Beach Haven, Long Beach Island, Manahawkin, and Little Beach. Stone (1937) reported 24 nests in Ocean, Atlantic, and Burlington Counties, and 80 nests were documented in the state in 1955. A black rail nesting population in Manahawkin contained 50 individuals in 1975 (Kerlinger and Sutton 1989).

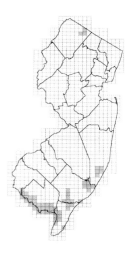

Marshes along the Delaware Bay coast of Cape May, Cumberland, and Salem Counties provide a stronghold for black rails in New Jersey. Surveys conducted in 1988 revealed that 75% of black rails detected were found along the Delaware Bay shore, particularly in Cumberland and Cape May counties (Kerlinger and Sutton 1989). Within this area, most black rails occur from Salem to Goshen and have been documented during the breeding season at Turkey Point, Greenwich Township, Fairfield Township, Dividing Creek, Heislerville Wildlife Management Area (WMA), Commercial Township, Jake's Landing, Dennis Creek, and Goshen.

In the past two decades, black rails have been observed along the Atlantic Coast during the nesting season at Nummy Island, Marmora, Upper Township, Lester G. MacNamara WMA, Edwin B. Forsythe National Wildlife Refuge, and Manahawkin. Most breeding records of this species occur south of the Raritan River. In 1993, the New Jersey Breeding Bird Atlas documented the state's first inland breeding population at Wallkill National Wildlife Refuge, Sussex County.

Black rails are nocturnal migrants that travel through New Jersey from September to mid-October and from mid-April to May. Although black rails typically winter in southern regions, they may rarely occur as far north as New Jersey during winter.

Habitat

Coastal salt and brackish marshes are home to the black rail, which nests in areas of elevated marsh that are flooded only during extremely high tides. Nests are typically located in marshes dominated by salt hay (*Spartina patens*). These marshes also may contain spike grass (*Distichlis spicata*), black rush (*Juncus gerardi*), or marsh elder (*Iva frutescens*). Salt-marsh cordgrass (*S. alterniflora*) and reed grass (*Phragmites communis*) may also occur within the marsh, but are not favored by black rails. Salt hay farming along the Delaware Bay shore inadvertently created habitat for breeding black rails. Marshes containing salt hay provide characteristically thick mats of overlapping vegetation, beneath which the rails traverse on pathways of flattened vegetation. During markedly high tides, black rails may seek cover within herbaceous vegetation in adjacent upland fields and meadows. Black rails occupy similar habitats throughout the year.

Diet

The black rail is an omnivorous species that consumes aquatic invertebrates, insects, and seeds. Isopods (aquatic crustaceans), mollusks, diving beetles, weevils, earwigs, grasshoppers, ants, and spiders have been documented in their diet. These rails often forage in wet areas, gleaning food items from above and below the high-tide line. Black rails are opportunistic and thus feed largely on seasonally abundant prey, such as insects in the summer and seeds in the winter.

Breeding Biology

During the breeding season, the *kee-kee-doo* calls of black rails can be heard on calm nights from within salt hay marshes along the shores of the Delaware Bay. Vocal activity of black rails typically peaks during the first 2 weeks of May, although courtship and nesting dates vary depending on water levels within the marsh. One "alpha" male may dominate the chorus, while other males call less frequently. Black rails typically vocalize in the evening and throughout the night but may infrequently call during the day.

Black rail breeding colonies can be ephemeral or transitory, suggesting that large areas of suitable habitat are necessary to maintain breeding populations of this species. In Maryland, territory size has been estimated at 3 to 4 hectares (7–9 acres).

The black rail constructs a cup nest woven of marsh grasses on the ground and concealed within mats of salt hay, spike grass, or black rush. Surrounding live grasses are intertwined into the nest structure, forming a canopy. Trampled pathways beneath tall grasses lead to and from the nest.

From late May to late June, the female lays a clutch of six to ten lightly speckled white eggs. Black rails may replace clutches that are lost to predation or flooding. Both the male and female incubate the eggs for 16 to 20 days. Although they are dependent upon their parents for food and brooding, the precocial chicks may leave the nest within a day of hatching. The age at which young gain independence is unknown.

Status and Conservation

The black rail, once considered a game bird, was historically a locally common breeding species in tidal marshes along the Atlantic and Delaware Bay coasts of New Jersey. Following the 1920s and 1930s, black rail numbers began to decline as coastal wetlands were filled, ditched, and polluted. From 1953 to 1973, nearly 25% of tidal marshes in New Jersey were filled or diked, with the most severe losses occurring throughout the range of the black rail in Cumberland, Salem, Cape May, Atlantic, and Ocean counties. Increased human recreational activities at coastal marshes further threatened already depressed populations of this rail. Consequently, this species was lost from many historic breeding locales, particularly along the heavily used and developed Atlantic coast.

Due to severe population declines and localized distribution resulting from habitat loss, alteration, and degradation, the black rail was listed as a threatened species in New Jersey in 1987. The New Jersey Natural Heritage Program considers the black rail to be "apparently secure globally," yet "rare in New Jersey" (Office of Natural Lands Management 1992). Because of its disjunct distribution and small population size, the black rail was included as a Migratory Nongame Bird of Management Concern in the United States by the U.S. Fish and Wildlife Service in 1992. Habitat loss and population declines have occurred in other northeastern states, such as Connecticut, where the black rail is listed as threatened, and New York and Maryland, where it is of special concern.

Limiting Factors and Threats

Habitat loss, flooding, human disturbance, and predation threaten black rails in New Jersey. Areas of high marsh and salt hay along the Delaware Bay shore are vulnerable to coastal erosion, tidal restoration activities, and marsh management activities. As water levels in the Delaware River rise, marshes erode, resulting in the succession of high marsh to low marsh as tidal inundation creeps inland. Recent restoration activities in Cumberland and Cape May counties have flooded large areas of salt hay, eliminating former black rail nesting habitat. Along the Atlantic coast, much of the high marsh has been filled and developed, severely limiting habitat for these rails. In addition, the invasive phragmites, which offers poor quality nesting habitat for black rails, has dominated many of New Jersey's marshes. Pesticides used for mosquito control may threaten the birds' invertebrate prey.

Because their ground nests are vulnerable to flooding, black rails typically breed in areas that do not experience regular tidal flow. As a result, nests are extremely susceptible to destruction during seasonally high tides. In some years, breeding activity may be delayed due to late spring flooding. Adult black rails and their young are also vulnerable to predators when vegetative cover is inundated during high tides.

Human activity in tidal marshes during the breeding season threatens black rails. During the summer months, many of New Jersey's coastal marshes receive high levels of human recreational activity that may result in nest abandonment or the trampling of nests and young. Frequent human activity may also deter this species from breeding at otherwise suitable sites. The harvesting of salt hay during the nesting season can destroy nests and kill both young and adult rails.

As a naturally elusive and infrequently encountered bird, the black rail is one of the most highly sought species by birders. Although often noninvasive, bird watchers may practice unethical methods in order to observe this species. Such activities in the marshes, which can trample birds, eggs, and habitat, may also alert predators to the locations of birds or nests. Call tapes, which are used to elicit responses from territorial or courting black rails, can disturb nesting birds and should only be used during legitimate scientific studies.

Predation and migration mortality limit black rail populations. Feral cats and dogs, hawks, owls, herons, gulls, raccoons, and rats may prey upon rail eggs, young, or adults. Flooding and human disturbance may increase the vulnerability of rails to such predators. Severe weather conditions encountered during migration or in the winter may result in elevated mortality rates for black rails. In addition, migrant rails may be killed during collisions with buildings, towers, lighthouses, or wires.

Recommendations

Management for black rails must include the preservation and protection of both occupied and potential habitat. Areas of potential habitat include sites that contain suitable habitat as well as locations where black rails have previously been documented. Because they occupy breeding sites ephemerally and have high juvenile dispersal rates, nesting black rails may be found at different locations in different years. Thus, large tracts of suitable habitat, including high marshes along the Delaware Bay shore, should be protected and considered high priority sites for this species. The protection of such locations from habitat alteration and human disturbance can also favor other endangered species such as the Northern harrier (*Circus cyaneus*) and the short-eared owl (*Asio flammeus*). In addition to large tracts of coastal marsh, adjacent upland buffers should be secured to provide shelter for black rails during floods. Habitat management should be implemented on public lands to create or maintain areas of high marsh that are safeguarded from regular tidal flooding. Pesticide use should be limited or restricted at black rail sites.

Human activity must be restricted at black rail nesting sites during the breeding season. Public outreach efforts should inform birders about the disturbances created by such activities as call tapes and walking through nesting habitat. In addition, the public must be made aware of the potential legal implications and fines for harassing endangered species. Cooperative efforts may be established in which birders can assist supervising biologists with black rail monitoring projects.

Because so little is known about the black rail, additional research is needed to study its nesting biology and monitor population trends. The effects of marsh management, tidal restoration, and mosquito control activities should also be investigated.

Sherry Liguori

Piping Plover, *Charadrius melodus*
Status: State: Endangered   Federal: Threatened (Atlantic Coast population)

Identification

The piping plover is a small shorebird with a black neck band and a black bar across the forehead. The upperparts are light sandy-brown and the underparts are white, providing the plover with camouflage against sandy beach backgrounds. The legs are bright orange and, in breeding plumage, the bill is also orange with a black tip. Although males and females are similar in appearance, males typically have darker, more extensive neck bands. The call of the piping plover is a ventriloquist-like *peep-lo* that is hard to pinpoint before the bird itself is sighted since it is often heard before it is seen.

Juvenile and winter-plumage adults are similar in appearance. Both lack the black neck and forehead bands characteristic of breeding adults. Rather,

Piping plover and chick. © Chris Davidson

there is a pale band around the neck. The bill is solid black and the legs are pale yellow.

Piping plovers may be confused with other shorebird species. The killdeer (*C. vociferus*), a larger plover of open uplands, has rich brown upperparts and two black neck bands. In both size and pattern, semipalmated plovers (*C. semipalmatus*) are similar to piping plovers but are much darker brown on the upperwing, back, and head. The sanderling (*Calidris alba*), which frequently feeds at coastal beaches along the water's edge, lacks neck bands and has a longer, black bill and a broad, white wing bar that is visible in flight.

Distribution

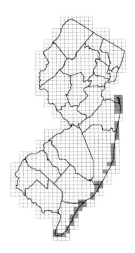

Three distinct breeding populations of piping plovers occur in North America: a northern Great Plains population, a Great Lakes population, and an Atlantic Coast population. The Atlantic Coast breeding population ranges from Newfoundland south to the Carolinas. Piping plovers winter in the Caribbean, Mexico, the Gulf Coast, and the southern Atlantic Coast north to North Carolina and Virginia.

In New Jersey, piping plovers breed on Atlantic Coast beaches from Sandy Hook to Cape May. Migrant plovers are uncommon and occur from early March to mid-April and from mid-July to late September. Females depart first during fall migration from their breeding grounds, followed by males, then juveniles.

Habitat

Piping plovers inhabit ocean-front beaches and barrier islands, typically nesting on the stretch of beach between the dunes and the high-tide line. Nests are often located in flat areas with shell fragments and sparse vegetation. The coloration of piping plovers and their eggs blend in remarkably with sand and broken pieces of shell. Sparse vegetation, such as American beach grass (*Ammophila breviligulata*) or sea rocket (*Cakile endentula*), is favored, as it provides cover against predators and the elements. However, areas with dense vegetation, such as dunes, are avoided by nesting plovers, since these sites provide cover for predators.

During the nonbreeding season, piping plovers inhabit coastal beaches, barrier islands, inlets, sandflats, mudflats, and dredged material islands. Piping plovers forage on intertidal beaches, washover areas, exposed mudflats and sandflats, wracklines, and shorelines.

Diet

The diet of the piping plover is dominated by marine invertebrates, including annelid and polychaete (marine) worms, small crustaceans, and mollusks. In addition, insects such as beetles and larvae are consumed. Adult piping plovers feed primarily during the day but may also forage at night. Foraging activity peaks during the hours before and after low tide, when intertidal areas are exposed.

Two piping plover chicks. © Clay Myers

Breeding Biology

During late March and April, piping plovers arrive at New Jersey's barrier islands and beaches. Males establish territories upon arrival, performing aerial displays and calling to mark their boundaries and attract mates. The male digs numerous scrapes throughout his territory, kicking sand, stones, and shells aside during the excavation. Prior to copulation, the female may join the male in nest scraping. Piping plovers are monogamous during each nesting season but may pair with different mates in successive years. Plovers exhibit fidelity to nesting sites and may return to a previously successful area in subsequent years.

The pair selects a scrape to be used as its nest. Located above the high-tide line among shells, pebbles, or clumps of beach grass, the shallow depression in the sand will soon contain eggs. The pair may leave the nest unlined or line it with shell fragments, pebbles, or small pieces of driftwood. Piping plovers may nest within colonies of least terns (*Sterna antillarum*) or common terns (*S. hirundo*). Terns, which aggressively attack intruders, afford plovers with an added method of defense and early warning of predators. Plovers that nest within tern colonies may experience increased reproductive success.

From late April to mid-May, piping plovers lay their eggs. The female deposits a clutch of three to four sandy-colored eggs that are speckled with brownish black spots, making them nearly invisible in the sand. If an intruder or predator should approach the nest, the adults feign injury to lure it away, leaving the camouflaged eggs concealed in the sand. While off the nest, adult plovers may also fake brooding to confuse a predator. Piping plovers generally lay one clutch of eggs per year but may replace lost clutches. Initial clutches are typically four eggs, while second nesting attempts often only produce three eggs.

Both adults incubate the eggs for 27 to 29 days. The precocial chicks, which are tiny, white, and downy, leave the nest within a few hours of hatching. Able to walk, the chicks follow their parents, pecking and running in search of food. The vulnerable chicks lay flat in the sand or hide among nearby vegetation when the adults sound an alarm call. In areas where several plovers nest in close proximity, neighboring pairs may assist one another in luring away predators.

Both the male and female plover brood the chicks for about three weeks. The young, which are able to fly at 30 to 35 days, fledge from early July to mid-August. Toward the end of the summer, adults and fledged juveniles form premigratory flocks, sometimes in the company of other shorebird species. The juveniles are able to breed the following year, but many do not breed until their second year. Often, young will return to their natal area to nest.

Status and Conservation

Although common during the 1800s, the piping plover was on the verge of extirpation by the 1890s and early 1900s due to market hunting and egg collecting. Protection afforded by the Migratory Bird Treaty Act of 1918 and changing fashion trends allowed plover populations gradually to recover during the 1920s and 1930s. However, since the late 1940s, coastal development

A plover shares the
Ocean City beach
with sunbathers.
© Richard Kuzminski

and the elevated recreational use of beaches have caused plover population declines. Human habitation along the shore has also resulted in elevated populations of many mammalian and avian predators.

In 1984, the piping plover was listed as an endangered species in New Jersey. The New Jersey Natural Heritage Program considers the piping plover to be globally "very rare and local throughout its range," and "critically imperiled in New Jersey because of extreme rarity" (Office of Natural Lands Management 1992). In 1986, the Atlantic Coast piping plover population was listed as threatened in the United States. A recovery goal of 2,000 pairs was set for the Atlantic Coast population, including 575 pairs in New Jersey and the New York region. Another goal set by the recovery plan is to achieve a five-year average productivity of 1.5 fledged young per pair. Active monitoring and management of the birds by the ENSP are integral parts of federal recovery efforts.

Since its date of listing, the Atlantic Coast piping plover population has increased, growing from 790 pairs in 1986 to 1,386 pairs in 1999 (U.S. Fish and Wildlife Service 2000). While numbers have increased in New England during the 1980s and 1990s, the number of plovers nesting in New Jersey has remained essentially stable at around 120 pairs. Due to its precarious existence, the piping plover remains one of New Jersey's most endangered species. The threats that it faces, including increased beach recreation and predation, continue to act as serious impediments to the recovery of this species. Without intense protection and management, it is unlikely that the piping plover would survive in New Jersey.

Limiting Factors and Threats

Human activity, predation, and "hardening" of our coast through the construction of jetties, groins, seawalls, and so on now threaten the piping plover in New Jersey. Human activity near nesting sites can disturb nesting plovers, flushing adults and leaving chicks vulnerable to predators. In addition, people may inadvertently trample the camouflaged eggs or chicks. Frequent disturbance may result in reduced foraging time, decreased reproductive success, or nest abandonment.

The use of vehicles on beaches may cause piping plover mortality, as the well-camouflaged eggs and chicks may be run over by passing automobiles. In addition, the small chicks may fall into tire ruts and be unable to climb out. The stranded chicks are then vulnerable to predators or passing vehicles. Recreational beach use, beach raking, and erosion have reduced the amount of suitable nesting habitat. Much of New Jersey's coast has been developed and "hardened," interfering with natural erosion and deposition processes that have historically created plover nesting and feeding habitat. Sea level rise, combined with coastal development, has acted to increase erosion and increase the threat of flooding. Stabilization of the coast and development also prevent natural creation of overwash areas that provide productive tidal flats for feeding.

Human development of coastal areas has also facilitated an increase in predator populations. Mammalian predators, such as raccoons (*Procyon lotor*), red foxes (*Vulpes fulva*), skunks (*Mephitis mephitis*), rats (*Rattus norvegicus*), and opossums (*Didelphis marsupialis*), thrive in areas where people feed them or leave garbage outdoors. Populations of some avian predators, for example, gulls (*Larus* spp.) and crows (*Corvus* spp.), have also increased along the coast as they have adapted to human habitation.

Feral and domestic cats (*Felis domesticus*) and dogs (*Canis familiaris*) also prey upon wild birds, including plovers. In addition, ghost crabs (*Ocypode quadrata*) may prey on plover eggs and young.

Because they feed along the water's edge, piping plovers are vulnerable to contamination resulting from oil spills. Plovers can become coated with oil while foraging and ingest oil during preening. Oil contamination is known to impair reproduction, cause negative physical effects, or result in mortality in avian species.

Recommendations

Piping plover populations have been monitored in New Jersey since 1976. In addition, New Jersey participates in the International Piping Plover Census, a count of breeding and wintering plovers conducted every five years and co-ordinated by the U.S. Fish and Wildlife Service.

As plovers arrive in New Jersey, Endangered and Nongame Species Program (ENSP) staff locate nesting areas and enclose them with string and posts. Educational and restricted area signs are displayed near nest sites and predator exclosures are erected around nests. When warranted, predator control is conducted near plover breeding areas. Personnel regularly monitor and patrol nest sites. In areas where chicks occur, restrictions on the use of recreational vehicles are enforced.

Cooperative relationships between wildlife managers and the municipalities that govern beach communities—some of which have been formalized through written agreements—are imperative to the conservation of beach-nesting birds. By protecting habitats for these birds, communities can benefit from ecotourism. Beach replenishment projects can be designed to incorporate the needs of piping plovers and to create additional habitat. Predator control should be implemented when necessary.

Sherry Liguori and Dave Jenkins

Upland Sandpiper, *Bartramia longicauda*
Status: State: Endangered   Federal: Migratory Nongame Species of Management Concern

Identification

Formerly known as the upland plover, the upland sandpiper is a slender, brown shorebird of dry, inland fields. It has a thin neck, long tail, and cryptic coloration. Adults are buff above and heavily marked with dark brown bar-

Upland sandpiper.
© F. K. Schleicher/
VIREO

ring. The throat is buff with dark brown chevron-shaped streaking that extends onto the white breast and flanks. The slender neck supports a small head with large, dark eyes. The bill is short and straight, with a slight decurve at the tip, and the legs are long and yellow. When the bird is perched, the tail extends beyond the wingtips. Juveniles appear similar to adults but have buff tips to the back feathers and less streaking on the flanks. The sexes are alike in plumage. The call of the upland sandpiper is a whistling *quip-ip-ip-ip, pulip-pulip,* or *whip-whee-ee-you.* In flight, the upland sandpiper appears dark above with a lighter brown innerwing that contrasts with the darker brown outerwing and rump. The underwing coverts are white with heavy dark brown barring. The feet do not extend beyond the tail in flight. Upon landing, the wings are stretched upward.

Distribution

Native to the prairies of the Midwest, the upland sandpiper expanded its range east as forests were cleared. The current range of the upland sandpiper spans from Alaska and Canada south to northeastern Oregon, Idaho, Colorado, Oklahoma, Texas, Illinois, Kentucky, Ohio, and along the Atlantic Coast states south to Maryland, West Virginia, and Virginia. These sandpipers

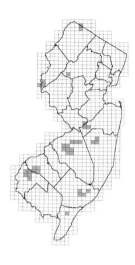

winter on the pampas of South America from Suriname and northern Brazil to central Argentina and Uruguay.

Breeding upland sandpipers have occurred at scattered grassland habitats throughout New Jersey. Within the past two decades, nesting birds have been documented at Alpha, Springfield, East Amwell, Hillsborough, Franklin, Linvale, Lumberton, Southampton, New Hanover, Mannington, Pilesgrove, Harrison, and South Harrison townships. Additional pairs have occurred at the Wallkill Valley, Assunpink Wildlife Management Area, McGuire Air Force Base, Lakehurst Naval Air Station, Burlington County Airpark, and Atlantic City International Airport. This airport held the largest breeding population in the state, about eight pairs, although numbers have dwindled in recent years. Likewise, the number of pairs and breeding sites throughout the state have recently declined.

Meanwhile, migrant upland sandpipers are rare in New Jersey. Fall migrants occur from mid-July to late August, with some individuals as late as the end of September. Spring migrants occur from mid-April to late May.

Diet

The upland sandpiper is a species beneficial to farmers, consuming many crop-damaging insects. The diet, which is dominated by insects and other small invertebrates, includes grasshoppers, crickets, weevils, locusts, beetles, larvae, flies, moths, ants and other Hymenoptera, centipedes, millipedes, spiders, earthworms, and snails. Plant matter, including weed and grass seeds, are consumed to a lesser extent.

Habitat

A bird of open countryside, the upland sandpiper inhabits grasslands, fallow fields, and meadows that are often associated with pastures, farms, or airports. Upland meadows and short-grass grasslands, containing vegetation 8 to 40 cm (3–16 in.) tall, provide habitat for nesting upland sandpipers. Such grasslands may include the following species: timothy (*Phleum* spp.), bluegrass (*Poa* spp.), needlegrass (*Stipa* spp.), bluestem (*Andropogon* spp.), quackgrass (*Argopyron* spp.), Junegrass (*Koeleria* spp.), and bromegrass (*Bromus* spp.). Habitats that contain a mix of tall and short grasses and forbs provide both foraging and nesting habitat. Upland sandpipers are sensitive to vegetation height and may not use sites with vegetation exceeding 70 cm (28 in.).

Pastures that receive light to moderate levels of grazing offer quality habitat for upland sandpipers. In addition, hayfields provide habitat so long as the hay is not cut during the breeding period. Large monocultures of row crops are of limited habitat value to this species due to the lack of cover and threat of farming operations. Smaller farms containing crops of wheat, rye, soybean, strawberries, or corn may offer habitat for upland sandpipers, especially if they are interspersed with fallow fields.

Airports often provide habitat for grassland birds such as the upland sandpiper, particularly if the habitat is managed to benefit these birds. Larger airports, such as the Atlantic City International Airport, support breeding colonies. Smaller airports, such as county airports, may support nesting pairs if they are surrounded by other areas of suitable habitat. Strips of short grasses located along runways and taxiways as well as adjacent areas of taller grasses are used by these birds. The characteristically low flight of upland sandpipers poses little threat to passing airplanes.

Regardless of the specific habitat type, upland sandpipers require several basic structural components. Habitats must be maintained at an early successional stage. Territories often contain telephone poles, fence posts, wires, or a few scattered small trees or shrubs, which are used as perches. Traditional nesting sites are often used in successive years, provided that suitable habitat remains.

Upland sandpipers require large home ranges. Of several New Jersey sites, nesting pairs occupied an average area of 87.5 hectares (216 acres). Breeding areas ranged in size from 44 hectares (109 acres) at Burlington County Airpark to 203 hectares (502 acres) at Featherbed Lane in Pilesgrove Township, Salem County (Plage 1983).

Upland sandpipers use similar habitats throughout the year. Migrants can be found in hayfields, pastures, airports, grasslands, sod farms, fallow fields, and vegetated landfills. Wintering sandpipers occur in mixed short and tall grasses on the pampas of South America.

Breeding Biology

From mid-April to early May, upland sandpipers return to breeding sites in New Jersey, where they form loose colonies or nest singly. Pairs nesting in colonies tend to experience greater reproductive success, possibly due to the increased vigilance of several sets of eyes. Displaying birds circle high above their territories while emitting a whistling call, after which they descend in a rapid dive to the ground.

The nest, located among tufts of grass, is a hollow scrape on the ground that is lined with grasses, twigs, and leaves. Overhanging vegetation conceals the location of the nest. Females begin laying eggs in early to mid-May. Clutch sizes average four eggs but may range from three to five. Both sexes incubate the eggs for 21 to 28 days. The precocial chicks, which hatch from mid-June to early July, leave the nest within a day of hatching. The adults care for them until they are able to fly at 30 to 34 days old. Around mid-July, adults and juveniles form flocks and depart for their southern wintering grounds. Juveniles are able to breed the following year.

Status and Conservation

The boom of agriculture in the northeastern United States during the 1800s provided habitat for upland sandpipers, enabling their populations to increase greatly in this region. Following the demise of the passenger pigeon (*Ectopistes migratorius*), gunners aimed their sights at the upland sandpiper, whose value began to increase in city markets. By the late 1800s and early 1900s, the upland sandpiper was on the verge of extinction, nearly wiped out by market hunters. In addition, severe hunting and habitat loss on the species' wintering grounds exacerbated population declines. Stone (1965a) noted that hundreds were shot in New Jersey, and nearly all of the migrants were gone from Cape May by 1903. Following the Migratory Bird Conservation Act of 1916, which afforded protection to upland sandpipers, populations began to recover gradually, although they probably never reached premarket-hunting levels. The decline of agriculture in the second half of the century prevented the upland sandpiper from achieving full recovery.

Since the 1950s, upland sandpiper populations in the eastern United States have declined due to habitat loss. Small farms and pastures have been replaced by suburban development and large monocultures that offer limited habitat value. In addition, early and more frequent crop harvests threaten sandpiper eggs and young.

From 1970 to 1987, the number of known active breeding sites in New Jersey fell from twenty-six to four. In 1982, the U.S. Fish and Wildlife Service designated the upland sandpiper as a Migratory Nongame Species of Management Concern, as populations in the East had declined due to habitat loss. The National Audubon Society included the upland sandpiper on its Blue List of Imperiled Species from 1975 to 1986, the final year of the list. In 1979, the upland sandpiper was listed as a threatened species in New Jersey. Due to further population declines and the increasing threat of habitat loss, the status of the upland sandpiper in New Jersey was changed to endangered in 1984. The New Jersey Natural Heritage Program considers this species to be "demonstrably secure globally," yet "critically imperiled in New Jersey because of extreme rarity" (Office of Natural Lands Management 1992). Breeding Bird Surveys have shown a reduction in the number of upland sandpipers in the Northeast from 1966 to 1999 (Sauer et al. 2000). Imperiled throughout this region, the upland sandpiper is listed as endangered in New Hampshire, Massachusetts, Connecticut, and Maryland, threatened in Vermont, Rhode Island, Pennsylvania, and Virginia, and of special concern in New York.

Limiting Factors and Threats

Habitat loss and fragmentation significantly threaten upland sandpiper populations. Upland habitats, including grasslands and fields, do not receive adequate regulatory protection in New Jersey and consequently are under severe development pressure. Many farms throughout the state have been lost to suburban development, resulting in small, fragmented patches of remaining habitat. Vegetative succession has also attributed to the decline in habitat, as fallow fields naturally mature into forests. Upland sandpipers require relatively large parcels of habitat and may not nest in small, fragmented patches. Within fragmented habitats, birds experience increased levels of predation and disturbance. Predators of eggs, young, and adults include dogs, cats, raccoons, skunks, foxes, coyotes, crows, hawks, and owls. Human activity at nesting sites may disturb breeding birds, isolate chicks from their parents, elevate the risk of predation, or result in the trampling of eggs and/or young.

Traditional farming techniques have been replaced with modernized agricultural practices, in which large monocultures are favored over a diversity of crops. Consequently, mosaics of pastures and farm fields have been replaced by expanses of row crops, which are of limited habitat value for upland sandpipers. In addition, early and more frequent harvesting threatens nests of grassland birds. High-intensity grazing is also detrimental as it can destroy the habitat and result in the trampling of eggs and young. Pesticides applied on the breeding and wintering grounds reduce prey populations and may result in physiological impacts on birds that consume contaminated prey.

In addition to the loss of breeding habitat, upland sandpipers have suffered from habitat loss on their wintering grounds and at migratory stopovers. Agriculture has replaced much of the native grasslands on the birds' wintering grounds. The modernization of farms has occurred in wintering countries as well. Although land is often protected by law, hunting regulations are difficult to enforce over the large, remote areas of land where the species winters. As a long-distance migrant, the upland sandpiper is vulnerable to mortality due to the stresses incurred during migration.

Recommendations

Habitat protection and management are imperative to the conservation of the upland sandpiper in New Jersey. Strengthened protection of open uplands and grasslands is necessary to maintain habitat for the species. Farmland preservation should be a high priority, and landowner incentives should be used to protect and maintain habitat. Educational programs should be implemented to increase awareness regarding the threats to and conservation of grassland birds. Landowners should be encouraged to delay haying and grazing until young birds have fledged. Public lands should be managed to create and maintain habitat for grassland birds. Currently, airports and military bases provide a substantial amount of habitat for grassland birds, including the upland sandpiper. Grassland management plans should be implemented at such sites. In addition, cooperative ventures should be established among countries in which upland sandpipers breed, migrate, and overwinter to ensure the protection of habitat for this species throughout its annual cycle.

Because they will naturally convert into forests, grassland habitats must be managed to maintain an early successional stage. Controlled burns, grazing, or mowing can be used as management tools. Controlled burns should be conducted during the fall, after breeding birds have departed. Although fall is preferable, burns can also be implemented during the spring. None of these techniques should be used during the breeding season, between May 1 to July 31. Grasslands should be burned at three-year intervals. To provide habitat during the year when burning is implemented, less than half of the site should be burned during one year. Upland sandpipers tend to prefer fields the second year after a burn is conducted. At sites larger than 40 hectares (100 acres), only 20% to 40% of the site should be burned in one year. If mowing is selected for habitat management, it should be conducted every year during the nonbreeding season. If habitats are grazed, cattle should be prohibited during the breeding season. Low to moderate intensity grazing should be conducted, as heavy and prolonged grazing is detrimental to the habitat.

At airports, short grass is maintained adjacent to runways and taxiways for traveling aircraft. In the surrounding fields, vegetation should be maintained at a height of 20 to 30 cm (8–12 in.). These areas of taller grass should not be mowed during the nesting season. In addition, grassland bird locations should be monitored and mapped, ensuring that personnel avoid these areas during the breeding season if possible.

Grasslands can be created or restored by planting a mixture of native and introduced grasses. To promote habitat diversity, a mosaic of fields should be established by using different management regimes and providing fields of differing ages. Upland sandpipers require grassland habitats of 40 to 80 hectares (100–200 acres) or more. As with the airports, a mixture of forbs and short and tall grasses at heights of 20 to 30 cm (8–12 in.) should be provided. Grass height should be a short 15 to 20 cm (6–8 in.) upon the spring arrival of birds. Timothy, bluegrass, needlegrass, bluestem, quackgrass, Junegrass, and bromegrass can be planted to create grassland habitat for upland sandpipers. Nesting sites should be fenced to minimize human disturbance and provide perches for displaying birds.

Sherry Liguori

Red Knot, *Calidris canutus*
Status: State: Threatened   Federal: Not Listed

Identification

After journeying from the southern tip of South America, the red knots that appear on the shores of Delaware Bay in May arrive so thin that they look like

Red knots swarm a Delaware Bay beach in search of horseshoe crab eggs.
© Clay Myers

sparrows. There they gorge themselves on the eggs of the horseshoe crab (*Limulus polyphemus*), putting on a layer of fat so thick that they leave for their Arctic breeding grounds looking like plump doves. At least five other shorebird species use the bay as a spring migratory stopover.

Among them, however, the red knot is the largest and stockiest. In its May to August breeding plumage, it also sports a distinctive breast of brilliant rusty red. Also described as pale salmon, this russet color extends up the neck and around the eyes, and bleeds somewhat into the patterned black, brown, gray, and white colorations on the wings and back. The rump is whitish. The knot has a short, straight black bill and, during breeding season, dark brown/black legs.

A small number of the adults arrive in the middle of their molt showing various amounts of the nonbreeding plumage that is typical between September and April: a washed-out gray look with scaly white feather edgings, whitish flanks with dark barring and greenish legs. Juveniles are primarily gray, with a scaly pattern on the wings and dull yellow-olive legs.

Passing through New Jersey again in August, adult red knots remain in breeding plumage and stay with many other species. During both the May and August migrations, whimbrels or Hudsonian curlews (*Numenius phaeopus*) look most similar to knots, but their breasts are duller, contrasting less with the rest of their bodies. Also, whimbrels are larger and their decurved bills are twice as long.

As with most shorebirds, the long-winged, strong-flying knots fly in groups, sometimes with other species.

Distribution

Red knots begin arriving on the Delaware Bay during the first week of May and gradually build to an average of approximately 55,000 birds by mid-May (Clark et al. 1993). Since then, the long-term peak average has declined to 42,000. While on the Delaware Bay, red knots range from Dyer's Cove (near Fortescue) in New Jersey and from Port Mahon in Delaware, south to Cape May and Cape Henlopen (Clark et al. 1993). Major concentrations are often found at Reed's Beach, Villas, Norbury's Landing, Moore's Beach, and Fortescue. The vast marsh and shoreline of Cumberland County's Egg Island appears to function as a staging area for birds about to leave for the Arctic. Red knots also occur on the coastal marsh of the Cape May peninsula, concentrating in the area from North Wildwood to Avalon. They roost primarily on isolated spits and islands of the area, with a major roost, numbering as many as 10,000 birds, on the sandbars of Hereford Inlet. In the last few years, red knots have been found feeding on the Atlantic Coast intertidal sand flats, primarily on mussel spat (Escudero and Niles 2001; Sitters 2001).

Their flight path to the Arctic is poorly understood, although birders in Toronto often see knots on the shore of Lake Ontario in late May and early June. Knots have also been sighted along the shores of James Bay in June, although snow and ice blanket most of the area. After extensive work using birds affixed with radio transmitters, biologists have recently determined that

Migration sites

most of the Delaware Bay red knots nest in the mid- to low-Arctic from King William Island to Southampton Island (Niles et al. 2001a). Nests of the New World knot have been found as far west as Victoria Island, as far east as Baffin Island, and as far north as Somerset Island. The population appears to center on King William and Southampton islands, perhaps because of the large concentration of suitable habitat.

Returning from the Arctic, red knots move slowly out to the Atlantic Coast, foraging in the tidal marshes and sandy flats from the Canadian Maritimes all the way to the island of Tierra del Fuego in Southern Chile and Argentina, a journey of more than 16,000 km (10,000 miles) (Morrison and Ross 1989). While wintering red knots can be found in significant numbers in two areas of the Argentine Atlantic Coast, Bahia San Sebastian and Rio Grande, by far the largest concentration uses the tidal flats of Bahia Lomas in Chile (Niles et al. 2001b). On the return flight, birds stop over in at least two sites, San Antonio Oeste in Argentina and in northern Brazil. Knots also concentrate on the coasts of Georgia, South Carolina, and Virginia before arriving on the Delaware Bay.

Habitat

Red knots on Delaware Bay depend primarily on horseshoe crab eggs and therefore occur more frequently in areas of dense horseshoe crab spawning, usually sandy beaches with gentle slopes and minimal wave action (Botton and Loveland 1992).

Red knots sometimes roost on the high portions of sandy beaches along Delaware Bay, but usually fly to roosts on the Atlantic side of the Cape May peninsula. The largest numbers use the long sandy spits at ocean inlets, although many birds roost in small numbers on the many marsh islands scattered between North Wildwood and Sea Isle City. Birds also roost on sandy beaches and spits on Egg Island and Fortescue.

In the Arctic, nesting red knots use a distinctive habitat type characterized by vast areas of sparsely vegetated, low-elevation tundra (Richard Lathrop, pers. comm. 2001). These areas remain mostly covered in snow until mid-June, so birds must build nests in areas swept free of snow by prevailing northeasterly winds. Foraging habitat often consists of extensive isolated or lacustrine wetlands (interconnected by streams) that are dominated by sedges.

In southbound migrations, birds are often found in marsh flats and sandy washes. In the wintering areas, the birds occur primarily on large tidal flats. Red knots roost in expansive sand flats that are only infrequently flooded by tides. Most of the wintering population occurs in Bahia Lomas, Chile, where birds feed on a large sandy flat 5 miles wide and more than 40 miles long (Niles et al. 2001b). Depending on the stage of the moon, varying portions of the flat flood at high tide. Even though the tide varies by 10 m (about 32 ft.), the tides barely flood the flats of Bahia Lomas. Shorebirds feed along the advancing tide line and roost along the water's edge.

Diet

Red knots arrive in New Jersey with little or none of the fat they accumulated while in South America. Many birds burn muscle to reach the bay, desperately gambling that sufficient resources exist at their destination. Gorging on crab eggs, the birds gain significant amounts of fat; sometimes this gain in fat weight equals their fat-free weight of 110 gm (3.85 oz.) (Myers et al. 1987; Baker et al. 1999). Birds often gain more than 10 gm (.35 oz.) per day, the equivalent of a normal adult human gaining 7.2 kg (16 lb.) per day. By the end of May, knots reach an average weight of about 185 gm (6.5 oz.), with some individuals reaching 220 gm (7.7 oz.).

Crabs dig about 25 cm (10 in.) into the sand to lay their eggs. However, red knots rely on exposed eggs, which result from many horseshoe crabs all trying to lay eggs in the same area. To create new nests, the crabs inadvertently dig up old nests and expose previously laid eggs on the beach surface. If crab numbers drop to a low density, then the eggs remain unavailable to most shorebirds. Ruddy turnstones (*Arenaria interpres*), which, like the knots, rely primarily on horseshoe crab eggs, often dig for egg masses; red knots and other species usually crowd in to feed with them. Extraordinary tides or high waves also expose egg masses, and discourage new spawning by crabs.

Knots have also been observed feeding on mussel beds on the Atlantic Coast marsh, particularly on intertidal sand flats around Hereford Inlet in Cape May County, but as a food resource the mussels are quite inadequate (Escudero and Niles 2001; Sitters 2001).

On arrival in the Arctic, knots probably don't feed for at least seven to ten days. Conditions remain cold, and most of the water and tundra are frozen, although there appears to be a growing trend toward earlier melting. As the wetlands warm, birds feed on insects as they become available, including mosquito larvae and tundra spiders.

During their southbound migrations, red knots feed on mussels, clams, and, to a lesser extent, marine worms. On their wintering grounds, they feed on mussels and small clams.

Breeding Biology

With sufficient fat resources accumulated in Delaware Bay, the birds leave by the beginning of June and arrive on the Canadian Arctic tundra by the second week of the month, often in wintry conditions and nearly 100% snow cover.

The nests the red knots soon build are situated in extremely barren, sparsely vegetated areas swept free of snow by prevailing northerly winds. The nests usually occur in small patches of dryas, a low grasslike plant less than one-half meter (about 19 in.) in diameter. Red knots create nest bowls approximately 15 cm (6 in.) in diameter and 6 cm (2.4 in.) deep and line them with lichen and dead dryas leaves. The sparse vegetation surrounding the nest usually amounts to 10% of the total area, though it may be as high as 20%. Establishing breeding territories in such forbidden areas probably reduces the

threat from predators such as the Arctic fox (*Alopex lagopus*), which concentrate on vegetated and thus more productive tundra.

Nests are often located on the northeast side of long ridges called eskers in close association with other species of early Arctic nesters, such as lesser golden plovers (*Pluvialis dominica*) and long-tailed jaegers (*Stercorarius longicaudus*). The red knots appear to establish small territories of about 1 km (0.6 mi.) in diameter that usually include small wetlands close to the nest and more extensive wetlands within 2 km (1.2 mi.) of the nest. Despite their relative isolation, knot nests sometimes fall prey to Arctic foxes, long-tailed jaegers, parasitic jaegers (*Stercorarius parasiticus*), and pomarine jaegers (*Stercorarius pomarinus*). The extent of predation varies with lemming cycles: in good lemming years, predators eat lemmings; in bad years they look for nests. A more significant threat to nests is extraordinary cold weather. In 2001, one nesting area underwent two days of hurricane-force winds that brought wind chills far below zero just as birds started incubation.

After laying their eggs, the females incubate without access to food for the first few weeks, relying once again on the fat accumulated in Delaware Bay. Invertebrate prey are unavailable until the third or fourth week of June, when the eggs begin to hatch. Four-egg clutches are the rule, and the precocial (independent) young will follow the adult male to wetland foraging areas within 48 hours of hatching. Adults sometimes lead the 7.6 cm (3 in.) tall chicks more than a mile through rocky, barren tundra to reach a suitable feeding site, while long-tailed jaegers and Arctic foxes regularly patrol for easy prey.

Females begin migrating south to wintering areas by the end of July, followed by males and then by the first-year offspring. The southward migration moves relatively slowly, with birds rarely concentrating together because of the abundant fall populations of clams and mussels. In South America the season shifts to early spring, but birds remain unhurried and unconcentrated. They arrive in the wintering areas beginning in October and through November. The first-year young will remain in the wintering areas for two seasons.

Status and Conservation

Conducted by a New Jersey Audubon team led by Peter Dunne (Wander and Dunne 1981), the first comprehensive surveys of red knots on the Delaware Bay began in 1981. Since 1986, the surveys have been conducted annually by the ENSP's Kathleen Clark, making the survey one of the longest-running surveys of shorebirds in North America. During the survey period, red knot numbers have fallen dramatically, from high counts of more than 90,000 birds in 1989 to about 32,000 birds in 2002. The numbers fluctuate cyclically, possibly related to Arctic weather or cyclic changes in the populations of snowy owls (*Nyctea scandiaca*), Arctic foxes, and jaegers.

The fall in numbers, however, parallels the decline in the Western Hemisphere flyway-wide population, estimated by the ratio of birds banded and eventually resighted throughout the flyway. Allan Baker has recently revised Brian Harrington's 1980s population estimate of 150,000 birds downward to just 70,000 birds. Moreover, counts of the winter population made by Niles et al. (2001b) suggest substantial declines of about 30%.

The red knot's status remains difficult to assess because the population remains relatively high, numbering in the tens of thousands. Most experts agree, however, that the decline of the knot, if it continues, will be abrupt and drastic. This is because the birds are relatively long lived and have adapted to substantial reductions in productivity resulting from periodically harsh Arctic nesting conditions. This ability to withstand temporary losses in the population would, in effect, mask other impacts until significant declines were well underway.

The status of the numbers of red knots prior to the 1980s surveys is poorly understood. As populations of horseshoe crabs were once more widespread, it is likely that knots also concentrated during their spring migration in other estuarine systems from Cape Cod Bay to Chesapeake Bay. In 1897 Charles Shriner noted that knots were "formerly very plentiful in migrations in New Jersey," having fallen easy prey to shorebird gunners. Both he and Witmer Stone found red knots on the Delaware Bay in the early twentieth century but made no remarks on unusual numbers. Red knots were probably found in similar numbers in Cape Cod Bay and the Atlantic coastal islands of Virginia, where large populations of crabs were once noted. As the horseshoe crab populations declined along the East Coast, birds probably concentrated around the Delaware Bay, currently their last remaining stronghold.

Due to the threat posed by the declining number of horseshoe crabs and the consequent effect on egg availability, the red knot was listed as threatened in New Jersey in 1999. Although the magnitude of the decline in horseshoe crab numbers remains uncertain, the long-term consequence of a decline in crabs—which do not breed until they are eight or nine years old—will require intensive monitoring of crab and red knot populations to enable biologists sufficient time to act if populations fall drastically.

The red knot is recognized as a high-priority species in the National Shorebird Conservation Plan (Brown et al. 2000), is on the Audubon Watch list, and is a U.S. Fish and Wildlife Service species of conservation significance.

Limiting Factors and Threats

With one of the longest migrations of all animals, the red knot is vulnerable in most areas of its 16,000 km (10,000 mi.) migration route. The Tierra del Fuego wintering area, Bahia Lomas, supports extensive land-based and offshore oil pumping and storage facilities. Although these oil operations have been active for decades, recent privatization by the Chilean government promises a significant increase in oil exploration, pumping, and storage. The extensive shallow sand flats of Bahia Lomas are extremely vulnerable to accidental oil spills. One significant oil spill in Bahia Lomas could cover the poorly drained flats and remain long enough to destroy food resources and directly threaten knots. One spill could cause extensive and lasting damage to most of the population of the New World red knots. The bay is at the mouth of the Straits of Magellan, notorious for bad weather and extreme tides. Controlling the effects of a major spill is unlikely.

In 1992, oil spill experts and biologists simulated the effects of a relatively small oil spill in Delaware Bay. It quickly became clear that the currents and geography of the bay made protection of the beaches during the shorebird migration unlikely. A spill in 1996 substantiated these conclusions. The tanker *Anitra* spilled less than 50,000 gallons of oil near the mouth of Delaware Bay. The oil submerged and, after reemerging, it washed up on Atlantic Coast beaches of the Cape May peninsula and oiled thousands of sanderlings. Studies by Burger and Tsipoura (1998) suggested that the ingestion of even slight amounts of oil, through preening, prevented birds from gaining weight.

The oil companies and the various government agencies involved in spills have reduced the threat of an oil spill on Delaware Bay in recent years with significant improvements in prevention and oil response planning. But the bay remains one of the most heavily used oil transport routes in the country. Moreover, most ships must "lighter" or off-load oil to barges to decrease draft for the trip upstream to Delaware River docks. This process creates a significant spill hazard that cannot be avoided until the channel is deepened to allow the larger tankers to reach the ports.

The declining availability of horseshoe crab eggs on the Delaware Bay represents another significant threat to red knots. Since 1990 their availability has declined by almost 90%, following similar declines in the number of horseshoe crabs as measured by trawl survey and spawning count data. At most beaches eggs have fallen by an order of magnitude, from 35,000 per square meter (10.76 sq. ft.) to 3,500 per square meter. Eggs have virtually disappeared from Moore's Beach and other smaller beaches, forcing birds to concentrate at an ever-decreasing number of beaches. Exacerbating the reduced number of eggs is increased competition with gulls, particularly laughing gulls.

The reduction in available horseshoe crab eggs is also expressed in the shorter periods of availability. Where eggs were once available on the beach surface every day from May through June, now they are available for only three or four days around the new and full moon tides. The consequence is the greater vulnerability of the birds to asynchrony in migration and egg availability. For example, the late arrival of birds in 1999 after the full moon and before the new moon left many birds without sufficient eggs. They were thus unable to build weight for the Arctic. The problem grew worse in 2000, but the timing improved in 2001. Insufficient or improperly timed supplies of horseshoe crab eggs reduces the number of birds reaching sufficient weight, which ultimately will decrease the production of offspring in the Arctic.

This decline in egg availability is obviously related to the reduction in the number of crabs, which are apparently declining because they are harvested as bait for the conch and eel fisheries. Approximately 90% of the horseshoe crab harvest goes to the conch fishery that moved into the area in the early 1990s, exactly paralleling the decline in eggs and horseshoe crab numbers. As there are no harvest limits governing the conch fishery, the demand for horseshoe crabs has been significant. The horseshoe crab harvest rose from a few hundred thousand animals in the early 1990s to more than 2.5 million in the Mid-Atlantic states in 2001. Although the Atlantic States Marine Fisheries Commission conducted a two-year effort to determine the status of horseshoe crabs, it failed to agree on a status. It did, however, impose a 25% reduction in the states' near-record harvests of 1996 and 1997. With high harvest levels, little information on horseshoe crab numbers or survival rates, and the crabs' high age before they reach sexual maturity, the fate of horseshoe crabs remains extremely uncertain and threatened. The Atlantic States Marine Fisheries Commission has banned harvesting horseshoe crabs in a 30-mile-square sanctuary outside the mouth of Delaware Bay. But it still allows a harvest that continues to place significant pressure on the Delaware Bay horseshoe crab population.

In addition, a 2001 survey of colonial waterbirds on the Atlantic Coast revealed a significant and growing population of laughing gulls (*Larus atricilla*). Laughing, herring (*Larus argentatus*) and greater black-backed (*Larus marinus*) gulls also rely on horseshoe crab eggs during their incubation and early hatchling nesting periods. The decreasing number of crab eggs has resulted in increased competition. Based on anecdotal observations, it appears that red knots are being out-competed by laughing gulls. Competition from laughing gulls is greatest just prior to their nesting, when adults of both sexes consume horseshoe crab eggs on Delaware Bay beaches. At egg laying, the number of laughing gulls feeding on crab eggs is significantly reduced, though still substantial.

Recommendations

The red knot is listed as threatened in New Jersey primarily because of the threat to horseshoe crabs and their eggs. The primary management need focuses on protecting horseshoe crabs. Studies conducted in 2000 and 2001 have confirmed that red knots rely primarily on horseshoe crab eggs, and that other foods are not available or, in the case of mussels, are inadequate. Without reduction in the total number of crabs harvested, it is likely that egg availability will continue to decline.

The impact of an oil spill during the month of May would have an incalculable negative effect on shorebirds. Not only would shorebirds be directly affected by being coated with oil, but ingesting small amounts through preening would stymie their ability to gain weight. Avoiding the impact of an oil spill would be virtually impossible because of the widespread areas used by shorebirds and the extreme currents along Delaware Bay shore and tidal creeks, which exceed the capacity of oil booms and other control measures. Although considerable planning and readiness improvements have been made by emergency response management agencies since 1992, the only way to avoid impacts on shorebirds is to avoid a spill.

The rising population of laughing gulls may represent an even greater threat to red knots as the availability of horseshoe crab eggs declines. Increased laughing gull populations on the Atlantic Coast also threaten other marsh nesting birds by increasing competition for food and nesting areas, and increasing predation of chicks. If the significant increase in laughing gulls counted during the 2001 survey can be independently verified, control must be considered.

Larry Niles

Roseate Tern, *Sterna dougallii*

Status: State: Endangered   Federal: Endangered (North Atlantic breeding population)

Identification

The roseate tern is a medium-sized, light-colored tern with a dark cap and long tail. In breeding plumage, the adult has a black cap and nape, a pale gray back and underwing, white underparts, and a white rump. Black tips on the outer primaries contrast with the otherwise pale upperwing. The tail is white and deeply forked with long streamers. On perched birds, the tail extends beyond the wingtips. The bill is black with a dark red base. The legs and feet are dark red and the iris is brownish black. Sexes are alike in plumage. The non-breeding adult has brown legs, a black bill, and a white forehead with a black mask extending from the eye to the nape.

The juvenile roseate tern has a dark brown cap, a black bill, and black legs. The back is brown and barred, making it appear scaly. On juveniles, there is a white trailing edge on the wing and a dark carpal bar on the upperwing. The tail lacks the long streamers present in adults.

The flight of the roseate tern is light and graceful with rapid wingbeats. The call is a soft *chew-ick* and the alarm call is a harsh *krack* that resembles the sound of ripping fabric.

The roseate tern can be confused with the similar-appearing common tern (*Sterna hirundo*) and Forster's tern (*S. forsteri*), both of which are fairly common in New Jersey. The roseate tern has paler upperparts and a longer tail than the common tern. The call of the common tern is a harsh, protracted, and descending *kee-earrr.* Unlike the roseate tern, the Forster's tern has a gray tail and silvery gray outer primaries. The call of the Forster's tern is a harsh, abrupt *kyarr.*

Distribution

The roseate tern occurs along coasts of both temperate and tropical seas throughout the world. In the Western Hemisphere, roseate terns occupy two isolated breeding populations, a North Atlantic population and a Caribbean population. The North Atlantic breeding population is located in the northeastern United States and southern Canada, from Nova Scotia to Long Island, New York, with historic nesting records occurring south to Virginia. The Caribbean population occurs in the Bahamas, the U.S. Virgin Islands, and the Dry Tortugas of Florida. Roseate terns from both populations winter on the coasts of the West Indies, the Caribbean, and northern South America.

Although the roseate tern has historically nested in New Jersey, breeding has not been documented since 1980. Consequently, it is currently considered extirpated as a breeding species in the state. Roseate terns are extremely rare summer transients and very rare fall migrants in New Jersey, occurring from late August to early September. They are also rare spring migrants, occurring from May to mid-June. Migratory and summer transient roseate terns have been seen in recent years at Cape May, Avalon, Corson's Inlet, Holgate, Sedge Island, and Sandy Hook.

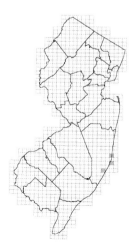

Habitat

The roseate tern is a coastal species that nests on barrier islands and salt marshes and forages over shallow coastal waters, inlets, and offshore seas. Nesting colonies are located above the high-tide line, often within vegetated dunes where dense concentrations of beach grasses and seaside goldenrod (*Solidago sempervirens*) provide cover. In comparison to other terns, roseates nest at sites with more vegetative cover. Infrequently, they may nest in open areas, especially when they are displaced from optimal sites by gulls.

Diet

Small schooling fish and sand eels (*Ammodytes americanus*) dominate the diet of the roseate tern. Roseate terns often forage over shallow waters and concentrate in areas where large fish, such as bluefish (*Pomatomus saltatrix*), force schools of smaller fish to the surface, making them vulnerable to the terns foraging above. Foraging birds may travel 30 km (18.6 mi.) or more from nesting sites in search of food (Gochfeld et al. 1998). Terns hunt by hovering over the water before diving in headfirst after fish.

Breeding Biology

By late April and early May, North Atlantic–breeding roseate terns arrive on their nesting grounds. In the absence of heavy predation pressure, roseate terns exhibit strong fidelity to breeding sites, as most adults return to the same colony in successive years. Courting terns engage in aerial chases and displays, and also feed their mates. Paired birds posture toward each other with necks stretched high, wings drooped, and tails elevated prior to copulation.

Roseate terns nest in colonies and often occur with other breeding terns. Within such mixed colonies, however, different tern species select different nesting habitats. For example, common terns nest on open beaches with sparse vegetation. But roseate terns prefer to nest within the dense vegetative cover provided by dunes. The nest of the roseate tern is a simple scrape or depression in the sand that may or may not be lined with dry grasses. Overhanging vegetation, driftwood, or stones may be used to conceal the location of the nest.

The female tern lays a clutch of one to two buff-colored eggs that are heavily patterned with brown markings. Both the male and female incubate the eggs, which hatch after 21 to 26 days. If disturbed by either a predator or a human, the entire colony will take to flight, diving and defecating on the intruder until the threat is gone. After hatching, both adults brood and feed the young. At 22 to 30 days old, the young are able to fly. The parents continue to care for them until they depart for their wintering grounds.

Roseate terns do not breed until they are three to four years of age. Consequently, nonbreeding immatures may remain on their wintering grounds during the summer.

Status and Conservation

Before 1890, the roseate tern nested along the New Jersey coast, although it was not common. From the late 1800s to the early 1900s, roseate tern populations along the Atlantic Coast were greatly reduced as a result of the millinery trade, in which birds were killed to acquire plumes for women's hats. The Migratory Bird Treaty Act of 1918, which afforded legal protection to all migratory birds, coupled with a change in fashion styles, reduced the pressure on roseate terns, enabling populations to reestablish and increase. Nesting roseate terns were observed at Hereford Inlet and Five Mile Beach in the 1930s and at Brigantine in the 1940s. However, by the 1950s, populations again began to decline and continued to do so for several decades. Breeding roseate terns were documented in New Jersey in the 1970s, when nesting pairs occurred at Little Egg Inlet, Brigantine, Sandy Hook, Holgate, and Barnegat Bay. The last nesting pair in the state was recorded in 1980. Unchecked development and high levels of recreational activity along the barrier islands have resulted in habitat loss and disturbance to beach-nesting birds, contributing to the decline of this species.

Due to severe population declines in the state, the roseate tern was listed as a threatened species in New Jersey in 1979. Because of a drastic worldwide decline in its population, the roseate tern was reclassified as an endangered species in New Jersey in 1984. The U.S. Fish and Wildlife Service included the North Atlantic breeding population on its list of federally endangered species in 1987 because of declines resulting from human activity, gull competition, and predation. The New Jersey Natural Heritage Program considers the roseate tern to be a nonbreeding species in the state and globally "very rare and local throughout its range" (Office of Natural Lands Management 1992). The National Audubon Society included the roseate tern on its Blue List of Imperiled Species in 1972 and from 1979 to 1986, the final year of the list. Depressed roseate tern populations are evident throughout other northeastern states, where the species is listed as endangered (Massachusetts, Connecticut, New York, Virginia) or threatened (Maine, New Hampshire).

Limiting Factors and Threats

Habitat loss, human disturbance, competition, and predation hinder roseate tern breeding activity and reproductive success. The development of barrier islands, the destruction of coastal dunes, and the frequent raking of beaches have greatly reduced habitat for beach-nesting birds in New Jersey. Likewise, high levels of human activity on beaches may preclude nesting, result in nest abandonment, or cause adults to flush from their nests, leaving eggs and chicks vulnerable to predators. Predators, including foxes, skunks, cats, dogs, crows, gulls, great horned owls (*Bubo virginianus*), and night-herons, decrease reproductive success and may result in colony abandonment. Competition, particularly with larger gulls, may displace nesting terns, forcing them into lower-quality sites where they are more vulnerable to human disturbance and predation. On their wintering grounds, roseate terns encounter predation by humans who trap them for food.

Recommendations

Management for breeding roseate terns must include the provision of high-quality habitat and the protection of nesting sites. Existing vegetated dunes must be protected to encourage nesting roseate terns. Additional dune habitat can be created through the deposition of dredge spoil and the planting of dune vegetation.

To minimize disturbance, nesting sites should be fenced, posted, and regularly monitored by wardens. In addition, areas of suitable habitat can be fenced in the spring, prior to the arrival of birds, to provide habitat that is safeguarded from human activity, trampling, and beach raking. Predator control should be implemented in areas where nest predation is a problem.

Sherry Liguori

Least Tern, *Sterna antillarum*
Status: State: Endangered   Federal: Not listed

Identification

The least tern is the smallest of the North American terns (about 23 cm, or 9 in. long), a black-capped tern with white underparts and gray upper body, wings, and forked tail. Unlike the common and Forster's terns that also inhabit New Jersey's coastal areas, the least tern has a white forehead with a black eye-line connecting to the black cap. The least tern is also distinguished by its sulfur-yellow bill, which is tipped black. In fall, the black cap retreats, with black covering only the back of the head and a line through each eye.

A least tern incubating its eggs.
© Chris Davidson

The bill and legs also lose their yellow color, turning dusky to black. Sexes are similar in coloration but females are slightly smaller than males.

Juvenile birds are similar to nonbreeding adults, but the upper body may be more brownish gray and there is even less black on the cap.

Least terns produce several calls, more musical and high pitched than other terns, and described variously as *kip, kip, kip* or *kit-kit-kit,* and *kid-ick, kid-ick,* and also a rasping *zr-e-e-e-p.* Calls are often given in such rapid succession that two or three birds can sound like a large flock.

Distribution

The least tern is widely distributed in North America. Populations occur along the Pacific Coast of California and Mexico, along the interior continental rivers, and along the Atlantic and Gulf coasts. The Atlantic and Gulf coastal population breeds from southern Maine to southern Florida and along the Gulf Coast west to the Texas-Mexico border. Central and South America and the Caribbean islands also host breeding populations. Least terns winter primarily in marine coastal areas, mostly in Central and South America, and occasionally as far north as the southern Gulf coasts of Texas and Florida.

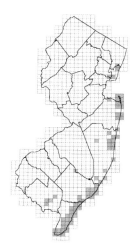

Along the Atlantic Coast of New Jersey, least terns nest on beaches, dredge disposal sites, and other sandy areas, from the New York Harbor and Newark Bay region south to Cape May and Cumberland counties. Over the past 20 years, the largest colonies have been found at Sandy Hook, Monmouth Beach, Barnegat Light, Holgate, Brigantine, Ocean City, Corson's Inlet State Park, Townsends's Inlet, Avalon, and Cape May.

Habitat

New Jersey least tern nest colonies of a few to several hundred pairs are found primarily along barrier island beaches or mainland beach strands. Bare sandy areas or areas sparsely vegetated with such typical beach vegetation as sea rocket (*Cakile endentula*), American beach grass (*Ammophila breviligulata*), beach clotbur (*Xanthium echinatum*), and seaside spurge (*Euphorbia polygonifolia*) that are just beyond the reach of normal spring tides are preferred. Nesting colonies are also found on sandy dredge disposal sites, especially after recent deposition before the establishment of dense vegetation. Least terns may also nest near sand and gravel pits where sand piles from mining operations provide suitable nesting habitat. Nesting on gravel rooftops has occurred in Florida, Mississippi, and other locations (Fisk 1975; Jackson and Jackson 1985) but has not been documented in New Jersey. The birds typically forage in bays, lagoons, estuaries, rivers, and lakes along the coast.

Diet

Small fishes, including killifish, mummichog (*Fundulus* spp.), herring (*Clupea* spp.), hake (*Urophycis* spp.), menhaden (*Brevoortia tyrannus*), and occasionally shrimp and other marine invertebrates are the main food items taken by least terns. Food is obtained during all times of the day by hovering 1 to

10 m (3.3–33 ft.) above the water and then plunge diving for prey. The prey is grasped with open mandibles, or jaws, and typically is swallowed in flight unless it is being delivered to the young or a mate.

Breeding Biology

During late April and early May, the first least terns are seen or, more often, heard flying over their coastal nesting beaches. Courtship and colony establishment begins in earnest during the first weeks of May when male terns are seen flying and calling—fish in bill—as they are pursued by other males or females. Courtship continues with the male often perched on an elevated location wagging the fish from side to side as he presents it to the female before or during copulation.

Shallow nesting scrapes are made by both male and female terns by sitting and kicking feet backward while rotating and using the breast to form the shallow depression. While the pairs make several scrapes, only one, selected by the female, is used. Egg laying begins in mid- to late May in New Jersey and is initially roughly synchronous within a nesting colony. The female lays two to three well-camouflaged, sand-colored, brown-speckled eggs. Egg laying peaks shortly after Memorial Day but may continue for several months as nests which are lost to predation and flooding are replaced.

Males and females share incubation duties for the three weeks it generally takes the eggs to hatch. Though hatched with their eyes open, the wet, down-covered chicks are mostly immobile and confined to the nest scrape for their first two to three days of life. Afterward, they clumsily scamper about the beach in search of cover or their food-bearing parents. Adults brood (cover and warm) the young in the nest scrape or nearby for the first several days after hatching, especially at night and during cool or rainy weather. Brooding behavior diminishes as chicks age, but brooding may be resumed at any time during the first two weeks or so after hatching when weather conditions warrant it. During hot and sunny conditions, the parents will often shade the chicks to help keep them cool. Both adults take part in feeding the young by delivering progressively larger fish as the young grow. About three weeks after hatching, the young are able to fly.

Juvenile terns, however, continue to depend on feeding by their parents for up to eight weeks after fledging as they acquire the flight and fishing skills needed to feed themselves. Especially in larger colonies, least tern fledglings may form "creches," large gatherings of chicks from several nests that are guarded by a few adult birds. Studies have shown that adult terns distinguish their own chicks from others in the colony by their chicks' response to the parents' calls. Chicks also quickly learn to recognize their parents' calls (Moosely 1979, and reviewed in Ehrlich et al. 1988).

As nests are often lost to predation and tidal flooding, renesting can extend the nesting season so that young are still fledging from colonies in late August and even early September. When whole colonies fail or are abandoned due to flooding or predation, the birds may establish new colonies or join a nearby nesting colony. Sites may be used for only one year or may remain active for several years. However, colony "turnover"—abandonment of old sites and colonization of new sites—is relatively high for least terns (Burger 1984; Kotliar and Burger 1984). Abandonment of nesting areas typically follows two or more successive years of low productivity or total colony failure.

Status and Conservation

Through most of the nineteenth century, the least tern was a common breeder along the New Jersey coast. However, as was true for so many of our coastal birds, by the early twentieth century, egg collecting and hunting for the millinery trade had decimated least tern populations. Protection afforded by the Migratory Bird Treaty Act of 1918 and changing fashion trends enabled least tern numbers to rebound, but, since the late 1940s, coastal development and the elevated recreational use of beaches began another population decline. Populations stabilized in recent decades as management measures were implemented; but recently, populations have begun declining again, due primarily to predation losses and increases in losses to coastal flooding.

Limiting Factors

Human disturbance, predation, and loss of habitat imperil least tern populations in New Jersey. Human activity near nesting colonies can disturb nesting terns, flushing adults and leaving chicks and eggs vulnerable to predators and to excessive heating or cooling. In addition, people may inadvertently trample the camouflaged eggs or chicks when nesting colonies expand or chicks wander outside protected colonies. Frequent disturbance may result in decreased reproductive success or whole colony abandonment. The use of vehicles on beaches may cause least tern mortality, as the well-camouflaged eggs and chicks may be run over by passing automobiles. In addition, the small chicks may wander into tire ruts and be unable to climb out. The stranded chicks are then vulnerable to predators or passing vehicles.

Much of New Jersey's coast has been developed and "hardened," interfering with natural erosion and deposition processes that have historically created least tern nesting habitat. Sea level rise, combined with coastal development, have acted to increase erosion and the frequency of colony flooding.

Human development of coastal areas has facilitated an increase in predator populations. Mammalian predators, such as raccoons (*Procyon lotor*), red foxes (*Vulpes fulva*), skunks (*Mephitis mephitis*), rats (*Rattus norvegicus*), and opossums (*Didelphis marsupialis*), thrive in areas where people feed them or leave garbage outdoors. Populations of some avian predators, for example, gulls (*Larus* spp.) and crows (*Corvus* spp.), have also increased along the coast as they have adapted to human habitation. Feral and domestic cats (*Felis domesticus*) and dogs (*Canis familiaris*) also prey upon wild birds, including tern chicks.

Recommendations

Least tern populations have been monitored in New Jersey since the mid-1970s. Monitoring programs track use of specific nesting areas, document the number of adults and nests, and attempt to determine overall colony success and causes of losses or nesting failure. As terns arrive in New Jersey, Endangered and Nongame Species Program (ENSP) staff locate nesting areas and enclose them with string and posts. Educational and restricted-area signs are displayed near nest sites. When warranted, predator control is conducted near plover breeding areas. Beach nesting bird "stewards" regularly monitor and patrol nest sites to provide an extra measure of protection and to serve as onsite educators to the beach-going public.

Cooperative relationships between wildlife managers and the municipalities that govern beach communities—some of which have been formalized through written agreements—are imperative to the conservation of beach-nesting birds. Management agreements between ENSP and local municipalities help to share the responsibilities of managing nesting areas and help to establish important lines of communication. By protecting habitats for these birds and participating in their management, communities can realize eco-tourism benefits.

Beach replenishment projects can be designed to incorporate the needs of beach-nesting birds. Decoys have been used to attract terns to previously abandoned nesting areas and to concentrate nesting interest in areas that can be more easily protected (Kotliar and Burger 1984). Decoys may also be useful in attracting birds to newly created habitat, although this remains to be seen. Predator control should be implemented when necessary.

Dave Jenkins

Black Skimmer, *Rynchops niger*
Status: State: Endangered   Federal: Not listed

Identification

Watching the strikingly colored black skimmer forage for food—flying low horizontally while its highly sensitive lower jaw sluices through the water—is one of the natural world's more remarkable sights. This rather unique skill is made possible by its long, laterally compressed bill, which has a lower mandible, or jaw, that extends beyond the upper mandible. Gull-like, with narrow, tapered wings, the black skimmer is graceful and buoyant in flight. Its call, meanwhile, is a distinct, repeated barking.

The breeding adult black skimmer has brown-black upperparts, contrasting with a white forehead and underparts. The upperwing shows a white trailing edge from the secondaries to the inner primaries. The tail is white, with dark central feathers. The bill is black with a reddish orange base. The legs and feet are also reddish orange. Male black skimmers are slightly larger than females. Nonbreeding adult plumage is similar, but duller, to that of breeding adults. In winter, the bill and upperparts are somewhat paler. In addition, white feathers on the nape form a light collar around the neck.

Juvenile skimmers look similar to adults but have duller brown upperparts

A pair of black skimmers and their chicks. © Clay Myers.

with light feather edges and streaked crowns. The legs, feet, and base of the bill are dusky red. Juveniles acquire adultlike plumage the following summer.

Distribution

Black skimmers breed along the Atlantic and Pacific coasts of North, Central, and South America. The western breeding population ranges from southern California to Mexico. The eastern population spans the Atlantic Coast from Massachusetts to Florida and the Gulf Coast south to northern Brazil. Wintering skimmers occur along coastal North Carolina and California south to Central and South America.

In New Jersey, black skimmers nest along the Atlantic Coast from Sandy Hook to Cape May. Substantial colonies exist, or have existed in the recent past, at Barnegat Light, Tow Island, Strathmere Natural Area, Stone Harbor Point, and, most recently, at the north end of Ocean City. Skimmers abandoned Champagne Island, which formerly held the state's largest colony with more than 1,000 individuals, following the winter storms of 1997 and 1998 that significantly reduced the size and height of the island.

Fall migration of black skimmers in New Jersey occurs from mid-August through October, with a few individuals seen into November. Wintering skimmers are very rare in the state. Spring migration occurs from mid-April through May.

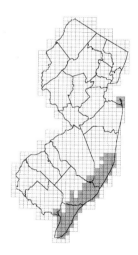

Habitat

The black skimmer nests on open sandy beaches, inlets, sandbars, offshore islands, and dredge disposal islands that are sparsely vegetated and contain shell fragments. The growth of dense vegetation may cause colony relocation. Skimmers also frequently nest on wrack mats (deposits of dead sea grasses and other vegetation) on marsh islands in the back bays; however, these colonies are typically much smaller than the beach colonies. Black skimmers forage in shallow-water tidal creeks, inlets, and ponds. Similar coastal and estuarine habitats are used throughout the year.

Diet

The diet of the black skimmer is comprised primarily of small fish such as minnows, killifish (*Fundulus* spp.), herring (*Clupea* spp.), and pipefish (*Sygnathus* spp.). Shrimp and other crustaceans constitute the remainder of the diet. Its unique hunting method has earned the skimmer its name. The skimmer glides low over the water, allowing its lower mandible to slice the water's surface. When the bird's bill strikes a fish, it snaps shut. The skimmer then aligns the prey headfirst before swallowing it whole. Skimmers may hunt during the day or at night, as foraging activity is correlated with tidal cycles. Foraging activity peaks near and during low tide.

Breeding Biology

From late April to late May, black skimmers arrive on their breeding grounds. Skimmers nest in colonies from a few pairs to several hundred. They return each year to areas where they have experienced past reproductive success, provided that suitable habitat remains. Often, nests are located within colonies of common (*Sterna hirundo*) and least (*S. antillarum*) terns, which nest earlier than the skimmers. Prior to copulation, the male skimmer presents his mate with a fish. Both the male and female dig shallow scrapes in the sand, one of which will be selected as the nest.

From mid-May to early June, the female lays a clutch of two to six eggs. Skimmers may replace lost clutches, particularly those destroyed by flooding.

A black skimmer in flight. Photo courtesy NJ ENSP

These birds may lay eggs as late as September, although they are unlikely to be successful. Sandy-colored with brown speckling, the eggs are well camouflaged within their scrape nest. Both adults incubate the eggs for 21 to 25 days, and they hatch during mid- to late June. The young are brooded for nearly all of their first week. By two weeks old, they are able to elude predators. Young chicks are fed regurgitant by their parents, but receive whole fish as they grow older. Initially, both the upper and lower mandibles of the bill are equal in length on young skimmers. The bill appears adultlike, with a longer lower mandible, by the time they fledge at 23 to 26 days.

Nesting at exposed sites, skimmer eggs and young are vulnerable to predation. If a predator or intruder threatens the colony, adults of both skimmers and terns take to the air and aggressively mob the intruder, using dives, pecks, calls, and defecation in their artillery. Adult skimmers may also perform a broken wing display, feigning injury to lure predators away from the nest. Skimmer chicks may hide among vegetation or lay flat in the sand, camouflaged by their plumage. After fledging in mid-July to early August, they remain in flocks prior to fall migration.

Status and Conservation

In the early 1800s, the black skimmer was a common breeder along the New Jersey coast. Egg collecting and hunting decimated skimmer populations in the state by the early 1900s. Protection afforded by the Migratory Bird Treaty Act of 1918 enabled skimmer numbers to rebound.

By the late 1970s, the black skimmer had declined, and concern arose over its status in the state. Consequently, the black skimmer was listed as an endangered species in New Jersey in 1979. The majority of the state's population remains in two to three large colonies that are threatened by habitat loss or human activity. The New Jersey Natural Heritage Program considers the black skimmer to be "demonstrably secure globally," yet "imperiled in New Jersey because of rarity" (Office of Natural Lands Management 1992).

Each year, the New Jersey Endangered and Nongame Species Program (ENSP) monitors the state's black skimmer population. Nesting colonies are enclosed and patrolled by personnel. Counts of adults and young are conducted to monitor population size and productivity. Despite annual fluctuations, the state's breeding population has remained relatively stable since the time of its original listing, although the number of active colonies has declined significantly. Human disturbance, beach raking, tidal flooding, and predation continue to threaten nesting skimmers and their habitat.

Limiting Factors and Threats

Human disturbance, degradation of nesting habitat, tidal flooding, and predation limit black skimmer breeding populations in New Jersey. Elevated levels of human recreational activity at beaches may cause colony abandonment, reduced nesting success, and increased predation risk. The skimmers' well-camouflaged eggs and chicks are susceptible to trampling by vehicular or foot traffic in nesting areas. Disturbance, resulting from people walking near or through nesting colonies or harassing birds, may cause adult skimmers to flush from their nests to drive intruders away. While the adults are away from the nest, the chicks are vulnerable to predators, temperature stress, and displacement. Chicks that are displaced from their parents may be killed by neighboring territorial adults. Defense displays conducted by adults may alert predators and attract them to eggs and/or young. Predators of skimmers and their eggs include Norway rats (*Rattus norvegicus*), herring gulls (*Larus argentatus*), laughing gulls (*L. atricilla*), dogs (*Canis familiaris*), cats (*Felis domesticus*), raccoons (*Procyon lotor*), red fox (*Vulpes fulva*), mink (*Mustela vison*), skunks (*Mephitis mephitis*), corvids, icterids, raptors, American oystercatchers (*Haematopus palliatus*), and black-crowned night-herons (*Nycticorax nycticorax*). High levels of predation can cause site abandonment and nesting failure.

Coastal beaches have been degraded due to heavy recreational pressure. The use of vehicles on beaches creates ruts in the sand, where chicks may become trapped. The great volumes of people at the Jersey Shore during the summer months has forced skimmers to nest in remote, low-lying areas where they are more susceptible to tidal flooding. Flooding can result in washouts of nests, eggs, and young of entire colonies. The erosion of coastal beaches intensifies the threat of flooding.

Black skimmers may be affected by environmental contaminants such as pesticides and metals, which are acquired in their diet. In addition, oil spills may impact skimmers that ingest oil while skimming for food. Skimmers bathing or wading in contaminated water may ingest oil during preening.

Recommendations

The ENSP conducts active management for beach-nesting birds, including black skimmers, each year. Prior to the arrival of nesting birds, known skimmer breeding sites are enclosed with fencing (posts and string). In addition, areas of suitable habitat and new breeding sites may be enclosed to encourage nesting. Nesting colonies are posted with educational and restricted-access signs. Personnel patrol skimmer colonies to minimize human disturbance and to educate the beach-going public. Biologists also conduct counts of nesting adults and young.

Cooperative relationships between wildlife managers and the municipalities that govern beach communities are imperative to the conservation of beach-nesting birds. By protecting habitats for these birds, communities can benefit from ecotourism. Beach management, including erosion control and beach replenishment, may be needed to provide or enhance habitat. In addition, beach vegetation may require thinning as skimmers abandon sites that become too densely vegetated. Predator control should be implemented when necessary.

Sherry Liguori

Barred Owl, *Strix varia*

Status: State: Threatened   Federal: Not listed

Identification

On still spring evenings, the hooting and eerie caterwauling of barred owls
resonate throughout the remote, swampy woodlands of New Jersey. The resounding song of the barred owl, often represented as *who cooks for you, who
cooks for you alllll,* is often accompanied by loud *hoo-ah* calls and yowling reminiscent of monkeys. Barred owls may vocalize throughout the year but are
most expressive during courtship, from late February to early April. These
owls often call at night but may also vocalize during the day.

The barred owl is a large fluffy-looking owl with brown barring on the upper breast and brown streaking on the lower breast and belly. The upperparts
are brown with buffy-white barring. The tail is patterned with alternating
bands of brown and buff-gray. The throat is white and the round head lacks
ear tufts. The facial disk is grayish white with a brown outline. The large facial disk funnels sounds toward the owl's proportionally gigantic ears, providing it with extraordinary hearing for detecting minute noises, such as the
rustling of mice in the dark. Unlike all other eastern owls excluding the barn
owl, the eyes of the barred owl are dark brown. The hooked bill is buff yellow.
The feet and toes are feathered and the talons are dark brownish black. Sexes
are similar in plumage and, although there is much overlap, females may be
larger than males. Juveniles resemble adults.

Barred owls fly with slow, mothlike wingbeats that are interspersed with
glides. In flight, the head appears large and the wings are broad and rounded.
Soft feathers and serrated edges on the outer wing feathers minimize noise,
enabling these and all other owls to fly silently—an advantage that enables
them to surprise their prey.

The barred owl can be distinguished from most other New Jersey owls by its plumage, large size, distinctive vocalizations, and habitat selection. The great horned owl (*Bubo virginianus*), a common breeding species in the state, is also a large owl but has rich brown plumage and yellow eyes. The ear tufts of great horned owls may not be noticeable in flight, making them appear round-headed like a barred owl. The call of the great horned owl is a melancholy *hoo-hoo-hoo*. Great horned owls, which often reside in forested uplands or near human habitation, are less restrictive in their habitat choice than barred owls. The barn owl (*Tyto alba*), the only other New Jersey owl with dark eyes, is white below and golden brown above. In addition, the barn owl, which resides in open fields and grasslands, has a narrow body, long, unfeathered legs, and a heart-shaped facial disk.

Distribution

The barred owl occurs throughout the eastern United States north to southern Canada and south to the Gulf Coast and Florida. In recent years this owl has expanded its range westward, overlapping with its imperiled cousin, the spotted owl (*Strix occidentalis*) in some western states.

The barred owl, a year-round resident, occurs in bottomland forests in southern New Jersey and riparian woodlands in northern New Jersey. Considerable populations occur in the Highlands region of North Jersey, the Pequannock watershed, High Point State Park, Stokes State Forest, Wawayanda State Park, Sterling Forest, Wanaque Wildlife Management Area, the Passaic River basin, and Great Swamp National Wildlife Refuge. In South Jersey, populations occur at Bear Swamp Natural Area, Belleplain State Forest, Great Cedar Swamp, and along tributaries of the Maurice River. In the Pine Barrens of Atlantic, Ocean, and Burlington counties, barred owls are restricted to Atlantic white cedar swamps and mixed hardwood swamps.

Habitat

Traditionally known as the "swamp owl," the barred owl is a denizen of remote, contiguous, old-growth wetland forests. These owls require mature wet woods that contain large trees with cavities suitable for nesting. Barred owl habitats typically have an open understory through which the owls can fly and hunt. The lack of large nesting cavities is often the primary limiting factor for barred owls. Consequently, these owls may nest immediately outside of a wetland or in subclimax wetland forests if adequate nest sites are unavailable within a mature wetland forest. Barred owls are typically found in remote wilderness areas that may also contain other rare species such as the red-shouldered hawk (*Buteo lineatus*) or the Cooper's hawk (*Accipiter cooperii*). Barred owls typically shun human activity by avoiding residential, agricultural, industrial, or commercial areas. In northern New Jersey, barred owls favored sites that were at least 500 m (1,640 ft.) from human habitation and had little or no forest clearings or trails (Bosakowski 1987).

In southern New Jersey, barred owls inhabit both deciduous wetland forests and Atlantic white cedar (*Chamaecyparis thyoides*) swamps associated with stream corridors. Often such lowland forests are buffered by surrounding pine or pine/oak uplands that may protect the owls from human disturbance and provide additional foraging habitat. Mixed hardwood swamps are often dominated by red maple (*Acer rubrum*) and black gum (*Nyssa sylvatica*) and may include highbush blueberry (*Vaccinium corymbosum*), swamp magnolia (*Magnolia virginiana*), or greenbrier (*Smilax* spp.) in the shrub layer. Although barred owls utilize white cedars for roosting, they infrequently provide cavities that are large enough for nesting owls.

In northern New Jersey, barred owls inhabit hemlock ravines and mixed deciduous wetland or riparian forests. Oak hardwood forests containing white oak (*Quercus alba*), red maple, black birch (*Betula lenta*), black willow (*Salix nigra*), hickory (*Carya* spp.), white ash (*Fraxinus americana*), basswood (*Tilia americana*), tulip poplar (*Liriodendron tulipifera*), black cherry (*Prunus serotina*), and black gum may be occupied. Barred owls may also inhabit northern hardwood forests that contain sugar maple (*A. saccharum*), birch (*Betula* spp.), and beech (*Fagus grandifolia*). Dense stands of hemlock (*Tsuga canadensis*), white pine (*Pinus strobus*), Norway spruce (*Picea abies*), or other conifers provide cover for roosting owls and protection from harsh weather. Barred owls prefer flat, lowland terrain and avoid rocky slopes and hillsides.

As a resident species, barred owls establish territories with fairly stable boundaries that are continuously maintained throughout the year. In eastern North America, home range sizes of 86 to 370 hectares (213–914 acres) have been documented for barred owls (Johnsgard 1990).

Diet

The diet of the barred owl consists predominantly of small mammals such as mice, voles, shrews, squirrels, rabbits, moles, rats, and chipmunks. As opportunistic predators, barred owls may also consume frogs, lizards, small snakes, salamanders, spiders, crayfish, snails, slugs, insects, fish, opossums, bats, or small birds. Small prey items are swallowed whole and later regurgitated as pellets of undigested bones, fur, and feathers. Feeding areas, which are often littered with pellets and whitewash, are telltale signs of an owl's presence. Much of what is known about owl diets has been revealed through the examination of pellets.

Barred owls hunt in the forest understory and in open areas within wooded tracts. They rely on keen vision and acute hearing to locate prey at night. When attending to a nest full of hungry chicks, adults may also hunt during the day.

Breeding Biology

From late February to mid-April, the calling of barred owls strengthen pair bonds and reinforce territories. During courtship, the male and female bow toward each other with wings fanned out, while rocking their heads from side to side. Vocal activity peaks during March, when the noisy, cackling calls of these owls can be heard echoing throughout their deep, swampy haunts. When incubating or caring for young, barred owls tend to be more secretive and vocalize less frequently.

Barred owls exhibit strong pair bonds and site fidelity. Consequently, a pair often occupies the same territory or nest in successive years. Large cavities within dead trees or dead limbs of live trees serve as nesting sites. Nesting trees must be large enough to provide cavities of adequate size. Often, a high-quality nesting site may be used until the bottom rots out beneath the cavity. If cavities are scarce, barred owls may use abandoned stick nests of hawks, crows, or squirrels. Barred owls may also accept man-made nest boxes.

From March to mid-April, the female barred owl deposits two to three round, white eggs within the unlined nesting cavity. Barred owls usually lay only one clutch per year but may replace clutches lost early in the breeding season. The male delivers food to the female, who incubates the eggs for 28 to 33 days. Because incubation begins with the first egg, the young hatch asynchronously and thus vary in size. If food is scarce, only the older, and consequently larger and stronger, chicks may survive.

The altricial (dependent) young, which are able to open their eyes within a week, are brooded until they are nearly three weeks old. Both adults care for the chicks, providing the begging nestlings with pieces of meat. At four to five weeks of age, the fledglings vacate the nest, branching out onto nearby limbs. At about six weeks, the young are able to fly but may continue to be fed by their parents for their first summer and possibly even longer.

Status and Conservation

The barred owl was traditionally a common resident within the deep wooded swamps of New Jersey. Historically, these owls were shot as trophies or because of alleged poultry predation. Collectors also looted young owls and eggs. Despite human persecution, the barred owl persisted virtually unscathed until the early 1940s, when the cutting of old-growth forests and the filling of wetlands greatly reduced habitat throughout the state. Rampant habitat loss and associated barred owl population declines continued for the next several decades. Consequently, these owls were lost from many historic breeding locales.

Due to population declines and habitat loss, the barred owl was listed as a threatened species in New Jersey in 1979. The New Jersey Natural Heritage Program considers the barred owl to be "demonstrably secure globally," yet "rare in New Jersey" (Office of Natural Lands Management 1992). Currently, barred owl populations appear to be declining due to development and fragmentation of large tracts of private forested lands. The barred owl population has been estimated at 37 pairs in South Jersey and 75 pairs in North Jersey (Sutton and Sutton 1986; Bosakowski 1988). But recent surveys in South Jersey indicate as much as a 30% decline there.

Limiting Factors and Threats

The loss, alteration, degradation, and fragmentation of forested habitats are the primary threats facing barred owls in New Jersey. Throughout the state, increasing development has eliminated upland forest buffers and encroached upon wetland forests, degrading habitat for these owls. The cutting of dead trees, stand thinning, and controlled burns can eliminate nesting cavities or render sites unsuitable for breeding owls. Younger second-growth forests rarely provide cavities that are large enough for nesting barred owls.

Barred owls require large, mature, contiguous forests and, consequently, are adversely affected by forest fragmentation. Habitat fragmentation can result in isolated populations that experience low recruitment and may suffer from localized extinctions. Within fragmented woodlots, barred owls are increasingly vulnerable to human disturbance and predation by great horned owls. In addition, expanding development may elevate road mortality of owls. Runoff and siltation resulting from the construction of buildings or roads may also degrade water quality within wetland habitats.

Recommendations

Barred owl conservation must include the preservation of extensive old-growth wetland forests. In addition, surrounding upland forests should be protected to afford buffers from human activity. Networks that connect existing forested tracts should be protected to enable movement between populations. Barred owl habitat protection should be incorporated into forest management plans for state and federal lands. Management practices, including thinning, selective cutting, and clear-cutting, should be prohibited within barred owl habitat. Large dead trees or live trees containing dead limbs must remain standing to provide nesting cavities. Human activity should be minimized or restricted at barred owl nesting areas.

Existing second-growth wetland forests should be allowed to mature to provide future barred owl habitat. Removing smaller trees to accelerate the growth of dominant trees can reduce competition, enabling these stands to mature quicker. When thinning young forests, snags should remain standing, and 80% of existing canopy cover should remain. In areas of suitable habitat, artificial nest boxes can be erected to provide supplemental cavity sites.

Sherry Liguori

Long-Eared Owl, *Asio otus*
Status: State: Threatened   Federal: Not listed

Identification

The long-eared owl is a slender, crow-sized owl with long "ear" tufts atop the head that are often visible when the owl perches. The ear tufts are not actual ears but rather clusters of feathers that aid in camouflaging the bird. The true ears are located on both sides of the head next to the round rusty-orange facial disk.

Long-eared owl.
© Blaine Rothauser

The breast of the long-eared owl is brown with irregular white spotting. The belly is buffy and crosshatched with dark brown markings. The upperparts are heavily marked with black and brown and have gray, buff, and white tones. The wings are long and rounded with a buff-orange patch at the base of the outer primaries on the upperwing. The flight feathers are grayish with dusky spots. The underwing shows a dark brown patch at the wrist. There is a small white patch on the throat below the black bill. The tail is buff colored with brown bands. The legs and feet are feathered to the talons, which are black. The iris is yellow to golden yellow. Sexes are alike in plumage, although males are often slightly paler than females.

The long-eared owl relies on its cryptic coloration to camouflage itself within its surroundings. When disturbed, the owl may elongate its body and raise its ear tufts to resemble a broken branch or part of a tree trunk. Long-eared owls also snap their bills if threatened. Vocal activity of the long-eared owl is primarily restricted to the breeding season when males emit a series of deep *hoo* notes during the nighttime hours. The call of the female is slightly higher pitched than that of the male. Both adults give a repeated barking *oo-ack* alarm call. Long-eared owls are skilled fliers that can maneuver among trees and migrate long distances.

The long-eared owl can be confused with other owl species. The great-horned owl (*Bubo virginianus*), which is similarly patterned and also has prominent ear tufts, can be distinguished from the long-eared owl by its larger size and stockier body. The eastern screech owl (*Otus asio*) is much smaller than the long-eared owl and differs in coloration, occurring in a rusty red or gray phase.

Distribution

The long-eared owl breeds throughout North America from southern Canada south to California, northern Texas, and Virginia. During the winter, these owls occur within suitable habitat throughout the contiguous United States. In years with harsh weather or limited prey, northern-wintering owls vacate their typical range and supplement populations to the south.

The long-eared owl is a rare breeding species in New Jersey and an uncommon migrant and winter resident. Breeding long-eared owls occur in northwestern, north-central, and southwestern Jersey. Nesting has been confirmed or suspected at Hopewell, Rockaway, Great Piece Meadows, the Pequannock Watershed, Harmony Township, Troy Meadows, Hatfield Swamp, Great Swamp, East Orange Water Reserve, Washington's Crossing, Lebanon State Forest, Mount Laurel, Medford, and Wharton State Forest.

Fall migration of long-eared owls in New Jersey occurs from late September to late November. During the winter, small numbers of these owls roost communally throughout the state in dense groves of conifers. Although long-eared owls exhibit strong fidelity to roost sites during a season, they may occupy different roosts in successive years. Wintering birds disperse from roosts by early April.

Habitat

Long-eared owls require a mosaic of wooded and open habitats. Both roosting and nesting sites may be located within dense stands of either natural or ornamental evergreens, such as Scotch pine (*Pinus sylvestris*), Austrian pine (*P. nigra*), Virginia pine (*P. virginiana*), eastern red cedar (*Juniperus virginiana*), Norway spruce (*Picea abies*), arborvitae (*Thuja orientalis*), eastern hemlock (*Tsuga canadensis*), red pine (*Pinus resinosa*), and white pine (*P. strobus*). Deciduous trees and impenetrable tangles of vines also provide cover for these owls. High foliage density is required at nesting and roosting sites to provide camouflage and protection from wind, cold temperatures, and precipitation. Roosting and nesting woodlots are located adjacent to upland or wetland open terrain. Open areas, such as fallow fields, farm fields, and marshes, are used for hunting and are integral components of long-eared owl habitat. Marshes may contain reed grass (*Phragmites australis*), cattail (*Typha* spp.), or sedges.

Diet

Long-eared owls are predators of small mammals, pursuing voles (*Microtus* spp.), mice (*Mus* spp., *Peromyscus* spp.), shrews (*Blarina* spp., *Sorex* spp., *Cryptotis* spp.), and rats (*Rattus* spp.) found in open areas. Songbirds, snakes, and insects may also be taken.

As nocturnal predators, owls rely on keen eyesight, acute hearing, and silent flight to detect, locate, and capture their prey. With the aid of facial disks that funnel sound to their large ears, owls are able to pinpoint the location of their prey in total darkness. Soft feathers and serrations on the outer wing feathers provide owls with silent flight, an adaptation that enables them to stalk prey undetected. Owls swallow their prey whole and regurgitate pellets of indigestible fur and bones that litter the ground at feeding and roosting sites.

Breeding Biology

Prior to their departure from winter roosts, long-eared owls begin to establish pair bonds. At their breeding territory, the courting male flies high within the forest and produces a clapping sound with his wings while the female calls to him from a perch below. The male also emits a courtship song, consisting of a series of *hoo* notes, to attract the female. Pairs may occupy the same nest site in successive years. Fairly tolerant of each other, long-eared owl pairs may form loose nesting colonies.

Long-eared owls do not build their own nests. Rather, they use abandoned crow and hawk nests and may on occasion breed in cavities, scrapes on the ground, or old squirrel nests. The female lays four to five round, white eggs at daily intervals between mid-April and mid-May. The eggs, which are incubated for 25 to 30 days, hatch asynchronously, resulting in young of staggered ages and sizes. The female, who rarely leaves the nest during this time, relies on her cryptic plumage for concealment. During incubation and brooding, the male delivers food to his mate. The chicks, unable to open their eyes for the first five days, are totally dependent upon their parents. If prey is scarce, only the older and consequently larger and more aggressive young may survive. At three or more weeks of age, the young, still unable to fly, leave the nest and perch on nearby branches. They typically roost separately from one another to reduce the chance of losing the entire clutch to predation. If predators, such as crows or raccoons, encroach upon the nest site, the adults may feign injury to lure them away. At five to six weeks of age, the young begin to fly. The parents continue to feed the fledglings until they are 10 to 11 weeks old. Family groups of long-eared owls may remain together into the winter.

Status and Conservation

Before the twentieth century, the clearing of eastern forests for agriculture resulted in a mosaic of farm fields and woodlands and may have enabled long-eared owl numbers to exceed presettlement populations. In the late 1800s and early 1900s, long-eared owls bred at scattered locations in New Jersey from Sussex County to Salem County. However, by the mid-1900s, vegetative succession, development of open and forested areas, and modern agricultural practices greatly reduced habitat for these owls in the state. The number of active long-eared owl winter roosts, as well as the number of birds per roost, has declined since the 1950s. Despite extensive surveys in the late 1980s, the number of known breeding pairs remained extremely low. Long-eared owls are currently absent from many nesting sites that were occupied prior to the 1960s. Expanding development has been responsible for the loss of traditional roosting and nesting sites. Due to population declines of breeding pairs and winter residents, habitat loss, and limited breeding distribution in the state, the long-eared owl was listed as a threatened species in New Jersey in 1991. The New Jersey Natural Heritage Program considers the long-eared owl to be "demonstrably secure globally," yet "rare in New Jersey" (Office of Natural Lands Management 1992).

Limiting Factors and Threats

The loss of forests, fallow fields, and farmlands to development and vegetative succession has reduced the amount of available habitat for long-eared owls in New Jersey. Over the past several decades, open areas have reverted to forest through vegetative succession. On the agricultural lands that remain, the transition to modern mechanized agriculture has replaced small farm fields with large monocultures that are treated with pesticides and rodenticides. Such practices reduce both habitat and prey for long-eared owls. In addition, rodenticides may be lethal to owls that consume contaminated prey.

Increased development has resulted in more roads and vehicular traffic, making long-eared owls vulnerable to road mortality. In addition, predation and competition by other raptors, especially great horned owls (*Bubo virginianus*), occurs in fragmented habitats. Raccoons (*Procyon lotor*) and American crows (*Corvus brachyrhynchos*) may also prey upon long-eared owl eggs or nestlings.

Recommendations

Management of long-eared owls must include the provision of suitable habitat, particularly dense stands of conifers and fallow open fields. Existing roost sites should be protected and additional evergreen groves should be planted. Cooperative management efforts for long-eared owls can be implemented on farms, airports, golf courses, wildlife management areas, and wildlife refuges. Grasslands, meadows, fallow fields, and low-impact agricultural lands should be maintained through cutting, low-intensity grazing, or controlled burns. On active farmlands, crops should be rotated annually with fallow fields, and rodenticide use should be limited. In addition, large monocultures should be avoided and a mosaic of smaller fields containing diverse species should be encouraged.

Sherry Liguori

Short-Eared Owl, *Asio flammeus*
Status: State: Endangered (breeding population only)   Federal: Migratory Nongame Bird of Management Concern (in the Northeast)

Identification

The short-eared owl is a medium-sized owl typically seen flying—with moth-like wingbeats—low over open marshes or fields. The wings of the short-eared

owl are long and have rounded tips, and the head, from a distance, appears stubby. In flight, white underwings contrast with dark wingtips and dark commas at the wrists.

The owl's body is tawny, with dark brown streaking. The upperparts are also tawny, with dark brown and white mottling. The tawny-colored flight feathers are bisected by dark brown bars and tips. A dark patch at the base of the primaries is visible on both the upperwing and underwing. The face is buff-colored or white, with areas of black surrounding the eyes. The rounded facial disk is bordered by tiny white feathers. The buff-colored tail is bisected by dark brown bars. The legs and feet are cloaked with small, tawny feathers. The talons and bill are black. The iris is yellow. Sexes are similar in appearance. The call of the short-eared owl is a raspy, repeated *wak-wak-wak* bark.

Distribution

The breeding range of the short-eared owl extends from Alaska, subarctic Canada, and the northern United States south to northern Virginia, Kansas, and central California. Wintering short-eared owls occur throughout the contiguous United States south to Baja California, Mexico, and Florida.

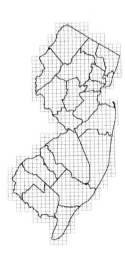

In New Jersey, the short-eared owl historically nested in marshes along the Atlantic and Delaware Bay coasts, including Elizabeth, Long Beach, Barnegat Bay, and Fortescue. By 1979–80, the only known breeding areas in the state were Barnegat, Turkey Point, and the Tuckahoe River. Since then, a probable nesting attempt was suspected at Supawna Meadows, Salem County, in 1989. In addition, birds observed during the breeding season may indicate possible nesting activity in Cumberland County at Bay Point (1976) and Turkey Point (1982), and in Cape May County at Ocean City (1984), Crow Creek (1984), Goshen Landing (1988), Jakes Landing (1988), and Stipsons Island Road (1993).

Migrant and wintering short-eared owls occur in marshes along the Delaware Bay shore and the Atlantic Coast and at inland fields and grasslands. Wintering owls are observed at the Hackensack Meadowlands, Manahawkin National Wildlife Refuge, Forsythe National Wildlife Refuge, Turkey Point, and Commercial Township. During the winter months, short-eared owls form communal roosts, occasionally in the company of northern harriers (*Circus cyaneus*). One historic roost located in grassy fields near Princeton contained 150 to 200 owls in the winter of 1878–1879 (Stone 1965b). Similarly, 24 wintering owls were tallied at Newark Meadows in 1947 (Bull 1964). In recent years, the number of wintering short-eared owls has declined, with an annual average of 42 birds recorded statewide on Christmas Bird Counts from 1976 to 1997 (Walsh et al. 1999).

The short-eared owl is a rare migrant in New Jersey, occurring from early October to late December, with a peak in late October. Spring migration occurs from mid-March to late April. Migrant short-eared owls may be seen during the day, particularly around dawn or dusk, at coastal beaches, dunes, and marshes as well as inland fields, landfills, and grasslands.

Habitat

In New Jersey, short-eared owls inhabit coastal tidal and brackish marshes, inland fields, pastures, and grasslands. Within coastal marshes, short-eared owls typically roost, forage, or nest in the drier portions of the marsh that do not experience regular tidal inundation. These marshes may contain salt-hay grass (*Spartina patens*), spike grass (*Disthchlys* spp.), black rush (*Juncus gerardi*), marsh elder (*Iva frutescens*), or phragmites (*Phragmites communis*). Infrequently, short-eared owls forage over salt-marsh cordgrass (*Spartina alterniflora*) or phragmites marshes, although vast areas of low marsh or thick stands of phragmites do not offer high-quality habitat for these owls. Large acreages of coastal high marsh adjacent to undisturbed upland fields serve as prime habitat for short-eared owls. Short-eared owls and northern harriers occupy similar habitats and, due to the crepuscular (dawn and dusk) and sometimes diurnal (daytime) nature of short-eared owls, the two species can be active at the same time.

Short-eared owls roost, forage, and nest at inland open areas, such as fallow fields, hay fields, grasslands, airports, and sedge meadows. Sensitive to human activity, short-eared owls require large tracts of undisturbed open areas. Territory size for breeding short-eared owls in southern Manitoba ranged from 73.9 to 121.4 hectares (182.6 to 300 acres), while territories for owls breeding in coastal Massachusetts ranged from 25 to 126 hectares (62–311 acres) (Clark 1975; Holt 1992; Holt and Leasure 1993).

Short-eared owls occupy similar habitats throughout the annual cycle. They form winter roosts on the ground within open areas. Wintering roosts of short-eared owls, occasionally in the company of long-eared owls (*Asio otus*), have also been documented in conifers such as yew (*Taxus* spp.), Austrian pine (*Pinus nigra*), and juniper (*Juniperus communis*), particularly during

periods of heavy snow cover. Wintering short-eared owls may concentrate at landfills where rodents are abundant.

Diet

The diet of the short-eared owl is dominated by small mammals, including voles (*Microtus*), mice (*Perosmyscus, Mus*), shrews (*Blarina*), rats (*Rattus*), and rabbits (*Sylvilagus*). Meadow voles (*Microtus pennsylvanicus*) constitute a large portion of their diet. These owls, which consume one to two voles per day, are essential in the control of rodent populations. Consequently, short-eared owl populations are strongly regulated by the availability of small mammalian prey. During the winter months, short-eared owls may resort to pursuing avian prey if snow cover prevents them from hunting small mammals.

Short-eared owls hunt primarily at night, although they may also forage at dawn or dusk. During the breeding season, these owls may hunt during the day as well to secure food for their clutch. Hunting short-eared owls either fly low over the ground in search of prey or scan for prey from a perch.

Breeding Biology

During late winter and early spring, short-eared owls begin to seek mates and establish pair bonds. The courting male performs an aerial display in which he soars upward in tight circles and then enters a steep dive, only to swoop upward again, producing a clapping noise with his wings. A courtship song, consisting of a series of *hoo* calls, typically accompanies the aerial display. The courtship flight and song may be performed during the day or at night.

Like its diurnal counterpart, the northern harrier, the short-eared owl builds its nest on the ground in an open habitat, such as a field or marsh. The nest is constructed by the female, who scrapes a cup in the existing vegetation and lines it with grasses and feathers. Nests are typically located on dry ground within herbaceous cover.

During May, the female lays a clutch of four to seven buff-colored eggs. She lays the eggs at two-day intervals, yet begins incubation with the first egg, resulting in young of staggered ages and sizes. If food is plentiful, all of the chicks may survive. However, only the larger, dominant chicks may endure lean years. After 24 to 28 days, the eggs hatch. The male hunts and provides food to the female, which feeds the owlets pieces of flesh.

At about two weeks of age, the owlets, not yet able to fly, leave the nest and seek cover in the surrounding vegetation. During this time, they explore their surroundings and observe the hunting behavior of their parents. The young fledge when they are approximately one month old, but they may continue to receive food from their parents for an additional three to four weeks.

Status and Conservation

Short-eared owls historically bred along the Atlantic and Delaware Bay coasts of New Jersey. During the early 1920s, numerous nests were documented in salt hay marshes in Elizabeth. In addition, large concentrations of short-eared owls occurred in New Jersey during the winter months, as evidenced by the Princeton roost of 1878–1879 that contained nearly 200 owls. Although shooting and egg collecting initially may have caused reductions in historic populations, habitat loss subsequently played a greater role in the species' decline. The filling of coastal marshes following World War II greatly reduced habitat for these owls. By the 1950s, the short-eared owl had declined as a breeding species in much of the Northeast, including New Jersey.

Due to habitat loss and severe population declines in the state, the short-eared owl was listed as a threatened species in New Jersey in 1979. Short-eared owls were last confirmed nesting in the state in 1979, with only a handful of sightings during the breeding season during the early 1980s. As a result, the status of the short-eared owl in New Jersey was changed from threatened to endangered in 1984. The New Jersey Natural Heritage Program considers the short-eared owl to be "demonstrably secure globally," yet "no extant occurrences are known in New Jersey" (Office of Natural Lands Management 1998).

Due to population declines, the National Audubon Society included the short-eared owl on its Blue List of Imperiled Species from 1976 to 1986, the final year of the list. The U.S. Fish and Wildlife Service designated the short-eared owl a Migratory Nongame Bird of Management Concern in the Northeast in 1992. Christmas Bird Counts revealed a significant decline in wintering owls surveywide from 1959 to 1988 (Sauer et al. 1996). Similarly, the Breeding Bird Survey detected a significant annual decline in short-eared owl populations surveywide from 1966 to 1999 (Sauer et al. 2001). In New Jersey, nesting was suspected in 1989 and birds were observed during the breeding season throughout the late 1980s and early 1990s, although nesting

was not confirmed. Field studies targeted specifically for this species and surveys conducted by New Jersey Breeding Bird Atlas participants (Walsh et al.
1999) indicate that the short-eared owl remains an extremely rare and possibly extirpated breeding species in the state. These owls have declined throughout the northeastern United States and consequently are listed as endangered
in Massachusetts and Pennsylvania, threatened in Connecticut, and of special
concern in New York and Maryland.

Limiting Factors and Threats

The loss of suitable habitat may be the primary factor limiting short-eared owl
nesting populations in New Jersey. High marsh habitats containing *S. patens*
have been destroyed through the encroachment of *S. alterniflora* resulting
from water level rises in the Delaware Bay, erosion of coastal marshes, open-
marsh water management, and restoration of tidal flow to salt-hay farms. The
invasive phragmites, which is of poor habitat value to short-eared owls, has
dominated many of New Jersey's marshes. In addition, fallow fields and grasslands are being rapidly lost to development and vegetative succession. The
ditching of marshes may negatively affect short-eared owls, as the pair nesting at Tuckahoe abandoned the site after the marsh was ditched. Habitat fragmentation may restrict breeding short-eared owls, which require large tracts
of contiguous habitat.

Despite the extensive loss of habitat, in areas such as the Delaware Bay
shore, apparently suitable habitat remains and species with similar habitat requirements such as the northern harrier occur. Yet the short-eared owl is absent. This indicates either that short-eared owls are more particular in their
habitat requirements than harriers or that there are unknown factors limiting
short-eared owl nesting.

Human disturbance may inhibit short-eared owl nesting activity. In agricultural areas, nests may be destroyed or abandoned due to the use of farm
machinery. At airports, mowing can destroy nests, and high noise levels may
deter owls from nesting. Human activity in coastal marshes, which increases
as tourism expands along the Jersey Shore, may preclude short-eared owls
from nesting in otherwise suitable habitats.

In addition to habitat loss and human disturbance, prey availability may
limit short-eared owl breeding populations. Short-eared owl abundance at
both wintering and breeding sites is strongly correlated with populations of
small mammalian prey.

Causes of short-eared owl mortality include collisions with automobiles, illegal shooting, predation of adults and juveniles by great horned owls (*Bubo
virginianus*), and nest predation by skunks (*Mephitis mephitis*), raccoons (*Procyon lotor*), and crows (*Corvus* spp.). A large population of great horned owls
along the Delaware Bay shore may deter short-eared owls from nesting.

Recommendations

The protection of large tracts of high-quality habitat, such as salt-hay marshes
and grasslands, is critical to the recovery of short-eared owl breeding popula-

tions in New Jersey. Existing salt hay marshes should be safeguarded from ditching, tidal restoration efforts, and human activity. Upland fields adjacent to salt-hay marshes should be targeted for acquisition and maintained as grasslands.

Management practices can be implemented on airports and grasslands to provide habitat for short-eared owls. Habitat management for short-eared owls will also benefit other marsh and grassland species, such as the northern harrier. Vegetative succession should be suppressed through mowing, grazing, or controlled burns. Management activities must be conducted during the nonbreeding season and should be implemented on a rotational scheme, ensuring that fields with vegetative cover are available for owls during the nesting season. If a short-eared owl nest is discovered, human activity should be restricted within a minimum buffer of 300 m (approximately 1,000 ft.) surrounding the nest.

Surveys for nesting short-eared owls should be conducted in areas of suitable habitat, particularly at sites where breeding has been suspected or confirmed in the past. Locations in which short-eared owls are sighted during late spring should be rechecked for nesting birds during the summer months.

Sherry Liguori

Red-Headed Woodpecker, *Melanerpes erythrocephalus*
Status: State: Threatened   Federal: Not listed

Identification

The red-headed woodpecker is a robin-sized bird, readily distinguished by its vibrant black, white, and red plumage. Brilliant red cloaks the head, neck, and throat and is separated from the white breast by a thin black border. The belly, undertail coverts, and rump are white, contrasting with the black tail, back, and upperwing coverts. White inner secondaries and tertials adjacent to black outer secondaries and primaries (flight feathers) form a white patch on the inner wing that is conspicuous in flight.

Though they lack the striking plumage of adults, juvenile red-headed woodpeckers are similarly patterned. The head and wings of juveniles are brown and the white belly has a variable amount of brown streaking. The back is brown with dark brown barring, and the white wing patch is also marked with dark barring. During their first fall and winter, juveniles molt into adult plumage.

Although the male is slightly larger, the sexes are indistinguishable by plumage. On all ages and sexes, the iris is brown and the legs are gray. The chisel-shaped bill is heavy and colored blue-gray. Like other woodpeckers, the red-headed has zygodactyl feet, in which two toes point forward and two point backward, enabling it to cling vertically to trees. In addition, the tail feathers are stiff and pointed, serving to prop the woodpecker up against a tree. Red-headed woodpeckers fly low over the ground in an undulating manner. The call of the red-headed woodpecker is a repeated *qweer*.

Red-headed wood-pecker. Photo courtesy NJ ENSP

Distribution

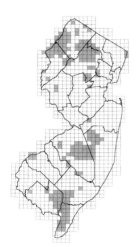

The red-headed woodpecker breeds in eastern North America from southern Canada west to central Texas and the eastern Rocky Mountains, east to the Atlantic Coast, and south to the Gulf Coast and Florida. Wintering birds occur in the eastern United States, south of Iowa and New Jersey.

In New Jersey, the red-headed woodpecker is an uncommon breeding species and a rare migrant and winter resident. Nesting occurs in the Pine Barrens of southern New Jersey and in the northern half of the state in Sussex, Bergen, Warren, Morris, Essex, Hunterdon, Somerset, and Monmouth counties. Southern New Jersey breeding locales include Lebanon State Forest, Colliers Mills Wildlife Management Area, Lakewood, Medford, Wharton State Forest, Tabernacle, Greenwood Forest, Batsto, Tuckerton, Galloway Township, Estelle Manor, Bevan Wildlife Management Area, Peaslee Wildlife Management Area, and Belleplain State Forest. Wild red-headed woodpeckers have also nested at the Cape May County Zoo since 1976, although few or no breeding birds have been seen in recent years. Northern New Jersey breeding locales include Stokes State Forest, Delaware Water Gap National Wildlife Refuge, Wallkill, Vernon, Green Brook, Whittingham Wildlife Management Area, Pohatchong Creek, Mount Olive, Great Swamp, and numerous sites in Sussex County. Historically, red-headed woodpeckers nested throughout the state, with substantial breeding populations in the Passaic River watershed, particularly Hatfield Swamp and Troy Meadows, and west-central Somerset County.

Spring migration of the red-headed woodpecker extends from late April to mid-May. Fall migrants occur from late August to mid-November and peak from mid-September to early October. Infrequently, small numbers of red-headed woodpeckers overwinter in New Jersey. For two years during the early 1980s, an unusually large number of approximately fifty birds remained throughout the year at Great Swamp. Because their diet in the nonbreeding season is dependent upon mast such as acorns, red-headed woodpeckers are nomadic in the winter, seeking areas with adequate food supplies.

Habitat

Red-headed woodpeckers inhabit open woods, both upland and wetland, that contain dead or dying trees and sparse undergrowth. Such habitat is often created by disturbances such as fire, flooding, or insect outbreaks. A sparse understory is favored for foraging and dead or dying trees are required for nesting. Red-headed woodpeckers occupy similar habitats throughout the year, seeking wintering sites such as open riparian or pine forests and orchards that contain nut and mast-producing trees.

In southern New Jersey, typical red-headed woodpecker nesting sites include upland oak or mixed oak/pine forests that contain both living and dead trees. Pitch pine (*Pinus rigida*), white oak (*Quercus alba*), and red oak (*Q. rubra*) are often found in the overstory and lowbush blueberry (*Vaccinium vacillans*) or huckleberry (*Gaylussacia* spp.) dominate the ground cover. In northern New Jersey, red-headed woodpeckers breed in open upland forests, beaver marshes, or wetland forests associated with floodplains or swamps. Such wetland habitats, which often provide an abundance of dead trees, may contain oak (*Quercus* spp.), hickory (*Carya* spp.), elm (*Ulmus* spp.), and hackberry (*Celtis occidentalis*) in the overstory and sedge (*Carex* spp.) on the ground.

Diet

The red-headed woodpecker is an omnivorous species, consuming invertebrates, acorns, beechnuts, chestnuts, fruit, berries, seeds, corn, lizards, mice, eggs, and the young of other birds. The seasonally variable diet is dominated by animal matter during the spring and summer months and shifts to plant matter during the fall and winter.

During the breeding season, red-headed woodpeckers consume beetles, ants, grasshoppers, caterpillars, bugs, earthworms, wasps, and bees. They often hunt in a flycatcher-like manner, gliding from a perch to secure flying insects in open areas. In addition, they glean insects from trees and forage on the ground. During the spring and summer months, red-headed woodpeckers also consume seasonally available fruits and berries. Young red-headed woodpeckers are fed insects, spiders, worms, and berries.

Acorns, nuts, seeds, and corn are the dietary staples of the red-headed woodpecker during the nonbreeding season. In the fall, acorns are collected and stored within crevices of trees. Competition from crows (*Corvus* spp.), blue jays (*Cyanocitta cristata*), and red-bellied woodpeckers (*Melanerpes carolinus*) forces red-headed woodpeckers to gather acorns rapidly. As the season progresses, the birds may re-store their acorns, distributing them farther apart to reduce the likelihood of piracy. These food caches are vigilantly guarded against potential thieves. Red-headed woodpeckers may further secure their stores by lodging strips of bark or rotten wood into crevices to seal any openings. During the winter months, red-headed woodpeckers may supplement their diet with sap.

Breeding Biology

Red-headed woodpecker courtship activity commences during May when the male initiates tapping and calling from within a potential nest cavity. He presents the female with several new or previously excavated cavities from which she selects a nest site. Red-headed woodpecker nesting cavities are located at varying heights within dead trees or dead limbs of live trees. Infrequently, red-headed woodpeckers may excavate nest cavities in utility poles. Entrance holes average 4.5 cm (1.75 in.) in diameter and cavity size ranges from 20 to 36 cm (8–14 in.) deep and 8 to 11 cm (3–4.5 in.) wide. The same nesting cavity may be used for several consecutive years, often until the tree rots or falls. Nesting cavities are aggressively defended against other woodpeckers as well as European starlings (*Sturnus vulgaris*), tufted titmice (*Parus bicolor*), and chickadees (*Parus atricapillus*, *P. carolinensis*).

Red-headed woodpeckers lay eggs from early May to late June in New Jersey. The female and male both incubate a clutch of four to five white eggs for approximately 14 days. Both adults care for the young, which fledge in about one month. Red-headed woodpeckers may produce a second brood, consequently forcing the first brood to leave the nesting area.

Status and Conservation

During the late 1700s and 1800s, the red-headed woodpecker was a common and widespread species in the Northeast. In the 1870s and 1880s, large concentrations of these birds, including flights of several hundred, were observed during fall migration at New York and Long Island, where it is now an uncommon migrant. Stone (1965b) stated that the red-headed woodpecker was a rare fall migrant at Cape May, with only one to two records, on average, per year. Currently, an average of eight per season is observed each fall at Cape May (Sibley 1997). This apparent increase in the number of birds recorded at Cape May is likely due to increased coverage by birders rather than an actual increase in red-headed woodpecker populations. Stone (1908) also described the red-headed woodpecker as a rare breeder in South Jersey that was "never found in the Pine Barrens." However, this again may reflect a lack of coverage during historic times.

By the turn of the twentieth century, red-headed woodpeckers had suffered population declines due to road mortality, competition with European starlings for nesting cavities, and harvesting for the millinery trade in which populations of many avian species were greatly reduced to provide feathers for women's hats. Farmers at this time also killed red-headed woodpeckers because they damaged fruit and berry crops. Further population declines resulting from habitat loss, limited availability of nesting sites, and road mortality were noted from the 1930s to the 1970s. Red-headed woodpeckers experienced declines surveywide on Christmas Bird Counts from 1959 to 1988 (Sauer et al. 1996). The Breeding Bird Survey detected annual declines of red-headed woodpeckers in New Jersey and the Northeast from 1966 to 1999 (Sauer et al. 2001). Currently, the species is considered to be rare in the Northeast.

Due to population declines, the red-headed woodpecker was listed as a threatened species in New Jersey in 1979. The New Jersey Natural Heritage Program considers the red-headed woodpecker to be "demonstrably secure globally," yet "imperiled in New Jersey because of rarity" (Office of Natural Lands Management 1998). Loss of breeding habitat and regional population declines in areas such as New Jersey and New York led the National Audubon Society to include the red-headed woodpecker on its Blue List of Imperiled Species in 1972 and from 1976 to 1981 (Arbib 1975; Tate 1986). In addition, the National Audubon Society has recognized the red-headed woodpecker as a species of special concern since 1982 (Tate 1986).

Limiting Factors and Threats

Habitat loss, the clearing of dead trees, road mortality, and competition for nesting sites continue to be the primary threats facing red-headed woodpecker populations today. Development, forestry practices, and vegetative succession have eliminated or reduced the quality of breeding habitat. Forest clearing has reduced the amount of available habitat, and the removal of standing dead trees (snags) has diminished nest sites for these woodpeckers in New Jersey.

The red-headed woodpecker has a limited breeding range in New Jersey because its required habitats are rare and discontinuous in the state. Its small population size and isolated distribution make the red-headed woodpecker especially vulnerable to threats such as removal of snags and rivalry for nest sites. In addition, chemical or pesticide use may contaminate the food supplies of this species. Creosote, which is used to coat utility poles, is lethal to red-headed woodpecker eggs and young in nests within creosote-treated poles.

Road mortality, which was recognized as a problem for this species as early as the beginning of the twentieth century, continues to pose a threat today. As forests become more fragmented, an increasing number of roads bisect red-headed woodpecker breeding habitats, where the bird's low flight style renders it vulnerable to passing vehicles.

Recommendations

Because red-headed woodpecker habitats are ephemeral, woodlots can be regularly managed to provide suitable conditions. Controlled burns and selective

Sedge wren. © Brian E. Small/VIREO

cutting can be implemented to reduce undergrowth and thin tree stands. Trees can be selectively girdled to provide dead snags. Existing dead, dying, and decaying trees, particularly those that are greater than 10 cm (3.9 in.) dbh (diameter at breast height) and taller than 2 m (6.6 ft.) should not be harvested. These snags may serve as nesting, perching, roosting, or food storage sites for red-headed woodpeckers as well as many other cavity-nesting species.

Sherry Liguori

Sedge Wren, *Cistothorus platensis*

Status: State: Endangered   Federal: Migratory Nongame Bird of Management Concern

Identification

Formerly known as the "short-billed marsh wren," the sedge wren is a small brown songbird with dark brown vertical streaking on the crown and back. The wings, rump, and tail are brown with dark horizontal barring. The underparts and undertail coverts are buffy. The bill is short, thin, and slightly decurved, and there is an inconspicuous pale eye stripe. Sexes are similar in plumage, although males are slightly larger than females. Juveniles resemble adults but are darker above, buffier below, and have less conspicuous streaking on the head. Like other wrens, the tail is short and often held upward. The diminutive sedge wren is extremely secretive and is often heard rather than seen. The insectlike song consists of three introductory notes, *tchip, tchip, tchip,* followed by a trill, *tchu, tchu, tchu.* The call note is a *tchip* or *chick.*

Distribution

The sedge wren breeds locally in eastern North America from southern Canada to Virginia and west to Kansas, Missouri, and Indiana. Nesting sedge wrens also occur from southern Mexico to southern South America. North

American–breeding sedge wrens winter along the Gulf and Atlantic coasts, north to Maryland, rarely wintering in New Jersey and Long Island.

In New Jersey, the sedge wren is an extremely rare breeding species. Historically, nesting sedge wrens were documented throughout the state in isolated wetlands in Sussex, Passaic, Bergen, Warren, Morris, Essex, Hunterdon, Burlington, Ocean, and Atlantic counties as well as along the coastal marshes of Cape May, Cumberland, and Salem counties. Undocumented nesting pairs probably occurred in additional counties as well. Breeding has been previously documented at Wallkill Valley, Newton, the Pequest River, Great Piece Meadow, Englewood, Great Swamp National Wildlife Refuge, Troy Meadows, Hatfield Swamp, Passaic Meadows, Hackensack Meadowlands, Double Trouble, Manahawkin, Tuckerton, Edwin B. Forsythe National Wildlife Refuge, and Turkey Point. In recent years, breeding has been confirmed or suspected at Wallkill (Sussex County), Birch Creek (Gloucester County), the Passaic River in Somerset County, and along the Delaware Bay shore of Cumberland County.

Migrant sedge wrens are scarce in New Jersey, occurring from mid-April to mid-May and from late August to October. Wintering sedge wrens, although rare, may also occur. Sedge wrens have been recently documented during the nonbreeding season at Cape May, Edwin B. Forsythe National Wildlife Refuge, Dividing Creek, Lincoln Park, and along the Delaware Bay shore.

Habitat

Wet meadows, freshwater marshes, bogs, and the drier portions of salt or brackish coastal marshes are home to sedge wrens throughout the year. Along the Delaware Bay shore, sedge wrens may be found in high marsh containing salt-meadow grass (*Spartina patens*), spike grass (*Distichlis spicata*), and marsh elder (*Iva frutescens*). Unlike its relative, the marsh wren (*Cistothorus palustris*), the sedge wren avoids cattail (*Typha* spp.) marshes. Rather, sedge wrens favor marshes containing sedges, grasses, rushes, scattered shrubs, and other emergent vegetation.

Sedge wrens typically exhibit low fidelity to breeding sites each year, possibly due to changes in water levels or vegetative structure and composition. Because they are sensitive to hydrology, sedge wrens may avoid nesting in areas that are too wet or too dry. Likewise, they may abandon sites if shrubby growth dominates due to vegetative succession.

Diet

The diet of the sedge wren is dominated by insects and spiders, including bugs, weevils, beetles, moths, caterpillars, ants, grasshoppers, crickets, locusts, flies, and mosquitoes. Sedge wrens may forage on the ground or glean insects from vegetation.

Breeding Biology

During late May, the song of the male sedge wren reiterates from within a breeding marsh. The male establishes and actively defends a territory, within which he constructs several nests. In addition to the true nest, the male builds several "dummy nests" that may confuse potential predators or may be used for roosting. Each nest is a woven ball of grasses and sedges with a side entrance. The nests are concealed among vegetation and located low above the ground or over water. The female selects one of the nests and lines it with thin grasses, hair, and feathers. Sedge wrens may nest in small colonies, but often only one or two pairs inhabit a site.

For 12 to 14 days, the female incubates a clutch of six to seven white, unmarked eggs. Although the female is the primary caretaker of the young, the male may also provide food. At about two weeks of age, the young are able to leave the nest. The female then may lay a second clutch. If so, the male will continue to care for the first brood while the female is incubating. Fledglings remain together until migration.

Status and Conservation

In the early 1900s, the sedge wren was a locally distributed and uncommon, although perhaps largely overlooked, breeding species in New Jersey. Since the 1950s, Christmas bird counts and breeding bird surveys have revealed alarming declines of this species in the Northeast. The draining and filling of wetlands, ditching of salt marshes, and spread of phragmites (*Phragmites australis*) have resulted in severe habitat loss and sedge wren population declines. Wet sedge or grass meadows, the habitat types required by sedge wrens, are among the most frequently destroyed wetlands in the United States.

Due to severe population declines and rapid habitat loss, the sedge wren was listed as a threatened species in New Jersey in 1979. The National Audubon Society included the sedge wren on its Blue List of Imperiled Species in 1979 and 1981. By the early 1980s, it was not known if any breeding sedge wrens remained in New Jersey. Due to its dire situation, the sedge wren was reclassified as an endangered species in New Jersey in 1984. The New Jersey Natural Heritage Program considers the sedge wren to be "demonstrably secure globally," yet "imperiled in New Jersey because of rarity" (Office of Natural Lands Management 1998). The sedge wren has been listed as a Migratory Nongame Bird of Management Concern by the U.S. Fish and Wildlife Service since 1992.

Currently, the sedge wren is a very rare breeding species in New Jersey despite the presence of apparently suitable habitat. Because this species occurs in small, isolated populations, it may take a long time for it to recover from precariously low levels. Sedge wrens have suffered severe declines throughout much of the northeastern United States and are consequently listed as endangered (Maine, New Hampshire, Massachusetts, and Connecticut), threatened (Vermont, Pennsylvania, Maryland, and Virginia), or of special concern (New York).

Limiting Factors and Threats

The loss of wetlands through draining, ditching, and filling has considerably reduced available habitat for sedge wrens. In existing marshes, vegetative succession and the proliferation of phragmites have degraded habitat quality for this species. Sedge wrens, which are often transitory, may occupy different nesting sites in successive years due to variations in water levels and changes in vegetative composition and structure. Because their specific habitat requirements are largely unknown, these wrens may be absent from areas that appear to contain suitable habitat.

Recommendations

Sedge wren conservation must include the protection and management of breeding habitat. Marshes, particularly those exceeding 5 hectares (12 acres) and containing tall, dense stands of sedges and grasses with scattered shrubs, must be preserved and managed for this species. The control of vegetative succession can be achieved through selective cutting of parcels during the nonbreeding season. Parcels should be cut on a rotating schedule, ensuring that areas of habitat remain in the interim. Herbicide and pesticide use should be prohibited on marshes occupied by sedge wrens. To minimize disturbance, human activity should be prohibited within 90 m (300 ft.) of nesting sites during the breeding season.

Additional research is needed to determine the specific habitat requirements of sedge wrens. This information can be used to develop habitat management plans for this species on state and federal wildlife refuges.

Sherry Liguori

Loggerhead Shrike, *Lanius ludovicianus migrans*
Status: State: Endangered   Federal: Nongame Migratory Bird of Management Concern

Identification

The loggerhead shrike is a robin-sized bird with a large gray head, a black hooked bill, and a black facial mask that extends across the forehead and behind the eyes. The back is gray and the wings are black with a white patch at the base of the outer flight feathers. The tail is black and the underparts are pale gray. Although a predator, the loggerhead shrike lacks the sharp talons of hawks, instead possessing legs and feet typical of passerines. The sexes are alike in plumage, yet male shrikes are larger than females. In comparison to adults, juvenile loggerhead shrikes are duller overall, have brown flight feathers, and are faintly marked with buff barring throughout the body. Loggerhead shrikes often perch in a horizontal posture on fence posts or wires and fly in a low, undulating flight with quick wingbeats.

The loggerhead shrike resembles both the northern mockingbird (*Mimus polyglottos*) and the northern shrike (*Lanius excubitor*). The mockingbird lacks the black mask and hooked bill of the loggerhead shrike and the tail and wings of the mockingbird are a lighter shade of gray. The wing patterns of these two species also differ, with the mockingbird displaying a white wing patch on the outer flight feathers as well as on its coverts. The northern shrike is larger than the loggerhead shrike, paler gray above, and heavier billed. The

The loggerhead shrike has a hooked bill.
© Mark Payne

northern shrike also has a more extensive rump patch, a pale lower mandible (jaw) during the winter, and a narrower black facial mask that does not extend above the eye or across the forehead. In addition, the northern shrike pumps its tail when perched.

The name shrike comes from the word "shriek," referring to the vocalizations of these birds. Shrikes emit both harsh, screeching calls as well as a musical song. Reminiscent of the brown thrasher's (*Toxostoma rufum*) melody, the song of the loggerhead shrike consists of a series of two-note liquid trills and guttural notes repeated over short intervals.

Distribution

The loggerhead shrike is widely distributed in North America, occurring from southern Canada throughout the United States south to Mexico. Along the eastern coast, the subspecies *L. ludovicianus migrans* occurs from southeastern Manitoba to Texas, and the subspecies *L. ludovicianus ludovicianus* occurs from North Carolina to Florida. The clearing of lands for farms and pastures before the twentieth century created breeding habitat for shrikes in the northeastern United States. However, breeding shrikes have declined in the Northeast and currently occur only as migrants throughout much of this region. Loggerhead shrikes winter in Mexico and the southern United States, north to Maryland.

In New Jersey, the loggerhead shrike is considered a rare transient, occurring infrequently during spring and fall migration and very rarely during winter. Records of fall migrants range from mid-August to mid-October, with most occurring mid-August to late September. Spring migrants have been documented from mid-March to May. Migrant shrikes have been observed at Troy Meadows, Great Swamp National Wildlife Refuge, Princeton, Freehold, Edwin B. Forsythe National Wildlife Refuge, Marmora, Goshen, and Cape

May. In addition, wintering shrikes have occurred at Rosedale Park and Princeton. Although loggerhead shrikes have bred nearby in New York and Pennsylvania, nesting has not been confirmed in New Jersey. Over the past few decades, loggerhead shrikes have been observed during the summer months, although breeding has not been confirmed, at Cape May, Spruce Run Reservoir, Boonton, Bound Brook, and Wharton State Forest.

Habitat

A bird of open countryside, the loggerhead shrike inhabits short-grass pastures, weedy fields, grasslands, agricultural areas, swampy thickets, orchards, and right-of-way corridors. Shrikes occupy sites containing hedgerows, scattered trees or shrubs, and utility wires or fence posts, which serve as perches. Nests are often situated in trees or shrubs bearing thorns, such as hawthorns (*Crataegus* spp.), osage orange (*Maclura pomifera*), and multiflora rose (*Rosa multiflora*). Red cedar (*Juniperus virginiana*) may also be used for nesting. Similar habitats are occupied year-round.

Diet

Loggerhead shrikes are opportunistic predators, consuming insects, small mammals, songbirds, snakes, frogs, lizards, and even small turtles. During the warm summer months, shrikes eat large quantities of insects, including grasshoppers, crickets, spiders, beetles, ants, wasps, bees, moths, caterpillars, and flies. Shrikes also prey upon small mammals, particularly mice, as well as fledgling songbirds during the breeding season. In the winter, small mammals and songbirds, such as sparrows, comprise the bulk of the diet.

Loggerhead shrikes hunt from conspicuous perches, such as fence posts or telephone wires, that offer wide, unobstructed views of the surrounding countryside. Shrikes scour their surroundings for prey and then pounce on it or, in the case of birds, pursue it in the air. Shrikes kill their prey instantly with a bite on the spinal column.

Due to their habit of impaling prey on thorns, branches, or wires, shrikes have earned the colloquial name of "butcher birds." However grisly it may appear, impaling prey serves several functions. Shrikes, which lack the sharp talons of raptors, rely on thorns to anchor and immobilize their prey during feeding. Impaling also enables shrikes to handle larger prey items than they could otherwise manage. Caches of impaled prey provide shrikes with food reserves and may serve as an attractant to potential mates. Shrikes may kill and impale noxious prey, such as monarch butterflies (*Danaus plexippus*) or toads (*Bufo* spp.), only to consume them several days later when the toxins have diminished.

Breeding Biology

Loggerhead shrikes occupy relatively large territories that they guard vigilantly. In New York State, home range sizes measured 3.4 to 9.3 hectares

A perched loggerhead shrike. Photo by Gary M. Stolz, courtesy US FWS.

(8.4–23 acres) (Novak 1989). During courtship, the male loggerhead shrike performs aerial displays and delivers food to the female. Both the male and female gather nesting materials, although the female typically builds the nest alone. Located within a thorny tree that provides adequate cover, the cup nest is constructed of rootlets, twigs, weeds, and bark and lined with grasses, lichens, moss, downy plant seeds, fur, feathers, hair, or string. As early as mid-April, the female lays a clutch of five to six white eggs that are speckled with brown. During the 16- to 20-day incubation period, the male delivers food to his mate. The young hatch asynchronously, resulting in young of staggered ages and sizes. This may result in brood reduction during years with limited prey availability. The female broods the altricial (dependent) chicks for four to five days. At 17 to 21 days of age, the chicks, flightless and dependent upon their parents for food, leave the nest on foot and seek cover in nearby vegetation. At about four weeks of age, the young are able to fly and learn to catch and impale prey on their own. Young shrikes are fed by their parents for an additional three to four weeks after fledging. Juvenile loggerhead shrikes are able to breed the following spring.

Status and Conservation

The clearing of eastern forests for agriculture during the nineteenth century created habitat for several species of grassland and edge birds, including the loggerhead shrike. The abundance of small farms, pastures, and hedgerows in the northeastern United States enabled this shrike to expand its breeding range. With the advent of mechanized agriculture, large monocultures with few shrubs or hedgerows replaced smaller fields, diminishing habitat quality for shrikes. In addition, open landscapes were lost to development or matured into forests. Consequently, the breeding range and the number of loggerhead shrikes in the Northeast began to decline by the early 1960s. Heavy use of pesticides, particularly DDT, accumulated in the prey of shrikes and resulted in eggshell thinning, reproductive failure, and contamination of adults and young.

Severe habitat loss, coupled with pesticide contamination, proved disastrous for nesting loggerhead shrikes in the northeastern United States. Since the 1970s, loggerhead shrike numbers have plummeted and breeding populations have been extirpated from much of this region. The Breeding Bird Survey has detected annual declines of this species in the Northeast from 1966 to 1999 (Sauer et al. 2000). Likewise, numbers of wintering shrikes detected on Christmas Bird Counts significantly declined surveywide from 1959 to 1988 (Sauer et al. 1996). The loggerhead shrike was included on the National Audubon Society's Blue List of Imperiled Species from 1972 to 1986, the final year of the list. This shrike was also listed as a Nongame Migratory Bird of Management Concern by the U.S. Fish and Wildlife Service in 1982 and 1987.

Due to severe population declines and habitat loss, the loggerhead shrike was classified as an endangered species in New Jersey in 1987. The New Jersey Natural Heritage Program considers the northeastern subspecies, *migrans*, to be "imperiled globally because of rarity." Rare throughout much of the Northeast, the loggerhead shrike is also listed as endangered in New Hampshire, Vermont, Massachusetts, New York, Pennsylvania, Maryland, and Virginia.

Limiting Factors and Threats

Habitat loss and pesticide use are largely responsible for the decline of loggerhead shrikes in the Northeast. In New York, shrike declines coincided with the reduction of pasture habitat (Novak 1989). In the Northeast, particularly in New Jersey, large acreages of farmland have been developed or grown into forests. The conversion to mechanized agriculture and the resulting trend toward large monocultures have reduced habitat quality for breeding shrikes. Large fields of row crops with few shrubs have replaced small farms interspersed with hedgerows. Increased motor vehicle traffic in rural areas has also resulted in greater road mortality of shrikes, which often fly low when hunting near roads. Feral cats, foxes, raptors, and corvids (crows and jays) are predators of eggs, young, and adults.

In some areas, suitable shrike habitat occurs, yet breeding shrikes remain absent, suggesting that factors other than habitat availability may limit shrikes. Additional research is needed to determine the precise requirements and limiting factors of the loggerhead shrike in order to adequately manage for this species.

Also, pesticides applied on the breeding and wintering grounds of loggerhead shrikes may have devastating effects on reproduction and prey availability. Elevated concentrations of organochlorines, such as DDT, can reduce eggshell thickness or hinder the development of young. Although DDT is banned in the United States, migratory birds such as the loggerhead shrike may encounter this contaminant on their wintering grounds.

Recommendations

Suitable habitat for loggerhead shrikes should be created and maintained. On private lands where quality habitat exists, landowner cooperation and incentive programs should be implemented to maintain suitable habitat. Habitat management plans should also be implemented on state and federal wildlife refuges. Open areas can be maintained through light grazing, mowing, or burning. Habitat management should be conducted during the nonbreeding season and parcels should be managed on a rotational scheme. Hedgerows containing thorny plant species such as hawthorn, osage orange, and multiflora rose should be planted along field edges. Pesticide use should be restricted or greatly reduced in areas where shrikes nest and forage.

Sherry Liguori

Bobolink, *Dolichonyx oryzivorus*
Status: State: Threatened   Federal: Not listed

Identification

Amid a sea of agriculture, the bubbly *bobo-o-link!* song of the bobolink echoes from within an overgrown weedy field. On a fall day at Cape May, a chorus of *plink* notes is heard overhead as a flock of bobolinks passes above a fallow grassland. These are the song and call of the bobolink, a sparrow-sized member of the blackbird family.

Bobolinks exhibit sexual dimorphism (gender differences) in plumage during the breeding season. The nuptial male is black overall with a creamy nape and hindneck, a white rump, and white scapulars (feathers at the base of the wing). The plumage of the female, which camouflages her during nesting, is

A male in striking breeding plumage. Photo by S. Maslowski, courtesy US FWS

relatively drab. The female is buffy with dark brown streaking on the back, sides, and rump and has dark stripes on the head. In nonbreeding plumage, adult males resemble females. Immature bobolinks also resemble adult females but are more yellow and lack streaking on the sides of the body. All ages and sexes have a short, finchlike bill and pointed tail feathers.

Distribution

The bobolink breeds in southern Canada and the northern United States, from the Atlantic Coast states south to West Virginia and west to Oregon and Washington. Bobolinks are long-distance migrants, traveling 10,000 km (6,200 mi.) to their South American wintering grounds in Brazil and Argentina. This 20,000 km (12,400 mi.) round-trip flight is one of the longest migrations undertaken by a North American passerine.

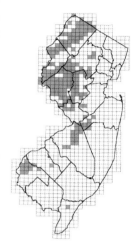

Breeding bobolinks occur in agricultural areas and grasslands in northwestern, central, and southwestern New Jersey. In late June and early July, postbreeding bobolinks concentrate in freshwater and coastal marshes, where they remain for several weeks to molt. From early August to late September, there is a second influx of migrant bobolinks, which abound along the Atlantic and Delaware Bay coasts. On September 3, 1996, a record daily count of 15,000 migrant bobolinks was recorded at Cape May Point (Sibley 1997). Bobolinks continue to migrate through New Jersey, albeit in lesser numbers, into October. Spring migrants are somewhat common and can be found throughout the state from late April through late May.

Habitat

Bobolinks inhabit low-intensity agricultural habitats, such as hay fields and pastures, during the breeding season. In addition, lush fallow fields and meadows of grasses, forbs, and wildflowers are occupied. Bobolink nests are often placed in areas of greatest vegetative height and density. Although small numbers of bobolinks may nest in grasslands of 2 to 4 hectares (5–10 acres), larger-sized fields support higher densities of nesting pairs (Jones and Vickery 1997a).

Similar habitats are occupied by bobolinks throughout their annual cycle. During migration, bobolinks inhabit fallow and agricultural fields, as well as coastal and freshwater marshes. On their South American wintering grounds, they occur in grasslands, marshes, rice fields, and farm fields.

Diet

The diet of the bobolink varies seasonally, with individuals consuming both animal and plant matter at different times throughout the year. In the spring and summer months, the abundance of insects dictates the bobolink's diet. Adult bobolinks glean insects from vegetation or from the ground and supplement their diet with seeds. They feed their young invertebrates such as caterpillars, grasshoppers, wasps, weevils and other beetles, ants, spiders, centipedes, and larval insects. During the nonbreeding season, plant matter, including rice, seeds, oats, grains, and corn, dominates the bobolink's diet.

Breeding Biology

In early May, male bobolinks arrive on their breeding territories, often returning to the same area in successive years if the site is of high quality. Within a week, the females arrive. Social at other times of the year, male bobolinks are territorial during the early breeding season. Bobolink nesting colonies bustle with activity: spirited courtship displays, lively songs, aerial chases, and vigorous competition for mates. If habitat conditions and food availability are favorable, bobolinks may exhibit polygyny, in which one male breeds with several females. Depending on their former nesting success, a female may pair with her mate of the previous year.

Once paired, the female bobolink plucks a small area of vegetation in preparation for her nest. The ground nest, which is often located at the base of a large forb or clump of grass, is well concealed within herbaceous cover. Grasses and weeds are woven together to form the cup nest, which is then lined with fine grasses. The female lays a clutch of five to six pale brown, blotched eggs that she incubates for 11 to 13 days. Although bobolinks lay eggs once a year, the female may nest and lay eggs again if her first nest fails. Occasionally, the brown-headed cowbird (*Molothrus ater*), a brood parasite, may lay its eggs within a bobolink nest. This forces the bobolink to rear the young of the cowbird, often at the expense of the bobolink's own young.

After the young bobolinks hatch, the male aids the female in brooding and feeding the young. Polygynous males typically provide more assistance to their primary females while offering limited parental care to females from secondary nests. However, if the secondary female is unable to adequately provide for the young, the male may focus his efforts toward caring for her brood.

Unable to fly, the chicks leave the nest at 10 to 14 days and hide in thick vegetation. At about 16 days old, the young begin to fly, but the parents continue to feed them for another four weeks. Following fledging, family groups from several nests join together in flocks and soon depart from their breeding territories. Large aggregations of bobolinks converge within marshes, where they may remain for several weeks to molt and feed in preparation for the fall migration.

Status and Conservation

Historic clearing of forests in the eastern United States during the 1700s and 1800s enabled numerous grassland species to expand their ranges, inhabiting the growing agricultural landscape. As a result, the bobolink became a common breeding species in the hayfields and pastures of New Jersey. However, by the early 1900s, bobolink population declines were noted in the Northeast. The slaughter of migrant bobolinks in rice fields of the southern United States, market hunting, and modernized farming techniques likely caused this decline. During the 1960s and 1970s, changing agricultural practices, the conversion of fallow fields to forests, and the development of agricultural lands further shrunk bobolink populations in New Jersey.

Modern farming techniques, including frequent rotation of hayfields, early mowing of hay, decreased vegetative diversity, and the change from warm-season to cool-season grasses, have rendered agricultural fields less favorable for nesting bobolinks. In addition, alfalfa (*Medicago sativa*) fields, which offer poor nesting habitat for bobolinks, have replaced many timothy (*Phleum* spp.) and clover (Fabaceae) fields. The area of land cultivated as hay fields in the northeastern United States declined from 12.6 to 7.1 million hectares (31.1 to 17.5 million acres) from 1940 to 1986 (Martin and Gavin 1995). During the same period, the percentage of sites where alfalfa replaced hay increased from 20% to 60% (Bollinger and Gavin 1992). Habitat loss is largely responsible for the decline of bobolink populations in the United States and New Jersey as detected by the Breeding Bird Survey from 1966 to 1999 (Sauer et al. 2000).

Due to population declines and habitat loss, the bobolink was listed as a threatened species in New Jersey in 1979. The New Jersey Natural Heritage Program considers the bobolink to be "demonstrably secure globally," yet "imperiled in New Jersey because of rarity" (Office of Natural Lands Management 1992).

Limiting Factors and Threats

Changing agricultural practices have played a major role in the decline of bobolinks in the Northeast. As mentioned above, many farms have shifted from timothy and clover to alfalfa, which is harvested earlier and offers lesser-quality habitat for nesting bobolinks. In addition, hay fields are currently harvested earlier and more frequently than during historic times, often resulting in nest failure through direct mortality of eggs and nestlings or through nest abandonment following mowing. Bobolink chicks also experience increased vulnerability to predation in mowed fields due to the lack of cover.

In addition to the change in farming methods, the overall acreage of land dedicated to farming in the Northeast has declined. Over the years, farmlands, pastures, grasslands, and fallow fields have been fragmented or lost to development and vegetative succession. Thus, bobolinks, as well as other grassland species, may be forced to nest in suboptimal habitats, such as small, fragmented grasslands, where the threats of predation and nest parasitism are greater than on larger tracts.

Historically, large flocks of bobolinks were shot during migration and brought to markets, where they were sold for 20 cents per dozen. Bobolinks were also collected alive and kept as pets in the United States. Fortunately, neither of these practices continues today. However, on their South American wintering grounds, bobolinks are shot by farmers who view them as agricultural pests and are also collected as pets. Furthermore, many environmentally hazardous pesticides are used on foreign farm fields, particularly in areas where strict environmental laws are lacking.

Recommendations

Conservation and management of grasslands in New Jersey is required to provide habitat for nesting bobolinks. Farmland preservation and cooperative efforts with farmers are critical to ensure the presence of breeding areas for bobolinks. Quality habitat should be maintained at existing nesting locales, and new sites should be created or restored. The cultivation of warm-season native grasses, such as little bluestem (*Schizachyrium scoparium*), poverty grass (*Danthonia spicata*), switchgrass (*Panicum virgatum*), and Indian grass (*Sorghastrum nutans*), should be encouraged.

Open habitats can be maintained either through mowing, grazing, or controlled burns. Mowing should be delayed until after the nesting season is completed (mid- to late July in New Jersey). Likewise, controlled burns should only be conducted during the nonbreeding season. Each area should be burned every two to five years. Regardless of the technique selected, management should be implemented on a rotating schedule, ensuring that vegetated habitat will be available for the breeding season.

Sherry Liguori

Savannah Sparrow, *Passerculus sandwichensis*
Status: State: Threatened   Federal: Not listed

Identification

The savannah sparrow is a small drab sparrow that is brown above and white below with brown streaking on the breast and sides. The back, nape, and crown are also patterned with variable amounts of dark brown streaking. There is a beige wing bar and the tail is short, brown, and notched. The head is brown with an obscure white crown stripe, a dark brown malar (mustache)

Savannah sparrow.
© A. Morris/VIREO

stripe, yellow lores (between the eyes and the bill) and eyeline, and a white throat. The legs and feet are pink and the bill is a light pinkish horn color. The sexes are similar in plumage. Juveniles resemble adults but are buffier colored with more streaking.

The savannah sparrow closely resembles the song sparrow (*Melospiza melodia*). However, the song sparrow lacks yellow lores, has a longer, rounded tail, and its streaking forms a distinctive spot on the upper breast. The Ipswich sparrow (*P. sandwichensis princeps*), a race of savannah sparrow that breeds on Sable Island, Nova Scotia, and winters along the Atlantic Coast, is larger and paler than the typical eastern race of savannah sparrow (*P. sandwichensis savanna*).

The song of the savannah sparrow consists of two to three chips followed by two buzzy trills. The insectlike melody is represented as *tsit tsit tsit, tseee tsaay.* The call is a mild *tsip.*

Distribution

The savannah sparrow breeds in the northern and central United States and Canada from Alaska and subarctic Canada south to California, New Mexico, Missouri, and New Jersey. The wintering range of the savannah sparrow extends from New York, southern Illinois, and Washington along the Atlantic, Gulf, and Pacific coasts south to Central America.

Savannah sparrows breed in the Ridge and Valley and Highlands regions of northern New Jersey and in the inner coastal plain of southwestern New Jersey. During the first half of the twentieth century, savannah sparrows were more common breeders along the New Jersey coast, where filling of wetlands created habitat for this species. In 1935, 125 pairs nested within filled wetlands at Newark Meadows. However, by the 1980s the species' distribution in the state shifted inland, probably due to regulations protecting coastal wetlands that eliminated the ephemeral habitats created by the filling in of wetlands. Currently, savannah sparrows nest in Sussex, Bergen, Warren, Morris, Essex, Hunterdon, Somerset, Mercer, Middlesex, Monmouth, Burlington, Ocean, Gloucester, Salem, and Cumberland counties, with strongholds in Hunterdon and southern Warren counties.

The savannah sparrow is a common fall migrant in New Jersey, occurring from mid-September through early November. Spring migrants occur from mid-March through late April. The savannah sparrow is an uncommon winter resident, found in small flocks along the coast, inland grasslands, and fields. The Ipswich sparrow is an uncommon migrant and winter resident along coastal New Jersey.

Habitat

Indigenous to open habitats, the savannah sparrow nests in hay and alfalfa fields, fallow fields, grasslands, upland meadows, airports, pastures, and vegetated landfills. The species also formerly nested within salt-marsh edges and coastal grasslands in New Jersey. Suitable tracts must provide a mix of short and tall grasses, a thick litter layer, dense ground vegetation, and scattered shrubs, saplings, or forbs. Because savannah sparrows are relatively tolerant of vegetative succession, they may occupy fields of varied ages, including those containing early woody growth. During the nonbreeding season, savannah sparrows inhabit coastal dunes, drier portions of salt marshes, roadside edges, agricultural and fallow fields, pastures, airports, vegetated landfills, and golf courses.

Diet

Savannah sparrows exploit seasonally abundant food sources, including insects during the summer months and grass and weed seeds during the winter. Throughout the nesting season, these sparrows feed on invertebrates such as insects, larvae, insect eggs, beetles, caterpillars, grasshoppers, ants and other Hymenoptera, flies, lepidopterans (butterflies and moths), odonates (dragonflies), snails, and spiders. Young sparrows are fed invertebrates along with fruit and berries.

Breeding Biology

Prior to the arrival of females, male savannah sparrows reach their breeding grounds and proclaim their territories from atop shrubs, tall forbs, or fence posts. Savannah sparrows require large grasslands of approximately 8 to 16 hectares (20–40 acres), within which males establish territories of 0.4 to 0.8 hectares (1–2 acres). In areas of high-quality habitat, they may nest semi-colonially, or polygyny—in which males service more than one female—may occur. Individuals often return to the same nesting site in successive years and mated pairs typically remain together in subsequent years.

One to three weeks after the arrival of male savannah sparrows, the females arrive and pairs are formed. The female constructs a cup nest, concealed by overhanging vegetation, in a slight depression on the ground. Located within clumps of grass or at the base of a shrub, the nest is woven of thick grasses and sedges and lined with thinner grasses, rootlets, and hair.

Egg dates for the savannah sparrow in the New Jersey/New York area span from mid-May to late June. The female lays a clutch of four to five pale eggs that are heavily marked with reddish brown mottling. The female alone incubates the eggs for 8 to 13 days. Both adults feed and guard the young, performing distraction displays to lure potential predators away from the nest. Monogamous males provide a greater amount of parental care than polygynous males. At 8 to 14 days, the young leave the nest but remain with their parents for an additional two weeks. By about 20 days old, they are able to fly.

The pair may produce a second clutch, extending the breeding season into late July or early August. If only one clutch is produced, the adults, especially the female, will spend a longer amount of time with their fledglings, remaining with them for an additional three weeks or more. If the female lays a second clutch, she may continue to care for the first brood while building a new nest and incubating the subsequent clutch. Savannah sparrows exhibit fidelity to their natal sites, where young may return to breed the following year.

Status and Conservation

At the southern edge of its breeding range, the savannah sparrow has been a traditionally local and uncommon breeding species in the Garden State. Historically, the clearing of forests for farmland and the filling of coastal marshes provided habitat for breeding savannah sparrows. As agriculture began to decline in the Northeast, farms were developed or left idle, slowly growing into forests. In areas where farming continued, agricultural practices shifted, resulting in large monocultures and earlier and more frequent mowing of hay fields. Wetlands protection regulations prohibited the filling of coastal marshes, resulting in an inland shift in the distribution of savannah sparrows.

With the decline in traditional agriculture, breeding populations of savannah sparrows also began to fall. From 1966 to 1999, the number of savannah sparrows detected on Breeding Bird Survey routes declined in the Northeast and throughout the United States (Sauer et al. 2000). Likewise, Christmas Bird Counts revealed a significant decrease in wintering savannah sparrows from 1959 to 1988 (Sauer et al. 1996). Due to population declines and habitat loss, the savannah sparrow was listed as a threatened species in New Jersey in 1979. The New Jersey Natural Heritage Program considers this species to be "demonstrably secure globally," yet "imperiled in New Jersey because of rarity" (Office of Natural Lands Management 1992).

From 1981 to 1982, the breeding population of savannah sparrows in New Jersey was estimated at 45 to 50 pairs. In the late 1990s, the New Jersey Breeding Bird Atlas confirmed nesting savannah sparrows in 21 blocks and located probable pairs in an additional 29 blocks (Walsh et al. 1999).

Limiting Factors and Threats

Habitat loss and modern agricultural practices threaten nesting savannah sparrows in New Jersey. The decline of farming, coupled with development of open areas and vegetative succession, has greatly reduced the amount of habitat available to this species. The development of many agricultural areas in New Jersey has resulted in small, fragmented patches of farmland, where nest predation is often elevated and habitation by savannah sparrows may be unlikely. On existing farms, modern agricultural practices such as monocultures reduce habitat quality. In addition, earlier and more frequent mowing can result in destruction of nests, eggs, and young.

Recommendations

Active management is needed to maintain grassland habitats for savannah sparrows. Vegetative succession can be suppressed through annual mowing, controlled burns, or light grazing, all of which should be implemented outside of the May 15 to August 1 nesting season. Fields should be grazed or burned on a rotational basis to provide habitat for nesting sparrows while implementing management. Controlled burns should be conducted at approximately four-year intervals. At grassland restoration sites, a mix of tall and short grasses and forbs should be planted. In addition, vegetated coastal dunes should be protected to provide habitat for wintering sparrows.

Sherry Liguori

Grasshopper Sparrow, *Ammodramus savannarum*
Status: State: Threatened   Federal: Not listed

Identification

A small, secretive songbird, the grasshopper sparrow is more often heard than seen as its insectlike melody emits from dense grasses. Its song consists of one to two chips followed by a buzzy trill reminiscent of a grasshopper. This sparrow also sings a series of buzzy notes.

The grasshopper sparrow has a stocky body that is brown above with buff streaking. On adults, the breast and sides are solid buff and the belly is white. The buff breast and sides of juveniles are marked with dark brown vertical streaking. Grasshopper sparrows have flat heads with relatively large bills. The crown is dark brown with light central stripes atop the head and behind the eye. The lores (between the eyes and the bill) are orange or golden. The tail is short and brown.

Distribution

During the breeding season, the eastern race of the grasshopper sparrow (*A. savannarum pratensis*) ranges from southern Canada to Georgia, east to the Atlantic Coast and west to the prairies of Oklahoma and Texas. Grasshopper

Grasshopper sparrow.
© M. Patrikeev/VIREO

sparrows winter in Central America, the West Indies, and the southern United States, seldom occurring as far north as New Jersey. Migrant grasshopper sparrows are rare in New Jersey, occurring from mid-September to mid-November and late April to early May.

Grasshopper sparrows nest in open habitats throughout New Jersey. Atlantic City International Airport, McGuire Air Force Base, Assunpink Wildlife Management Area (WMA), Mercer County Park, and Sharptown grasslands have all supported substantial breeding colonies. Controlled mowing schedules implemented for grassland birds at airports have enabled grasshopper sparrows to thrive at such sites, as evidenced by 75 pairs at McGuire Air Force Base in 1994 and 50 pairs at Atlantic City International Airport in 1987. In 1981, Assunpink WMA supported at least 15 pairs, and Mercer County Park and Sharpton each contained ten pairs. Historically, temporary habitat for grasshopper sparrows was inadvertently created when coastal wetlands were filled. For example, in 1935 the Newark Meadows supported 19 nesting pairs.

Habitat

Grasshopper sparrows breed in grassland, upland meadow, pasture, hay field, and old field habitats. Nesting grasshopper sparrows may occur on agricultural lands and airports where such habitats occur. Although grasshopper sparrows may use small grasslands, open areas of over 40 hectares (100 acres) are favored. Optimal habitat for these sparrows contains short- to medium-height bunch grasses interspersed with patches of bare ground, a shallow litter layer, scattered forbs, and few shrubs. Clumped grasses, such as poverty grass (*Danthonia spicata*) and broom-sedge (*Andropogon virginicus*), provide cover and foraging areas and are consequently favored over sod or matting grasses. In addition, orchardgrass (*Dactylis glomerata*), alfalfa (*Medicago sativa*), red clover (*Trifolium pratense*), lespedeza (*Lespedeza* spp.), and dewberry (*Rubus* spp.) provide sparrow habitat. Shrubs, fence posts, and tall forbs are used as song perches. However, habitats may become unsuitable for nesting grasshopper sparrows if shrub cover becomes too dense. Consequently, the presence and density of grasshopper sparrows at breeding sites vary annually due to habitat changes. Habitat use during the nonbreeding season is similar, although less restrictive, to that of the breeding season, as these sparrows may inhabit thickets, weedy lawns, vegetated landfills, fence rows, open fields, or grasslands.

Diet

The diet of the grasshopper sparrow includes both animal and plant matter. During the spring and summer, these sparrows consume grasshoppers, spiders, snails, myriapods (many-legged insects, such as millipedes and centipedes), earthworms, beetles, caterpillars, ants, larvae, and other invertebrates. Adult grasshopper sparrows feed caterpillars to their young. Grains, weed seeds, and grass seeds supplement the diet throughout the year.

Breeding Biology

From mid-April to early May, grasshopper sparrows arrive at their breeding grounds. Males arrive several days prior to females and sing atop perches to establish their territory boundaries. Territory size averages 0.8 to 1.6 hectares (2–4 acres); however, the species may nest semicolonially at high-quality sites that offer habitat for numerous pairs.

The female grasshopper sparrow constructs a nest at the base of a clump of grass in a shallow depression. The rim of the nest may be even with or slightly above the ground. Stems and grasses are woven together to form the nest, which is lined with finer grasses and rootlets. A clutch of four to five eggs, which are white with reddish brown speckling, is incubated by the female for 11 to 12 days. The female broods the newly hatched chicks, and both adults feed the young. Pathways leading to and from the nest enable the adults to land a distance away and run to the nest while concealed within ground cover. If disturbed, the adults may feign injury to distract potential predators away from the nest or chicks. After about nine days, the young leave the nest and hide in nearby vegetation. The parents continue to care for them for an additional one to two weeks. Grasshopper sparrows may lay two clutches of eggs during the same year, in which case the female builds a new nest for the second clutch. High levels of nest predation may necessitate the production of more than one clutch in this species. Double-brooding extends the breeding season into early August.

Status and Conservation

In the eastern United States, the historic distribution of grasshopper sparrows was restricted to natural grasslands created by fires or flooding. However, the boom in agriculture during the late 1800s and early 1900s enabled this species to spread its range and increase in numbers, making it a fairly common breeder in New Jersey. By the 1950s and 1960s, expanding development of open areas, coupled with dwindling acreage of land devoted to farming or pasture, led to decreases in grasshopper sparrow populations. Continued declines in the Northeast were noted in the 1970s and 1980s, when the species was considered locally distributed and uncommon. The number of grasshopper sparrows detected on Breeding Bird Survey routes in New Jersey, the eastern United States, and throughout the country declined from 1966 to 1999 (Sauer et al. 2000).

As the result of population declines and severe habitat loss, the grasshopper sparrow was listed as a threatened species in New Jersey in 1979. The New Jersey Natural Heritage Program considers this species to be "apparently secure globally," yet "imperiled in New Jersey because of rarity" (Office of Natural Lands Management 1992). Currently, grasshopper sparrows occur in small, localized, and unstable populations in the Northeast. Consequently, other nearby states have listed this species as endangered (Maine, Connecticut), threatened (Massachusetts, Rhode Island), or of special concern (New York). In New Jersey, the survival of grasshopper sparrows is critically linked with management practices for grassland birds on airports, agricultural lands, and pastures.

Limiting Factors and Threats

Habitat loss is the primary threat facing grasshopper sparrow populations in New Jersey. Many open areas that previously supported nesting pairs have been lost to development and vegetative succession. Consequently, much of the remaining grasslands are small and fragmented. Fragmented habitats may not support breeding grasshopper sparrows; however, if nesting does occur, birds are often vulnerable to elevated levels of nest predation.

Changing agricultural practices such as earlier and more frequent mowing, the use of crop species of limited habitat value, and the trend toward monocultures have negatively affected grasshopper sparrows. Frequent mowing, which may be initiated during nesting, can destroy eggs and young or expose them to the elements and predators. The shift from warm-season native bunch grasses to cold-season matting grasses degrades habitat quality for nesting sparrows. Likewise, monocultures lack the habitat heterogeneity required by these birds. Areas that are intensively grazed may also be unsuitable for breeding grasshopper sparrows, as excessive grazing can destroy the habitat and render nests vulnerable to trampling.

Recommendations

As inhabitants of fallow fields and grasslands, grasshopper sparrows are dependent on active management to maintain open areas. Habitat management for grassland birds should be implemented on state and federal wildlife refuges, airports, and farmlands using incentive programs and management plans. Burning, mowing, or light- to moderate-intensity grazing can be implemented to suppress vegetative succession and remove shrubs and woody growth. Such management practices should only be conducted after the nesting season (May 1 to August 5) is complete. Controlled burns should be carried out on a five- to seven-year rotation, and adequate areas (approximately 50%) of unburned habitat must be provided each year. Mowing, which should not be implemented until all chicks have fledged, can be conducted annually. At grassland restoration sites, warm-season native bunch grasses, such as little bluestem (*Schizachyrium scoparius*), big bluestem (*Andropogon gerardii*), poverty grass, broom-sedge, switchgrass (*Panicum virgatum*), and side-oats gramma (*Bouteloua curtipedula*), along with a mixture of forbs and some scattered shrubs, should be planted.

Sherry Liguori

Henslow's Sparrow, *Ammodramus henslowii*
Status: State: Endangered   Federal: Not listed

Identification

Within a wet sedge meadow, a sparrow briefly perches atop a clump of grass, only to quickly disappear within the lush ground cover. A secretive species,

the Henslow's sparrow will often run on the ground, concealed by vegetation, rather than fly. The song of this sparrow is a two-note, buzzy *tse-lick* or *tse-zik*, accented on the second syllable.

The Henslow's sparrow has a large, flat head with a heavy, pale gray bill. The head is a distinctive olive green color with dark brown crown, short, dark lateral throat stripe (or malar stripe), and white eye ring. The wings are chestnut brown, the breast is buffy with black streaks, and the belly is white. The chestnut brown tail is short and appears rounded in flight. The sexes are alike in plumage. Juvenile Henslow's sparrows resemble adults but are duller overall, lack a malar stripe, and have little, if any, streaking below.

Distribution

The breeding range of the Henslow's sparrow extends from southeast Ontario into New England and the northeastern United States southward to Kentucky and North Carolina, and westward across the central United States to Kansas. It winters from South Carolina to Florida and along the Gulf Coast.

Historically, the Henslow's sparrow bred sporadically in New Jersey. It nested in Salem, Cumberland, Cape May, Ocean, Somerset, Sussex, Mercer, Monmouth, Morris, Middlesex, Hunterdon, Burlington, Camden, and Gloucester counties. Former breeding sites included the Passaic Valley, Great Swamp, New Brunswick, Princeton, and marsh/field edges along the Delaware Bay and Atlantic coasts. Until the mid-1960s, there was also a stable breeding population in northwestern Hunterdon County. Sites in Cumberland County, including Thompsons Beach, Turkey Point, East Point, and Port Norris, supported breeding pairs during the 1960s and 1970s. In the early 1980s, a pair of Henslow's sparrows was observed during the breeding season in the Stony Brook–Millstone Watershed, although nesting was not suspected.

Henslow's sparrows are nearly extirpated in New Jersey due to habitat alteration and loss. The only recent confirmed New Jersey nesting of a Henslow's sparrow was at the Lakehurst U.S. Naval Air Station in 1994 (Walsh et al. 1999).

In New Jersey, the Henslow's sparrow is an extremely rare migrant. Fall migrants may occur from October to early December and spring migrants from mid-April to mid-May.

Habitat

Open fallow and grassy fields, sedge meadows, and pastures are home to breeding and migrating Henslow's sparrows. Henslow's sparrows prefer lush habitats containing high, dense herbaceous vegetation and a thick layer of ground litter. Such habitats are dominated by grasses, sedges, forbs, or clover and contain little or no woody vegetation and few scattered shrubs. Unmowed agricultural fields or ungrazed pastures are preferred for their thick cover. Henslow's sparrows are tolerant of a variety of moisture regimes and thus will occupy both wet and dry habitats. Large open areas are preferred; fields of 10 to 100 hectares (25–250 acres) may be needed to support breeding populations (Samson 1980).

Historically, Henslow's sparrows nested in coastal dunes and wet fallow fields situated between salt marshes and upland fields along the Delaware Bay and Atlantic coasts. Cranberry bogs in southern New Jersey also served as nesting habitats during the late 1800s.

Diet

The diet of the Henslow's sparrow is comprised of invertebrates and seeds. The bird consumes crickets, grasshoppers, katydids, beetles, bugs, caterpillars, spiders, wasps, ants, and other *Hymenoptera*, as well as snails. In addition, these sparrows forage on seeds of grass, sedge, forb, and weeds. Young sparrows are primarily fed insects.

Breeding Biology

During late April and May, Henslow's sparrows arrive on their breeding grounds. Singing males perch atop tall forbs to define their territory boundaries and advertise for mates. Often, only isolated pairs will nest at one site. However, this species may nest semicolonially if sufficient habitat exists. Henslow's sparrow territories average 0.4 to 0.8 hectares (1–2 acres) per pair.

The female constructs a cup nest of grasses, forbs, and dead leaves and lines it with fine grasses and hair. The nest is located either at the base of a clump of grass on the ground or within vegetation above the ground. Overhanging grasses conceal the nest.

In late May or early June, the female lays a clutch of three to five pale eggs with reddish brown spotting. Incubation is conducted solely by the female for 10 to 11 days. Both adults care for the young, which fledge at 9 to 10 days of age. Henslow's sparrows may raise two broods per season, provided that sufficient time and food resources exist.

Status and Conservation

In the early 1800s, John James Audubon noted that the Henslow's sparrow was abundant in New Jersey. In addition, numerous pairs were documented throughout the Garden State in the late 1800s and early 1900s (Rising 1996). After the mid-1950s, Henslow's sparrow populations began to decline and continued to drop throughout the 1970s and 1980s. Declines were noted surveywide on Christmas Bird Counts from 1959 to 1988 (Sauer et al. 1996). The Breeding Bird Survey detected annual decreases in Henslow's sparrows from 1966 to 1999 both in the Northeast and throughout the United States, with the greatest declines occurring after 1980 (Sauer et al. 2001). Habitat loss may be partially attributed to the decline, although Henslow's sparrows remain absent from numerous traditional locales where apparently suitable habitat still exists.

Because of population declines and restricted habitat requirements, the Henslow's sparrow was listed as a threatened species in New Jersey in 1979. With fears that the Henslow's sparrow may have been extirpated in the state, its status was changed to endangered in 1984. The New Jersey Natural Heritage Program considers this species to be "apparently secure globally," yet "critically imperiled in New Jersey because of extreme rarity" (Office of Natural Lands Management 1998). Declines of the Henslow's sparrow have occurred throughout its range, particularly in the East, where it is listed as threatened (Maryland, Virginia), endangered (New Hampshire, Vermont, Massachusetts), or of special concern (Connecticut, New York).

Limiting Factors and Threats

Habitat loss and fragmentation have contributed to the decline of Henslow's sparrows and continue to limit breeding populations. Vegetative succession, development, the draining and filling of wetlands, and the invasion of phragmites (*Phragmites australis*) have reduced the availability and quality of breeding habitat. Few agricultural areas or pastures remain idle, limiting nesting habitat. Intensive mowing and overgrazing can reduce the ground cover required for nesting. In addition, early mowing can destroy nests, eggs, and young.

Recommendations

Grasslands should be actively managed to provide breeding habitat for Henslow's sparrows as well as other grassland birds. Active management, either through mowing or grazing, is necessary to maintain an early successional stage and prevent the growth of woody vegetation and the eventual transition to forest. Mowing should not be conducted during the breeding season, from mid-April to mid-August. If pastures are to be grazed during the breeding season, cattle should be present prior to the birds' arrival so that they may select an alternative breeding site. Each year or two, some pasture fields should be allowed to go fallow while others are actively grazed. These fallow fields will provide future feeding grounds for cattle while offering breeding habitat to grassland birds in the interim.

Cooperative efforts and incentive programs must be implemented in order to provide habitat for grassland birds and preserve open space and farmland in New Jersey. If available, large tracts of suitable habitat should be acquired as public land, rather than be lost to development.

Sherry Liguori

Vesper Sparrow, *Pooecetes gramineus*
Status: State: Endangered   Federal: Not listed

Identification

The "bay-winged bunting," as it was formerly known, was given the name "vesper sparrow" because it frequently sings during the early evening hours and well into the night. The rich, musical song of the vesper sparrow, which is reminiscent of the song sparrow's (*Melospiza melodia*) melody, consists of a pair of repeated notes, represented as *here-here where-where,* followed by a series of descending trills. The first two notes are long, slurred, low-pitched

Vesper sparrow.
© R. & N. Bowers/
VIREO

whistles while the latter two notes are higher pitched. The call of the vesper sparrow is a short *hsip*.

The vesper sparrow is a stocky, short-tailed, grayish brown sparrow with a streaked breast. The upperparts are pale gray-brown and marked with black streaking. The breast is grayish white and streaked with black. A brown cheek patch, which reaches behind the eye, is adjacent to a white submustachial stripe that extends down from the bill. A thin, dark malar stripe (mustache) also extends from the bill, separating the white submustachial stripe from the white throat. There is a white eye ring that stands out against the brown cheek. Rich brown lesser coverts appear as chestnut shoulder patches on adults. However, the brilliance of these patches is variable and, depending on the view of the bird, may be difficult to see. The wings are marked with a pair of narrow, white wing bars. The tail, which is a key diagnostic indicator in flight, is notched and black with white outer tail feathers, similar to that of a junco (*Junco hyemalis*). The bill is conical-shaped with a dark upper mandible (jaw) and a flesh-colored lower mandible. Likewise, the legs are flesh colored. The iris is reddish brown to dark brown. Although males are slightly larger, the sexes are otherwise similar. Juveniles resemble adults but are buffier overall, have broader wing bars, and lack the chestnut shoulder patches.

Distribution

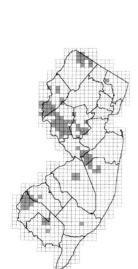

The breeding range of the vesper sparrow spans from Canada south to the central United States, including North Carolina, Illinois, Arizona, New Mexico, and California. Wintering vesper sparrows occur in Central America, Mexico, the Gulf Coast, and the southern United States north to Virginia in the East.

Locally, the vesper sparrow breeds in the inner coastal plain of South Jersey and the Piedmont, Highlands, and Ridge and Valley regions of northern and central New Jersey. Nesting is concentrated in Warren, Hunterdon, and Sussex counties, although breeding has also been documented in Somerset, Mercer, Bergen, Monmouth, Ocean, Atlantic, Burlington, Gloucester, Salem, and Cumberland counties. The vesper sparrow has withdrawn from much of its former range in the state. Sites in Somerset, Mercer, and Atlantic counties that contained breeding pairs in the early 1980s were unoccupied by the mid-1990s when the New Jersey Breeding Bird Atlas surveys were conducted.

Vesper sparrows are rare fall migrants in New Jersey, occurring from mid-October to mid-November, with an average of ten records each fall at Cape May Point. During 1992, an unusually high number of 35 migrants were observed at Cape May Point during fall migration. Vesper sparrows rarely overwinter along the southern coastal region of New Jersey. The vesper sparrow is an extremely rare spring migrant, with less than one migrant, on average, documented each season. Spring migrants occur from early April to mid-May.

Habitat

Inhabitants of open areas, vesper sparrows reside in cultivated fields, grasslands, fallow fields, and pastures. Agricultural fields containing crops of corn, soybean, alfalfa (*Medicago sativa*), hay, timothy (*Phleum* spp.), wheat (*Agropyron* spp.), or strawberry may be occupied. Farmed areas that are adjacent to fallow fields or contain uncultivated strips along fence-rows are favored. These fallow areas provide nesting habitat, cover, foraging sites, and singing perches. On active farmlands, human disturbance and crop harvesting can threaten nesting sparrows. Fallow fields and grasslands provide a safer haven for nests.

Vesper sparrow habitats are typically sparsely vegetated with patches of bare ground, low vegetation 2.5 to 20 cm (1–8 in.), and scattered shrubs or saplings. Habitats are typically dry and well drained. Nests are placed within clumps of herbaceous cover that afford protection from predators. Elevated perches such as fence posts, shrubs, or weeds provide singing posts from which males can advertise their territories and attract mates. Territory size may range from 0.5 to 3.2 hectares (1.2–7.9 acres). Similar habitats are used throughout the year.

Diet

The diet of the vesper sparrow consists of invertebrates and seeds. During the summer months, the diet is comprised largely of invertebrates such as beetles, weevils, grasshoppers, caterpillars, *Hymenoptera* (wasps, bees, and ants), other insects, and insect larvae. Weed and grass seeds are also consumed during this time, although in a smaller proportion. The young sparrows are fed invertebrates almost exclusively. Vesper sparrows are a beneficial species in agricultural areas, as they consume many crop-destroying insects. As insect populations wane during the fall and winter, seeds of ragweed (*Ambrosia* spp.), bristlegrass (*Chaetochloa* spp.), smartweed (*Persicaria* spp.), panic grass (*Panicus* spp.), oats (Gramineae), and other plants are sought. Vesper sparrows forage on the ground in weedy fields, brushy edges, and recently mowed fields.

Breeding Biology

During April, male vesper sparrows arrive on their breeding grounds and establish territories. About one week later, the females return. Vesper sparrows exhibit site fidelity, as pairs may return to the same nesting location during consecutive years. They often form small colonies, with three to six pairs nesting in an area.

Over a one- to two-week period, the female vesper sparrow constructs a cup nest of grasses, rootlets, and weeds and lines it with thinner grasses, rootlets, and hair. The ground nest often is concealed in a hollow at the base of a weed or grass tuft.

By the second or third week of May, the female lays a clutch of three to five greenish white eggs that are blotched with brown. Both parents, although primarily the female, incubate the eggs for 11 to 13 days. The protective incubating adult will not flush from the nest until nearly stepped upon, at which time it will feign injury to lure an intruder away. At 9 to 13 days, the chicks, not yet independent, leave the nest. The adults continue to care for the young, which seek cover in the surrounding vegetation, for several weeks. If a pair produces a second clutch, the male will tend to the first brood while the female begins incubating the subsequent clutch.

Status and Conservation

The vesper sparrow was formerly a common, widespread breeding species within agricultural fields and pastures in the Garden State. Turnbull (1869), Stone (1894a,b), Griscom (1923), Hausman (1935), and Cruickshank (1942) considered it to be a common to abundant summer bird in open cultivated areas of northern New Jersey and the Pine Barrens. However, even at this time, these authors noted its rarity in areas with suburban development. By the 1950s and 1960s, the vesper sparrow, which was by then considered an uncommon breeding species, had undergone population declines resulting from increased development of rural farmlands. Further declines in the Northeast were noted during the mid-1970s and early 1980s. The number of vesper sparrows detected on New Jersey Christmas Bird Counts plummeted from an average of 44 per year in 1971–73 to four per year in 1983–85. Likewise, numerous breeding populations documented in the state in the early 1980s were absent by the mid-1990s. The Breeding Bird Survey has shown a significant annual decline in the number of vesper sparrows detected on surveys in New Jersey from 1966 to 1999 (Sauer et al. 2000).

Due to its dependence on habitats created by farming, the vesper sparrow has suffered significant population declines resulting from the ebb of agriculture in New Jersey. Consequently, the vesper sparrow was listed as a threatened species in New Jersey in 1979. As the breeding population continued to decline and nesting habitat dwindled, the status of the vesper sparrow was reclassified as endangered in 1984. Currently, it is a rare and local breeding species in the state. The New Jersey Natural Heritage Program considers the vesper sparrow to be "demonstrably secure globally," yet "imperiled in New Jersey because of rarity" (Office of Natural Lands Management 1992). The National Audubon Society included the vesper sparrow on its Blue List of Imperiled Species from 1978 to 1980 and listed it as a local problem species in 1982 due to declines in the eastern population. Throughout much of the Northeast, the vesper sparrow has declined and, as a result, has been listed as endangered in Connecticut and Rhode Island, threatened in Massachusetts, and of special concern in New York.

Limiting Factors and Threats

The vesper sparrow has been adversely impacted by the conversion of farmlands to development. In addition, habitat loss has resulted in the fragmentation of agricultural areas. Habitat fragmentation may impede vesper sparrows from nesting, as they require large tracts of suitable habitat.

Within cultivated areas, vesper sparrows may be negatively affected by agricultural operations. Early or frequent harvesting may destroy nests and kill sparrow eggs or young. Likewise, the cultivation of fallow strips and edges surrounding farm fields eliminates foraging habitats, song perches, and areas of protective cover. A reduction in cover may render vesper sparrows and their young more vulnerable to predators such as birds, snakes, and mammals. The vesper sparrow is also a common host for the brown-headed cowbird (*Molothrus ater*), a nest parasite that lays its eggs in the nests of other birds at the expense of the host bird.

Recommendations

Management for vesper sparrows must include the preservation of breeding habitats such as farmlands, grasslands, and open fields. Large, contiguous tracts of suitable habitat, particularly those exceeding 30 acres, should receive the highest conservation priority. Habitat protection and management for vesper sparrows will also benefit other imperiled grassland-nesting birds. Within cultivated areas, management practices can be implemented to benefit vesper sparrows. Mowing within nesting habitats should be restricted during the April-to-August breeding season to protect vesper sparrow eggs and young. Fence rows and fallow strips of herbaceous or shrubby vegetation should be set aside as uncultivated land, yet should be maintained as early successional habitats, either through selective cutting or mowing. No-tillage or low-frequency tillage programs can be implemented to minimize nest destruction. The increase in crop residue resulting from such practices will provide supplemental cover for wildlife.

In uncultivated lands such as fallow fields or grasslands, management practices must be implemented in order to maintain the successional stage. Controlled burns, selective cutting, mowing, or grazing can be implemented as habitat management tools. Management, which must be conducted outside of the breeding season, can be executed during the late fall or early spring, prior to the birds' arrival. Fields should be managed on a rotational scheme, ensuring that no more than half of the grassland area is burned or cut in one year. To enhance managed habitats for vesper sparrows, a mixture of native warm-season grasses, such as little bluestem (*Schizachyrium scoparius*), big bluestem (*Andropogon gerardii*), switchgrass (*Panicum virgatum*), and Indian grass (*Sorghastrum nutans*), should be planted.

Sherry Liguori

Three REPTILES

Bog Turtle, *Clemmys muhlenbergii*
Status: State: Endangered   Federal: Threatened

Identification

The bog turtle is a tiny, dark turtle with a distinct orange patch behind the tympanum (ear membrane) on either side of the head. The scutes (scalelike horny layers) of the carapace (upper shell) are brown or black and may have yellow or reddish centers. Likewise, the plastron (underneath shell) is brownish black with a light yellow or mahogany center. The limbs are brown and may be mottled with variable amounts of dark yellow, orange, or red blotching. Bog turtles, one of the smallest and most secretive of North America's turtles, measure only 7.6 to 10 cm (3.0–3.9 in.) long as adults. The male bog

Bog turtle. © Robert Zappalorti

turtle has a concave plastron while that of the female is flat or slightly convex. In addition, the male has a long, thick tail and long foreclaws.

Distribution

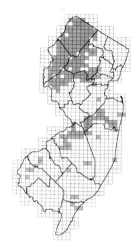

The bog turtle occurs in disjunct populations throughout the eastern United States, ranging from New York and southwestern Massachusetts south to western North Carolina. In New Jersey, the bog turtle occurs in Sussex, Warren, Morris, Hunterdon, Somerset, Union, Monmouth, Burlington, Ocean, Gloucester, and Salem counties. Although the bog turtle historically occupied nearly all counties in New Jersey, by the early 1990s habitat loss had limited their distribution to the above counties. Currently, the largest populations occur in northwestern New Jersey within the Wallkill and Paulinskill River watersheds.

Habitat

Bog turtles inhabit calcareous (limestone) fens, sphagnum bogs, and wet, grassy pastures that are characterized by soft, muddy substrates (bottoms) and perennial groundwater seepage. Bog turtle habitats are well drained and water depth rarely exceeds 10 cm (4 in.) above the surface. Flora associated with bog turtle habitats include sedges (*Carex* spp.), rushes (*Juncus* spp.), mosses, and grasses. These habitats may also contain red maple (*Acer rubrum*), alder (*Alnus* spp.), skunk cabbage (*Symplocarpus foetidus*), cattail (*Typha* spp.), willow (*Salix* spp.), highbush blueberry (*Vaccinium corymbosum.*), jewelweed (*Impatiens capensis*), swamp rose (*Hibiscus palustris*), dogwood (*Cornus* spp.), shrubby cinquefoil (*Potentilla fruticosa*), buttonbush (*Cephalanthus occidentalis*), rice-cut grass (*Leersia oryzoides*), wool-grass (*Scirpus cyperinus*), arrowhead (*Sagittaria* spp.), watercress (*Nasturtium officinale*), Saint-John's-wort (*Hypericum* spp.), blue vervain (*Verbena hastata*), sundew (*Drosera* spp.), pitcher plant (*Sarracenia purpurea*), cinnamon fern (*Osmunda cinnamomea*), and sensitive fern (*Onoclea sensibilis*). Because open areas are favored for basking and nesting, vegetative succession may cause the dispersal or loss of bog turtle colonies.

Many of the emergent wetlands inhabited by bog turtles have served as pastures during historic or current times. Grazing by livestock maintains the successional stage and softens the ground, creating favorable conditions for these turtles. Although controlled grazing is beneficial, overgrazing can result in excessive fecal runoff that may degrade water quality or encourage the growth of undesirable plant species.

Linear drainage ditches provide an alternative habitat for bog turtles in some areas of the state. These ditches, which have healed over time, may support remarkably high bog turtle densities.

Diet

Invertebrates, including insects and their larvae, crayfish, mollusks, worms, snails, and slugs are part of the bog turtle's diet. Seeds, berries, and shoots, as well as amphibians and carrion, are also eaten.

Bog turtle from above.
© Blaine Rothauser

Breeding Biology

As daytime air temperatures warm during March or April, bog turtles emerge from hibernation and bask atop sedge tussocks and sphagnum hummocks. Basking increases their body temperature and, in turn, stimulates the urges for foraging and mating. In New Jersey, mating activity occurs in May and early June as air temperatures exceed 25°C (77°F). Males seek females and bite at the limbs, tail, head, and neck of a prospective mate. If she is receptive, copulation ensues, either on land or in shallow water. Throughout the course of a season, one male may mate with several females. It is not until they are at least six years of age, or have a minimum plastron length of 7 cm (2.8 in.), that bog turtles are sexually mature (Ernst 1977).

From mid-June to early July, females seek open areas with raised hummocks, such as sedge tussocks or clumps of sphagnum moss, to deposit their eggs. These elevated sites offer a drier microhabitat within the marsh that allows for proper gas exchange to the developing embryos. Nest dimensions average 4.6 cm (1.8 in.) deep and 3.0 cm (1.2 in.) wide. Within the nest, the female lays a clutch of three to four tiny, white oblong eggs that measure only 2.4 to 3.4 cm (0.94–1.34 in.) in length. Sunlight incubates the eggs for 48 to 58 days. Barely over an inch long, the recently hatched turtles, as well as the eggs, are preyed upon by an array of mammalian predators. If a young turtle survives, it may live for 30 to 50 years.

During the summer months, bog turtles may occupy home ranges of several acres. In Pennsylvania, the mean home range of bog turtles encompassed an estimated 1.3 hectares (3.2 acres) (Bury 1979). Cold temperatures for one to two consecutive weeks during late October to late November compel bog turtles to retreat to their wintering sites. These turtles hibernate within subterranean burrows, where springs ensure that water will flow during the winter, preventing the turtles from freezing. Bog turtles may excavate their own burrows, utilize old muskrat holes, or enlarge existing tunnels of small mammals. Within these subterranean shelters, the turtles may hibernate singly or in small groups at depths of 5 to 55 cm (2–22 in.) (Ernst et al. 1989). Bog turtles exhibit fidelity to their wintering sites, as individuals have been documented using the same burrows in successive years.

Status and Conservation

Due to population declines, restricted habitat preference, habitat loss, and collecting, the bog turtle was listed as an endangered species in New Jersey in 1974. Declining throughout its range, this turtle is also listed as threatened in Maryland, North Carolina, South Carolina, and Georgia and endangered in Massachusetts, Connecticut, New York, Pennsylvania, Delaware, and Virginia. In 1997, the U.S. Fish and Wildlife Service included the bog turtle on its list of federally threatened species. The New Jersey Natural Heritage Program considers the bog turtle to be "globally, either very rare and local throughout its range or found locally in a restricted range or because of other factors making it vulnerable to extinction throughout its range," and "imperiled in New Jersey because of rarity" (Office of Natural Lands Management 1992).

Since the 1970s, biologists have studied the life history, habitat use, and distribution of the bog turtle in New Jersey. Current conservation efforts include

A fen favored by bog turtles. Photo courtesy NJ ENSP

habitat management, population monitoring, land acquisition, and landowner outreach. Since most bog turtle populations occur on private lands, biologists devote a substantial amount of time educating private landowners about bog turtle conservation. Private landowners can benefit from having bog turtles on their land through various federal cost-sharing programs, which provide funding for habitat management and improvement. Biologists from the New Jersey Endangered and Nongame Species Program (ENSP) are presently implementing a watershed-based management strategy for the protection of critical bog turtle areas.

Limiting Factors and Threats

Habitat loss, pollution, and illegal collecting are the primary threats facing bog turtle populations in New Jersey. Development, vegetative succession, and the invasion of undesirable alien plants have resulted in the destruction and degradation of bog turtle habitat. Habitat fragmentation isolates turtle colonies, potentially resulting in decreased genetic diversity and limited colonization of new sites. The construction and improvement of roads may lead to petroleum and salt runoff as well as turtle mortality during roadway crossings. Vegetative succession and the invasion of aggressive plant species such as phragmites (*Phragmites australis*) and purple loosestrife (*Lythrum salicaria*) negatively affect bog turtles by eliminating open areas and thereby reducing suitable nesting and basking habitats.

Illegal collecting has long been a serious problem for this species, as bog turtles are highly sought as pets on the black market. Currently, evidence of human activity at colonies exists, although the extent of collection activity in New Jersey remains unknown. Collecting bog turtles violates both state and federal endangered species laws and is punishable by severe fines and/or imprisonment.

Recommendations

Bog turtle management efforts must include the protection of occupied sites, the control of vegetative succession and alien plant invasions, and law enforcement. Networks of wetlands containing bog turtle colonies must be protected to allow movement of turtles and encourage dispersal and gene flow between otherwise isolated populations. These watersheds should be monitored to ensure high levels of water quantity and quality. Furthermore, efforts must be made to apprehend and prosecute illegal collectors.

Management of bog turtle habitat must include the suppression of vegetative succession and the control of undesirable plant species. Succession can be arrested by periodic cuttings, herbicidal treatments, or prescribed grazing. Currently the ENSP, in cooperation with cattle farmers, is grazing bog turtle sites that are threatened with invasive plant encroachment. Specific leaf, flower, and root-eating beetles are used to control purple loosestrife.

Sherry Liguori and Jason Tesauro

Wood turtle. © Robert Zappalorti

Wood Turtle, *Clemmys insculpta*
Status: State: Threatened   Federal: Not listed

Identification

As the taxonomic name *insculpta* indicates, the wood turtle is distinguished by the sculpted or grooved appearance of its carapace, or upper shell. Each season a new annulus, or ridge, is formed, giving each scute (a scalelike horny layer) a distinctive pyramid-shaped appearance. As the turtle ages, natural wear smoothes the surface of the shell. While the scutes of the carapace are brown, the plastron, or underneath shell, consists of yellow scutes with brown or black blotches on each outer edge. The legs and throat are reddish orange. The male wood turtle has a concave plastron while that of the female is flat or convex. The male also has a thicker tail than the female. Adult wood turtles measure 14 to 20 cm (5.5–8.0 in.) in length (Conant and Collins 1991).

Distribution

The wood turtle is found in eastern North America, ranging from Nova Scotia south to the Virginias and west to Michigan and eastern Minnesota. In New Jersey, the range is primarily limited to the northern and central portions of the state, although there have been a few occurrences within the Pine Barrens.

Wood turtles historically inhabited nearly all counties in northern and central New Jersey. However, habitat loss has restricted their distribution to disjunct populations associated with particular drainages. The largest populations in the state currently exist in Hunterdon, Morris, Sussex, Passaic, and Warren counties.

Habitat

Unlike other turtle species that favor either land or water, the wood turtle resides in both aquatic and terrestrial environments. Aquatic habitats are required for mating, feeding, and hibernation, while terrestrial habitats are used for egg laying and foraging. Freshwater streams, brooks, creeks, or rivers that are relatively remote provide the habitat needed by these turtles. Consequently, wood turtles are often found within streams containing native brook trout (*Salvelinus fontinalis*). These tributaries are characteristically clean, free of litter and pollutants, and occur within undisturbed uplands such as fields, meadows, or forests. Open fields and thickets of alder (*Alnus* spp.), greenbrier (*Smilax* spp.), or multiflora rose (*Rosa multiflora*) are favored basking habitats. Lowland, midsuccessional forests dominated by oaks (*Quercus* spp.), black birch (*Betula lenta*), and red maple (*Acer rubrum*) may also be used. Wood turtles may also be found on abandoned railroad beds or agricultural fields and pastures. Nevertheless, wood turtle habitats typically contain few roads and are often over one-half of a mile away from developed or populated areas. Individuals from relict or declining populations are also sighted in areas of formally good habitat that have been fragmented by roads and development.

Diet

An omnivorous species, the wood turtle consumes a variety of animal and plant matter. Insects and their larvae, worms, slugs, snails, fish, frogs, tadpoles, crayfish, and carrion are included in their diet. In addition, these turtles forage on leaves, algae, moss, mushrooms, fruit, and berries.

Breeding Biology

During early March, wood turtles emerge from hibernation and bask along stream banks. Breeding activity begins as water temperatures warm to about

A newly hatched
wood turtle.
© Robert Zappalorti

A wood turtle stream with adjacent basking and foraging areas. Photo courtesy NJ ENSP

15°C (59°F). During April, the turtles mate within streams and, by mid-May, move to dry land, where they will spend the next several months. Females seek elevated, well-drained, open areas where they can dig their nests. Nests are often excavated at depths of 9.0 to 11.5 cm (3.5–4.5 in.).

The female wood turtle lays a clutch of eight to nine smooth, white eggs that are incubated for 70 to 71 days. The eggs, hatchlings, and adults may fall prey to raccoons or skunks. At a mere 4 cm (1.5 in.) in length, hatchling wood turtles are distinguished by their long tails, which can be nearly equal in length to the carapace. If the young turtles survive, they can live 20 to 30 years, reaching sexual maturity in their fourteenth year.

During the summer months, adult wood turtles wander along stream corridors while foraging in open fields and woodlands. In New Jersey, marked wood turtles have been observed at locations up to 0.9 km (0.56 mi.) from their wintering streams. One turtle traversed nearly 1.6 km (1 mi.) within two months. During this nomadic period, the turtles are especially vulnerable to mortality during roadway crossings.

Wood turtles return to streams and creeks and begin hibernating by late November. They winter in muddy stream bottoms, within creek banks, or in abandoned muskrat holes. Individuals may overwinter in the same stream or embankment during successive years.

Status and Conservation

Historically, the wood turtle was a fairly common species within suitable habitat in New Jersey. By the 1970s, however, declines were noted as wood turtles were absent from many historic sites due to habitat loss and stream degradation. Consequently, the wood turtle was listed as a threatened species in New Jersey in 1979. The New Jersey Natural Heritage Program considers the wood turtle to be "demonstrably secure globally," yet "rare in New Jersey" (Office of Natural Lands Management 1992).

Since the late 1970s, biologists have monitored and surveyed wood turtle sites in New Jersey, providing valuable data regarding the life history, reproduction, and habitat use of these turtles in the state. There is, however, a continuing need to examine the productivity and juvenile survival of wood turtles, which may be threatened by disturbance or predation.

In 1995, the wood turtle was proposed for inclusion on the federal endangered species list. Despite declines in several northeastern states, populations were considered stable enough throughout the species' entire range to deny listing. However, the wood turtle was considered by the U.S. Fish and Wildlife Service as a species that "although not necessarily now threatened with extinction may become so unless trade in them is strictly controlled" (U.S. Fish and Wildlife Service 1995). As a result, international trade of these turtles is strictly monitored and regulated through the CITES Act (Convention on International Trade in Endangered Species of Wild Flora and Fauna Act). The New Jersey Endangered Species Conservation Act prohibits the collection or possession of wood turtles.

Limiting Factors and Threats

The degradation and loss of both riparian and terrestrial habitats continue to be the primary threats facing wood turtle populations in New Jersey. Pesticides, sewage effluent, runoff, illegal dumping and other pollutants jeopardize water quality of streams and creeks. As terrestrial habitats become more fragmented, road mortality and predation may pose increased threats to these turtles. Collecting of wood turtles as pets, a problem that may be abating due to increased public awareness, can result in reduced population size or local extirpations.

Recommendations

Streams that are currently occupied by wood turtles as well as sites offering suitable habitat should be protected from destruction and degradation. Buffer zones surrounding tributaries should be preserved to provide upland habitat for wood turtles. In locations where open areas are sparse or lacking, uplands can be managed to provide fields and meadows. Watersheds should be monitored to ensure high levels of water quality. Management practices for brook trout can improve stream quality, benefiting both trout and wood turtles.

Sherry Liguori

MARINE TURTLES

Atlantic Loggerhead Turtle, *Caretta caretta*
Status: State: Endangered   Federal: Threatened

Atlantic Leatherback Turtle, *Dermochelys coriacea*
Status: State: Endangered   Federal: Endangered

Kemp's Ridley Turtle, *Lepidochelys kempi*
Status: State: Endangered   Federal: Endangered

Atlantic Green Turtle, *Chelonia mydas*
Status: State: Threatened   Federal: Threatened/Florida and Mexico
breeding populations endangered

Atlantic Hawksbill Turtle, *Eretmochelys imbricata*
Status: State: Endangered   Federal: Endangered

Identification

Loggerhead: The loggerhead sea turtle's carapace (upper shell) is a distinguishing reddish brown for both adults and subadults. Scales on the top and sides of the head and top of the flippers are also reddish brown but have yellow borders. The scutes (scalelike, horny layers) on the carapace are thin, but very hard and very rough, and often covered with barnacles. The neck, shoulders, and limb bases are dull brown on top and medium yellow on the sides

A loggerhead equipped with a radio transmitter to track it. Photo by Ryan Hagerty, courtesy US FWS

and bottom. The plastron (underneath shell) is also medium yellow. The very strong horny beak is comparatively thicker than in other sea turtles. The fore-flippers are relatively short and thick, with two visible claws; rear flippers have two to three claws.

Generally, the mean straight carapace length of mature females is between 81.5 and 105.3 cm (32.6–42.12 in.), with a mean weight near 75 kg (65.7–101.4 kg) or 165 lb. (144–223 lb.) (FAO 1990).

Hatchlings are dark brown, with flippers that are pale brown on their edges and underneath, and with a plastron that usually is much paler. The hatchlings and juveniles have blunt spines on the scutes on their carapace; the spines disappear during the juvenile stage. (Unless otherwise noted, all physical descriptions in this section rely upon FAO 1990.)

Leatherback: The largest of all sea turtles, the leatherback is one of the largest living reptiles; only some species of crocodiles are larger. It is easily distinguished by its black, leathery skin, huge spindle- or barrel-shaped body, and long flippers. As Archie Carr wrote, "This extraordinary turtle . . . could be confused with nothing else" (Carr 1995). Rather than having horny shields, the body is covered with a layer of rubbery skin that has seven longitudinal ridges (keels) on the back and five underneath.

The dorsal or upper side of adults is predominantly black. Scattered white blotches arranged along the keels become more numerous along the sides and even more so underneath, with the ventral side primarily whitish. Pinkish blotches on the neck, shoulders, and groin intensify when the turtle is out of the water.

The head and neck are black or dark brown, mottled with white or pink blotches. Each side of the upper jaw has a toothlike cusp, giving the turtle a W-shaped beak. Paddlelike, clawless limbs are black with white margins and might have white spots. Males can be distinguished from females by their much longer tails and narrower and less deep bodies.

Hatchlings are dark brown or black, with white or yellow carapace keels and flipper margins. Their skin is covered with small scales that become thinner with each molt, which starts about three weeks after hatching. Claws may be visible in hatchlings, but they vanish in subadults and adults.

Adults generally weigh 290 to 590 kg (638–1,298 lb.) but can weigh up to 2,000 pounds; the average carapace length is 155 cm (62 in.) (USFWS 1980a, 1998).

Kemp's Ridley: This is the smallest of all sea turtles. From above, the short, chunky shell appears broadly heart-shaped to nearly round, with high vertebral projections and serrated edges. The turtle has a moderate-sized subtriangular head and a somewhat hooked beak with large crushing surfaces. The plastron has several small pores on each side, which lead to Rathke's glands (secretory structures that release an odiferous substance that may play a pheromonal role when females mass together off their nesting beaches). Each foreflipper has one visible claw, with one or two claws on the rear flippers.

Dorsally, the color of the adult skin and shell is plain olive-gray above and white or yellowish underneath.

When wet, hatchlings are jet black on both sides, with two visible flipper claws. As the turtle matures, the hingeless plastron changes to white, then yellow while the carapace changes to gray, then olive green.

Adults weigh 35 to 42 kg (77–92 lb.) and have a carapace length of 56 to 70 cm (22.4–28 in.) (USFWS 1980d).

Green Sea Turtle: This is the largest cheloniid sea turtle, with a low, broadly oval carapace and small head with one pair of prefrontal scales that are unique to green turtles. Single-clawed flippers are paddle-shaped. Color varies widely.

Kemp's ridley sea turtle.
Photo courtesy US FWS

Adults have a smooth carapace that ranges from pale to very dark and from plain colors to brilliant mixtures of yellows, browns and yellows that radiate in stripes or are splattered with dark splotches. The plastron is whitish to light yellow. The upper surface of the head is light brown with yellow markings; sides of the head are brown with broad yellow margins. The neck is dusky above and yellow near the shell below. The tail and flippers are colored like the carapace and plastron. Each flipper has one visible claw.

Hatchlings are dark brown or nearly black on the upper side, with white plastrons and white margins on the shell and limbs. In juveniles, the carapace has radiant patterning similar to hawksbills, and the scales of the head and upper side of the flippers are fringed by a narrow, clear yellowish margin. Adults weigh 100 to 200 kg (220–440 lb.) and range between 91 and 122 cm (36.4 and 48.8 in.) (USFWS 1980b).

Hawksbill Turtle: The most colorful sea turtle, the medium-sized hawksbill turtle has an elongated, oval shell distinguished by overlapping scutes on the carapace. The overlapping is most pronounced at maturity but often disappears in older individuals. Barnacles are often found on the carapace and plastron. Its medium-sized head is narrow, with a pointed beak. There are two claws on each fore and rear flipper. As is true of other sea turtles, males have stronger, more curved claws and longer tails than females.

Color varies widely, from very bright colors to heavy dark brown (in the eastern Pacific). The scales of the head have creamy or yellow margins, while the carapace has an amber "ground" color overlaid with spots or stripes of brown, red, black, and yellow, usually arranged in a radiant, fan-shaped pattern. Underneath, the plastron is amber colored. The dorsal, or upper, part of the head and flippers are darker, with less variation in color.

The carapace of hatchlings and juveniles is wider than the shell of adults, with three keels of spines along the carapace that disappear with age. Hatch-

Green sea turtle.
Photo by David Vogel,
courtesy US FWS

Hawksbill sea turtle.
Photo by Anja G. Burns,
courtesy US FWS

lings are mostly brown, with paler blotches on the rear part of the carapace, with small pale spots on the top of each scute along the plastron's two keels (FAO 1990). Juveniles, though, are the most vibrantly colored, with bold amber/brown/greenish/gold variegation (Cheryl Ryder, pers. comm. 2001).

Adults are 76 to 89 cm long (30.4–35.6 in.) and weigh between 43 and 75 kg (94.6 and 165 lb.).

Distribution

Though most sea turtles inhabit warm tropical and subtropical waters, they migrate northward as water temperatures increase in the late spring and summer and remain in northern waters until late fall. Leatherbacks routinely migrate as far north as Newfoundland.

From late May until November, New Jersey coastal waters provide important seasonal foraging habitat to several species of sea turtles. Since 1978, the Marine Mammal Stranding Center in Brigantine, New Jersey, has reported numerous strandings of sea turtles in New Jersey, including 452 loggerheads, 214 leatherbacks, 47 Kemp's ridleys, and eight green sea turtles (Vikki Socha, pers. comm. 2001). In addition, both the Salem Nuclear Power Plant and the Oyster Creek Nuclear Generating Station have reported impingements of sea turtles trapped at cooling water intake sites. Sea turtles have also been recorded in state waters by the Rutgers University Marine Field Station, the New Jersey Division of Fish and Wildlife, and other marine agencies.

Migratory sites

According to Morreale and Standora (1998), New York's coastal waters provide important developmental habitat for young loggerheads, Kemp's ridley, and green sea turtles during the warmer months. The most pelagic of sea turtles, the leatherbacks, which range in the Atlantic from Newfoundland to Argentina, are often found near the edge of the continental shelf. But in northern waters, they sometimes frequent shallow estuaries. Adult leatherbacks occur annually in New York waters (Morreale and Standora 1998). The less common green sea turtles, which are found in tropical and subtropical waters around the world, inhabit North American coastal waters from Massachusetts to Mexico. Found in the tropics throughout the world, hawksbills range from southern Brazil to Massachusetts in the Atlantic.

Based on extensive satellite telemetry studies, Morreale and Standora (1998) hypothesize that juvenile sea turtles migrate through narrowly defined corridors along the Atlantic Coast between Florida and New England. It is suspected that New Jersey waters factor highly into successful sea turtle migration and development (Stephen Morreale, pers. comm. 1999).

Habitat

Unlike land turtles from which they evolved more than 150 million years ago, sea turtles spend almost their entire lives in the sea. When active, they often come to the surface to breathe but can remain underwater for several hours at a time while resting. Leatherbacks can dive to more than 914 m (3,000 ft.) below sea level (USFWS 1998). Preferred estuarine habitat of sea turtles—deeper or shallower water—directly relates to their preferred diet. Adult green sea turtles are herbivores, or plant eaters. All the other sea turtles are either carnivores (meat eaters) or omnivores which eat both plant matter and meat.

Diet

While little is known of the foraging of sea turtles in New Jersey waters, studies of the Chesapeake Bay and other northeastern areas indicate that the abundance of invertebrates, particularly crabs, attract sea turtles to shallower waters. One diet analysis indicated that more than 75% of the diets of both loggerhead and ridley turtles consisted of blue crabs, with the rest comprised of mollusks, algae, synthetics, and natural debris (Burke et al. 1990). Another study indicated loggerheads tended to be in deeper Chesapeake Bay waters, such as the mouths of rivers and in open water, to target their key prey, horseshoe crabs, while ridley turtles preferred shallower areas in search of blue crabs (Keinath et al. 1987).

Adult green sea turtles are largely herbivores, feeding primarily on marine algae and marine grasses. Juvenile green sea turtles, meanwhile, eat both invertebrates and aquatic vegetation such as eelgrass, which grows in beds in Barnegat Bay.

Breeding Biology

Sea turtles share similar life histories. After mating offshore, the females come ashore to lay clutches of eggs on sandy beaches. The clutch sizes vary widely between and within species, ranging between 23 and 195 eggs per clutch. The number of clutches laid in each active nesting season also varies, from an average of 1.5 times for Kemp's ridley to as often as five times for loggerheads. Intervals between the nesting seasons for individual adult females range between one and four years for green sea turtles and between two and three years for loggerheads, leatherbacks, and hawksbills; 58% of Kemp's ridleys nest each year (FAO 1990).

The marine turtles found in U.S. waters are regionally faithful to their natal beaches in the southeastern United States, the Caribbean, and the Gulf of Mexico, meaning that they return to nest on the same beaches or beaches within the region, where they had originally hatched. After hatching, anywhere from 50 to 90 days after the eggs are laid (Cheryl Ryder, pers. comm. 2001), hatchlings scramble to the water and engage in a swimming frenzy that can last two to three days. They spend their first year of life offshore, presumably in mats of aquatic vegetation propelled by oceanic currents. The juveniles then move inshore to bays, estuaries, and coastal areas, where they remain until they reach sexual maturation. Maturation varies widely by species, ranging from just three to four years for leatherbacks to 12 to 30 or more years for loggerheads and 25 to 30 years for green sea turtles (FAO 1990; Schoelkopf and Stetzar 1995).

Status and Conservation

Overharvesting of eggs for food, intentional killing of adults and immatures for their shells and skin, and incidental drowning caused by commercial fishing gear are primarily responsible for the worldwide decline in sea turtle populations. Coastal residential and resort development have also degraded nesting habitat, and pollution of oceans threatens foraging habitats.

In one striking case, the number of Kemp's ridley females at the species' primary nesting site, a beach on the Gulf of Mexico near Rancho Nuevo, Mexico, plummeted from 40,000 in 1947 to just 200 by 1978 (USFWS 1980d). As a result of such declines, the federal government listed the Kemp's ridley as endangered in 1970, the same year it also listed hawksbill and leatherback turtles as endangered. In 1978, it listed loggerheads and green sea turtles as threatened and, in the case of the green sea turtle's Florida and Mexico breeding populations, as endangered. In response, in 1979 the state of New Jersey classified the Atlantic hawksbill, loggerhead, ridley, and leatherback turtles as endangered and listed the Atlantic green sea turtle as threatened.

Limiting Factors and Threats to Populations

Sea turtle nests can be destroyed by natural events such as tidal surges or hurricanes. Raccoons, ghost crabs, and other predators prey upon the eggs. Although adult sea turtles have few natural predators, sharks and killer whales do prey on them. In such cases, sea turtles, unlike land turtles, cannot protect themselves by pulling their head inside their shells.

Human activity, however, is the primary cause of the decline in sea turtles. Modifications to nesting areas—many such sites are also prime real estate—can have devastating effects on sea turtle populations. Coastal modifications, such as jetties, sea walls, rip rap, revetments, sand fences, and groins, can also cause nesting beach habitat to erode. If a nesting site is destroyed or altered, females may nest in inferior locations where hatchlings are less likely to survive, or they may not lay eggs at all.

Artificial lighting from developed beachfront often disorients both nesting females and emerging hatchlings, which mistakenly head inland, leaving them vulnerable to predation, exhaustion, dessication, or being crushed by vehicles. Adult females may also avoid brightly lit beaches that otherwise might prove suitable for nesting.

Beach driving is another major threat. Headlights and vehicular movement at night can deter females from coming ashore to nest. Vehicles can collide with turtles or run over nests, and the tracks they leave in the sand can be deep enough to prevent hatchlings from taking a direct route to the ocean —again leaving them vulnerable (USFWS 1998).

Besides being a threat to nesting habitat, human activities in the water also pose a significant threat to sea turtles. They are incidentally captured in commercial fishing gear such as commercial shrimp trawls, gill nets, longlines, pound nets, as well as whelk, crab, and lobster pot gear and recreational hooks and lines. Although turtles can hold their breath, they die from drowning, stress, and catastrophic injuries associated with these interactions. Turtles surfacing to breathe are killed or injured by ships, small boats, and jet skis (USFWS 1998).

Commercial exploitation of sea turtles for food and leather products has caused many sea turtle populations to decline. As a result of international demand for turtle shells, between 1970 and 1989, 1.2 million hawksbill turtles were killed. Japan alone imported the shells of more than 670,000 hawksbills in that period, with more than half coming from the Caribbean and Latin America. Today the shells, which are used to make combs, brushes, jewelry, and other ornamental items, are still worth $225 per kilogram (NMFS, Hawksbill Sea Turtle, n.d.).

Sea turtles often mistake balloons, plastic pieces, and other debris for prey. Consuming marine debris can lead to nutritional deficiencies and death. Many sea turtles, particularly those in Florida and Hawaii, are afflicted with fibropapillomatosis, a disease that can cause large tumors on the turtle's skin, eyes, and mouth, and sometimes affects internal organs. Turtles with heavy tumor burdens can become debilitated and die. The disease affects primarily green sea turtles, but is emerging as a serious threat to loggerheads and several other sea turtle species. It is thought that environmental alteration of sea turtle foraging habitat by pollution and contaminants might play a role in this disease (USFWS 1998).

Recommendations

The requirement that shrimp trawlers in the United States and Mexico use turtle excluder devices in their trawler nets, combined with the protection of nesting females and their nests, has resulted in an increase of females at the primary Kemp's ridley nesting site to an estimated 1,500 (USFWS 1998).

Although previous efforts to study sea turtles have focused on tagging stranded and power-plant-impinged turtles, data on movement patterns within New Jersey state waters are incomplete. Location and movement-pattern information is critical for targeting areas for protection. Additionally, there are no long-term scientific investigations into the importance of the state's coastal environment as a sea turtle feeding and developmental area. Finally, threats to New Jersey sea turtle populations need to be identified and a management plan developed so that protective measures can be undertaken.

The goals of a proposed New Jersey Endangered and Nongame Species Program (ENSP) project are as follows:

- Determine growth rates, primary food sources, distribution patterns, and seasonal activity cycles of sea turtle species that occur in New Jersey coastal waters.

- Identify threats to populations and take appropriate measures to ensure protection.

- Develop a New Jersey Sea Turtle Management Plan that will (1) define our state's role in sea turtle migration and development and identify critical areas; (2) identify threats such as boat strikes and commercial fishing gear entanglements; (3) recommend and seek to enact protective measures such as no-wake zones and critical areas designations, as well as commercial fishing gear modifications.

By establishing an Endangered Species Act (ESA), Section 6 Cooperative Agreement with the National Marine Fisheries Service (NMFS), the ENSP hopes to better address sea turtle recovery objectives in New Jersey state waters. Possible sea turtle projects we would like to pursue through the agreement include the following:

1. Work with the N.J. Bureau of Marine Fisheries to tag sea turtles during coastwide trawl surveys.
2. Tag and collect information on sea turtles entrapped in commercial pound nets.
3. Explore the effectiveness of utilizing modified trap nets and other gear types to capture, tag, weigh, measure, and release sea turtles in appropriate habitats.

Bruce E. Beans

Corn Snake, *Elaphe g. guttata*
Status: State: Endangered   Federal: Not listed

Identification

Also known as the red rat snake, the corn snake is a strikingly beautiful and docile serpent. Highly variable in coloration, the upperparts range from brown to light orange or red and are marked with brick-red blotches outlined in black. Two red lines extend from a blotch on the back of the neck and merge at the top of the head, forming a spear-shaped mark. In addition, a red line extends from both sides of the head, through the brown eyes, and across the

Corn snake. © Robert Zappalorti

snout. The underside of the corn snake is checkered with black and white rectangular markings, which have been likened to corn kernels or piano keys. The undertail is striped with black and white lines. Corn snakes have weakly keeled scales and a divided anal plate. The sexes may be distinguished externally by the size of the tail, which is longer and thicker in males. Adults measure 0.76 to 1.2 m (2.5–4 ft.) in length, with a record individual of 1.8 m (6 ft.) long (Conant and Collins 1991).

The corn snake molts several times a year, shedding its outer layer of skin to accommodate the growing animal. Prior to shedding, the snake appears duller overall and the eyes become cloudy. During this vulnerable time, the corn snake seeks and rubs against bark, logs, or rocks to dislodge the old skin. Once a tear is made, the snake crawls out of the old skin, leaving its shed behind. After shedding, the snake appears more vibrantly colored and resumes normal behavior. The complete process of shedding, from clouding to sloughing off the old skin, spans about a week or longer.

Distribution

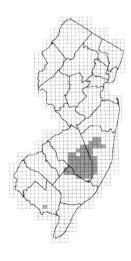

A species of the southeastern United States, the corn snake reaches its northern limit in central New Jersey. Its range extends from New Jersey south to Florida and west to Mississippi and southeastern Louisiana, with disjunct populations in Kentucky.

Native to the Pine Barrens of southern New Jersey, the corn snake historically inhabited sites in Ocean, Burlington, Cumberland, and Atlantic counties. The species was first discovered in the state in 1912 at Chatsworth, Burlington County. Although both Burlington and Ocean counties continue to hold the largest corn snake populations in the state, this reptile has been lost from many traditional sites because of habitat destruction.

The only recorded specimen for Atlantic County, which is presently held in the American Museum of Natural History in New York City, was obtained in Hammonton Township in 1924. Since the habitat was subsequently developed, however, corn snakes have not been found in this area in recent years. Although several sightings from Maurice River Township, Cumberland County, occurred during the 1970s, the species was not documented in the county again until a gravid (pregnant) adult female was discovered dead on a road in Downe Township in 1990. Due to their secretive nature, corn snakes may remain undetected in areas containing suitable habitat.

Habitat

Corn snakes inhabit mature, upland pine-dominated forests that contain uprooted trees, stump holes, and rotten logs. Soil types typically include sands and loams. Pitch pine (*Pinus rigida*), blackjack oak (*Quercus marilandica*), lowbush blueberry (*Vaccinium vacillans*), highbush blueberry (*V. corymbosum*), greenbrier (*Smilax* spp.), bracken fern (*Pteridium aquilinum*), Pennsylvania sedge (*Carex pennsylvanica*), and heather (*Hudsonia* spp.) often comprise corn snake habitats. In addition, shortleaf pine (*P. echinata*), Virginia pine (*P. virginiana*), black oak (*Q. velutina*), scarlet oak (*Q. coccinea*), and common hairgrass (*Deschampsia flexuosa*) may be present. Corn snakes inhabit locations containing a water source such as a stream or pond. Open field and forest edges are used for foraging. The home range of a marked corn snake in Ocean County encompassed 4.6 hectares (11.3 acres).

A highly fossorial (burrowing) species, the corn snake seeks cover within subterranean burrows, stump holes, or old, rotten, and hollowed railroad ties. These snakes also tunnel beneath sand mounds, boards, logs, rubbish, or concrete slabs. Abandoned buildings or foundations may be used for nesting or hibernating. In some areas of New Jersey, corn snakes have shown a preference for abandoned, hollowed-out railroad ties, where they concentrate due to increased prey, protection from predators, and shelter for eggs and hatchlings.

Diet

The corn snake's diet is dominated by small mammals but also includes birds, reptiles, and insects. In the New Jersey Pine Barrens, white-footed mice (*Peromyscus leucopus*) and fence lizards (*Sceloporus undulatus*) constitute the majority of the corn snakes' diet. Adult snakes also prey upon small birds, eggs, chicks, moles, mice, chipmunks, and voles. Hatchling snakes feed primarily on fence lizards and insects.

Snakes are highly adapted predators, specialized at detecting and subduing small mammals. The snake's tongue is used to detect airborne molecules, which are then transferred to the Jacobson's organ, located in the roof of the mouth. This organ, unique to reptiles, is used in conjunction with the brain to identify odors associated with prey. Thus, when a snake flicks its tongue, it is actually using this sense to interpret its surroundings. The corn snake is a constrictor, meaning that the snake suffocates its quarry by tightly wrapping its body around the prey. Corn snakes stealthily stalk their prey until they are

A corn snake hatchling.
© Robert Zappalorti

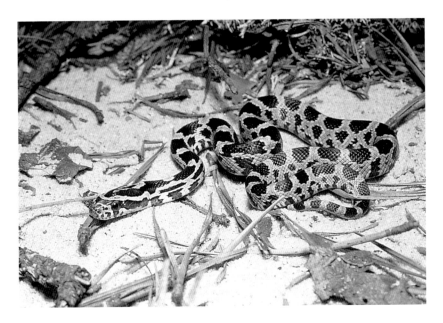

within striking range. With one lightning-speed motion, the snake lunges at its target, grabbing the animal with its mouth and constricting its body around the prey. Once the prey is dead, the snake begins to consume it, swallowing it whole, headfirst. Snakes are able to consume sizeable prey by unhinging their jaw bones while swallowing and stretching their skin to accommodate their prey. The corn snake requires at least several days for digestion.

Breeding Biology

Warming temperatures in late April and early May arouse corn snakes from hibernation. From May to early June, the snakes mate. The exact date of egg laying, which ranges from mid- to late July, varies with environmental conditions, the physical state of the female, and the date of mating. Clutch sizes also vary, ranging from 5 to 14 eggs, depending on prey availability and the health of the female. The female, which may deposit her eggs at the same location each year, nests in old railroad ties, hollow logs, or stump holes. The heat generated from the rotting of wood or logs may facilitate incubation. The eggs, which incubate for five to seven weeks, hatch in September. Hatchling corn snakes measure only 27.5 cm (10.8 in.) in length.

Triggered by cooling temperatures in October and November, corn snakes retreat to their wintering sites. Underground burrows, stump holes, or hollow railroad ties located beneath the frost line serve as hibernacula. Typically, corn snakes use the same hibernaculum in consecutive years.

Status and Conservation

Due to habitat loss, limited range in the state, illegal collecting, and population declines, the corn snake was listed as a threatened species in New Jersey in 1979. Although the species was afforded protection, severe habitat loss continued, particularly in Ocean and Atlantic counties. Likewise, this handsome and docile snake was highly prized by illegal collectors, who continued to excavate denning sites in search of these snakes. Many historic corn snake populations were lost due to habitat destruction and poaching, and, despite extensive surveys, no new populations were found during the early 1980s. As a result of the continued and increased threats to this species and its habitat, the corn snake was reclassified as an endangered species in New Jersey in 1984.

The New Jersey Natural Heritage Program considers the corn snake to be "demonstrably secure globally," yet "critically imperiled in New Jersey because of extreme rarity" (Office of Natural Lands Management 1992). Documented corn snake sites are currently protected through the Pinelands Protection Act and environmental reviews of proposed development. The collection or possession of wild corn snakes is prohibited by the New Jersey Endangered Species Conservation Act and is punishable with fines and/or imprisonment.

Limiting Factors and Threats

Due to its specialized habitat requirements and limited range, the corn snake is especially vulnerable to habitat destruction and alteration. Although documented sites containing corn snakes are afforded protection within the Pinelands Protection Area, upland forests often receive less protection than wetland areas. Upland forests that lie outside the Pinelands Protection Area are highly vulnerable to destruction. The loss of potentially suitable upland forests reduces the overall amount of available habitat for corn snakes and magnifies the detrimental impacts of habitat fragmentation and patch size reduction. As habitats are fragmented or reduced in size, corn snakes become increasingly vulnerable to genetic isolation, road mortality, human persecution, and illegal collecting. Off-road vehicle use may result in road mortality of basking or traveling snakes.

Both corn snakes and northern pine snakes prefer sandy pinelands. © Robert Zappalorti

Illegal collecting of corn snakes is a persistent problem. Because of its beauty and ease of care in captivity, the corn snake is highly prized by collectors. Poachers often destroy nesting sites and hibernacula to remove adult snakes, eggs, and young.

Recommendations

The protection of upland forest habitats is critical to the conservation of corn snakes in New Jersey. Parcels that contain corn snakes or suitable habitat, or are adjacent to known corn snake sites, should be protected from habitat destruction. In addition, the use of off-road vehicles should be seasonally prohibited near known corn snake sites.

Forest management and the creation of man-made hibernacula can be used to improve habitat for corn snakes. Corn snakes inhabit pine-dominated forests that rely on fire to suppress the growth of oaks, which would otherwise out-compete the pines. Controlled burns or selective cutting can be implemented to maintain the pine-dominated successional stage. If selective cutting is implemented as a management tool, the resulting logs and branches can be used to create denning mounds for snakes or brush piles for their prey. Because corn snakes accept man-made hibernacula, they can be created within areas of suitable habitat.

New hibernacula, as well as established sites, should be monitored regularly by conservation officers. If poaching is suspected, strong efforts must be made to apprehend illegal collectors and prosecute them to the fullest extent of the law.

Sherry Liguori

Northern Pine Snake, *Pituophis melanoleucus melanoleucus*
Status: State: Threatened   Federal: Not listed

Identification

The northern pine snake is a relatively large (122–172 cm, or 48–68 in.), black and dull white to yellowish or light gray snake. These snakes have blotches that are dark toward the front of the body but may fade to brown near and on the tail. Pine snakes have keeled scales and a single anal plate. Known for their noisy hiss, pine snakes are typically ground dwellers and rarely climb vegetation. Since this species is both secretive and fossorial, meaning it burrows underground, it can easily go undetected even in locations where it is known to be common (Mitchell 1994).

Distribution

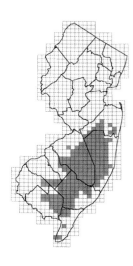

In New Jersey, the pine snake occurs exclusively within the Pinelands habitats of the outer coastal plain. This population of pine snake is disjunct and distant from populations in other parts of this species' range, which includes the western Appalachians of Virginia, North Carolina, southern Kentucky, Tennessee, northern Alabama, northern Georgia, as well as the Piedmont of south-

Northern pine snake.
© Blaine Rothauser

ern North Carolina and nearly all of South Carolina (Conant and Collins 1991). Throughout its range the pine snake nearly always occupies dry upland forests usually comprised of pines (Conant and Collins 1991).

Habitat

Pine snakes in New Jersey require dry pine-oak forest types growing on very infertile sandy soils such as Lakehurst or Lakewood sands (Burger and Zappalorti 1988, 1989). Both human-caused and natural disturbances (e.g., agriculture, forestry, and fire) are probably involved in creating the types of openings important for nesting and basking. Sandy infertile soil not only provides for persistent openings in disturbed sites, but may also be important because pine snakes are the only snakes known to dig hibernacula and summer dens.

Diet

Adult pine snakes feed on a variety of rodents and other small mammals. Younger snakes prey upon small mammals and lizards (Tennant and Bartlett 2000).

Breeding Biology

Female pine snakes lay eggs in nests excavated in sandy clearings with high sun exposure. The large eggs of this species are usually laid between mid-June and mid-July, with eggs incubating for a minimum of 60 days before hatching (Burger and Zappalorti 1992). An average of 3 to 12 eggs are laid per clutch (Martof et al. 1980), and females appear to exhibit a high degree of nest fidelity, returning to the same nests in subsequent years to lay eggs (Burger and Zappalorti 1992). Hatchling pine snakes range in length from 27 to 38 cm (10.5–15 in.) (Wright and Wright 1957) and may stay close to the nest until

A northern pine snake and her eggs. © Robert Zappalorti

their first shed (Zappalorti, pers. comm.). In New Jersey, this species is active from April to October (Zappalorti et al. 1983) and overwinters in underground dens.

Status and Conservation

The secretive nature of this snake has led to some degree of uncertainty about its overall status in the northeastern United States. However all indications seem to suggest that pine snake abundance has decreased throughout its northeastern range. It is also believed that pine snakes have been extirpated from West Virginia and Maryland. The New Jersey Pinelands may hold some of the largest populations of pine snakes in the Northeast, but even in the Pinelands this species is at risk.

Limiting Factors and Threats

The pine snake is an example of a species that is facing multiple threats. While habitat loss and alteration appear to be the primary threats to this species in New Jersey, illegal collecting and off-road recreation vehicle use have also negatively impacted pine snakes. For example, while monitoring pine snake nests for a scientific study, Burger and Zappalorti (1992) reported poachers excavating 8 of 20 nests and 7 of 19 nests during 1988 and 1989, respectively.

The development of Pinelands habitats leads to an overall loss of pine-oak forest habitat as well as an increase in human encounters with pine snakes. Too often, such encounters prove fatal to these snakes, and reports of pine snake road kills are common. Some forestry practices may also have negative impacts on pine snakes. For example, forestry practices that favor oak-dominated systems with closed canopies or dense shrub layers probably decrease the amount of suitable pine snake habitat in an area.

Recommendations

Because this species suffers from multiple threats, multiple recommendations would benefit pine snakes. First, increased efforts to limit development in suitable pine snake habitat is important to protect unidentified populations of pine snakes. Because this species is very secretive, conventional methods of surveying for reptiles may be inadequate to determine whether or not pine snakes occupy a particular location. Taking a "habitat-based" approach to pine snake protection may therefore be justified. Management for the pine-oak forest habitat that is required by this species would also be helpful for maintaining known populations of pine snakes and possibly increasing pine snake abundance in locations where this species is likely to exist. On state-owned lands, this type of management would include appropriate silviculture methods and prescribed burns intended to thin the forest understory and impede succession. Finally, increased vigilance and penalties for poachers would further protect pine snakes in the Pinelands landscape region.

David M. Golden and Dave Jenkins

Queen Snake, *Regina septemvittata*
Status: State: Endangered   Federal: Not listed

Identification

This slender snake can reach lengths of 41 to 61 cm (16–24 in.) when fully grown. The dorsal (or upper) surface of a queen snake is a solid grayish brown color. A yellow band is present on the lower half of the body and extends from the snake's chin to its tail. The belly of the snake is a white to yellow color with four characteristic stripes that make for easy identification. Of these four

A male queen snake.
© Rudolf G. Arndt

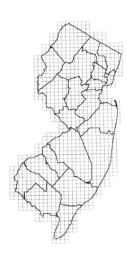

stripes, the two outer stripes are visibly thicker than the inner pair. Queen snakes have keeled scales and an anal plate that is divided.

Distribution

The queen snake is present in most of the eastern states, with the exception of the states in the extreme Northeast (Connecticut through Maine), where it is absent. In New Jersey, this species has a very narrow distribution that is believed to comprise only a 10-mile-wide strip along the Delaware River from Hunterdon County southward to Gloucester County. Within this range, isolated populations may exist in areas with appropriate habitat, but some experts believe that this species has actually been extirpated from the state.

Habitat

This species is highly aquatic and a very adept swimmer. Authorities report that swiftly flowing creeks, brooks, and streams are the preferred habitat for queen snakes (Wright and Wright 1957). But finding them along the edges of more slowly flowing rivers and streams, and sometimes lakes, is not uncommon in some states. The queen snake's diet (see below) always keeps it close to water, where it can sometimes be seen with just its head above the surface. On occasion, a lucky observer might find these snakes basking in high numbers along the banks of streams and even hanging from streamside vegetation (Golden, pers. obs.). Such aggregations are probably unlikely in New Jersey, however. The best strategy for finding this species in the state would be to look under flat rocks and other debris along the banks of the Delaware River and its tributaries.

Diet

Crayfish are the queen snake's primary food source. The local abundance of crayfish in an area can regulate the presence or absence of this snake. Supplements to the diet include minnows and amphibian larvae. Queen snakes forage for their prey during both day and night (Tennant and Bartlett 2000).

Breeding Biology

Queen snakes give birth to live young during midsummer, with the typical litter size ranging from 5 to 15 snakes. At birth, the young range from 15 to 23 cm (6–9 in.) in length. Active from early May to early October in our area, large numbers of individuals of this species may form aggregations along stream banks just prior to hibernation (Wright and Wright 1957).

Status and Conservation

With its selective diet, this species is uncommon in areas where crayfish are not abundant. In some areas, however, it can be locally abundant and easily observed. As of October 2001, the last recorded sighting of this species in New Jersey dated back to 1977. Queen snakes are also listed as endangered in New York and are absent from all other northeastern states.

Limiting Factors and Threats

The physical characteristics of a habitat can greatly influence the presence and absence of this species. Shallow, swiftly flowing streams and creeks with rocky bottoms appear to comprise more suitable habitat for queen snakes than deep, slowly flowing rivers with smooth bottoms. This may be linked to the higher abundance of crayfish in swift, rocky streams and creeks. Declines in crayfish populations throughout the Northeast may partially explain the queen snake's decline in our region. Water pollution, channelization of streams and rivers, and stream bank erosion may be contributing to the decline of both crayfish and queen snakes.

Recommendations

Studies focusing on the distribution and biology of queen snakes are needed to better understand the potential threats to this species. With no recorded queen snake sightings in the state since 1977, the possibility exists that this species has been extirpated from New Jersey. Basic survey work is therefore needed to determine if this species is still present in our area. Once viable populations are identified, management plans can be developed to maintain or increase the abundance of queen snakes in New Jersey.

David M. Golden

Timber Rattlesnake, *Crotalus horridus*
Status: State: Endangered   Federal: Not listed

Identification

The timber rattlesnake is one of only two venomous reptiles found in the Garden State. The only other venomous reptile is the northern copperhead,

Timber rattlesnake.
© Breck P. Kent

Agkistrodon contortrix mokasen. The rattlesnake is unique in that it is the only animal that nature has equipped with a rattle, which is found at the end of its black-colored tail. The timber rattlesnake is a member of the family Viperidae and subfamily Crotalinae, or pit vipers. Pit vipers are aptly named for the two facial pits found midway between the nostrils and the eyes on each side of the head. In addition, its head is noticeably wider than the body portion directly behind the head. Other distinguishing characteristics include a single row of scales on the ventral, or underneath, side of the snake from the vent to the end of the tail, and vertical, elliptically shaped pupils. These features are found only on our two venomous snakes and are not found on any non-venomous species of snake found in New Jersey.

Timber rattlesnakes have dark brown to black blotches on the body section just behind the head. Moving backward from the head and neck, the blotches generally become connected and form primarily unbroken lateral crossbands, or chevrons, by the midsection of the body. The dark bands are typically outlined with a lighter color. There are actually three different color phases. On light-phase snakes, the background colors vary from brilliant to pale to brownish yellow. Intermediate-phase snakes have shades of grays, blacks, and white. Dark-phase timber rattlesnakes are almost completely black, revealing their skin patterns only from a close distance. Although difficult to see on most specimens in the Northeast, light-phase rattlesnakes have a reddish brown to olive green stripe running down the center of the dorsal (or upper) side; the intermediate-phase rattlers have an olive green stripe, while the dark phase's darkened stripe is less discernible.

In addition to the shovel-shaped head and rattle, a dark-phase rattlesnake can be differentiated from a black rat snake or black racer by its keeled scales. Black rat snakes and black racers have smooth scales. A black racer also has a small patch of white on its chin, while the black rat snake has traces of white showing throughout its body.

Distribution

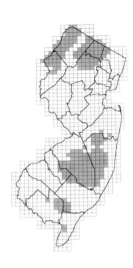

Historically, timber rattlesnakes ranged from Maine to the northern tip of Georgia. Their range extended westward to Wisconsin, Kansas, and eastern Texas (Galligan and Dunson 1979; Klauber 1997). Development, human encroachment, and wanton killings have limited the timber rattlesnakes' range, extirpating them from some of these states and endangering the survival of populations in others. The species once thrived throughout New Jersey, but currently only three disjunct regional populations remain.

Timber rattlesnake populations remain in the northwestern and north-central portion of the state and in the Pinelands of southern New Jersey. In the north, they can be found along the entire length of the Kittatinny Ridge from the Delaware Water Gap to High Point. Moving east from the Kittatinny Ridge, timber rattlesnakes are absent from the Wallkill and Paulinskill River valleys. Another population exists along the Highland ridges of eastern Sussex County, northern Morris and Passaic counties, and northwestern Bergen

County. Southern New Jersey is home to timber rattlesnakes primarily in Burlington and Ocean counties, in addition to a few sightings in Atlantic and southern Cumberland counties.

Habitat

Timber rattlesnake habitat varies greatly between northern and southern New Jersey. In the north, rattlesnakes are primarily associated with deciduous upland forest habitats (Reinert 1984a). Here rattlesnakes use hardwood and hemlock forests, seeps, open fields, floodplains, talus slopes, and rock outcrops to varying degrees based on the season and their physiological state (e.g., ecdysis—shedding their skins—their current reproductive state, etc.) (Schantz, pers. comm. 2000). In northern New Jersey the typical timber rattlesnake den is located on a rocky, sparsely to moderately wooded steep slope that faces southeast to southwest. Extensive survey work by Martin (1992) described dens in the mountainous habitat of the northeastern United States as being either a fissure in a ledge or crevice between the ground and a rock outcrop, talus slopes, or fallen rock partially covered by soil. Here snakes are able to gain access to underground cavities and voids below the frost line.

Populations in southern New Jersey are typically found in pinelands habitats that consist primarily of pitch pine (*Pinus rigida*), short-leaf pine (*P. echinata*), scrub oak (*Quercus ilicifolia*), blackjack oak (*Q. marilandica*), and blueberry (*Vaccinium* spp.). Dens in the Pinelands are usually found in cedar swamps and along stream banks.

The summer ranges of male and nongravid (not pregnant) female timber rattlesnakes typically includes forested habitats with greater than 50% canopy cover and approximately 75% vegetative ground cover (Reinert and Zappalorti 1988). Gravid females prefer areas with approximately 25% canopy cover,

A typical rattlesnake basking area in the Appalachians. © Randy Stechert

nearly equal amounts of vegetation and leaf litter covering the ground, and numerous fallen logs (Reinert and Zappalorti 1988).

Both populations hibernate in communal dens, sharing the hibernacula with other rattlesnakes as well as northern copperheads (northern population only), black rat snakes, and others (Martin 1992).

Diet

The rattlesnakes' diet consists of small mammals, including white-footed mice, red-backed voles, chipmunks, and cottontail rabbits (Reinert 1984b). Timber rattlesnakes are ambush predators. They typically lie coiled or semi-coiled at fallen logs and rocks awaiting their prey. Timber rattlesnakes will occasionally make use of man-made structures such as old barns, wood piles, and stone rows that provide good "hunting grounds" for small mammals. However, when foraging they rarely stay in one location for extended periods.

Timber rattlesnakes use hemotoxic venom to kill their prey. Hemotoxic venom is composed of numerous chemical compounds that, once injected into rattlesnake prey, travels through the bloodstream and/or lymphatic system, where it is rapidly absorbed and carried throughout the body. It affects the victim's tissues, organs, and blood. The amount of time it takes to affect prey depends on the amount of venom injected, the location of the bite, and the size of the prey.

These rattlesnakes deliver their venom—their only means of killing prey—through hollow fangs that are connected to the venom glands by elongated ducts. The snake is able to control the amount of venom injected through each fang by controlling the contraction of the muscles connected to the venom glands. The amount of venom injected is determined by the size of the prey; a snake will never completely deplete its reserve. Defensive strikes almost always result in less injection of venom than a strike made at prey.

Breeding Biology

Few studies have attempted to explain the factors that stimulate snakes to emerge from their dens in spring; however, surface air temperature does influence egress (Brown 1992). Egress from the winter den is variable among individuals and generally occurs over a period of a few weeks in the spring. Snakes generally emerge as conditions allow, basking in the early and late sunlight and returning to their crevices at night. In general, timber rattlesnakes emerge when mild weather and the surface air temperature exceed approximately 15°C (59°F) for two to seven days (Brown 1992; Martin 1992). Migration to summer ranges begins as daytime and evening temperatures remain consistently warm. Males and nongravid females generally return to the same summer range each year. Between May and July their time is spent foraging and basking, and they may shed their skins. Mature male timber rattlesnakes typically have larger home ranges than females.

Toward the end of July, the breeding season begins, and males begin to move long distances in search of mature females. Males are able to locate females by following scent trails. Females do not seek out males to breed, but continue foraging until a male locates them (Reinert and Zappalorti 1988). If the female is mature and receptive, breeding takes place, and the snakes may remain together anywhere from several hours to several days. Once breeding has concluded, the snakes separate. Male timber rattlesnakes will continue to search for receptive females. By mid- to late September, mating activity slows and mature males return their focus to foraging.

Gravid females, having bred the previous summer, emerge from their dens and forage in wooded areas near their dens or basking areas. By mid- to late June, foraging ceases and they move to basking areas, where, during the summer, they will incubate the eggs they are carrying. During this time they move into and out of the sunlight to thermoregulate their bodies to assist embryonic development. The young are born sometime between late August and early September.

Timber rattlesnakes have soft egg casings that form inside the female. When the young (neonates) are ready to be born, the egg casings break open and the female gives birth to live young.

The female stays with the young until their first shed, which occurs when they are approximately 10 to 14 days old. The female will then attempt to forage in preparation for hibernation. The neonates also forage and eventually follow scent trails of either their mother or another rattlesnake to the winter den site.

As the weather cools, timber rattlesnakes begin moving back toward their den sites. During this migration, snakes will remain in wooded areas for a better opportunity to forage (Martin 1992). Ingress—entering the den to begin hibernation—varies among individuals and occurs between mid-September and late October. After their initial entry, some individuals may periodically come out of the dens to bask before final entry into the den to hibernate.

Female timber rattlesnakes reach reproductive maturity between five and eleven years of age, usually nine or ten years in the Northeast (Brown 1993). They give birth to between six and ten young and may breed only one or two times in their lifetime. Females breed only at three- to four-year intervals because they require that much time to recover from this stressful event, during which they may lose up to 40% of their body weight (Brown 1995). At best, these traits lead to very slow population growth.

Status and Conservation

The status of timber rattlesnake populations varies among the states within its range. The timber rattlesnake is listed as a threatened or endangered species in Connecticut, Massachusetts, New Hampshire, New York, Vermont, Indiana, and Ohio (Rubio 1998). Although not listed in Pennsylvania, they are considered a candidate species for listing.

Once thriving throughout New Jersey, loss of habitat and wanton killings have limited the populations. The timber rattlesnake was listed as an endangered species in New Jersey in 1979. Under state endangered species laws, it is illegal to harm, harass, or collect the timber rattlesnake.

The entrance to this rattlesnake den in the Pine Barrens is the dark hole (lower left-center) underneath a tree root. Photo courtesy NJ ENSP

Timber rattlesnake research has been limited to the efforts of only a few biologists over the past few decades. This research has attempted to determine their habitat use, breeding biologies, activity ranges, and population genetics. Over the past two decades, research involving the timber rattlesnake in New Jersey has increased with studies being conducted along the Kittatinny Ridge and in the Pinelands. This research has helped wildlife managers and Endangered and Nongame Species Program (ENSP) biologists to better understand the needs and requirements of this cryptic and elusive species. Efforts by the ENSP are being made to limit the impact of development on rattlesnake habitat, minimize human-rattlesnake interaction, and educate the public about rattlesnakes.

The ENSP is conducting research to identify timber rattlesnake den locations and map critical habitat surrounding dens. The information is used to protect habitat through the Land Use Regulation Program within the Department of Environmental Protection.

The ENSP has instituted a nuisance venomous snake response program in areas of the state where timber rattlesnakes live in close proximity to people. Volunteers, under the authority and supervision of the state, capture and remove nuisance timber rattlesnakes that find their way into areas inhabited by people. This results in saving snakes that might normally be destroyed and provides an opportunity for the public to learn more about the species. These interactions often result in people becoming more tolerant of the species.

Limiting Factors and Threats

The primary threats to rattlesnake populations in New Jersey include habitat loss resulting from development, disturbance caused by human encroachment into rattlesnake habitat, population isolation due to development, wanton killings, and illegal collection.

Habitat loss and alteration are the most significant threats to timber rattle-snake populations in New Jersey. Unfortunately, there is little regulatory protection for upland habitat in New Jersey. Today, most viable populations of timber rattlesnakes are found relatively far from areas of dense human habitation. As development encroaches on timber rattlesnake habitat, losses increase from vehicular traffic and deliberate killings around housing developments. Given the snake's reproduction characteristics, even slight increases in mortality can remove enough adults to negate any growth in a population. Increased losses to females could have an even more profound impact on a population.

Human disturbance in and around key snake habitat (e.g., basking areas and dens) appears to have an effect on their behavior and may alter their habits. Snake behaviors at a den site in northern New Jersey appeared to be affected by the presence of researchers over a three-year period. Snakes were observed less frequently at the den talus in successive years after the research began. It is unclear what, if any, impact this disturbance could have on a population over the long term.

Recommendations

It is imperative that critical habitat for timber rattlesnakes be properly identified and protected. Critical habitat includes the den site, basking and transient habitat, and an area surrounding a den that provides suitable habitat for foraging. These areas must be protected from the pressures of human population expansion. Critical habitat can be protected through direct acquisition, conservation easements, and cooperative agreements with public and private land managers. A radius of 2.4 km (1.5 mi.) around a den is the minimum area recommended for protecting a population (Brown 1993). However, on a regional basis, sufficient areas beyond this should be protected to ensure genetic flow between individuals from surrounding dens.

Under most circumstances, the locations of dens should be kept confidential to prevent the exploitation of timber rattlesnake populations. Timber rattlesnakes are especially vulnerable during two times of the year: (1) During egress from the den in the spring (April to mid-May), and (2) in June through August, when gravid females are gestating and giving birth. At these times it is recommended that these habitats be patrolled to prevent illegal collecting by poachers.

Many people are not sympathetic to the protection and conservation of timber rattlesnake populations. Public education programs are needed to dispel current misconceptions about venomous snakes and to provide an understanding of the importance of snakes in the ecosystem (Brown 1993). As people are exposed to more accurate information about timber rattlesnakes, they are more likely to become tolerant of them and even become advocates for their protection.

Kris Schantz and Michael Valent

Four   AMPHIBIANS

Blue-Spotted Salamander, *Ambystoma laterale*
Status: State: Endangered   Federal: Not listed

Tremblay's Salamander, *A. (2) laterale-jeffersonianum*
Status: State: Endangered   Federal: Not listed

Identification

The blue-spotted salamander is a member of a group of subterranean amphibians known as "mole salamanders." Likened to the coloration and pattern of old-time enameled pots and pans, blue-spotted salamanders are dark blue with light blue flecking on the sides and tail. These salamanders have large heads with protruding eyes and robust, stocky bodies supported by sturdy limbs. Adults measure 10 to 14 cm (4–5.5 in.) in length (Conant and Collins 1991).

Blue-spotted
salamander.
© Robert Zappalorti

Distribution

The blue-spotted salamander occurs throughout southern Canada and the northeastern United States, ranging from the Gulf of St. Lawrence south to New York. In addition, disjunct populations exist in Labrador (Canada), Iowa, Long Island, and New Jersey. In New Jersey, the blue-spotted salamander is distributed in Sussex and Warren counties and within the Passaic River basin of Somerset, Essex, Morris, and Passaic counties.

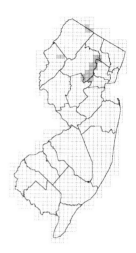

Once thought to be a distinct species, Tremblay's salamander has long been the focus of taxonomic dispute (see Lowcock et al. 1987). Because the all-female hybrid is dependent upon the blue-spotted salamander for breeding, Tremblay's salamander occurs exclusively in areas containing blue-spotted salamanders. Consequently, the only known locations of breeding Tremblay's salamanders in New Jersey are in Morris County.

Habitat

Blue-spotted salamanders inhabit mature hardwood forests such as red maple (*Acer rubrum*) swamps and oak/birch woodlands. These forests, which provide ponds suitable for breeding, are often slightly above swamp or marshland levels. They contain a deep humus layer with sandy and silt loams, gravelly, loamy sand, or muck soil types. Tree species may include pin oak (*Quercus palustris*), black oak (*Q. velutina*), northern red oak (*Q. rubra*), red maple, black willow (*Salix nigra*), and gray birch (*Betula populifolia*). Typically, the ground is littered with rotting logs, boards, rocks, or leaves, beneath which the salamanders dwell within moist depressions or subterranean burrows.

Temporary woodland ponds, marshy sedge ponds, and roadside ditches may serve as breeding pools. Ephemeral breeding ponds typically have a muddy substrate (bottom) and contain leaf litter and fallen twigs with limited wetland vegetation. Marshy breeding ponds consist of dense submergent (underwater) vegetation and tussocks of emergent vegetation. The water must be deep enough to prevent the ponds from drying up before the juveniles emerge from the water, yet be shallow enough to avoid inhabitation by predatory fish. One breeding pond located in Morris County measured 35 m (115 ft.) long by 27 m (89 ft.) wide and was 98 cm (39 in.) deep at the lowest point. Other occupied ponds in this county contained water at depths of 15 to 25 cm (6–10 in.) (Nyman et al. 1988).

Diet

The diet of adult blue-spotted salamanders includes worms, insects, snails, slugs, centipedes, and spiders. The salamander larvae feed on plankton, crustaceans, and aquatic insects. As larvae reach maturity, they are able to capture larger prey items such as tadpoles and other larval salamanders.

Breeding Biology

Warming temperatures and increased precipitation during mid- to late March trigger the movement of adult blue-spotted salamanders to breeding ponds.

Although most mating activity occurs during the first few nights affording op-timum weather conditions, reproduction may continue into early April.

Blue-spotted and Tremblay's salamanders exhibit strong fidelity to the na-tal ponds where they were born. Therefore, it is to these same ponds that the salamanders return to breed when they reach sexual maturity at two to three years of age. Their loyalty to breeding sites extends into the terrestrial stage; in New Jersey, individuals have been located 1 to 250 m (3.3 to 820 ft.) from their breeding ponds.

Following courtship, the male deposits spermatophores at the base of the pond. After collecting and fertilizing them, the female lays small clusters of eggs on twigs, leaves, or aquatic vegetation. Upon completion, the female may lay a total of 300 to 400 eggs. When breeding activity has concluded, the adults retreat to their subterranean haunts, leaving the eggs to incubate for 14 to 21 days. The larvae, which measure 12 to 15 mm (0.45–0.6 in.) upon hatching, spend the next 90 to 100 days within the pond. During June or July, the juveniles emerge and disperse to terrestrial locations.

Status and Conservation

Due to its restricted range within the state and the severe threats of habitat loss and pesticide use, the blue-spotted salamander was listed as an endan-gered species in New Jersey in 1974. The New Jersey Natural Heritage Program considers the blue-spotted salamander to be "demonstrably secure globally," yet "critically imperiled in New Jersey" (Office of Natural Lands Management 1992).

At the end of the last ice age, the ranges of the blue-spotted and another species of mole salamander, the Jefferson salamander, overlapped, which pro-duced a series of hybrids that share many of the physical characteristics of the two parent species. One of the hybrids was found to be an all-female species that required male blue-spotted salamanders to reproduce. This hybrid was known as "Tremblay's salamander." Because of its close association and supposed reliance upon blue-spotted salamanders for reproduction, Tremblay's salamander was once listed as an endangered species in New Jersey. However, recent investigation into the genetics of the hybrids demonstrated that the Tremblay's salamander was not a true species but instead part of a dynamic hybrid complex that is still in taxonomic debate (Bogart and Klemens 1997).

Limiting Factors and Threats

The primary threats facing blue-spotted salamanders in New Jersey are the loss, alteration, and degradation of quality habitat. Specialized habitat requirements and strong fidelity to breeding ponds render these salamanders especially vulnerable to habitat loss. In addition, restricted range and isolated populations can hinder their ability to recover from localized extirpations or declines. Within the Passaic River basin, a stronghold for these salamanders in New Jersey, a considerable amount of habitat has already been lost to development. An expanding network of roads bisecting forests may impede salamander movement to breeding ponds or result in road mortality of migrating adults and dispersing juveniles. These salamanders are sensitive to water quality and may therefore be negatively affected by ditching and runoff, insecticide spraying, and other pollutants.

Recommendations

Blue-spotted salamander locales, including both breeding ponds and terrestrial habitats, should be protected from development, habitat degradation,

Among the species that breed in vernal pools are blue-spotted and eastern tiger salamanders. Photo courtesy NJ ENSP

and reduction of water quality. In addition, mosquito control efforts, including insecticide spraying, should be restricted in areas where these salamanders occur.

Sherry Liguori and Jason Tesauro

Eastern Tiger Salamander, *Ambystoma tigrinum tigrinum*
Status: State: Endangered   Federal: Not listed

Identification

Each winter a prehistoric-like scene unfolds as adult tiger salamanders, resembling miniature dinosaurs, converge upon woodland ponds to breed. As its name implies, the tiger salamander is a robust amphibian with dark brown or black upperparts marked with yellow, gold, or olive blotches. The belly is olive or yellow with dark mottling. Tiger salamanders belong to a group of fossorial (burrowing) amphibians known as mole salamanders, which characteristically possess broad heads with blunt, rounded snouts that enable them to burrow underground. Tiger salamanders are equally adept in the water, using their laterally compressed tails for propulsion and steering during swimming.

The tiger salamander is the largest salamander species in New Jersey, measuring 18 to 21 cm (7–8.25 in.) long, with a maximum recorded length of 33 cm (13 in.) (Conant and Collins 1991). Adult males average 20 cm (8 in.) in length while females measure 18 cm (7 in.) (Bishop 1994). The male also has a longer tail and longer, stouter hind legs than the female.

Distribution

The tiger salamander is found throughout the United States and southern Canada. The eastern race, *tigrinum,* occurs in disjunct populations in the east-

Eastern tiger salamander.
© Blaine Rothauser

ern United States, ranging from New York south to the Gulf Coast and west to Minnesota.

In New Jersey, the eastern tiger salamander historically occurred in eight counties along the coastal plain from Toms River to Cape May and along the Delaware River south of Trenton. Although this species has been recorded in six counties within the past few decades, its current range is primarily limited to Cape May and southern Atlantic and southeastern Cumberland counties, with Cape May County serving as a population stronghold.

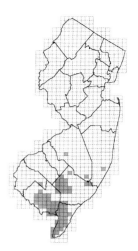

Habitat

Tiger salamanders require both upland and wetland habitats that contain suitable breeding ponds, forests, and soil types appropriate for burrowing. Subterranean throughout much of the year, these salamanders reside in underground tunnels and burrows or beneath logs. Loamy sand and sandy loam soil types are preferred for burrowing.

As natural woodland breeding ponds have been destroyed through development, dumping, and pollution, old gravel pits and farm ponds have come to serve as breeding sites for the eastern tiger salamander. These ponds must contain clean, unpolluted water and be free of fish that prey upon salamander eggs and larvae. Like numerous other vernal pond breeding species, tiger salamanders require pools that contain water long enough during the season to allow for metamorphosis, but dry up late in the summer, preventing the establishment of predatory fish populations. Consequently, breeding ponds are typically only 0.6 to 1.2 m (2–4 ft.) deep.

Terrestrial habitats occupied by the eastern tiger salamander include old fields and deciduous or mixed woods such as oak/pine or oak/holly forests. These woodlands typically have sandy or gravelly soil types and may contain willow (*Salix* spp.), holly (*Ilex opaca*), oaks (*Quercus* spp.), and pitch pine (*Pinus rigida*). Vegetation surrounding breeding ponds, such as sedges (*Carex* spp.) and sphagnum moss (*Sphagnum* spp.), as well as aquatic vegetation within the pond, provide cover for the salamanders. Ponds may have gravel, mud, sand, or clay substrates (bottoms) and pH water levels ranging from 3.5 to 7.9.

Diet

Adult tiger salamanders are opportunistic feeders, consuming various invertebrates such as insects and their larvae, fairy shrimp, worms, and spiders. Tiger salamander larvae feed on fairy shrimp, plankton, insects, insect larvae, crustaceans, mollusks, and other small invertebrates. In addition, tiger salamander larvae may consume tadpoles and larval salamanders of both their own and other species.

Breeding Biology

Mild temperatures and rain from late October to March trigger the nocturnal movement of adult tiger salamanders to their breeding ponds. Exhibiting strong site fidelity, these salamanders return to breed in the same ponds from which they metamorphosed. Tiger salamanders that are at least two to three

years of age are able to breed. Some research has suggested that individual adults may breed only every two years.

During courtship, a male swims to a female and nudges her with his snout. If receptive, the female will nudge the male, which deposits spermatophores on the bottom of the pond. The female then picks up the spermatophores in her cloaca, where the eggs are fertlilized. She then deposits egg masses within the water. The eggs are typically laid from January to mid-March. Clutch sizes range from 5 to 122 eggs and average about 50 eggs per mass. One female may lay a total of 250 to 350 eggs in five to eight different masses. The eggs are attached to twigs, stems, or rooted vegetation within the water, often at depths of 30 to 45 cm (11.8 to 17.7 in.) (Hassinger et al. 1970). Because the eggs are vulnerable to mortality from desiccation and freezing, they are deposited in areas of the pond that are less susceptible to the elements but are still warmed by sunlight.

The eggs incubate for 30 to 50 days and hatch from late March to April when water temperatures exceed 9°C (48°F). The larvae, which have feather-like external gills, measure 1.3 to 1.7 cm (0.5 to 0.7 in.) at hatching (Bishop 1994). They transform in 75 to 118 days, depending on temperature and weather conditions. Following metamorphosis, the juveniles, which measure 5.5 to 9.0 cm (2.2–3.5 in.) in length, are vulnerable to predation as they emerge from ponds (Zappalorti 1980). Most juveniles emerge during July but may occur from June to September. From the ponds, they disperse to underground tunnels or burrows.

Following breeding, adult tiger salamanders may either remain within ponds or move to uplands, seeking cover in subterranean burrows or beneath rubbish, stumps, or logs. They may excavate their own tunnels or use those of small mammals such as mice or moles. Both adults and juveniles show fidelity to breeding sites, occupying a small home range and remaining near larval

ponds outside of the breeding season. To reduce the risk of freezing, tiger salamanders may overwinter within the mud of their breeding ponds.

Status and Conservation

Habitat loss and the pollution of breeding ponds led to declines of tiger salamander populations in New Jersey. By the mid-1970s, the known historic
breeding sites had been roughly halved, to 19 sites. Consequently, the eastern
tiger salamander was listed as an endangered species in New Jersey in 1974.
The New Jersey Natural Heritage Program considers the tiger salamander to
be "demonstrably secure globally," yet "imperiled in New Jersey because of
rarity" (Office of Natural Lands Management 1992).

Currently, the status of the tiger salamander population in New Jersey remains endangered. Population stability varies by site. At many locations, numbers have declined and habitat, particularly on private land, is increasingly
threatened by encroaching development. Protected sites, such as those on
state land, appear to have stable populations.

Despite the loss of much of their natural breeding habitat, the tiger salamander has been saved from localized extinction by its ability to utilize
man-made pools as breeding ponds. As a result, management efforts have
been implemented to create additional habitat for this species. In one case,
a new population was successfully established in a pond excavated on state
land specifically for tiger salamanders. Egg masses were transferred from local ponds threatened by habitat destruction. The population has been self-
sustaining since 1988.

Efforts have been made to monitor eastern tiger salamander populations
statewide. In 1995, surveys revealed that tiger salamanders occurred at only a
limited number of sites in Atlantic and Cumberland counties.

The larvae exhibit
feathery gills. © Breck P.
Kent

Limiting Factors and Threats

The loss and degradation of both vernal ponds and wooded uplands are the primary threats facing tiger salamanders in New Jersey. Illegal dumping, in addition to filling and pollution of vernal ponds, have led to the destruction or degradation of many tiger salamander breeding sites throughout the state. Wetland disturbance favors the growth of phragmites, an invasive plant species that can dominate native emergent vegetation needed by tiger salamanders to anchor their egg masses. Pollution resulting from insecticides, runoff, and fertilizers may kill salamander eggs and larvae or render ponds uninhabitable. Development of upland forests within 300 m (approximately 1,000 ft.) of breeding ponds destroys critical habitat for nonbreeding salamanders. In addition, salamanders are more susceptible to road mortality during migration to and from breeding ponds as development increases.

Recommendations

Thorough surveys must continue to determine population trends and monitor habitat conditions. Protection or acquisition of breeding ponds and surrounding habitats is critical to the continued survival of tiger salamanders in New Jersey. Currently, wetland breeding habitats are protected through the Coastal Area Facilities Review Act (CAFRA), the Freshwater Wetlands Act, and the Pinelands Protection Act, which consider endangered species habitats in their regulations. Wooded uplands near ponds, however, receive less regulatory protection and are increasingly vulnerable to development.

The long-term survival of tiger salamander populations requires the protection of suitable habitat and the connection of sites through wooded corridors to facilitate the movement of animals between sites.

Sherry Liguori and Kathleen Clark

Long-Tailed Salamander, *Eurycea longicauda longicauda*
Status: State: Threatened   Federal: Not listed

Identification

Well deserving of its name, the long-tailed salamander has a tail that accounts for nearly two-thirds of its total length. In addition to tail size, these salamanders can be recognized by their coloration and pattern. The slender, bright yellow body is unmarked below and speckled above with black spots that form a herringbone pattern on the tail. Although typically yellow, individuals may range from orange to reddish orange and, in older specimens, brown. Speed, agility, and the ability to regenerate their tails enable long-tailed salamanders to evade potential predators. Adults measure 10 to 16 cm (4.0–6.25 in.) in length (Conant and Collins 1991).

Distribution

The long-tailed salamander occurs in the eastern United States, ranging from southern New York to Georgia, west to Arkansas, and north to Missouri and

Long-tailed salamander.
© Blaine Rothauser

Illinois. Locally, this species is found in limestone areas within the Ridge and Valley, Highlands, and Piedmont regions of northern New Jersey. Although the long-tailed salamander historically occupied a greater range in the state, since the 1990s the species has been documented only in Sussex, Warren, Hunterdon, and Union counties.

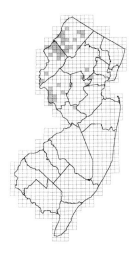

Habitat

Long-tailed salamanders inhabit clean, calcareous (limestone) spring-fed seepages, spring kettleholes, swampy floodplains, artesian wells, and ponds associated with springs. They may also reside in abandoned mines or caves that are permeated by calcareous groundwater.

Aquatic habitats occupied by long-tailed salamanders often occur within upland deciduous forests that may also contain calcareous fens, limestone outcrops, or caves. Forest types typically include mature, closed canopy maple/mixed deciduous, mixed hardwood, or hemlock/mixed deciduous woodlands. Overstory vegetation may include silver maple (*Acer saccharinum*), red maple (*A. rubrum*), yellow birch (*Betula alleghaniensis*), white oak (*Quercus alba*), sugar maple (*A. saccharum*), black walnut (*Juglans nigra*), sycamore (*Platanus occidentalis*), American elm (*Ulmus americana*), tulip poplar (*Liriodendron tulipifera*), gray birch (*B. populifolia*), basswood (*Tilia americana*), slippery elm (*Ulmus rubra*), red cedar (*Juniperus virginiana*), eastern cottonwood (*Populus deltoides*), willow (*Salix* spp.), or eastern hemlock (*Tsuga canadensis*). In addition, alder (*Alnus* spp.), sumac (*Rhus* spp.), poison ivy (*Toxicodendron radicans*), spicebush (*Lindera benzoin*), sassafras (*Sassafras albidum*), wild grape (*Vitis* spp.), rhododendron (*Rhododendron* spp.), or maple-leaved viburnum (*Viburnum acerifolium*) may comprise the shrub layer.

Herbaceous species that make up the ground cover include jewelweed (*Impatiens capensis*), smartweed (*Polygonum* spp.), skunk cabbage (*Symplocarpus foetidus*), Solomon's seal (*Polygonatum biflorum*), violets (*Viola* spp.), pickerel-weed (*Pontederia cordata*), sedge (*Carex* spp.), cattail (*Typha* spp.), may apple (*Podophyllum peltatum*), columbine (*Aquilegia canadensis*), bloodroot (*Sanguinaria canadensis*), cardinal flower (*Lobelia cardinalis*), and bulrush (*Scirpus* spp.), as well as numerous grasses and ferns. Stony loam, gravelly sandy loam, silt loam, stony silt loam, and muck gravelly loam soil types may be found at long-tailed salamander sites. On the ground, rotting logs, stones, moss, and leaf litter provide cover for the salamanders.

Diet

Comprised of an array of invertebrates, the diet of the long-tailed salamander varies with habitat type, prey abundance, and individual preference. In forests, spiders, beetles, and beetle larvae, which are found beneath bark or within crevices of rotting logs, are consumed. In mines, spiders are often abundant and therefore constitute a large portion of the diet, which may also include isopods (freshwater crustaceans), pseudoscorpions, and crickets.

Breeding Biology

During January and February, adult long-tailed salamanders mate in subterranean tunnels near springs and seepages. The female secures her clutch of approximately 90 eggs to stones or boards within water. From February to early March, the eggs hatch and the larval salamanders seek cover among rocks, moss, aquatic vegetation, leaf litter, and crevices near the seepage. If the surface dries, the salamanders may trek through crevices in search of underground water.

The larval stage of the long-tailed salamander averages 100 days but may span up to five months. Some individuals may undergo an additional year of development, transforming 14 to 15 months after hatching. In New Jersey, metamorphosis typically occurs during May and June. Following metamorphosis, the juvenile salamanders seek cover under bark, twigs, logs, and rocks near seepages.

Throughout the summer months, both adult and juvenile long-tailed salamanders remain near water, moving regularly between subterranean crevices and feeding areas on the surface. By late September and October, they retreat from pond margins and migrate to wintering sites within caves, mines, or the surrounding forest.

Status and Conservation

Due to habitat loss and pollution of larval ponds, the long-tailed salamander was listed as a threatened species in New Jersey in 1979. The New Jersey Natural Heritage Program considers this species to be "demonstrably secure globally," yet "imperiled in New Jersey because of rarity" (Office of Natural Lands Management 1992).

From the 1960s to the 1980s, biologists have conducted studies to determine the distribution, habitat use, life history, and breeding ecology of the

Clean, spring-fed streams in upland deciduous forests are prime long-tailed salamander habitat. © Robert Zappalorti

long-tailed salamander in New Jersey. Currently, surveys are conducted to monitor known sites and locate additional populations, enabling biologists to document changes in the range of this species throughout the state. The Freshwater Wetlands Protection Act and environmental reviews of proposed development afford protection to long-tailed salamander habitats in New Jersey.

Limiting Factors and Threats

Habitat loss and water-quality degradation are the primary threats facing long-tailed salamander populations in New Jersey. Unchecked development results in both direct habitat destruction as well as secondary impacts such as sedimentation and nutrient loading of freshwater ponds. Removal of trees near breeding ponds eliminates the sources of cover and shade favored by this species and results in siltation of ponds. Actions that alter the hydrology, such as filling ponds or blocking springs and seepages, jeopardize breeding habitats. In addition, draw-downs of the water table may alter spring flow and, in turn, adversely affect long-tailed salamanders. Groundwater contamination resulting from pesticides, herbicides, and roadway runoff degrades the streams and ponds needed for larval development.

Recommendations

Both the aquatic and terrestrial habitats occupied by long-tailed salamanders should be protected from development and degradation. Watersheds should be safeguarded from changes in hydrology that may alter or reduce spring flow. In addition, breeding ponds should be monitored to ensure high levels of water quality.

Sherry Liguori

Eastern Mud Salamander, *Pseudotriton montanus montanus*

Status: State: Threatened   Federal: Not listed

Identification

The eastern mud salamander is a vibrant red amphibian marked with small black spots. Body coloration and spotting vary with age, as juveniles are often bright red and lightly marked with a few, tiny spots. In contrast, the brick red or brown skin of older individuals is patterned with larger spots, which may be obscured by the darker body coloration. Adults measure 7.5 to 19.5 cm (3.0–7.7 in) in length (Petranka 1998).

Although similar in appearance to the northern red salamander (*Pseudotriton ruber*), the eastern mud salamander can be distinguished by eye color and the pattern of spotting on the body. The mud salamander has brown eyes, while those of the northern red salamander are yellow. In addition, the spots of the eastern mud salamander are separate and defined, while those of the northern red tend to fuse together.

Distribution

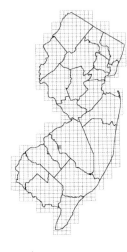

The eastern mud salamander occurs in the southeastern United States, ranging from southern New Jersey to the Carolinas and northeastern Georgia. In New Jersey, at the northern terminus of the species' range, there have only been two documented records of this salamander. The first record in the state, a specimen collected in Marlton, Burlington County, in 1953, is currently held in the American Museum of Natural History (Conant 1957). A more recent specimen was documented at Atlantic County Park when it was disgorged by a garter snake (*Thamnophis sirtalis*) captured by researchers in March 1988. Fortunately, the salamander revived and swam away in a pond.

Habitat

True to its name, the mud salamander inhabits low-elevation swamps, bogs, springs, and streams that provide a muddy substrate (bottom) as well as clear, clean water. A fossorial (burrowing) species, this salamander seeks shelter in burrows beneath leaf litter, logs, stones, or bark and may also excavate tunnels in creek banks. Mud salamanders spend much of their time in close proximity to water, yet also burrow in the soil of the surrounding forest. The specimen obtained in Burlington County was excavated from the mud of a densely vegetated ditch within a cranberry bog (Conant 1957).

Diet

The diet of adult mud salamanders is comprised of small invertebrates such as arthropods (such as insects and spiders) and earthworms and may also include salamanders. Larval mud salamanders likely feed on small aquatic invertebrates.

Breeding Biology

Due to its rarity and difficulty to detect, much information regarding the life cycle of the mud salamander in New Jersey is lacking. In other parts of its range, courtship and mating occur during late summer and early fall.

The clutch size, which increases with age, may range from 65 to nearly 200 small white eggs. The eggs are clumped together and attached to leaf litter and aquatic vegetation on the bottoms of slow-moving streams or in underwater channels within stream banks. The eggs hatch during the winter months. Female mud salamanders may skip breeding during some years, possibly due to the energetic strain of producing such a large clutch.

Mud salamanders require approximately 14 to 17 months of larval development. Some individuals undergo an additional year of growth, metamorphosing at 29 to 32 months. The larvae dwell in sluggish streams, seepages, and ponds. Newly hatched young subsist on their yolk sacs for several weeks, after which they forage on aquatic invertebrates. Although most mud salamanders transform in July and August, metamorphosis can occur from mid-May to early September. Recently transformed salamanders typically hide under leaf litter near the water's edge or beneath logs and rocks. Sexual maturity is attained at two to three years for males and at four to five years for females.

Status and Conservation

Due to its extreme rarity in the state, the eastern mud salamander was listed as a threatened species in New Jersey in 1979. The New Jersey Natural Heritage Program considers this species to be "demonstrably secure globally," yet "critically impaired in New Jersey because of extreme rarity" (Office of Natural Lands Management 1992).

Throughout the 1980s, surveys were conducted to locate mud salamander populations in southern New Jersey, particularly in the Burlington County area, where the species was first documented. Despite these efforts, there remain only two sightings of this species in the state.

Limiting Factors and Threats

Because so little is known about the eastern mud salamander in New Jersey, it is difficult to assess potential threats to this species. However, factors that endanger other salamanders, such as degradation of water quality and habitat loss, would also likely affect the mud salamander. The impacts of such threats would be compounded by this species' small population size in the state.

Recommendations

Additional surveys are needed to determine the distribution, habitat requirements, and life cycle of the eastern mud salamander in New Jersey. If the species is located, sites should be acquired or protected, high levels of water quality should be ensured, and the population should be monitored.

Sherry Liguori

Pine Barrens Treefrog, *Hyla andersonii*
Status: State: Endangered   Federal: Not listed

Identification

Vibrant green and boldly marked, the Pine Barrens treefrog is arguably one of New Jersey's most beautiful amphibians. A purple stripe with a yellowish white border extends from the snout through the eye down each side of the body. Although the underparts are white, there is a vibrant orange patch beneath each hind leg that shows a flash of color when the frog jumps. Its throat

Pine Barrens treefrog.
© Clay Myers

has a purplish tinge, which is particularly visible on the male. Adults measure 2.8 to 4.4 cm (1.13–1.75 in.) in length (Conant and Collins 1991).

The call of the Pine Barrens treefrog is a rapid and nasal *quonk-quonk-quonk*, which is repeated frequently. The series may be reiterated faster on warm evenings and slower on cool nights.

Distribution

The Pine Barrens treefrog occurs in disjunct populations within the pine barrens of the southeastern United States, residing in southern New Jersey, North Carolina, South Carolina, south-central Alabama, and along the Florida panhandle. One of the last strongholds for this species exists in the New Jersey Pinelands, where healthy populations occur in state forests, wildlife management areas, and on some private lands.

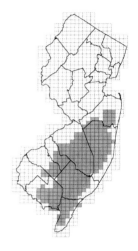

In New Jersey, the Pine Barrens treefrog is distributed within and along the periphery of the Pine Barrens ecosystem. Although the species historically occupied ten counties, it currently inhabits only nine of these: the Middlesex County population is believed to be extirpated.

Habitat

The Pine Barrens treefrog requires specialized acidic habitats, such as Atlantic white cedar (*Chamaecyparis thyoides*) swamps and pitch pine (*Pinus rigida*) lowlands that are carpeted with dense mats of sphagnum moss (*Sphagnum* spp.). Plant species found at breeding sites include those mentioned above as well as highbush blueberry (*Vaccinium corymbosum*), greenbrier (*Smilax* spp.), red maple (*Acer rubrum*), swamp azalea (*Rhododendron viscosum*), swamp magnolia (*Magnolia virginiana*), viburnums (*Viburnum* spp.), inkberry (*Ilex glabra*), mountain laurel (*Kalmia latifolia*), sheep laurel (*K. angustifolia*), blackjack oak (*Q. marilandica*), scrub oak (*Q. ilicifolia*), sundew (*Drosera* spp.), pitcher plant (*Sarracenia purpurea*), sweet pepperbush (*Clethra alnifolia*), and various orchids (*Habenaria* spp.). Structural characteristics of preferred habitats include an open canopy, a dense shrub layer, and heavy ground cover. Soil types include sands and muck.

Temporary woodland ponds, white cedar or cranberry bogs, and seepage areas along tributaries of major rivers and streams serve as breeding ponds for the Pine Barrens treefrog. Occasionally, disturbed areas—such as burrow pits, roadside ditches, vehicle ruts, or pools found along power line corridors—may be used as breeding sites, provided that appropriate shrubby and herbaceous vegetation is available. Treefrogs prefer ponds that support sphagnum moss, sedges, grasses, or aquatic plants and are surrounded by dense, woody vegetation. Breeding ponds, which may dry up by midsummer, contain shallow water, with depths often less than 60 cm (23.6 in.) and in some cases less than 10 cm (3.9 in.) (Freda and Morin 1984). The water is clean, yet acidic, with pH values ranging from 3.38 to 5.9. The preference for acidic water serves to reduce competition with other frog species that cannot tolerate this low pH.

Diet

Small invertebrates, including grasshoppers, crickets, beetles, spiders, ants, flies, and other insects, comprise the diet of adult Pine Barrens treefrogs. Tadpoles consume algae, microscopic invertebrates, and aquatic vegetation.

Breeding Biology

Warming temperatures and increased rainfall during early May stimulate the calling of male Pine Barrens treefrogs. Vocal activity, which may be initiated prior to sunset, peaks during humid June evenings when temperatures exceed 20°C (68°F) (Hulmes et al. 1981). Males may vocalize from the ground or within vegetation near the breeding pond. Tagged individuals in New Jersey have been heard from the same location on different evenings (Freda and Morin 1984; Freda and Gonzalez 1986). During the breeding season, Pine Barrens treefrogs hide within ground cover or perch in trees during the day and emerge at night to forage. Although a few individuals may call into mid-July, vocal activity typically concludes by the beginning of the month.

To minimize the risk of losing an entire clutch, female treefrogs lay each egg singly. Upon completion, one female may deposit a total of 1,000 eggs. The eggs, which are then fertilized by the male, may either be attached to

Pine Barrens treefrog breeding habitat.
© Robert Zappalorti

aquatic vegetation or deposited on the bottom of a pond. Within one to two weeks, they hatch into tadpoles.

Depending on weather conditions and rainfall, the tadpoles transform into tailed "froglets" within 80 to 100 days. Fat reserves stored in the tail sustain the froglets until they are able to capture their own prey. Following transformation during late July, August, or sometimes September, juvenile frogs disperse into woods, bogs, and wet meadows.

After breeding activity has been completed, adult treefrogs move to the surrounding forest, where they remain for the duration of the season. They may disperse more than 106 m (348 ft.) from breeding ponds (Freda and Gonzalez 1986).

Although little is known about the wintering ecology of Pine Barrens treefrogs, it is believed that they hibernate under bark, amid tree root holes, or in the muddy bottoms of ponds.

Status and Conservation

In 1979, the Pine Barrens treefrog was listed as an endangered species in New Jersey due to its restricted range and declining population, habitat loss, and the pollution of breeding ponds. The New Jersey Natural Heritage Program considers this species to be "apparently secure globally," yet "rare in New Jersey" (Office of Natural Lands Management 1992).

Although endangered, the Pine Barrens treefrog is currently considered stable in New Jersey. Because of large expanses of protected habitat within the Pinelands National Reserve of southern New Jersey, the state serves as a stronghold for this species throughout its entire range. In areas of suitable habitat, particularly on public land, Pine Barrens treefrogs may seem abundant. However, protection of this species is warranted, as suitable habitat is limited to specialized Pine Barrens ecosystems that are patchily distributed throughout the southeastern United States.

Limiting Factors and Threats

Habitat loss, wetlands draining and filling, and water pollution, especially from nonpoint sources such as residential and agricultural runoff, are the primary threats facing the Pine Barrens treefrog in New Jersey. Throughout its range, unchecked development has resulted in the degradation and eradication of high-quality wetlands and increases in nonpoint source water pollution that alters water quality and may increase pH levels. These changes improve habitat conditions for predators and competitors of the Pine Barrens treefrog. Factors that threaten the Pine Barrens aquifer, including pollution and lowering of the water table, may also endanger this frog. For example, habitat loss, coupled with chemical and waste water pollution, is thought to have caused the extirpation of the Middlesex County population. Specialized habitat requirements and fragmented populations render the Pine Barrens treefrog especially vulnerable to habitat destruction.

Because the Pine Barrens treefrog prefers acidic water, changes in pH may restrict breeding activity or prohibit larval development. Increased pH levels favor the inhabitation of bullfrogs (*Rana catesbeiana*), a competitor and predator of both larval and adult Pine Barrens treefrogs. As a late breeding species, the Pine Barrens treefrog is especially vulnerable to predation from tadpoles of earlier breeding species.

Recommendations

Because it is critically linked to the Pine Barrens ecosystem, the Pine Barrens treefrog serves as a barometer for the health of this region. Thus, efforts that favor this species, such as water-quality protection and habitat preservation, will benefit a distinct community that relies on this unique ecosystem.

Sherry Liguori

Southern Gray Treefrog, *Hyla chrysoscelis*
Status: State: Endangered   Federal: Not listed

Identification

The southern gray treefrog is an arboreal amphibian equipped with large toe pads enabling it to cling to trees. Also known as Cope's gray treefrog, this species has a robust body, stubby limbs, and a short rounded head with large eyes. Ranging in pigment from dark gray, brown, and light gray to nearly white, these treefrogs can alter their coloration based on their activities or environmental conditions. Dark blotches that speckle the warty gray skin of the upperside resemble bark and help camouflage the treefrog when it is perched on a trunk or branch. Although the underside is white, the inner thigh is brilliant orange or gold with black speckling, radiating a flash of color when the frog

Southern gray treefrog.
© Robert Zappalorti

jumps that may startle potential predators. Gray treefrogs also have a white or yellow mark beneath each eye. The male has a dark throat while that of the female is white. The largest treefrog in the state, the southern gray measures 3.2 to 5.1 cm (1.25–2.0 in.) in length (Conant and Collins 1991).

In New Jersey, two species of gray treefrogs occur—the northern (*Hyla versicolor*) and the southern (*H. chrysoscelis*). Nearly identical in appearance, these treefrogs can be differentiated only by vocal or chromosomal analysis. The call of the southern gray, a resounding trill, is faster and higher pitched than that of the northern gray.

Distribution

The composite range of both gray treefrog species spans eastern North America from southern Maine to northern Florida, west to southern Manitoba and central Texas. Further vocal analysis is needed to accurately separate the ranges of these two similar species.

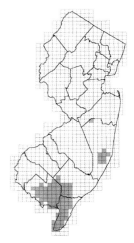

In New Jersey, the southern gray treefrog is limited to Cape May, Cumberland, Atlantic, and Ocean counties. Within this area, most populations are located in Middle and Lower townships of southern Cape May County. The southern gray treefrog, which was historically recorded in Cape May and Cumberland counties, was not discovered in Atlantic County until 1991 and in Ocean County until 1995. Its counterpart, the northern gray treefrog, occurs throughout New Jersey and overlaps with the southern gray in the southerly counties.

Habitat

Southern gray treefrogs require both aquatic and terrestrial habitats, relying on small freshwater ponds, old fields, and hardwood forests throughout their annual cycle. Accepting both natural and man-made basins, they breed in vernal ponds, gravel pits, retention basins, floodplain corridors, bogs, weedy lakes, cattail (*Typha* spp.) or sedge (*Carex* spp.) marshes, and farm ponds. Breeding pools must contain water long enough to ensure metamorphosis but often dry up by the end of summer, thereby prohibiting the establishment of predatory fish.

Breeding ponds are located within or near deciduous or mixed woodlands such as climax oak/pine forests. Tree species found in the forest overstory at New Jersey southern gray treefrog locales may include scarlet oak (*Quercus coccinea*), willow oak (*Q. phellos*), white oak (*Q. alba*), scrub oak (*Q. ilicifolia*), blackjack oak (*Q. marilandica*), red maple (*Acer rubrum*), sweet gum (*Liquidambar styraciflua*), black gum (*Nyssa sylvatica*), pitch pine (*Pinus rigida*), shortleaf pine (*P. echinata*), Virginia pine (*P. virginiana*), willow (*Salix* spp.), white cedar (*Chamaecyparis thyoides*), and American holly (*Ilex opaca*). Low shrubs and brushy wet thickets consisting of buttonbush (*Cephalanthus occidentalis*), huckleberry (*Gaylussacia* spp.), highbush blueberry (*Vaccinium corymbosum*), alder (*Alnus* spp.), inkberry (*Ilex glabra*), greenbrier (*Smilax* spp.), and cattail may comprise the understory. Ground cover may consist of sphagnum moss

(*Sphagnum* spp.), star moss (*Mnium* spp.), club moss (*Lycopodium* spp.), sundew (*Drosera* spp.), and pitcher plant (*Sarracenia purpurea*), as well as various species of forbs and grasses.

Diet

Southern gray treefrogs rest during the day and emerge at night to forage. As skilled climbers, they feed on flying insects as well as those found hidden amid branches and leaves. Flies, mosquitoes, gnats, spiders, and ants, in addition to other insects and insect larvae, are included in the diet. Southern gray treefrog tadpoles feed on algae within their natal ponds.

Breeding Biology

In late April and early May, nighttime temperatures exceeding 17°C (63°F) stimulate the vocal activity of southern gray treefrogs. Although they may call from late April to mid-August, choruses peak during warm, humid evenings in May or June. Males may vocalize from trees, shrubs, or the ground to attract females to breeding ponds.

The female deposits individual eggs or groups of up to 40 eggs on aquatic vegetation and leaf litter within a breeding pond; they are then fertilized by the male. When complete, the female will have laid a total of nearly 2,000 eggs. By laying eggs singly or in small clumps, the female reduces the likelihood of losing an entire clutch to predation or desiccation. The eggs hatch in four to five days and metamorphosis occurs in 80 to 100 days. Following emergence, the young frogs disperse into nearby fields and forests.

During July and August, adult treefrogs migrate to terrestrial habitats where they have been documented more than 91 m (300 ft.) from their breeding ponds. Here, they dwell in tree cavities, underneath bark, in rotting logs, beneath leaf litter, or inside underground burrows, where they will remain over the winter. Gray treefrogs are able to withstand freezing and thawing due to an "antifreeze" present in their blood.

Status and Conservation

Because of its limited distribution in the state and the destruction of its habitat, the southern gray treefrog was listed as an endangered species in New Jersey in 1979. The New Jersey Natural Heritage Program considers the southern gray treefrog to be "demonstrably secure globally," yet "imperiled in New Jersey because of rarity" (Office of Natural Lands Management 1992).

Over the past 20 years, biologists have conducted research to determine the distribution, habitat use, and breeding ecology of the southern gray treefrog in New Jersey. Currently, efforts are being made to protect treefrog habitats on a comprehensive landscape level as well as on an individual wetland basis. Documented breeding ponds, as well as surrounding buffers of 150 to 300 feet, are protected under New Jersey land-use regulations, including the Freshwater Wetlands Act and the Coastal Area Facilities Review Act (CAFRA).

Limiting Factors and Threats

As industrial and residential development encroach upon vulnerable habitats, the destruction of both forests and woodland ponds threatens southern gray treefrog populations in New Jersey. Small ponds, particularly those on private property, are vulnerable to illegal filling. Although current land-use regulations protect wetlands, many upland habitats remain vulnerable: treefrogs require both wetlands and the adjacent forested uplands. In the Cape May peninsula alone, 40% of forest, scrub-shrub, and grassland habitat was lost between 1972 and 1992. Habitat loss is often coupled with degradation of water quality, as runoff, wastewater effluent, leaching of toxic chemicals, and illegal dumping all pollute ponds.

Predation of treefrog eggs and larvae within breeding ponds may limit populations. Mosquito fish (*Gambusia affinis*), which are released into ponds to control mosquitoes, are predators of anuran (frog and toad) eggs and larvae.

Recommendations

Because the southern gray treefrog and the endangered eastern tiger salamander (*Ambystoma tigrinum tigrinum*) occupy similar habitats, management and protection efforts can benefit both of these imperiled species. To maintain genetic diversity, the southern gray treefrog has the ability and long-term necessity to move between breeding ponds and colonize suitable new ponds within the same wetland complex. Thus, management for viable, sustained populations must include the protection of wetland areas surrounding occupied ponds in order to provide additional habitat and to maintain genetic diversity.

In suitable habitat where southern gray treefrogs occur, artificial ponds can be excavated in fields near wooded edges to provide additional breeding habitat. Such ponds should be dug approximately 60 m (200 ft.) long by 30 m (100 ft.) wide, with a bottom that gradually slopes from 0.3 to 1.5 m (1–5 ft.) (Zappalorti and Johnson 1981). In addition, a 1.8 m (6 ft.) wide and 2.1 m (7 ft.) deep trench should be excavated in the center of the pond to provide water during extremely dry seasons (Zappalorti and Johnson 1981). Although artificial ponds may provide supplemental habitat, they should not be created as a substitute for existing natural ponds. Habitat protection must be the highest priority.

Sherry Liguori

Five   *FISH*

Shortnose Sturgeon, *Acipenser brevirostrum*
Status: State: Endangered   Federal: Endangered

Identification

The shortnose sturgeon has a short and bluntly rounded snout, wide mouth, barbels, numerous dorsal, lateral, and ventral scutes (bony or horny plates), and a heterocercal tail (the upper lobe of the tail fin is larger and contains the upturned end of the spinal column). Typically, the body is yellowish brown to nearly black on the head, back, and sides level to lateral plates, and whitish to yellowish below. Length at initial maturity for this species is 45 to 55 cm (18–22 in.) fork length, from the snout to the middle of the tail for males and females (Dadswell et al. 1984). Maximum known fork lengths are nearly 124 cm (49 in.) for a female and nearly 99 cm (39 in.) for a male. In New Jersey, 28 tagged males ranged between 53 and nearly 89 cm (21–35 in.) fork length.

Genevieve E. O'Herron with a shortnose sturgeon captured in the nontidal portion of the Delaware River north of Trenton, N.J. Photo by Joshua D. Ingram, courtesy John C. O'Herron II

Distribution

The shortnose sturgeon is an anadromous species (migrates from salt to fresh waters to spawn) that inhabits large estuaries and near-shore waters along the Atlantic Coast from New Brunswick, Canada, to the St. John River, Florida (Brundage and Meadows 1982). In New Jersey, specimens have been recorded from the Delaware River, Delaware Bay, Maurice River, Dividing Creek, and Sandy Hook Bay (Dadswell et al. 1984).

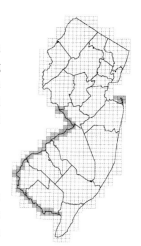

Habitat

River mouths, tidal rivers, estuaries, and bays serve as prime habitat for the shortnose sturgeon. In addition, individuals occasionally enter the open ocean. A significant portion of New Jersey's shortnose sturgeon population occurs in the upper tidal Delaware River (Dadswell et al. 1984).

Diet

Feeding shortnose sturgeon, especially young, vacuum the bottom with a protruding mouth, extracting substrate along with animals. Adult sturgeon have also been observed feeding off plant surfaces. According to Dadswell et al. (1984), juvenile shortnose sturgeon eat available benthic (bottom-dwelling) crustaceans and insects, whereas prey items of adults are more variable and reflect the prey base of certain regions. Adults of the species have been reported to consume insects, bivalve mollusks, snails, polychaetes (marine worms), benthic crustaceans, small flounder, and a variety of other organisms.

Breeding Biology

Eggs of the shortnose sturgeon are demersal (found on or near the bottom) and adhesive, hatching about 13 days after fertilization (Meehan 1910). Hatching larvae are tadpole-like and about 7.3 to 11.3 mm (2.9–4.5 in.) with an attached yolk sac (Taubert 1980; Dadswell et al. 1984). Larvae and juveniles are benthic, typically occupying deep channels with strong currents (Dadswell 1979). Depending on latitude, sturgeon may grow between 14 and 30 cm by the end of the first growing season. Young sturgeon remain juveniles until they are 3 to 10 years old, or until 45 to 55 cm (49.5–60.5 in.) fork length (Dadswell et al. 1984). Males typically begin spawning one to two years after maturity, but female spawning can be delayed for five years (Dadswell 1979). Once sturgeon achieve adult size, they begin migratory behavior, moving upstream in spring to spawn and downstream in fall. The oldest individuals of the species ever recorded were a 67-year-old female and a 32-year-old male, both from the St. John River, Canada (Dadswell 1979).

According to O'Herron et al. (1993), shortnose sturgeon in the Delaware River overwinter from November to late March in the area of Duck and Newbold islands but extensively use the channel area immediately off Duck Island. Analysis of sonic tagging data showed that sturgeon become active in mid- to late March and move upstream between Trenton Rapids and

Scudders Falls, where spawning presumably occurs from late March through April. After spawning, the fish apparently travel downstream into the tidal portion of the river near Philadelphia, remaining in the area through May. Sturgeon of both sexes were observed to move upstream near Trenton by the end of June, reentering the upper tidal river and remaining for the summer and winter. In 1987 Hastings et al. reported a population of 6,000 to 14,000 shortnose sturgeon inhabiting the upper tidal Delaware River.

Status and Conservation

The shortnose sturgeon has been federally listed as endangered since the inception of the Endangered Species Act in 1973, when it was also considered endangered in New Jersey. The Office of Natural Lands Management (1992) ranks the species as "rare in New Jersey" and "either very rare and local throughout its range or found locally in a restricted range or because of other factors making it vulnerable to extinction throughout its range."

This species is afforded protection under both federal and state Endangered Species acts, Clean Water acts, fishing regulations, and environmental review of proposed development projects.

Limiting Factors and Threats

Maintenance dredging and water quality degradation associated with development are potential threats to the Delaware River shortnose sturgeon. Predation of early life stages by other fish species may be an additional limiting factor to the population. There is also a potential risk for early life stages to be inadvertently caught up in water intake systems from the vicinity of Scudders Falls seaward. The population is especially at risk during the winter and early spring, when shortnose sturgeon occur in dense aggregations that may number a few thousand individuals (more than a significant portion of the population) within localized areas of the overwintering and spawning grounds (John O'Herron, pers. comm. 1994).

Recommendations

Data on the occurrence of shortnose sturgeon eggs and larvae in the Delaware River are lacking. Also, locations and habits of smaller juvenile sturgeon have yet to be documented in the river and are necessary in order to determine critical areas for these early life stages. This lack of information remains a serious problem in completely assessing impacts of human activities such as maintenance dredging on the species.

Critical areas in the Delaware River for early-life-stage shortnose sturgeon should be identified through intensive sampling for eggs, larvae, and younger juveniles. In addition, research on sturgeon movement patterns should be conducted to determine if this species is utilizing more southern portions of the river as a result of improved water quality in the vicinity of Philadelphia.

Jeanette Bowers-Altman

Northeastern Beach Tiger Beetle, *Cicindela d. dorsalis*
Status: State: Endangered   Federal: Threatened

Identification

Distinguishing features of the northeastern beach tiger beetle include a bronze green head and thorax and white to light tan elytra (forewings), often with dark lines. Typically 1.2 to 1.5 cm (0.5–0.6 in.) in length, it is considered to be one of four subspecies of *C. dorsalis* (Cazier 1954; USFWS 1994).

Distribution

Although once abundant along beaches from Martha's Vineyard to New Jersey, the northeastern beach tiger beetle is now extirpated in Rhode Island, Connecticut, and New York. There are only two natural populations of the species north of the Chesapeake Bay: Buzzard's Bay and Martha's Vineyard,

A pair of northeastern beach tiger beetles mate on a N.J. beach. Photo courtesy USFWS.

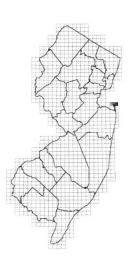

both in Massachusetts. In New Jersey, there is a small northeastern tiger beetle population at Gateway National Recreation Area at Sandy Hook due to ongoing translocation experiments sponsored by the USFWS (Knisley and Hill 1998). Despite regional extirpations, the Chesapeake Bay area has exhibited an increase in the number of known occurrences for the species (USFWS 1994).

Habitat

Although there are no definable indicators of northeastern beach tiger beetle habitat, this species is found on long, wide, dynamic, relatively undisturbed sandy beaches of the Atlantic Coast or Chesapeake Bay (Hill and Knisley 1994).

Diet

According to Knisley and Hill (pers. obs., as cited in USFWS 1994), northeastern beach tiger beetles scavenge much of their food from dead amphipods (marine invertebrates), crabs, and fish. They are also successful predators, using sicklelike mandibles to capture small amphipods, flies, and other beach arthropods such as spiders (USFWS 1994).

Breeding Biology

Northeastern beach tiger beetles mate and lay eggs from late June through August. Ovipositing females are thought to lay their eggs at night in shallow, vertical burrows within the mid- to above-high tidal drift zone (Knisley and Hill pers. obs., as cited in USFWS 1994).

After hatching from eggs laid by the breeding adults, northeastern beach tiger beetle larvae appear in late July and August, with larvae passing through three developmental stages (instars). The larvae of this species inhabit vertical burrows, where they sit and wait for small prey to pass by (USFWS 1994).

Tiger beetle larvae reach their second instar by September, remaining active for most of November (some larvae are third instar by this month). Third instar larvae also become active during the fall, after a period of inactivity during the summer. All larvae of the species hibernate in winter and emerge in mid-March (USFWS 1994).

For those beetles that haven't already done so, progression to third instar larvae will continue for an additional year. Most third instar tiger beetle larvae will emerge in June, almost two years after they were laid as eggs (early hatchers with an abundant food source may emerge after one year). Third instar larvae from the previous year will emerge in June as adults (USFWS 1994).

Status and Conservation

Listed as federally threatened in 1990 and state endangered in 1991, the northeastern beach tiger beetle receives regulatory protection from both federal and state Endangered Species acts. In addition, habitat protection is afforded through the Coastal Areas Facilities Review Act and other coastal regulations. The Natural Heritage Program ranks the species as "critically imperiled in New Jersey because of extreme rarity."

Since 1994, the USFWS has supported studies designed to reestablish populations of the northeastern beach tiger beetle in the Northeast. Experiments to establish translocation techniques were conducted at the Gateway National Recreation Area at Sandy Hook by researchers from Randolph-Macon College in Virginia. During these studies, tiger beetle larvae from the Chesapeake Bay area were translocated to several beach sites within the recreation area and routinely monitored. Initial results from the experiments indicated that the translocation techniques employed could be used to establish a population of northeastern beach tiger beetles at Sandy Hook and possibly at other sites in the Northeast (Knisley and Hill 1997). A program to reintroduce the species at Gateway National Recreation Area has been under way since 1997 (Knisley and Hill 1998).

Limiting Factors and Threats

The northeastern beach tiger beetle is most susceptible to disturbance during its two-year larval stage. During this time, larvae live in vertical burrows in the intertidal zone of the beach (USFWS 1994). Human activities associated with recreational beach use, destruction and disturbance of natural beach habitat from shoreline development, and beach stabilization structures are contributing factors leading to larval disturbance and, ultimately, to the tiger beetle's extirpation throughout most of its range (Knisley et al. 1987). Other threats to the species include off-road vehicles (Knisley and Hill 1992); beach erosion, both natural and human induced (USFWS 1994); oil slicks; flood tides; and hurricanes (Stamatov 1972, as cited in USFWS 1994).

Recommendations

Efforts to reintroduce the northeastern beach tiger beetle through translocation techniques should continue at Gateway National Recreation Area and be expanded to other coastal areas with suitable habitat.

Jeanette Bowers-Altman

American Burying Beetle, *Nicrophorus americanus*
Status: State: Endangered   Federal: Endangered

Identification

The American burying beetle is the largest native member of the carrion beetle family Silphidae, of which there are 31 species in North America and 570 species worldwide (Ratcliffe 2001). Adults range in length from 25 to 35 mm (1.0–1.5 in.) and average 30 mm (1.2 in.). Its coloration, orange-red on shiny black, is distinctive. One colored mark covers the frons, an upper frontal head plate, and another covers the pronotum, the shieldlike area just behind the head (Ratcliffe 2001). The black wings have two pairs of scalloped red spots, and the antenna tips are orange. Below the frons, males have a distinguishing

large orange-red rectangular facial mark, while females have a smaller triangular mark.

Swarms of orange-colored mites, which keep the beetles and carcasses they feed upon clean of microbes and fly eggs, are often present on the beetles' bodies (NYDEC 2001).

Distribution

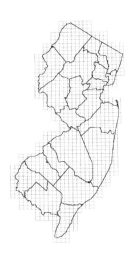

Historically, the American burying beetle ranged from the southern fringes of Ontario, Quebec, and Nova Scotia through 35 eastern and central U.S. states, including New Jersey. Based on dated collection specimens, the beetles became quite rare east of the Appalachians between the late 1800s and the 1920s, with the last known historic locations documented in the early 1940s. In the Midwest, the decline occurred later, proceeding from the center of its range outward. During the 1960s and 1970s, all collections in this region occurred on the periphery of the range.

In New Jersey, the most recent record was a specimen collected in Hightstown, Mercer County, in 1919. Between 1896 and 1910, beetles were also recorded in Camden, Gloucester, Ocean, and Sussex counties, with two undated records attributed to Essex County (Raithel 1991).

Today, the beetle is found in just seven states and is absent from more than 90% of its historic range. East of the Mississippi the only known naturally occuring population exists on Block Island, Rhode Island. Reintroduced populations of captively bred American burying beetles are present on Penikese and Nantucket islands in Massachusetts. American burying beetles from Arkansas also have been translocated and released in southeastern Ohio (1998–2000) in a three-year effort to reestablish the species there (Michael Amaral, pers. comm. 2001). West of the Mississippi, the beetle's stronghold appears to be centered in 14 eastern Oklahoma counties and four western Arkansas counties. Other smaller populations have been located in Kansas, Nebraska, and South Dakota.

Habitat

Whether it is coastal grassland/scrub in the East or prairie or savannah-like oak/hickory forests with open understories in the Midwest, American burying beetles require landscapes that are open enough to allow a large beetle with limited flight maneuverability to be active at night.

Diet

American burying beetles consume a wide range of food, from vertebrate carrion of varying size to insects. The antennae of American burying beetles have receptors capable of detecting chemicals emitted by dead vertebrates. From as much as two miles away, they can locate a dead mouse within an hour of its death (Ratcliffe 2001). When not brood rearing, adults may also feed on live insects. In captivity, adults consume about one live mealworm per day, while newly enclosed (emerged) adult beetles consume four to six live mealworms per day (Wetzel 2001).

Breeding Biology

To reproduce successfully, the American burying beetle requires the largest vertebrate carcass of any member of the burying beetle genus. Adults are active between late April and September; on Block Island, most breeding activity occurs in June and July. Airborne only at night, usually only when nighttime temperatures exceed 15.6°C (60°F), the adults fly about seeking odors of recently deceased vertebrates (Raithel 1991). If the carcass is of the right size —80 to 200 g (2.8–7 oz.), about the size of a mourning dove, an American woodcock, a ring-necked pheasant chick, or small mammal such as a young cottontail rabbit—a male and female pair up (Amaral and Prospero 1999). The process usually begins soon after dark. Even though the carcass can weigh 200 times their body weight, the pair moves the carcass as much as a meter and buries it, or they bury it where they found it, usually before dawn to stymie competing predators and flies.

The pair also cleans the carcass of feathers or fur and coats it with anal and oral secretions to preserve it. The female then lays 10 to 30 eggs in a brood chamber adjacent to the carcass, which then becomes food for the larvae (Ratcliffe 2001). The size of the carcass is critical: the larger the carcass, the greater the number of larva that survive. Adults may cannibalize some larvae if the carcass is not of sufficient size to support all of the growing brood.

Showing a degree of parental care quite rare in nonsocial insects, the female stays with the larvae and tends and feeds them for 10 to 14 days until the carcass is completely consumed and the larvae development is completed. Males also remain for about a week, also regurgitating food and guarding the brood and carcass from other beetles and intruders (Raithel 1991).

Crawling up into the soil and encasing themselves into a pupa case, the larvae metamorphose into beetles and emerge as adults about 48 to 60 days after the carcass burial. These teneral (just-emerged) adults are capable of breeding four to six weeks later, and might do so during the same season in the central United States. But during the shorter season on Block Island, they overwinter as adults and breed the following year. As for the adults, males and females might breed once more, but both will soon die (Raithel 1991).

Status and Conservation

The prevailing theory indicates habitat fragmentation was largely responsible for the American burying beetle's decline (Raithel 1991). Such fragmentation reduced or eliminated prey species favored for breeding carrion, such as passenger pigeons, wild turkeys, and prairie chickens. Meanwhile, the resulting increase in "edge" habitat increased the number of scavengers competing with the beetles for the carrion, such as the American crow, raccoon, fox, opossum, and skunk (Michael Amaral, pers. comm. 2001).

The American burying beetle was listed as federally endangered in 1989. Even though it apparently has been extirpated from New Jersey, the state listed the beetle as threatened in the same year due to the federal listing.

At the time of the federal listing, the beetle was known to occur naturally only on Block Island off Rhode Island and in one Oklahoma county. Subsequently, the USFWS required surveys during environmental planning for proposed developments in eastern Oklahoma and western Arkansas. As a result of these surveys, several additional populations were found.

In the East, attempts have been made to expand the population by breeding adults captured on Block Island and reintroducing their offspring on two Massachusetts islands, Penikese and Nantucket. Building on the early experience of Boston University, zookeepers at the Roger Williams Park Zoo in Providence, Rhode Island, have since raised more than 25 generations of American burying beetles.

Like Block Island, both Penikese and Nantucket islands are free of predators such as foxes, raccoons, skunks, and coyotes, which would compete with the beetles for carcasses. As of 2001, it was still unclear, however, whether the reintroduced populations had become self-sustaining. Eight years after the end of a four-year reintroduction program on 70-acre Penikese Island, beetles could still be found. But, considering adults appear capable of traveling a kilometer per night, determining the status of the reintroduced population on much-larger Nantucket Island is much more difficult (Michael Amaral, pers. comm. 2001).

Limiting Factors and Threats

Loss and fragmentation of habitat and increase in predators that compete with beetles for decreasing numbers of species that provide carrion for the American beetle continue to limit the potential for recovery of the country's largest carrion beetle. Pesticide use, light pollution, the spread of fire ants, and population isolation are additional threats that must be overcome for a successful recovery.

Recommendations

Existing populations should continue to be monitored and protected from development and habitat alteration. In areas of likely habitat, more surveys should be conducted, particularly in states such as Kentucky and Missouri, where the beetles were documented fairly recently (1974 and the early 1980s, respectively). Particular attention should be paid to large military bases and protected lands, such as state wildlife management areas and state and national forests and parks, which appear to have acted as refuge "islands" in some areas for the beetles. Likely habitats free of predators should also be considered for the reintroduction of captively bred beetles.

Research into other potential factors, such as the impact of artificial lights —which attract and disorient many species of nocturnal insects—might also aid recovery efforts.

Bruce E. Beans

LEPIDOPTERA

Appalachian Grizzled Skipper, *Pyrgus wyandot*
Status: State: Endangered   Federal: Not listed

Identification

The Appalachian grizzled skipper is a small (29–33 mm, or 1.1–1.3 in.) grayish black skipper that is endangered within New Jersey. This skipper is difficult to distinguish from the more ubiquitous common checkered skipper (*P. communis*), but the Appalachian grizzled skipper is slightly smaller and has fewer white markings on its wings. The white markings on the upperwing surface

Appalachian grizzled skipper. © Rick Cech

also tend to be somewhat less aligned in the Appalachian grizzled skipper. The flight period of the adults can also be helpful in distinguishing this species from the common checkered skipper (see Breeding Biology, below). Once considered a subspecies of the grizzled skipper (*P. centaureae*), the Appalachian grizzled skipper's status as a separate species was proposed by Shapiro (1974) and is now accepted by many lepidopterists based on differences in the genitalia, larval characteristics, and habitat preferences of the two species.

Distribution

The distribution of this species is largely restricted to the Mid-Atlantic region of the United States, with the western boundary of its range extending into Michigan, Ohio, and Kentucky. Its north-south range extends from New York to North Carolina.

Habitat

The Appalachian grizzled skipper is found in open, sparsely grassed and barren areas in close proximity (usually less than 30 m, or 100 ft.) to oak or pine forests (Schweitzer 1989a). The presence of its larval host plant, dwarf cinquefoil (*Potentilla canadensis*), is also an important habitat requirement for this species (but see Diet).

Diet

According to Iftner et al. (1992), the larval host plant for the Appalachian grizzled skipper in Michigan appears to be wild strawberry (*Fragaria virginiana*). Throughout the rest of its species range, however, larvae feed exclusively on dwarf cinquefoil. Adults are less host specific and will feed on the nectar of a variety of plants, including dwarf cinquefoil, wood vetch (*Vicia caroliniana*), coltsfoot (*Tussilago farfara*), spring beauty (*Claytonia virginica*), and birdsfoot violet (*Viola pedata*) (Iftner et al. 1992; Schweitzer 1989b).

Breeding Biology

Adults become active in early April and may remain active throughout the month of May in the northern portions of their range. In New Jersey, most of the adult flight activity has ceased by early to mid-May. Flight activity of the adults also appears to be restricted to cool days during this period (Schweitzer 1994). The flight period of this species is a helpful diagnostic feature in differentiating the Appalachian grizzled skipper from the common checkered skipper, which can be seen flying into early November. Adults lay eggs singly on the leaves of host plants, and the tan to pinkish caterpillars (Allen 1998) have an active period of about 100 days (Schweitzer 1994).

Status and Conservation

This skipper was once distributed throughout the northern quarter of the state, with the greatest number of records coming from the Paterson/Great Notch area of Passaic County. From specimen records, this species began to show a rapid decline in the 1940s and 1950s. The last New Jersey specimens were collected in Warren County in 1960. Insecticide applications to control Dutch elm disease, gypsy moths, and mosquitoes have probably eliminated this species from our fauna. Increasing deer populations may also have had an impact on this species by overbrowsing its host plants (David Iftner, pers. comm. 2001).

The Appalachian grizzled skipper was listed as endangered under the New Jersey Endangered Species Conservation Act in 2001.

Limiting Factors and Threats

With its ability to disperse long distances, this species could respond to management programs quite well. Currently, a major limiting factor for this species is the availability of suitable habitat that is not sprayed for gypsy moths.

Recommendations

Existing populations of Appalachian grizzled skippers must be monitored, and suitable habitats throughout the state should be surveyed in an effort to identify new populations. Furthermore, because this species will likely respond well to management efforts, a reasonable recommendation would be to manage suitable areas for the proliferation of this species. Such an effort would no doubt involve limiting insecticide spraying for gypsy moth caterpillars as well as maintaining appropriate host-plant communities. Additional research on the life history of this species would also contribute to the overall success of any proposed management plan.

David M. Golden

Arogos Skipper, *Atrytone arogos arogos*
Status: State: Endangered   Federal: Not listed

Identification

Arogos skippers range in size from 35 to 41 mm (1.3–1.4 in.) and look very similar to the more abundant Delaware skipper (*Anatrytone logan*). Both species have a light orange base color with black wing margins on their upper surface, but the margins on the arogos tend to be slightly thicker than those of the Delaware skipper. The white fringe on the underside of the arogos skipper's hindwing and deeper orange coloration on the undersurface of the wings are also useful characteristics to help naturalists distinguish between the two species. Because differentiating between arogos skippers and Delaware skippers can be difficult, readers should refer to the field guides by Opler and Malikul (1998) and Glassberg (1999) for additional help with identification.

Distribution

This species has a very spotty distribution with populations restricted to a few states along the Atlantic Coast. Strongholds for this species occur in New

Arogos skipper on Deptford pink in Morris County, N.J. © Wade and Sharon Wander

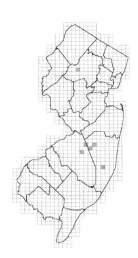

Jersey, Florida, and North Carolina, but more survey work is required to confirm the locations and size of extant populations throughout the East. New Jersey's Pinelands may hold some of the largest single populations of this species worldwide.

Habitat

The habitat requirements for this species vary regionally, even within the state. Northern populations inhabit xeric to dry-mesic grasslands dominated by its host plant, little bluestem (*Schizachyrium scoparius*). Little bluestem communities typically occur in abandoned agricultural fields, derelict parking lots, abandoned gravel pits, and power line right-of-ways. Arogos skippers in the Pinelands inhabit postburn wetland habitats dominated by Pine Barrens reed grass (*Calamovilfa brevipilis*), which serves as its host plant (Schweitzer 1992). The disparity between arogos skipper habitat in northern and southern portions of New Jersey suggests that each population may differ genetically. The ENSP, in cooperation with the USFWS, began investigating this possibility in 2001.

Diet

In northern New Jersey, arogos skipper caterpillars feed on little bluestem, while Pine Barrens reed grass is the host plant for this species in the Pinelands. Adults will feed on nectar of knapweeds (*Centaurea* spp.), milkweeds (*Asclepias* spp.), thistles (*Cirsium* spp.), and blazing-stars (*Liatris* spp.). According to Schweitzer (1992), in some years no nectar sources are available for adult arogos skippers in the Pinelands.

Breeding Biology

In New Jersey, the flight period for this species is brief, extending only from mid/late July into August. Northern New Jersey arogos fly during the first two to three weeks of July. Adults can be observed in flight during late morning to early afternoon on sunny days when temperatures are below 26.7°C (80°F). In the Pinelands, adults fly during late July/early August and are most active and easily flushed from vegetation in the late afternoon/early evening when temperatures are below 32.2°C (90°F). Schweitzer (1992) reports that the egg and pupal stages are probably about one and two weeks long, respectively. The larval stages are much more extensive, lasting from roughly late July to mid-June of the following year.

Status and Conservation

This species is experiencing major declines across most (if not all) of its range and may be extirpated from major portions of its original range (Glassberg 1999). The little bluestem-feeding arogos populations that occur in northern New Jersey are currently the only extant populations of its kind in the Northeast. The Pine Barrens reed grass-feeding arogos is known from four locations in the Pinelands, which are the four largest of the five known populations of the ecotype in its entire range (Schweitzer, pers. comm. 2001). In 2001 the species was listed as endangered under the New Jersey Endangered Species Conservation Act, and the USFWS was considering listing populations of arogos skipper that occur in the eastern United States.

Limiting Factors and Threats

Destruction of habitat and changes in natural fire regimes appear to be the two major causes of this species' rapid decline. In the Pinelands it appears that the reed grass-feeding arogos is dependent on ephemeral grasslands that establish after fires. However, because of efforts to suppress fires, these grasslands have become extremely rare, and arogos skipper populations have become isolated. Northern New Jersey arogos populations are threatened by land development and the natural encroachment of woody vegetation in their grassland habitats. Periodic burning may have also been historically associated with northern New Jersey populations; however, it appears that anthropogenic disturbances such as mowing, selective cutting, and small-scale soil disturbance can effectively maintain little bluestem grasslands.

Recommendations

Additional survey and natural history research are needed to fully understand the range and biology of the arogos skipper. Other research on how this species responds to different types of management (e.g., mowing and prescribed burning) is essential for developing a long-term conservation plan. However, because of the rarity of the species, extreme care must be taken to avoid adversely affecting populations in the pursuit of such information.

David M. Golden and Jason Tesauro

Bronze Copper, *Lycaena hyllus*

Status: State: Endangered   Federal: Not listed

Identification

The bronze copper is one of the largest species of coppers (subfamily Lycaeninae), with adults obtaining sizes from 37 to 47 mm (1.5–1.9 in.). The sexual dimorphism exhibited by this species is especially apparent in the patterning on the upper surface of the forewing. In males, the upper side of the forewing is a solid purple iridescent color. Females have orange forewings with several black spots, and only the forewing margin exhibits the purple iridescence. In both sexes, the upper surface of the hindwing is purple with an orange margin. The appearance of the underside of the wings is also similar in males and females of this species. The underside of the forewing is an orange base color with black spots and a white margin. The hindwings also have black spots on the underside, but the base color is off-white. An orange margin is present on the ventral, or underside, surface of the hindwings in both sexes.

Distribution

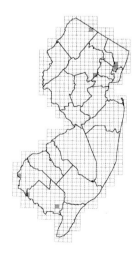

The bronze copper is locally rare, but fairly widespread in its distribution. It is found in most states, including New Jersey, above the Mason-Dixon Line. Although it is not present in the extreme northwestern states (Washington and Oregon), the range of the bronze copper does extend into many Canadian provinces.

Habitat

Bronze coppers are found in moist or wet areas, including brackish and freshwater marshes, bogs, fens, seepages, wet sedge meadows, riparian zones, wet grasslands, and drainage ditches.

Diet

Host plants for the larvae include water dock (*Rumex orbiculatus*), curled dock (*Rumex crispus*), and knotweeds (*Polygonum* spp.) (Iftner et al. 1992; Opler and Malikul 1998). Adults of this species feed on the nectar of red clover (*Trifolium pratense*), milkweeds (*Asclepias* spp.), asters (*Aster* spp.), thistles (*Cirsium* spp.), and a variety of other herbs and grasses.

Breeding Biology

In New Jersey, each summer the bronze copper goes through two broods, with the two generations of adults dying after they reproduce. Adults typically are flying from mid-June to mid-September. Caterpillars are yellowish green with a dark dorsal stripe down their backs and feed on leaves of water dock, curled dock, and knotweeds (Iftner et al. 1992). Each year, this species' second generation of adults lays eggs that overwinter and hatch the following season.

Status and Conservation

Historically, this species was scattered in pockets throughout much of New Jersey. It occurred primarily in the northern third of the state, but also sparingly in the coastal areas of the lower-tier counties. Relatively common throughout the 1940s, few individuals of this butterfly have been recorded since. Although this species is widespread, it often exists in small isolated populations and it is doubtful that the few extremely small colonies that still occur in the northern part of the state have the potential to recolonize adjacent areas of suitable habitat. The southern populations are also comprised of few individuals with limited recolonizing ability (David Iftner, pers. comm. 2001). This butterfly was listed as endangered under the New Jersey Endangered Species Conservation Act in 2001.

Limiting Factors and Threats

Agricultural herbicides, loss of habitat, and insecticide applications to control mosquitoes have all had serious impacts on the bronze copper. Habitat loss for this species can be directly related to the draining and filling of wetlands in New Jersey.

Recommendations

Protecting wetlands throughout the state is crucial for the long-term success of this species. New Jersey is committed to preserving and protecting wetlands for this and other wetland-dependent species. Toward this end, New Jersey has recently recommended higher protection for isolated freshwater wetlands that cover less than one acre. The bronze copper is just one example of a species that will benefit from New Jersey's more stringent recommendations.

David M. Golden

Mitchell's satyr.
© Rick Cech

Mitchell's Satyr, *Neonympha mitchelli mitchelli*
Status: State: Endangered   Federal: Endangered

Identification

The Mitchell's satyr butterfly is a small (3.8 cm, or 1.5 in. wingspan) brownish butterfly that can be identified by the presence of a continuous series of five yellow-ringed dark ocelli (eye spots) on the underside of the wing surfaces (Scott 1986).

Distribution

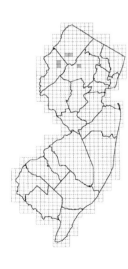

The Mitchell's satyr is considered one of the rarest butterflies in North America. It occurs in a disjunct geographic range encompassing New Jersey, Indiana, Michigan, and Ohio. Within that range, there are an estimated 15 to 20 populations, mostly in southern Michigan (USFWS 1997). The butterfly has been documented at two, possibly three, locations in northern New Jersey, but it has not been observed since 1988.

Habitat

The species inhabits calcareous (limestone) wet meadows and fens that feature a dense cover of sedges and scattered shrubs.

Diet

Larvae feed on sedges of the genus *Carex,* most likely *Carex stricta* (tussock sedge), which flourish in open wetlands. Although experts are unclear whether the adults feed at all during their short flight period, if they do feed it would be on fermenting sap or rotting fruit.

Breeding Biology

The Mitchell's satyr flies for a brief period from late June through mid-July, at which time it mates, lays eggs, and dies. It generally flies during warm 26.7°C (80°F), overcast days. Males are the more active sex, patrolling through the sedges and low-growing shrubs for mates. According to observations made in captivity, eggs hatch within 7 to 11 days, and the larvae feed on sedges through late summer. By fall, larvae go into diapause (dormancy) and resume feeding the following spring. Pupation takes place in June and lasts approximately two weeks (Shuey et. al 1987).

Status and Conservation

Much like the bog turtle, which shares many of the same habitat requirements, the Mitchell's satyr historically relied upon natural agents to maintain the open conditions of its habitat, including beavers, grazing herbivores, and fire (USFWS 1997). Today, however, as trees and shrubs invade open wet meadows and fens, sedges are outcompeted, which can ultimately affect the species' reproductive success.

The loss of habitat due to plant succession, wetland draining, filling, and impounding, fragmentation of the landscape, and the spraying of biocides for agricultural purposes are the primary reasons the USFWS and the state of New Jersey listed the Mitchell's satyr as endangered in 1991.

In Warren and Sussex counties, New Jersey, where the last two populations historically occurred, suitable calcareous sedge meadow habitats are common; however, extensive surveys conducted at these potential habitats over the past decade have failed to reveal the presence of any Mitchell's satyrs. It is possible that the species was always relatively rare in New Jersey. Nonetheless, each year Endangered and Nongame Species Program biologists discover new Mitchell's satyr habitats, thus the species cannot be considered extirpated from New Jersey until each site is thoroughly surveyed.

Limiting Factors and Threats

Many of the known Mitchell's satyr sites are poor in quality and/or are threatened by human land-use practices, natural ecological changes in plant community composition, and the invasion of exotic flora, for example, purple loosestrife. Because of the butterfly's rarity, excessive collecting is also a problem. The extirpation of New Jersey's two known occurrences has been attributed to overcollecting.

Recommendations

The ENSP will continue to survey all newly discovered calcareous sedge meadow habitats. Should a Mitchell satyr's population be identified, strategies will be employed to manage the habitat to maintain its present condition and prevent plant succession. Such management techniques might include strategies currently being employed on behalf of bog turtles, including prescribed low-density livestock grazing and the deployment of biological controls to arrest the spread of purple loosestrife.

Jason Tesauro

Checkered White, *Pontia protodice*
Status: State: Threatened   Federal: Not listed

Identification

Similar in size and appearance to the much more common cabbage white (*Pieris rapae*), adult checkered whites reach sizes of 44 to 62 mm (1.75–2.4 in.). Both sexes have a similar chalky white base color on the wings. The black spots on the upper surface of the wings are restricted to forewings in the males but extend onto the hindwings in females. Although the number of spots differs between the sexes, both males and females of this species have a greater number of spots on the upper surface of the forewing than cabbage whites, which only have one (male) or two (female) spots present. A characteristic black patch exists along the bottom front margin of the forewing in both sexes of checkered whites; the undersurface of the hindwing is a solid off-white color.

Checkered white.
© Wade and Sharon
Wander

Distribution

The checkered white is found throughout all of the southern United States. While New Jersey may represent the northern extent of its range along the East Coast, migratory transients of this species have been documented in many Canadian provinces, and some northern states, such as Montana and Michigan, appear to have resident populations.

Habitat

Mainly restricted to open areas such as savannahs, old fields, vacant lots, and power-line right-of-ways, checkered whites can sometimes be found along forest edges, especially in the spring.

Diet

Various species of mustards (Cruciferae) and peppergrasses (*Lepidium* spp.) are the major host plants of this species. Adults will actively feed on nectar from a variety of plants such as red clover (*Trifolium pratense*), ironweed (*Vernonia* spp.), dogbane (*Apocynum* spp.), Canada thistle (*Cirsium arvense*), and asters (*Aster* spp.), but usually stay in the vicinity of their host plants (Iftner et al. 1992).

Breeding Biology

With two to five generations a year, adults of this species can be seen flying throughout the season. Adults may appear as early as late April in the South, but in New Jersey the first adults are more typically seen mid- to late July. Adults continue to be active into early October.

Status and Conservation

The checkered white has decreased in abundance in many northeastern states despite the fact that it is still quite common in many southern and western states. Checkered whites have been reported in almost every county in New Jersey, with most records coming from the Piedmont and inner coastal plain regions. Based on specimen records, this species began to decline during the late 1940s to early 1950s, and by the late 1960s it was seldom encountered. While most current records probably represent migrants or their offspring, a resident population still occurs at the Newark International Airport in Essex County. This species was listed as threatened by the state of New Jersey in 2001.

Limiting Factors and Threats

While no clear answers exist regarding the root causes behind this species' decline in the Northeast, herbicides and changing land-use practices have likely contributed to its overall decline (David Iftner, pers. comm. 2001). It has also been speculated that the introduction of the very abundant cabbage white (*P. rapae*) has contributed to the decline of checkered whites as a result of direct competition and parasite transmission (Iftner et al. 1992; Schweitzer 2001; but see Gochfeld and Burger 1997).

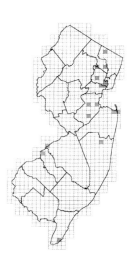

One interesting hypothesis regarding this species' decline blames the introduction of yet another exotic species, exotic mustards. According to Chew (1977), adult checkered whites may be unable to distinguish between native species of mustard and other exotic mustards. Adult checkered whites may therefore lay eggs on whatever mustard species are abundant in a given area. Many exotic species of mustard contain lethal quantities of mustard oils, which can kill checkered white caterpillars before they are able to fully develop. This becomes a problem when exotic species of mustards become more abundant than native mustards, a situation that unfortunately occurs in many northeastern states.

Recommendations

Suggestions of active management plans for this species may be somewhat premature since so much uncertainty still exists about the circumstances leading to the checkered whites' decline. Proposed explanations regarding its decline (see limiting factors and threats), however, do direct important attention to the potential consequences of exotic species introductions. Until more definitive answers about the threats to this species are revealed, continued research and monitoring of checkered white populations throughout the state is highly recommended.

David M. Golden

Frosted Elfin, *Callophrys irus*
Status: State: Threatened   Federal: Not listed

Identification

Slightly larger than most elfins of similar morphological appearance, adult frosted elfins obtain sizes in the range of 26 to 32 mm (1–1.25 in.) and both

Frosted elfin in Monmouth County, N.J. © Chris Williams

sexes of this species look alike. The upper surface of the wings are a drab brown color and provide naturalists with little help in distinguishing this species from other closely related elfins. A small "tail" extending from the hindwings is one diagnostic feature that can be used to differentiate this species from others. The underside of the hindwing also contains distinctive markings that can be helpful in positively identifying frosted elfins. For example, the posterior margin of the hindwing often has a white "frosting," which is the characteristic from which this species has derived its name. A black spot near the "tail" on the hindwing is almost always present and is an important field mark for proper identification. Another characteristic feature of the underside of the hindwing is a very crooked white line that runs roughly parallel to the body and divides the wing in half.

Distribution

The frosted elfin is present along most of the eastern seaboard (excluding Maine, where it is presumed extirpated), with isolated populations existing in southeastern Texas (and surrounding areas), Michigan, Indiana, and Wisconsin. New Jersey may be a stronghold for this species (Schweitzer 1994), with Assunpink Wildlife Management Area (WMA) and Bellplain State Forest having well-known colonies in the state (Gochfeld and Burger 1997).

Habitat

The frosted elfin dwells in dry clearings and open areas that are natural (e.g., savannahs) or of human origin (e.g., power-line right-of-ways and roadsides). The presence of food plants (see Diet) is also of importance.

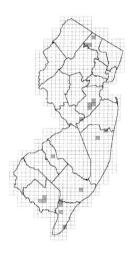

Diet

Lupine (*Lupinus perennis*) and indigo (*Baptisia* spp.) are the major food and host plants of this species. Regional differences in the exclusivity with which larvae and adults feed on these plants has led some experts to believe that this species should actually be divided into two separate species (Schweitzer 1994). Larvae feed on the flowers or fruits of the host plants, and the adults are nectarvores, or nectar feeders.

Breeding Biology

Frosted elfins produce a single brood each year, with adults flying from late May to mid-June in New Jersey. The larvae are a pale blue-green color with three faint white lines extending along the dorsal surface (Scott 1986). The caterpillars move into the litter a few weeks after the adults stop flying for the season, and there the larvae develop into pupae (Schweitzer 1994). Individuals of this species overwinter as small brown pupae in the soil or in litter bound together by silk (Scott 1986).

Status and Conservation

The frosted elfin is often locally rare and occurs in small isolated populations throughout much of its range. It is believed to be extirpated from historic locations, including Maine, Ontario, and possibly Texas. In New Jersey, this tiny butterfly also has a scattered distribution. It has been recorded from the extreme northern part of the state and from the inner coastal plain southward. The northern populations disappeared during the early 1980s, probably as a result of insecticide applications to control gypsy moths. A number of small isolated populations still exist in southern New Jersey. While these populations appear to be stable, natural succession could impact them.

This species was listed as threatened by the state of New Jersey in 2001. Currently it is not listed for federal protection, but its rarity throughout its range might justify a federal status of threatened or endangered in the near future.

Limiting Factors and Threats

Suitable habitat for the frosted elfin is being lost throughout most of its range. In New Jersey, the early successional habitats required by frosted elfins are being lost to natural succession (as a result of fire suppression) and overgrazing by white-tail deer. Some evidence also suggests that improperly planned prescribed burns have actually had a negative impact on frosted elfin populations in midwestern states.

Recommendations

The development of a monitoring program of frosted elfin populations in New Jersey is an important first step in understanding the local and regional population dynamics of this species. In the absence of such baseline data, strategically planned (and placed) controlled burns could be an effective technique to manage early successional plant communities and therefore increase the presence of suitable habitat for frosted elfins in the state.

David M. Golden

Silver-Bordered Fritillary, *Bolaria selene myrina*
Status: State: Threatened   Federal: Not listed

Identification

Like all lesser fritillaries within its range, the wings of the silver-bordered fritillary are orange with black markings. This species reaches sizes of 39 to 45 cm (1.6–2.75 in.) and can be distinguished from other closely related species by the presence of silver spots on the underside of the hindwing. The black margin, which encloses several small orange spots, on the upper surface of the forewing is another very useful diagnostic characteristic.

Distribution

In contrast to the checkered white (for which New Jersey comprises the northeastern limit of its range), New Jersey is the southeastern range limit for the silver-bordered fritillary. Its range extends west to Oregon and north throughout most Canadian provinces.

Silver-bordered fritillary in Middlesex County, N.J. © Wade and Sharon Wander

Habitat

This fritillary is most frequently observed in moist open areas such as sedge meadows, wet grasslands, and other wet areas with herbaceous growth.

Diet

The larvae feed exclusively on the leaves of violets (*Viola* spp.) but do not appear to be restricted to a single violet species. The flowers of red clover (*Trifolium pratense*), alfalfa (*Medicago sativa*), common milkweed (*Asclepias syriaca*), butterfly-weed (*Asclepias tuberosa*), and purple coneflower (*Echinacea purpurea*) represent nectar sources for the adults (Iftner et al. 1992).

Breeding Biology

This species is active from late May to early September in New Jersey, with peaks in flight activity around late June and August. This species has been documented to have two broods per year in New Jersey (Gochfeld and Burger 1997). Larvae are a dark grayish black with many black spots. An orange lateral line and orange spines with black tips are also visible on the larvae (Scott 1986). Adult females appear to haphazardly lay their pale greenish yellow eggs on vegetation close to (but not on) the larval host plant, *Viola* spp. Once hatched, the larvae will move onto the host plant to begin feeding. This species overwinters as larvae.

Status and Conservation

The silver-bordered fritillary is widespread and abundant across much of its range. Because New Jersey is located along the southeastern limit of this species' range, silver-bordered fritillaries are less common in New Jersey than in many northern states and Canadian provinces. While this butterfly has been recorded in almost every county, it has been reported most often from the northern half of the state. This species has experienced a dramatic decline since the mid-1960s and has disappeared from most of its former locales. The few populations that still exist are widely scattered, and it is unlikely that these few remaining colonies have the potential to recolonize other suitable habitats (David Iftner, pers. comm. 2001). As a result, it was listed as threatened in New Jersey in 2001.

Limiting Factors and Threats

As with most wetland species, silver-bordered fritillary populations in New Jersey have been impacted by habitat loss and destruction. Insecticide applications to control mosquitoes and gypsy moths have also contributed to the silver-bordered fritillary's decline in New Jersey (David Iftner, pers. comm. 2001). Finally, the natural succession of mesic (moist) grasslands to mesic or dry forests negatively impacts this species by reducing the availability of its larval host plant.

Recommendations

Anything that can be done to protect wetlands statewide and impede the natural succession of wetlands with known populations of silver-bordered fritillaries will be helpful toward the protection of this species. Surveying for this species throughout the state is an important first step in identifying wetlands, where managing succession might benefit silver-bordered fritillary populations.

David M. Golden

Seven BIVALVES
Freshwater Mussels

Dwarf Wedgemussel, *Alasmidonta heterodon*
Status: State: Endangered   Federal: Endangered

Brook Floater, *Alasmidonta varicosa*
Status: State: Endangered   Federal: Species of Special Concern

Green Floater, *Lasmigona subviridis*
Status: State: Endangered   Federal: Species of Special Concern

Yellow Lampmussel, *Lampsilis cariosa*
Status: State: Threatened   Federal: Species of Special Concern

Eastern Lampmussel, *Lampsilis radiata*
Status: State: Threatened   Federal: Not listed

Eastern Pondmussel, *Ligumia nasuta*
Status: State: Threatened   Federal: Not listed

Tidewater Mucket, *Leptodea ochracea*
Status: State: Threatened   Federal: Not listed

Triangle Floater, *Alasmidonta undulata*
Status: State: Threatened   Federal: Not listed

Freshwater mussels are filter-feeding bivalve mollusks that occur in rivers, streams, lakes, and ponds. They are most diverse in North America, where there are about 300 species. New Jersey is home to 12 native freshwater mussel species.

Mussels are vital components of freshwater ecosystems, providing food for raccoons, muskrats, ducks, herons, and sportfish. As natural filters, they improve water quality by straining particles and pollutants from the water column. Also, since mussels have a low tolerance for waterborne pollutants, they are excellent indicators of water quality and overall stream health.

Identification

All freshwater mussels have a calcium-carbonate bivalve shell that is divided into a left and right half. The shell consists of three layers; the outer periostracum, the middle calcium carbonate, and the inner nacre. The periostracum (or epidermis) protects underlying calcium carbonate from the corrosive action of low pH water and damage from moving sand and gravel. A thin prismatic layer of crystalline calcium carbonate lies beneath the periostracum. The nacre or mother-of-pearl is the innermost and often thickest layer of the shell. It is comprised of thin, stacked calcium-carbonate plates that lie parallel to the shell's surface. In many species, the color and texture of the nacre are important for identification.

Lateral and pseudocardinal teeth, separated by an interdentum, are located dorsally inside the shell. Lateral teeth are elongated and raised interlocking structures along the hinge line of a valve, whereas pseudocardinal teeth are triangular-shaped hinge teeth near the shell's anterior-dorsal margin. The interdentum is a flattened area of the hinge plate between the lateral and pseudocardinal teeth. The three points of apposition, which are taxonomically important in most species, serve to hold the two valves together. Some groups entirely lack lateral and pseudocardinal teeth. The umbo, or beak, is the dorsally raised, inflated area of the bivalve shell. Representing the oldest part of the shell, umbos appear as external swellings and are often points of taxonomic significance.

The valves are held closed by internal muscles. Empty shells show scars of former muscle attachment areas. Freshwater mussels have a large, muscular foot that extends between the valves and functions in locomotion and anchorage. The anterior and posterior retractor muscles draw the foot into the shell, while the anterior protractor helps in foot extension. Large anterior and posterior abductors draw the shell together.

New Jersey's Endangered and Threatened Freshwater Mussel Species

The dwarf wedgemussel is a rare freshwater mussel with a trapezoid-to-ovate, or "humpbacked," shell rarely exceeding 3.8 cm (1.5 in.) in length. It is characterized by having two lateral teeth on the right valve of the shell, but only one on the left (thus the species name *heterodon*). The ventral margin is mostly straight. The beaks are low and rounded, projecting only slightly above the hinge line. The periostracum, or outer shell or epidermis, is dark brown or yellowish brown and often exhibits greenish rays in young mussels. The nacre, or inner shell, is bluish or silvery white.

The dwarf wedgemussel once existed in 70 localities within 15 major Atlantic slope drainage basins from New Brunswick, Canada, to North Carolina

(USFWS 1993). Today, however, this species is thought to be extirpated from all but approximately 30 small sites in New Hampshire, Vermont, Maryland, North Carolina, New York, Connecticut, Virginia, and New Jersey.

In New Jersey, the dwarf wedgemussel historically inhabited areas of the Delaware, Hackensack, and Passaic rivers. These populations, however, are thought to be extirpated because of water-quality degradation and other factors. There are only three known active state occurrences of this elusive species: the Paulins Kill, Pequest River, and a portion of the upper Delaware River.

Preferred habitat of the dwarf wedgemussel ranges from muddy sand to sand and gravel/pebble bottoms in rivers and creeks with slow to moderate current. Favoring clean and relatively shallow water with little silt deposition, this species is known to co-occur with other freshwater mussels such as the eastern elliptio (*Elliptio complanata*), triangle floater (*Alasmidonta undulata*), creeper (*Strophitus undulatus*), eastern floater (*Pyganodon cataracta*), and eastern lampmussel (*Lampsilis radiata*).

Fish species identified as suitable hosts for the dwarf wedgemussel include the tessellated darter (*Etheostoma olmstedi*), mottled sculpin (*Cottus bairdi*), and Johnny darter (*Etheostoma nigrum,* not found in New Jersey) (Michaelson and Neves 1995).

The brook floater has a small, kidney-shaped shell that is slightly thicker toward the anterior. There is a conspicuous posterior slope with wavy ridges perpendicular to the growth lines. The ventral margin is straight and slightly concave centrally. The outer shell color ranges from yellowish brown to dark brown and the nacre is a glossy bluish white to orange in the umbo region. The pseudocardinal teeth exist as weak knobs and lateral teeth are absent. The species has a bright orange to pinkish foot.

The brook floater ranges from the Savannah River basin in South Carolina

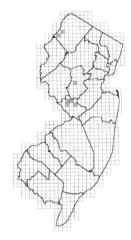

north to the St. Lawrence River basin in Canada and west to the Ohio River Basin of West Virginia. In New Jersey, there are reported occurrences in the Stony Brook, Musconetcong, Raritan, Lamington, and upper Delaware rivers.

Habitat of the brook floater includes rapids or riffles on rock and gravel substrates. The species prefers small streams and is commonly associated with the eastern elliptio (*Elliptio complanata*) (Clarke 1981). Reported host fishes for the species that occur in New Jersey include the slimy sculpin (*Cottus cognatus*), longnose dace (*Rhinicthys cataractae*), golden shiner (*Notemigonus crysoleucas*), and pumpkinseed (*Lepomis gibbosus*).

The green floater is a small, rare mussel with an ovate trapezoid shell that is fragile and thin. The posterior ridge is rounded. The outer shell is light yellow or brown with many green rays, especially in juveniles. The pseudocardinal

and lateral teeth are small and delicate. The beak cavity is shallow. The nacre can be white to blue and is iridescent toward the posterior end.

The green floater can be found from the Cape Fear River basin in North Carolina north to the Hudson River basin and westward to the St. Lawrence River basin in New York. In New Jersey, the species once occurred in the Passaic, Raritan, Delaware, and Pequest rivers, but is now represented by a single known individual in the Stony Brook in Mercer County.

This species can be found in smaller streams, most often in pools and eddies with gravelly and sandy bottoms (Ortmann 1919). It is averse to strong currents (Clarke 1985). The host fish is not known. There is some evidence that the green floater may not require a host fish in order to complete its life cycle (Barfield and Watters 1998; Lellis and King 1998).

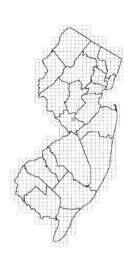

The yellow lampmussel has a medium-sized shell, with males elliptical and somewhat elongate and females more ovate. Shells are moderately inflated and thick. The anterior margin is rounded and the ventral margin is slightly curved. The umbos are swollen and raised above the hinge line. The pseudocardinal teeth are compressed and the beak cavity is somewhat deep. The periostracum is smooth, shiny, and usually yellow with brown patches. The nacre is white to bluish white. There may be green or black rays on the posterior slope.

The species ranges from Georgia to the Lower Ottawa River in Canada and eastward to Nova Scotia. New Jersey occurrences of the yellow lampmussel are restricted to the Delaware River.

The yellow lampmussel prefers large rivers that drain more than 1,200 sq. km (463 sq. mi.) (Strayer 1993), and is often found in sand/silt substrates. Although the host fish has not been identified, a migratory species such as the alewife is the suspected host.

Shells of the eastern lampmussel are elliptical and have a rounded posterior ridge. The posterior and anterior ends are rounded, and swollen umbos extend

Yellow lampmussel (exterior). Photo courtesy North Carolina Wildlife Resources Commission

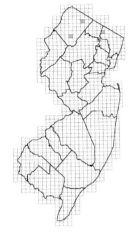

above the hinge line. The periostracum is brown and extensively rayed. The nacre is white and may be tinged with pink or salmon. This species has long lateral teeth and two pseudocardinal teeth on the left and right valves.

The eastern lampmussel ranges from South Carolina north to the St. Lawrence River basin. In New Jersey, the species is known from locations in the Ramapo, Pequannock, and Wallkill rivers.

The eastern lampmussel is found in a variety of habitats. It is reported to prefer medium to coarse sands. The host fish is unknown.

The eastern pondmussel can be distinguished by its bluntly pointed posterior and distinctive posterior ridge. The shells are elongate and twice as long as wide. The dorsal margin is straight and the ventral margin (the side that opens) is curved. The beaks are low and located in the anterior quarter

of the shell. The lateral teeth are long and straight. The pseudocardinal teeth are compressed. The nacre is white but can also vary from an iridescent blue to salmon. The periostracum is greenish yellow to dark olive or brown.

The eastern pondmussel occurs from Cape Fear River basin, North Carolina, to the St. Lawrence River basin, Canada, and westward through northern parts of the continent's Interior basin. In New Jersey, the species can be found in the Delaware River and several of its tributaries.

The eastern pondmussel is often associated with tidewaters. The host fish is unknown.

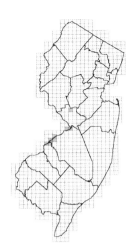

The tidewater mucket appears similar to the yellow lampmussel. The shell is small; males are elliptical and females are ovate, subinflated, and thin. The anterior end is rounded, the posterior margin is evenly rounded, somewhat pointed in males and truncated in females. The beaks are moderately swollen, raised above the hinge line, and are located near the middle of the shell. The periostracum is yellow to brown or olive green and is often covered with fine green rays. The pseudocardinal teeth are compressed; the lateral teeth are short and curved. The beak cavity is shallow, and the nacre is bluish white and sometimes pink.

The tidewater mucket ranges from the Savannah River Drainage basin in Georgia north into Nova Scotia. In New Jersey, the species occurs in the Delaware River.

This species is associated with tidewaters and can be found in sand/silt substrates. The host fish is undetermined.

The triangle floater is a small, ovate- to triangular-shaped mussel. The lateral teeth are absent, but there is an interdental projection in the left valve. The pseudocardinal teeth are large and well developed. The periostracum is yellowish green to black and is extensively rayed. The nacre is pinkish salmon posteriorly and whitish on the anterior portion.

Tidewater mucket (exterior). Photo courtesy North Carolina Wildlife Resources Commission

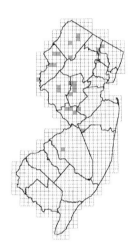

The triangle floater is a generalist and can be found in a variety of stream and river habitats. The host fish is thought to be the black nose dace.

Diet

Freshwater mussels filter a wide variety of food particles from the water column such as zooplankton, phytoplankton, algae, diatoms, and organic debris. Water is inhaled by mussels through an incurrent aperture where it is passed over mucus-covered gills. Small food collects in the gills and is then transferred to the mouth. Waste particles and unpalatable items are released through the excurrent siphon.

Breeding Biology

Eggs from female freshwater mussels are released from the ovaries and carried by water currents to the outer gills (marsupium), where they are fertilized by the male. The marsupial pouch in Unionoida, or freshwater mussels, is a brood pouch for eggs and developing larvae (glochidia). The pouch is formed by the restricted portion of the outer gill, the complete outer gill, or all four gills. Mussels that retain glochidia in their gills for only part of the summer are termed tachytictic (short-term breeders). In bradytictic (long-term breeders) mussels, such as the dwarf wedgemussel (*A. heterodon*), females typically retain glochidia in their gills over the winter (Michaelson and Neves 1995). The release of glochidia depends on temperatures (Miller and Nelson 1983).

Glochidia are separable into three main types: hooked, hookless, and axe-head (Kat 1984). Hooked glochidia are the largest of the three types, possessing a well-developed, hook-shaped, hinged projection at the ventral margin of each valve. Hookless glochidia, which are round to subelliptical, are characteristic of most North American freshwater mussels. Axe-head glochidia are only known in the genus *Proptera* and are distinguished by a flaring ventral margin (Kat 1984).

Once the female releases the glochidia through her excurrent siphon, these motile larvae must attach to a suitable host fish in order to survive into adulthood. Without the host fish, the species is unable to complete its reproductive life cycle. Points of glochidial attachment on the host fish include gills, fins, body surface, and eyes.

Freshwater mussels have evolved effective methods of ensuring glochidial attachment to host fishes. For example, pocketbook mussels (*Lampsilis* spp.) possess an appendage that waves in the currents and resembles a minnow. Largemouth bass attracted to the appendage are then doused by a cloud of glochidia exuded by the female mussel. Also, according to Kat (1984), members of the genera *Elliptio* release a wormlike conglutinate from the excurrent siphon that effectively attracts hosts such as the yellow perch and the white crappie.

Movement of host fishes bearing glochidia is by far the main mechanism of freshwater mussel dispersal (Watters 1992). After acquiring the necessary nutrients, usually between one to four weeks of infestation, the parasitic juvenile drops off the host fish. During this stage, the essentially nonmotile mussel is subject to an extremely high mortality rate. In order to survive, it must fall at a place with suitable substrate (or stream bottom), water chemistry, and flow. Once the mussel has traveled through the water column, it uses the newly developed foot to anchor into the substrate.

Freshwater mussels are among the longest-living organisms on Earth, with some individuals reaching ages in excess of a century (Bauer 1992; Anthony and Downing 1999).

Status and Conservation

Since 1990 the dwarf wedgemussel has been afforded protection through federal and state Endangered Species acts, federal and state Clean Water acts, Flood Hazard Area Control Act rules (stream encroachment), and environmental reviews of proposed development projects. The other species listed above were listed as state endangered or threatened in late 2002. Federal and state Clean Water acts, stream encroachment rules, environmental reviews of proposed development projects and the state Endangered Species Conservation Act will serve to help protect existing populations.

Limiting Factors and Threats

One in ten of North America's freshwater mussel species has gone extinct in this century, while 75% of the remaining species are either rare or imperiled (Sawhill 1992). In addition, a number of the endangered species are functionally extinct, with individuals surviving but not reproducing (Bogan 1993). This alarming decline is directly tied to the degradation and loss of essential habitat and the invasion of exotic species such as the Asian clam (*Corbicula fluminea*) and the zebra mussel (*Dreissena polymorpha*).

Destruction of freshwater mussel habitat has ranged from dam construction, channelization, and dredging to siltation and contaminants. Dams alter the physical, chemical, and biological stream environment, sometimes destroying 30% to 60% of the mussel fauna upstream and downstream of the construction (Layzer et al. 1993; Williams et al. 1992). The most detrimental effect of dams, however, is the elimination of host species and resulting disruption in the reproductive cycle (Williams et al. 1992). Increased silt loads and shifting stream bottoms caused by erosion also threaten mussel habitats, as do contaminants such as heavy metals and pesticides (Fuller 1974), and effluent from sewage treatment plants (Goudreau et al. 1993). Further, dwarf wedgemussels are threatened by overcollecting and loss of genetic diversity due to small, geographically isolated populations (USFWS 1993).

The introduction of nonindigenous mollusks has also impacted freshwater mussel populations. The Asian clam, *Corbicula,* was introduced to the West Coast in the 1930s and is now the most widespread mollusk in North America (McMahon 1983). Often competing for space and food with native mussels, *Corbicula* in high densities have been implicated in the decline of native freshwater mussels (Williams et al. 1992). Zebra mussels, which were accidentally introduced into the Great Lakes in 1988 via the ballast water of a European tanker, are now engaged in the worst aquatic invasion ever to hit North America (Stolzenburg 1992).

Recommendations

Continue surveys for endangered and threatened freshwater mussel species and determine population sizes and age distributions. Identify threats to populations, including barriers to host fish and glochidial movement. Create sufficient buffer areas along riparian banks and up and downstream of population boundaries. Upgrade the protection classifications of streams with endangered and threatened freshwater species in order to protect water quality. Identify critical stream and riparian habitat through Geographic Information Systems (GIS) mapping as part of the ENSP's Riparian Landscape Project. Develop protection guidelines for endangered and threatened species and work with federal, state, and local municipalities and private landowners in order to protect critical areas. Encourage stream bank restoration efforts.

Jeanette Bowers-Altman

Bibliography

In instances where references have been cited or referred to more than once within each class, such as birds, these references are grouped at the head of each reference section under the title General References. References specific only to individual species are listed under each particular species.

MAMMALS

Indiana Bat

Barbour, R.W., and W.H. Davis. 1969. *Bats of America.* Lexington: University Press of Kentucky.

Evans, J.E., N. Drilling, and R.L. Henson. 1992. *Element Stewardship Abstract for Myotis sodalis.* Minneapolis: Nature Conservancy.

Garner, J.D., and J.E. Gardner. 1992. Determination of summer distribution and habitat utilization of the Indiana bat (*Myotis sodalis*) in Illinois. Final Report: Project E-3. Division of Natural Heritage, Department of Illinois Conservation and Center for Biogeographic Information, Illinois Natural Heritage Survey.

Harvey, M.J. 1992. *Bats of the United States.* Little Rock: Arkansas Game and Fish Commission.

Hobson, C.S., and J.N. Holland. 1995. Post-hibernation movement and foraging habitat of a male Indiana bat *Myotis sodalis* (*Chiroptera: Vespertilionidae*) in western Virginia. *Brimleyana* 23:95–101.

Kurta, A., J. Kath, E.L. Smith, R. Foster, M.W. Orick, and R. Ross. 1993. A maternity roost of the endangered Indiana bat (*Myotis sodalis*) in an unshaded, hollow, sycamore tree (*Platanus occidentalis*). *American Midland Naturalist* 130(2):405–7.

N.J. Department of Environmental Protection. 2002. Protocols for the Establishment of Exceptional Resource Value Wetlands Pursuant to the Freshwater Wetlands Protection Act (N.J.S.A.13:9B-1 et seq.). Based on Documentation of State or Federal Endangered or Threatened Species.

Tuttle, M.D. 1999. Former home of more than a million endangered Indiana bats protected. *BATS* 17, no. 3:8–9.

U.S. Fish and Wildlife Service (USFWS). 1999. Agency Draft: Indiana bat (*Myotis sodalis*). Revised Recovery Plan. Fort Snelling, Minn.

———. Indiana Bat, Endangered Species Facts. U.S. Fish Wildl. Serv. Region 3 Website. *http://midwest.fws.gov/Endangered/mammals/ibat_fctsht.htm* (accessed November 5, 2001).

Allegheny Woodrat

Godin, A.J. 1977. *Wild Mammals of New England*. Baltimore: Johns Hopkins University Press.

Hamilton, W.J., Jr. 1963. *The Mammals of the Eastern United States*. New York: Hafner.

Hamilton, W.J., Jr., and J.O. Whitaker, Jr. 1979. *Mammals of the Eastern United States*. Ithaca, N.Y.: Cornell University Press.

Hicks, A.P. 1989. Whatever happened to the Allegheny woodrat? *New York State Conservationist,* March–April 1989, 34–38.

LoGiudice, K. 2000. *Baylisascaris procyonis* and the decline of the Allegheny woodrat (*Neotoma magister*). Ph.D. diss., Rutgers University, New Brunswick, N.J.

Poole, E.L. 1940. A life history sketch of the Allegheny woodrat. *J. Mammal.* 21:249–318.

Rainey, D.G. 1956. Eastern woodrat, *Neotoma floridana:* Life history and ecology. *Univ. Kansas Publ., Mus. Nat. Hist.* 8:535–646.

Reichman, O.J. 1988. Caching behavior by eastern woodrats, *Neotoma floridana,* in relation to food perishability. *Anim. Behav.* 36:1525–1532.

Whales

Audubon Society. 1983. *The Audubon Society Field Guide to North American Fishes, Whales, and Dolphins*. Chanticleer Press Edition. New York: Alfred A. Knopf.

Grzimek, B., ed. 1979. *Grzimek's Animal Life Encyclopedia*. Vol. 11, *Mammals II*. New York: Van Nostrand Reinhold.

Marine Mammal Center. 2001. Blue whales. The Marine Mammal Center, Sausalito, Calif. Website, *http://www.tmmc.org/blue.htm*. Revised 6/00 (accessed September 7, 2001).

National Marine Fisheries Service (NMFS). 1991. Recovery plan for the humpback whale (*Megaptera novaeangliae*). Prepared by the Humpback Whale Recovery Team for the National Marine Fisheries Service, Silver Spring, Md.

N.J. State Museum. 1907. Annual Report of the N.J. State Museum.

Rhoads, S.N. 1903. *The Mammals of Pennsylvania and N.J.* Philadelphia: Privately published.

Van Gelder, R.G. 1984. The mammals of the state of N.J.: A preliminary annotated list. N.J. Audubon Soc., occasional paper no. 143, November 1, 1984, 11–14.

Waring, G.T., J.M. Quintal, and S.L. Swartz, eds. 2000. U.S. Atlantic and Gulf of Mexico marine mammal stock assessments—2000. NOAA Technical Memorandum NMFS-NE-162, November 2000, 1–300.

Bobcat

Bailey, T.N. 1972. Ecology of bobcats with special reference to social organization. Ph.D. diss., University of Idaho, Moscow.

Crowe, D.M. 1975. Bobcats: Out of sight, out of mind. *Wyoming Wildlife* 37(11):8–12.

Godin, A.J. 1977. Bobcat. In *Wild Mammals of New England*. Baltimore: Johns Hopkins University Press.

Koehler, G. 1987. The bobcat. *Audubon Wildlife Report,* 399–409.

Leopold, B.D., L.M. Conner, and K.J. Sullivan. 1995. Ecology of the Bobcat (*Felis rufus*) within a Forest Management System. Completion Report for Federal Aid in Wildlife Restoration, Project W-48, Study 29.

Marshall, A.D., and J.H. Jenkins. 1966. Movements and home ranges of bobcats as determined by radio-tracking in the upper coastal plain of West-Central South Carolina. *Proc. 20th Conf. Southeast Assoc., Game and Fish Commissioners,* October, 206–214.

Marston, M.A. 1942. Winter relations of bobcats to white-tailed deer in Maine. *J. Wildlife Mgt.* 6:328–337.

McCord, C. 1977. The bobcat in Massachusetts. *Mass. Wildlife,* September–October, 2–8.

N.J. Division of Fish, Game, and Wildlife. 1980. Bobcat Restoration Project: Literature Review of Bobcat Behavior, Food Habits, Range, and Capture and Marking Techniques. Furbearer Research, Study No. II—Bobcat Restoration; Job No. II-A—Literature Review.

———. 1995. Taxonomy, Life History, and Management Report: Bobcat, Species ID 050051. NINJA database.

Pollack, E.M. 1951. Food habits of the bobcat in the New England states. *J. Wildlife Mgt.*15:209–213.

Wassmer, D.A., D.D. Guenther, and J.N. Layne. 1988. Ecology of the bobcat in South-Central Florida. *Bull. Florida State Mus., Biol. Sci.* 33(4):159–228.

BIRDS

General References

Anderson, J.M. 1978. Protection and management of wading birds. 99–103. In *Wading birds.* A. Sprunt, J.C. Ogden, and S. Winckler, eds. Natl. Audubon Soc. Research Report No. 7. New York.

Arbib, R. 1975. The blue list for 1976. *Amer. Birds* 29:1067–1072.

———. 1976. The blue list for 1977. *Amer. Birds* 30:1031–1039.

———. 1977. The blue list for 1978. *Amer. Birds* 31:1087–1096.

———. 1979. The blue list for 1980. *Amer. Birds* 33:830–835.

Babson, W. 1901. *The Birds of Princeton, N.J., and Vicinity.* Princeton, N.J.: Princeton Bird Club.

Baicich, P.J., and C.J.O. Harrison. 1997. *A Guide to the Nests, Eggs, and Nestlings of North American Birds,* 2nd edition. San Diego: Academic Press.

Bent, A.C. 1921. Life histories of North American gulls and terns. *U.S. Natl. Mus. Bull.* 113:270–279.

———. 1937. Life histories of North American birds of prey. Part 1. *U.S. Natl. Mus. Bull.* 167.

———. 1963. *Life Histories of North American Marsh Birds.* New York: Dover.

———. 1964. *Life Histories of North American Woodpeckers.* New York: Dover.

———. 1968. *Life Histories of North American Cardinals, Grosbeaks, Buntings, Towhees, Finches, Sparrows, and Allies.* New York: Dover.

Benzinger, J., and R. Speiser. 1982. Breeding birds of N.J.'s Ramapo Mountains. *Rec. N.J. Birds* 8:24–26.

Benzinger, J., P. Bacinski, D. Miranda, and T. Bosakowski. 1988. Breeding birds of the Pequannock Watershed, 1986–87. *Rec. N.J. Birds* 14:22–27.

Bird, D.M., ed. 1983. *Biology and Management of Bald Eagles and Ospreys.* Ste. Anne de Bellevue, Quebec: Harpell Press.

Boyle, W.J., Jr. 1986. *A Guide to Bird Finding in N.J.* New Brunswick: Rutgers University Press.

———. 1991. *A Guide to Bird Finding in N.J.* New Brunswick: Rutgers University Press.

Bratton, S.P. 1990. Boat disturbance of ciconiiformes in Georgia estuaries. *Col. Wat.* 13:124–128.

Bull, J. 1964. *Birds of the New York Area*. New York: Harper and Row.

Bull, J.L. 1974. *Birds of New York State*. Ithaca, N.Y.: Cornell University Press.

———. 1975. *Birds of the New York Area*. New York: Dover.

Burger, J. 1978. The pattern and mechanism of nesting in mixed-species heronries. In *Wading Birds*, ed. A. Sprunt, J.C. Ogden, and S. Winckler, 45–58. National Audubon Society Research Report No. 7, New York.

Cromartie, W.J., ed. 1982. N.J.'s endangered and threatened plants and animals. In *Proc. Second Symposium on Endangered and Threatened Plants and Animals of N.J.* Pomona, N.J.: Stockton State College, Center for Environmental Research.

Cruickshank, A.D. 1942. *Birds around New York City: Where and When to Find Them.* American Museum of Natural History Handbook Series No. 13, New York.

Custer, T.W., R.G. Osborn, and W.F. Stout. 1980. Distribution, species abundance, and nesting-site use of Atlantic Coast colonies of herons and their allies. *Auk* 97:591–600.

DeGraaf, R.M., and J.H. Rappole. 1995. *Neotropical Migratory Birds: Natural History, Distribution and Population Change*. Ithaca, N.Y.: Comstock.

Dove, L.E., and R.M. Nyman, eds. 1975. *Living Resources of the Delaware Estuary*. Philadelphia: Delaware Estuary Program.

Ehrlich, P.R., D.S. Dobkin, and D. Wheye. 1988. *The Birder's Handbook: A Field Guide to the Natural History of North American Birds*. New York: Simon and Schuster.

Fables, D. 1955. *Annotated List of N.J. Birds*. Urner Ornithological Club.

French, T.W., and D.M. Pence, eds. 1996. *Endangered, Threatened and Special Concern Animal Species in the Northeastern States: A List of Species Recognized by State and Federal Laws*. Compiled by the Northeast Nongame Technical Committee, Northeast Wildlife Administrators Association, and the U.S. Fish and Wildllife Service. Hadley, Mass.

Griscom, L. 1923. *Birds of the New York City Region*. New York: American Museum of Natural History.

Johnsgard, P.A. 1990. *Hawks, Eagles, and Falcons of North America: Biology and Natural History*. Washington, D.C.: Smithsonian Institution Press.

Jones, A.L., and P.D. Vickery. 1997a. *Conserving Grassland Birds: Managing Agricultural Lands Including Hayfields, Crop Fields, and Pastures for Grassland Birds*. Lincoln, Mass.: Massachusetts Audubon Society.

———. 1997b. *Conserving Grassland Birds: Managing Small Grasslands Including Conservation Lands, Corporate Headquarters, Recreation Fields, and Small Landfills for Grassland Birds*. Lincoln, Mass.: Massachusetts Audubon Society.

———. 1997c. *Conserving Grassland Birds: Managing Large Grasslands Including Conservation Lands, Airports, and Landfills over 75 Acres for Grassland Birds*. Lincoln, Mass.: Massachusetts Audubon Society.

Kane, R., W.J. Boyle, and A.R. Keith. 1985. Breeding birds of Great Swamp, 1983–84. *Rec. N.J. Birds* 11:29–33.

Kane, R., P. Kerlinger, and R. Radis. 1991. Birds of the Arthur Kill Tributaries, 1990. *Rec. N.J. Birds* 17:22–33.

Kushlan, J.A. 1978. Feeding ecology of wading birds. In *Wading Birds*, ed. A. Sprunt, J.C. Ogden, and S. Winckler, 249–298. National Audubon Society Research Report No. 7, New York.

Leck, C.F. 1975. *Birds of N.J.: Their Habits and Habitats*. New Brunswick: Rutgers University Press.

———. 1984. *The Status and Distribution of N.J.'s Birds*. New Brunswick: Rutgers University Press.

————. 1986. Population changes in recent N.J. Christmas counts. *Rec. N.J. Birds* 12: 18–19.

Martin, A.C., H.S. Zim, and A.L. Nelson. 1961. *American Wildlife and Plants: A Guide to Wildlife Food Habits.* New York: Dover.

Mott, D.F. 1978. Control of wading bird predation at fish-rearing facilities. In *Wading Birds,* ed. A. Sprunt, J.C. Ogden, and S. Winckler, 131–132. National Audubon Society Research Report No. 7, New York.

Office of Natural Lands Management. 1992. *Special Animals of N.J.* Trenton: Department of Environmental Protection and Energy.

————. 1998. *Special Vertebrate Animals of N.J., Updated September 1998.* Trenton: N.J. Natural Heritage Program, Division of Parks and Forestry, Department of Environmental Protection.

Ogden, J.C. 1978. Recent population trends of colonial wading birds on the Atlantic and Gulf coastal plains. In *Wading Birds,* ed. A. Sprunt, J.C. Ogden, and S. Winckler, 137–154. National Audubon Society Research Report No. 7, New York.

Palmer, R.S., ed. 1962. *Handbook of North American Birds,* vol. 1: *Loons through flamingos.* New Haven and London: Yale University Press.

Parnell, J.F., D.G. Ainley, H. Blokpoel, B. Cain, T.W. Custer, J.L. Dusi, S. Kress, J.A. Kushlan, W.E. Southern, L.E. Stenzel, and B.C. Thompson. 1988. Colonial waterbird management in North America. *Col. Wat.* 11:129–169.

Parnell, J.F., and R.F. Soots, Jr. 1978. The use of dredge islands by wading birds. In *Wading Birds,* ed. A. Sprunt, J.C. Ogden, and S. Winckler, 105–111. National Audubon Society Research Report No. 7, New York.

Parsons, K.C. 1995. Heron nesting at Pea Patch Island, Upper Delaware Bay, USA: Abundance and reproductive success. *Col. Wat.* 18:69–78.

Peachey, J. 1985. Grassland breeding birds at Thompson Grove Park, 1984. *Rec. N.J. Birds* 11:26–28.

Peterson, R.T. 1980. *A Field Guide to the Birds of Eastern and Central North America.* Boston: Houghton Mifflin.

Poole, A., and F. Gill, eds. Various years. *The Birds of North America.* Philadelphia: Academy of Natural Sciences, and Washington, D.C.: American Ornithologists' Union.

Sauer, J.R., S. Schwartz, and B. Hoover. 1996. *The Christmas Bird Count Home Page.* Version 95.1. Patuxent Wildlife Research Center, Laurel, Md. *http://www.mbr_pwrc. usgs.gov/bbs/cbc.html.*

Sauer, J.R., J.E. Hines, G. Gough, I. Thomas, and B.G. Peterjohn. 1997. *The North American Breeding Bird Survey Results and Analysis.* Version 96.4. USGS Patuxent Wildlife Research Center, Laurel, Md.

Sauer, J.R., J.E. Hines, I. Thomas, J. Fallon, and G. Gough. 2000. *The North American Breeding Bird Survey, Results and Analysis, 1966–1999.* Version 98.1. USGS Patuxent Wildlife Research Center, Laurel, Md.

Sauer, J.R., J.E. Hines, and J. Fallon. 2001. *The North American Breeding Bird Survey, Results and Analysis 1966–2000.* Version 2001.2. USGS Patuxent Wildlife Research Center, Laurel, Md.

Schneider, K.J., and D.M. Pence, eds. 1992. *Migratory Nongame Birds of Management Concern in the Northeast.* Newton Corner, Mass.: U.S. Department of the Interior, Fish and Wildlife Service.

Shick, C.S. 1890. Birds found breeding on Seven Mile Beach, N.J. *Auk* 7:326–329.

Shriner, C.A. 1897. *The Birds of N.J.* Trenton: State of N.J. Fish and Game Commission.

Sibley, D. 1997. *The Birds of Cape May.* Cape May, N.J.: N.J. Audubon Society's Cape May Bird Observatory.

————. 2000. *The Sibley Guide to Birds.* National Audubon Society. New York: Chanticleer Press.

Sprunt, A., J.C. Ogden, and S. Winckler, eds. 1978. *Wading Birds.* National Audubon Society Research Report No. 7, New York.

Stone, W. 1892. Winter birds of Cape May, N.J. *Proc. Acad. Nat. Sci. Philadelphia* 44:203.

————. 1894a. Summer birds of the Pine Barrens of N.J. *Auk* 15:133–140.

————. 1894b. The Birds of Eastern Pennsylvania and N.J. Delaware Valley Ornithological Club, Philadelphia.

————. 1908. The Birds of N.J., Their Nests and Eggs. Report of the N.J. State Museum. Trenton: John L. Murphy Publishing.

————. 1965a. *Bird Studies at Old Cape May, an Ornithology of Coastal N.J.* Vol. 1. New York: Dover.

————.1965b. *Bird Studies at Old Cape May.* Vol. 2. New York: Dover.

Sutton, C., and P. Sutton. 1986. Breeding birds of Bear Swamp, Cumberland County, 1981–1985. *Rec. N.J. Birds* 12:21–24.

Tate, J.J. 1981. The Blue List for 1981. *Amer. Birds* 35:3–10.

————. 1986. The Blue List for 1986. *Amer. Birds* 40:227–236.

Tate, J.J., and D.J. Tate. 1982. The Blue List for 1982. *Amer. Birds* 36:126–135.

Tiner, R.W., Jr. 1985. *Wetlands of N.J.* Newton Corner, Mass.: U.S. Fish and Wildlife Service, National Wetlands Inventory.

Turnbull, W.P. 1869. *The Birds of east Pennsylvania and New Jersey.* Glasgow: Printed for private circulation.

Walsh, J., V. Elia, R. Kane, and T. Halliwell. 1999. *Birds of N.J.* Bernardsville, N.J.: N.J. Audubon Society.

Wiens, J.A. 1969. An approach to the study of ecological relationships among grassland birds. American Ornithologists' Union, *Ornith. Monogr. No. 8.*

Pied-Billed Grebe

Coulter, M.L. 1957. Predation by snapping turtles upon aquatic birds in Maine marshes. *J. Wildl. Mgt.* 21:17–21.

Forbes, M.R.L., and C.D. Ankney. 1988. Nest attendance by adult pied-billed grebes, *Podilymbus podiceps. Can. J. Zool.* 66:2019–2023.

Gibbs, J.P., and S.M. Melvin. 1992. Pied-billed grebe, *Podilymbus podiceps.* In K.J. Schneider and D.M. Pence, eds., *Migratory Nongame Birds of Management Concern in the Northeast,* 31–49. Newton Corner, Mass.: U.S. Department of the Interior, Fish and Wildlife Service.

Harrison, P. 1983. *Seabirds: An Identification Guide.* Boston: Houghton Mifflin.

Klein, M.L. 1993. Waterbird behavioral responses to human disturbances. *Wildl. Soc. Bull.* 21:31–39.

Black-Crowned Night-Heron

Andrews, R. 1990. *Coastal Waterbird Colonies: Maine to Virginia, 1984–85.* An update of an atlas based on 1977 data, showing colony locations, species, and nesting pairs at both time periods. Newton Corner, Mass.: U.S. Fish and Wildlife Service.

Beaver, D.L., R.G. Osborn, and T.W. Custer. 1980. Nest-site and colony characteristics of wading birds in selected Atlantic Coast colonies. *Wilson Bull.* 92:200–220.

Burger, J., M. Gochfeld, and L.J. Niles. 1995. Ecotourism and birds in coastal N.J.: Contrasting responses of birds, tourists, and managers. *Env. Cons.* 22:56–65.

Byrd, M.A. 1978. Dispersal and movements of six North American Ciconiiforms. In *Wading Birds,* ed. A. Sprunt, J.C. Ogden, and S. Winckler, 161–186. National Audubon Society Research Report No. 7, New York.

Carney, K.M., and W.J. Sydeman. 1999. A review of human disturbance effects on nesting colonial waterbirds. *Waterbirds* 22:68–79.

Custer, T.W., and W.E. Davis. 1982. Nesting by one-year-old black-crowned night-herons on Hope Island, Rhode Island. *Auk* 99:784–786.

Custer, T.W., C.M. Bunck, and T.E. Kaiser. 1983a. Organochlorine residues in Atlantic Coast black-crowned night-heron eggs, 1979. *Col. Wat.* 6:160–167.

Custer, T.W., G.L. Hensler, and T.E. Kaiser. 1983b. Clutch size, reproductive success, and organochlorine contaminants in Atlantic Coast black-crowned night-herons. *Auk* 100:699–710.

Custer, T.W., G. Pendleton, and H.M. Ohlendorf. 1990. Within- and among-clutch variation of organochlorine residues in eggs of black-crowned night-herons. *Env. Monitor. Assess.* 15:83–89.

Davis, W.E., Jr. 1993. Black-crowned night-heron (Nycticorax nycticorax). In *The Birds of North America,* no. 74, ed. A. Poole and F. Gill. Philadelphia: Academy of Natural Sciences; Washington, D.C.: American Ornithologists' Union.

DeMauro, M.M. 1993. Colonial nesting bird responses to visitor use at Lake Renwick Heron Rookery, Illinois. *Natural Areas J.* 13:4–9.

Erwin, R.M. 1979. *Coastal Waterbird Colonies: Cape Elizabeth, Maine to Virginia*. U.S. Fish and Wildlife Service, Biological Services Program, FWS/OBS-79/10.

———. 1989. Responses to human intruders by birds nesting in colonies: Experimental results and management guidelines. *Col. Wat.* 12:104–108.

Erwin, R.M., and C.E. Korschgen. 1979. *Coastal Waterbird Colonies: Maine to Virginia, 1977.* An atlas showing colony locations and species composition. Newton Corner, Mass.: U.S. Fish and Wildlife Service, Biological Services Program, FWS/OBS-79/08.

Fleury, B.E., and T.W. Sherry. 1995. Long-term population trends of colonial wading birds in the southern United States: The impact of crayfish aquaculture on Louisiana populations. *Auk* 112:613–632.

Henny, C.J., and L.J. Blus. 1986. Radio-telemetry locates wintering grounds of DDE-contaminated black-crowned night-herons. *Wildl. Soc. Bull.* 14:236–241.

Henny, C.J., L.J. Blus, A.J. Krynitsky, and C.M. Bunck. 1984. Current impact of DDE on black-crowned night-herons in the intermountain West. *J. Wildl. Mgt.* 48:1–13.

Hoffman, D.J., B.A. Rattner, C.M. Bunck, A. Krynitsky, H.M. Ohlendorf, and R.W. Lowe. 1986. Association between PCBs and lower embryonic weight in black-crowned night herons in San Francisco Bay. *J. Toxicol. Env. Health* 19:383–391.

Jenkins, D., and L.A. Gelvin-Innvaer. 1995. Colonial wading birds. In *Living Resources of the Delaware Estuary,* ed. L.E. Dove and R.M. Nyman, 335–345. The Delaware Estuary Program.

Kane, R., and R.B. Farrar. 1976. 1976 coastal colonial bird survey of N.J. *N.J. Audubon* 2:8–14.

Kaufman, K. 1988. Immature night-herons. *Amer. Birds* 42:169–171.

L'Arrivee, L.P., and H. Blokpoel. 1990. Seasonal distribution and site tenacity of black-crowned night-herons, *Nycticorax nycticorax,* banded in Canada. *Canada Field-Nat.* 104:534–539.

Office of Natural Lands Management. 2000. *Special Vertebrate Animals of N.J.* Trenton: N.J. Natural Heritage Program, Division of Parks and Forestry, Department of Environmental Protection.

Ohlendorf, H.M., E.E. Klaas, and T.E. Kaiser. 1978. Environmental pollutants and eggshell thinning in the black-crowned night heron. In *Wading Birds,* ed. A. Sprunt, J.C. Ogden, and S. Winckler, 63–82. New York: National Audubon Society Research Report No. 7.

———. 1979. *Environmental Pollutants and Eggshell Thickness: Anhingas and Wading*

Birds in the Eastern United States. Special Scientific Report—Wildlife No. 216. Washington, D.C.: U.S. Department of Interior, Fish and Wildlife Service.

Ohlendorf, H.M., D.M. Swineford, and L.N. Locke. 1979. Organochlorine poisoning of herons. *Proc. Colonial Waterbird Group* 3:176–185.

Osborn, R.G., and T.W. Custer. 1978. *Herons and Their Allies: Atlas of Atlantic Coast Colonies, 1975 and 1976.* Newton Corner, Mass.: U.S. Fish Wildl. Serv., Biological Services Program, FWS/OBS-77/08.

Parsons, K.C., and J. Burger. 1981. Nestling growth in early- and late-nesting black-crowned night herons. *Col. Wat.* 4:120–125.

Peterson, R.T. 1969. Population trends of ospreys in the northeastern United States. In *Peregrine Falcon Populations—Their Biology and Decline,* ed. J.J. Hickey, 333–337. Madison: University of Wisconsin Press.

Riegner, M.F. 1982. The diet of yellow-crowned night-herons in the eastern and southern United States. *Col. Wat.* 5:173–176.

Rodgers, J.A., and H.T. Smith. 1995. Set-back distances to protect nesting bird colonies from human disturbance in Florida. *Cons. Biol.* 9:89–99.

Tremblay, J., and L.N. Ellison. 1979. Effects of human disturbance on breeding of black-crowned night herons. *Auk* 96:364–369.

Wiese, J.H. 1978. Heron nest-site selection and its ecological effects. In *Wading Birds,* ed. A. Sprunt, J.C. Ogden, and S. Winckler, 27–34. New York: National Audubon Society Research Report No. 7.

Yellow-Crowned Night-Heron

Bagley, F.M., and G.A. Grau. 1979. Aspects of yellow-crowned night heron reproductive behavior. *Proc. Colonial Waterbird Group* 3:165–175.

Burger, J., M. Gochfeld, and L.J. Niles. 1995. Ecotourism and birds in coastal New Jersey: Contrasting responses of birds, tourists, and managers. *Env. Cons.* 22:56–65.

DeMauro, M.M. 1993. Colonial nesting bird responses to visitor use at Lake Renwick Heron Rookery, Illinois. *Natural Areas Journal* 13:4–9.

Erwin, R.M. 1989. Responses to human intruders by birds nesting in colonies: Experimental results and management guidelines. *Col. Wat.* 12:104–108.

Niethammer, K.R., and M.S. Kaiser. 1983. Late summer food habits of three heron species in northeastern Louisiana. *Col. Wat.* 6:148–153.

Niethammer, K.R., T.S. Baskett, and D.H. White. 1984. Organochlorine residues in three heron species as related to diet and age. *Bull. Environ. Contam. Toxicol.* 33:491–498.

Price, H.F. 1946. Food of a yellow-crowned night heron. *Auk* 63:441.

Riegner, M.F. 1982. The diet of yellow-crowned night-herons in the eastern and southern United States. *Col. Wat.* 5:173–176.

Rodgers, J.A., and H.T. Smith. 1995. Set-back distances to protect nesting bird colonies from human disturbance in Florida. *Cons. Biol.* 9:89–99.

Watts, B.D. 1988. Foraging implications of food usage patterns in yellow-crowned night-herons. *Condor* 90:860–865.

———. 1989. Nest-site characteristics of yellow-crowned night-herons in Virginia. *Condor* 91:979–983.

———. 1991. Yellow-crowned night-heron. In *Virginia's Endangered Species,* ed. K. Terwiliger, 493–496. Blacksburg, Va.: McDonald and Woodward.

———. 1995. Yellow-crowned night-heron (*Nyctanassa violacea*). In *The Birds of North America,* no. 161, ed. A. Poole and F. Gill. Philadelphia: Academy of Natural Sciences; Washington, D.C.: American Ornithologists' Union.

American Bittern

Gibbs, J.P., and S.M. Melvin. 1992. American bittern, *Botaurus lentiginosus*. In *Migratory Nongame Birds of Management Concern in the Northeast,* ed. K.J. Schneider and D.M. Pence, 51–69. Newton Corner, Mass.: U.S. Department of Interior, Fish and Wildlife Service.

Gibbs, J.P., S. Melvin, and F.A. Reid. 1992. American bittern. In *The Birds of North America,* no. 18, ed. A. Poole, P. Stettenheim, and F. Gill. Philadelphia: Academy of Natural Sciences; Washington, D.C.: American Ornithologists' Union.

Harlow, R.C. 1913. Bittern breeding in N.J. *Auk* 30:268.

Kane, R. 1984. Breeding birds of Troy Meadows, 1984. *Rec. N.J. Birds* 10:77–80.

National Geographic Society. 1987. *Field Guide to the Birds of North America.* Washington, D.C.: National Geographic Society.

Temple, S.A., and B.L. Temple. 1976. Avian population trends in central New York state, 1935–1972. *Bird Banding* 47:238–257.

Thomas, S. 1982. The birdfinder's guide: Allendale Celery Farm. *Rec. N.J. Birds* 8:18–19.

Northern Goshawk

Block, W.M., M.L. Morrison, and M.H. Reiser, eds. 1994. The northern goshawk: Ecology and management. *Stud. Avian Biol.* 16.

Bosakowski, T., and R. Speiser. 1994. Macrohabitat selection by nesting northern goshawks: Implications for managing eastern forests. *Stud. Avian Biol.* 16:46–49.

Bosakowski, T., D.G. Smith, and R. Speiser. 1992. Niche overlap of two sympatric-nesting hawks, Accipiter spp. in the N.J.–New York Highlands. *Ecography* 15:358–372.

Crocker-Bedford, D.C. 1990. Goshawk reproduction and forest management. *Wildl. Soc. Bull.* 18:262–269.

Forbush, E.H. 1927. *Birds of Massachusetts and Other New England States.* Boston: Massachusetts Department of Agriculture.

Hausman, L.A. 1927. The hawks of N.J. and their relation to agriculture. *N.J. Agric. Exp. Sta. Bull.* 439:1–48.

Speiser, R., and T. Bosakowski. 1984. History, status, and future management of goshawk nesting in N.J. *Rec. N.J. Birds* 10:29–33.

———. 1987. Nest site selection by northern goshawks in northern N.J. and southeastern New York. *Condor* 89:387–394.

Squires, J.R., and R.T. Reynolds. 1997. Northern goshawk (*Accipiter gentilis*). In *The Birds of North America,* no. 298, ed. A. Poole and F. Gill. Philadelphia: Academy of Natural Sciences; Washington, D.C.: American Ornithologists' Union.

Cooper's Hawk

Benzinger, J., and R. Speiser. 1982. Breeding birds of N.J.'s Ramapo Mountains. *Rec. N.J. Birds* 8:24–26.

Bosakowski, T., and R. Speiser. 1992. Niche overlap of two sympatric-nesting hawks, Accipiter spp. in the N.J.–N.Y. highlands. *Ecography* 15:358–372.

Bosakowski, T., R. Speiser, D.G. Smith, and L.J. Niles. 1993. Loss of Cooper's hawk nesting habitat to suburban development: Inadequate protection for a state-endangered species. *J. Raptor Res.* 27:26–30.

Dodson, S.I., T.F.H. Allen, S.R. Carpenter, A.R. Ives, R.L. Jeanne, J.F. Kitchell, N.E. Langston, M.G. Turner. 1998. *Ecology.* New York: Oxford University Press.

Forman, R.T.T. 1995. *Land Mosaics: The Ecology of Landscapes and Regions.* Cambridge, U.K.: Cambridge University Press.

Holms, J., and C. Leck. 1993. Breeding bird survey of the D&R Canal State Park, 1990 and 1991. *Rec. N.J. Birds* 19:26–35.

Jones, S. 1979. The Accipiters—Goshawk, Cooper's Hawk, Sharp-shinned Hawk. Habitat Management Series for Unique or Endangered Species. Report No. 17, U.S. Bureau of Land Management, Technical Note 335.

Pattee, O.H., M.R. Fuller, and T.E. Kaiser. 1985. Environmental contaminants in eastern Cooper's hawk eggs. *J. Wildl. Mgt.* 49:1040–1044.

Rosenfield, R.N., and J. Bielefeldt. 1993. Cooper's hawk (*Accipiter cooperii*). In *The Birds of North America,* no. 75, ed. A. Poole and F. Gill. Philadelphia: Academy of Natural Sciences; Washington, D.C.: American Ornithologists' Union.

Rosenfield, R.N., and R.K. Anderson. 1988. Effectiveness of broadcast calls for detecting breeding Cooper's hawks. *Wildl. Soc. Bull.* 16:210–212.

Rosenfield, R.N., and W.A. Smith. 1985. Taped calls as an aid in locating Cooper's hawk nests. *Wildl. Soc. Bull.* 13:62–63.

Schriver, E.C. 1969. The status of Cooper's hawks in western Pennsylvania. 356–359. In *Peregrine Falcon Populations: Their Biology and Decline,* ed. J.J. Hickey. Madison: University of Wisconsin Press.

Snyder, N.F.R., H.A. Snyder, J.L. Lincer, and R.T. Reynolds. 1973. Organochlorines, heavy metals, and the biology of North American accipiters. *Bioscience* 23:300–305.

Temple, S.A., and B.L. Temple. 1976. Avian population trends in central New York state, 1935–1972. *Bird Banding* 47:238–249.

Red-Shouldered Hawk

Bednarz, J.C., and J.J. Dinsmore. 1981. Status, habitat use, and management of red-shouldered hawks in Iowa. *J. Wildl. Mgt.* 45:236–241.

Bosakowski, T., and R. Speiser. 1986. Apparent great horned owl predation on nesting red-shouldered hawks in N.J. *Rec. N.J. Birds* 12:44–45.

Brown, W.H. 1971. Winter population trends in the red-shouldered hawk. *Amer. Birds* 25:813–817.

Crocoll, S.T. 1994. Red-shouldered hawk (*Buteo lineatus*). In *The Birds of North America,* no. 107, ed. A. Poole and F. Gill. Philadelphia: Academy of Natural Sciences; Washington, D.C.: American Ornithologists' Union.

Dowdell, J., and C. Sutton. 1993. The status and distribution of breeding red-shouldered hawks in southern N.J. *Rec. N.J. Birds* 19:6–9.

Senchak, S.S. 1991. Home ranges and habitat selection of red-shouldered hawks in central Md.: Evaluating telemetry triangulation errors. Master's thesis, Virginia Polytechnic Institute and State University, Blacksburg.

Sutton, C.C., and P.T. Sutton. 1986. The status and distribution of barred owls and red-shouldered hawks in southern N.J. *Cassinia* 61:20–29.

Titus, K., and J.A. Mosher. 1981. Nest-site habitat selected by woodland hawks in the central Appalachians. *Auk* 98:270–281.

Titus, K., M.R. Fuller, D.F. Stauffer, and J.R. Sauer. 1989. Buteos. In *Proc. Northeast Raptor Management Symposium and Workshop,* 53–64. Washington, D.C.: National Wildlife Federation.

Windfelder, F. 1996. Taylor Wildlife Preserve. *Rec. N.J. Birds* 22:24–25.

Bald Eagle

Beans, B.E. 1996. *Eagle's Plume: The Struggle to Preserve the Life and Haunts of America's Bald Eagle.* New York: Scribner.

Brown, L.H., and D. Amadon. 1968. *Eagles, Hawks and Falcons of the World,* vol. 1. New York: McGraw-Hill.

Clark, K., and L. Niles. 1998. The making of a bald eagle nest. *N.J. Outdoors,* Spring 1998.

Clark, K.E., L.J. Niles, and W. Stansley. 1998. Environmental contaminants associated with reproductive failure in bald eagle (*Halieaeetus leucocephalus*) eggs in N.J. *Bull. Env. Contam. Toxicol.* 61:247–254.

Niles, L.J. 1995. Bald Eagle. In *Living Resources of the Delaware Estuary,* ed. L.E. Dove and R.M. Nyman, 359–366. Philadelphia: Delaware Estuary Program.

Nye, P.E. 1988. Bald eagle restoration in the Northeast United States, 1972–1987. In *Proceedings of the Northeast Raptor Management Symposium and Workshop,* ed. B.G. Pendleton, 264–269. National Wildlife Federal Scientific and Technical Series No. 13. Washington, D.C.: National Wildlife Federation.

Northern Harrier

Dunne, P. 1984. 1983 Northern harrier breeding survey in coastal N.J. *Rec. N.J. Birds* 10:3–5.

———. 1995. Northern harrier. In *Living Resources of the Delaware Estuary,* ed. L.E. Dove and R.M. Nyman, 381–385. Philadelphia: Delaware Estuary Program.

Fernandez, C. 1993. Human disturbance affects parental care of marsh harriers and nutritional status of nestlings. *J. Wildl. Mgt.* 57:602–608.

Godfrey, R.D., and A.M. Fedynich. 1987. Northern harrier (*Circus cyaneus*) predation on wintering waterfowl. *J. Raptor Res.* 21:72–73.

Harlow, R.C. 1913. The marsh hawk nesting in N.J. *Auk* 30:272.

Serrentino, P. 1989. Survey techniques for the northern harrier. In *Proceedings of the Northeast Raptor Management Symposium and Workshop,* 295–300. Washington, D.C.: National Wildlife Federation.

Simmons, R.E. 1983. Polygyny, ecology and mate choice in the Northern Harrier *Circus cyaneus (L.)*. Master's thesis, Acadia University, Wolfville, Nova Scotia.

Urner, C.A. 1925. Notes on two ground-nesting birds of prey. *Auk* 42:31–41.

Osprey

Clark, K.E. 1995. Osprey. In *Living Resources of the Delaware Estuary,* ed. L.E. Dove and R.M. Nyman, 395–400. Philadelphia: Delaware Estuary Program.

Clark, K.E., and C.D. Jenkins. 1993. Status of ospreys nesting in N.J., 1984 through 1993. *Rec. N.J. Birds* 19:74–77.

Henny, C.J., and W.T. VanVelzen. 1972. Migration patterns and wintering localities of American ospreys. *J. Wildl. Mgt.* 36:1133–1141.

Henny, C.J., M.A. Byrd, J.A. Jacobs, P.D. McLain, M.R. Todd, and B.F. Halla.1977. Mid-Atlantic coast osprey population: Present numbers, productivity, pollutant contamination, and status. *J. Wildl. Mgt.* 41:254–265.

Hughes, K.D., P.J. Ewins, and K.E. Clark. 1997. A comparison of mercury levels in feathers and eggs of osprey (*Pandion haliaetus*) in the North American Great Lakes. *Arch. Environ. Contam. Toxicol.* 33:441–452.

Peterson, R.T. 1969. Population trends of ospreys in the northeastern United States. In *Peregrine Falcon Populations: Their Biology and Decline,* ed. J.J. Hickey, 333–337. Madison: University of Wisconsin Press.

Poole, A.F. 1989. *Ospreys: A Natural and Unnatural History.* New York: Cambridge University Press.

Rymon, L.J. 1988. Osprey restoration in three northeastern states. In *Proceedings of the Northeast Raptor Management Symposium and Workshop,* 259–263. Washington, D.C.: National Wildlife Federation.

Spitzer, P.R. 1988. Osprey. In *Proceedings of the Northeast Raptor Management Symposium and Workshop,* 22–29. Washington, D.C.: National Wildlife Federation.

Steidl, R.J., and C.R. Griffin. 1991. Growth and brood reduction of mid-Atlantic coast ospreys. *Auk* 108:363–370.

Steidl, R.J., and L.J. Niles. 1991. Contaminant levels of osprey eggs and prey reflect regional differences in reproductive success. *J. Wildl. Mgt.* 55:601–608.

———. 1991. Differential reproductive success of ospreys in N.J. *J. Wildl. Mgt.* 55:266–272.

Wiemeyer, S.N., D.M. Swineford, P.R. Spitzer, and P.D. McLain. 1978. Organochlorine residues in N.J. osprey eggs. *Bull. Env. Contam. Toxicol.* 19:56–63.

Peregrine Falcon

Berger, D.D., C.R. Sindelar, and K.E. Gamble. 1969. The status of breeding peregrines in the eastern United States. In *Peregrine Falcon Populations: Their Biology and Decline,* ed. J.J. Hickey, 165–173. Madison: University of Wisconsin Press.

Cade, T.J. 1985. Peregrine recovery in the United States. In *Conservation Studies on Raptors,* ed. I. Newton and R.D. Chancellor, 331–342. ICBP Technical Publication No. 5. Cambridge: I.C.B.P.

Cade, T.J., J.H. Enderson, C.G. Thelander, and C.M. White, eds. 1988. *Peregrine Falcon Populations: Their Management and Recovery.* Boise, Idaho: Peregrine Fund.

Hickey, J.J. 1942. Eastern population of the duck hawk. *Auk* 59:176–204.

———, ed. 1969. *Peregrine Falcon Populations: Their Biology and Decline.* Madison: University of Wisconsin Press.

Hunter, R.E., J.A. Crawford, and R.E. Ambrose. 1988. Prey selection by peregrine falcons during the nestling stage. *J. Wildl. Mgt.* 52:730–736.

National Wildlife Federation. 1989. *Proceedings of the Northeast Raptor Management Symposium and Workshop.* Washington, D.C.: National Wildlife Federation.

Ratcliffe, D. 1980. *The Peregrine Falcon.* San Diego: Academic Press.

Rice, J.N. 1969. The decline of the peregrine falcon in Pennsylvania. In *Peregrine Falcon Populations: Their Biology and Decline,* ed. J.J. Hickey, 155–163. Madison: University of Wisconsin Press.

Schueck, L.S., M.R. Fuller, and W.S. Seegar. 1989. Falcons. In *Proceedings of the Northeast Raptor Management Symposium and Workshop,* 71–80. Washington, D.C.: National Wildlife Federation.

Steidl, R.J., C.R. Griffin, L.J. Niles, and K.E. Clark. 1991. Reproductive success and eggshell thinning of a reestablished peregrine falcon population. *J. Wildl. Mgt.* 55:294–299.

Black Rail

Braislin, W.C. 1900. Breeding of the little black rail (*Porzana jamaicensis*) in N.J. in 1844 and 1845. *Auk* 17:172–173.

Eddleman, W.R., F.L. Knopf, B. Meanley, F.A. Reid, and R. Zembal. 1988. Conservation of North American rallids. *Wilson Bull.* 100:458–475.

Eddleman, W.R., R.E. Flores, and M.L. Legare. 1994. Black rail (*Laterallus jamaicensis*). In *The Birds of North America,* no. 123, ed. A. Poole and F. Gill. Philadelphia: Academy of Natural Sciences; Washington, D.C.: American Ornithologists' Union.

Evans, J., and G.W. Page. 1986. Predation on black rails during high tides in salt marshes. *Condor* 88:107–109.

Harlow, R.C. 1913. Nesting of the black rail (*Creciscus jamaicensis*) in N.J. *Auk* 30:269.

Kerlinger, P., and C.C. Sutton. 1989. Black rail in New Jersey. *Rec. N.J. Birds* 15:22–26.

Kerlinger, P., and Widjeskog, L. 1995. Rails. In *Living Resources of the Delaware Estuary,* ed. L.E. Dove and R.M. Nyman, 425–431. Philadelphia: Delaware Estuary Program.

Kerlinger, P., and D.S. Wiedner. 1990. Vocal behavior and habitat use of black rails in south Jersey. *Rec. N.J. Birds* 16:58–62.

Sanderson, G.C. 1980. *Management of Migratory Shore and Upland Game Birds in North America*. Lincoln: University of Nebraska Press.

Stone, W. 1937. *Bird Studies at Old Cape May*. Philadelphia: Delaware Valley Ornithological Club.

Piping Plover

Burger, J. 1987. Physical and social determinants of nest-site selection in piping plover in N.J. *Condor* 89:811–818.

———. 1991. Foraging behavior and the effect of human disturbance on the piping plover (*Charadrius melodus*). *J. Coastal Res.* 7:39–52.

———. 1994. The effect of human disturbance on foraging behavior and habitat use in piping plover (*Charadrius melodus*). *Estuaries* 17:695–701.

Cairns, W.E. 1982. Biology and behavior of breeding piping plovers. *Wilson Bull.* 94:531–545.

Flemming, S.P., R.D. Chiasson, P.C. Smith, P.J. Austin-Smith, and R.P. Bancroft. 1988. Piping plover status in Nova Scotia related to its reproductive and behavioral responses to human disturbance. *J. Field Ornithol.* 59:321–330.

Haig, S.M. 1992. Piping plover. In *The Birds of North America*, no. 2, ed. A. Poole, P. Stettenheim, and F. Gill. Philadelphia: Academy of Natural Sciences; Washington, D.C.: American Ornithologists' Union.

Melvin, S.M., C.R. Griffin, and L.H. MacIvor. 1991. Recovery strategies for piping plovers in managed coastal landscapes. *Coastal Mgt.* 19:21–34.

Melvin, S.M., L.H. MacIvor, and C.R. Griffin. 1992. Predator exclosures: A technique to reduce predation at piping plover nests. *Wildl. Soc. Bull.* 20:143–148.

Melvin, S.M., A. Hecht, and C.R. Griffin. 1994. Piping plover mortalities caused by off-road vehicles on Atlantic Coast beaches. *Wildl. Soc. Bull.* 22:409–414.

Urner, C.A., and R.W. Storer. 1949. The distribution and abundance of shorebirds on the north and central N.J. coast, 1928–1938. *Auk* 66:177–194.

U.S. Fish and Wildlife Service. 1996. *Piping Plover (Charadrius melodus), Atlantic Coast Population, Revised Recovery Plan*. Hadley, Mass.

U.S. Fish and Wildlife Service. 2000. *1999 Status Update: U.S. Atlantic Coast Piping Plover Population*. Sudbury, Mass. http://pipingplover.fws.gov/status/.

U.S. Fish and Wildlife Service and N.J. Division of Fish, Game, and Wildlife. 1996. *Endangered Beach Nesting Bird Management on N.J.'s Municipal Beaches*. Pleasantville, N.J.

Vaske, J.J., D.W. Rimmer, and R.D. Deblinger. 1994. The impact of different predator exclosures on piping plover nest abandonment. *J. Field Ornithol.* 65:201–209.

Upland Sandpiper

Bowen, B.S., and A.D. Kruse. 1993. Effects of grazing on nesting by upland sandpipers in south-central North Dakota. *J. Wildl. Mgt.* 57:291–301.

Bowen, D.E., Jr. 1976. Coloniality, reproductive success, and habitat interactions in upland sandpipers (*Bartramia longicauda*). Ph.D. diss., Kansas State University, Manhattan, Kansas.

Carter, J.W. 1992. Upland sandpiper, *Bartramia longicauda*. In *Migratory Nongame Birds of Management Concern in the Northeast*, ed. K.J. Schneider and D.M. Pence, 235–252. Newton Corner, Mass.: U.S. Department of Interior, Fish and Wildlife Service.

Jones, A.L., and P.D. Vickery. 1997. Conserving Grassland Birds: Managing Large Grasslands Including Conservation Lands, Airports, and Landfills over 75 Acres for

Grassland Birds. Grassland Conservation Program, Center for Biological Conservation, Massachusetts Audubon Society, Lincoln, Mass.

Kirsch, L.M., and K.F. Higgins. 1976. Upland sandpiper nesting and management in North Dakota. *Wildl. Soc. Bull.* 4:16–20.

White, R.P. 1988. Wintering grounds and migration patterns of the upland sandpiper. *Amer. Birds* 42:1247–1253.

Red Knot

Baker, A.J., P.M. Gonzalez, T. Piersma, C.D.T. Minton, J.R. Wilson, H. Sitters, D. Graham, R. Jessop, P. Collins, P. de Goeij, M.K. Peck, R. Lini, L. Bala, G. Pagnoni, A. Vila, E. Bremer, R. Bastida, E. Ieno, D. Blanco, I. de Lima do Nascimento, S.S. Scherer, M.P. Schneider, A. Silva, and A.A.F. Rodrigues. 1999. Northbound migration of red knot *Calidris canutus rufa* in Argentina and Brazil. *Wader Study Group Bull.* 88:64–75.

Botton, M.L., R.E. Loveland, and T.R. Jacobsen. 1992. Overwintering by trilobite larvae of the horseshoe crab, *Limulus polyphemus,* on a sandy beach of Delaware Bay (New Jersey, USA). Marine Ecology Progress Series 88:289–292.

Brown, S., C. Hickey, and B. Harrington, eds. 2000. United States Shorebird Conservation Plan. Manomet Center for Conservation Sciences, Manomet, Mass.

Burger, J., and N. Tsipoura. 1998. Experimental oiling of sanderlings (*Calidris alba*): Behavior and weight changes. *Envir. Toxicol. and Chem.* 17:1154–1158.

Clark, K.E., L.J. Niles, and J. Burger. 1993. Abundance and distribution of migratory shorebirds in Delaware Bay, N.J. *Condor* 95:694–705.

Escudero, G., and L.J. Niles. 2001. Are there alternative food resources for knots in Delaware Bay? (abstract). *Wader Study Group Bull.* 95 (August 2001):13–14.

Harrington, B., with C. Flowers. 1996. *The Flight of the Red Knot: A Natural History Account of a Small Bird's Annual Migration from the Arctic Circle to the Top of South America and Back.* New York: W.W. Norton.

Morrison, R.I.G., and R.K. Ross. 1989. *Atlas of Nearctic Shorebirds on the Coast of South America.* 2 vols. Ottawa: Canadian Wildlife Service.

Myers, J.P., R.I.G. Morrison, P.Z. Antas, B.A. Harrington, T.E. Lovejoy, M. Salaberry, S.E. Senner, and A. Tarak. 1987. Conservation strategy for migrating species. *Amer. Sci.* 75:18–26.

Niles, L.J., M. Peck, and R. Lathrop. 2001a. Breeding habitat of the red knot in Nunavut, Canada (abstract). *Wader Study Group Bull.* 95 (August 2001):14.

Niles, L.J., K. Ross, and R.I.G. Morrison. 2001b. Survey of red knots in Tierra del Fuego (abstract). *Wader Study Group Bull.* 95 (August 2001):10.

Sitters, H. 2001. Behavioral evidence that shorebirds may suffer shortages of available horseshoe crabs' eggs in Delaware Bay (abstract). *Wader Study Group Bull.* 95 (August 2001):14.

Wander, W., and P. Dunne. 1981. Species and numbers of shorebirds on the Delaware Bayshore of N.J.—Spring 1981. Occas. Paper no. 140. *Rec. N.J. Birds* 7(4):59–64.

Roseate Tern

Buckley, P.A., and F.G. Buckley. 1981. The endangered status of North American roseate terns. *Col. Wat.* 4:166–173.

———. 1982. Population success and site-tenacity in saltmarsh-nesting common and roseate terns. *Col. Wat.* 5:57.

Burger, J., and M. Gochfeld. 1988a. Nest-site selection and temporal patterns in habitat use of roseate and common terns. *Auk* 105:433–438.

———. 1988b. Nest-site selection by roseate terns in two tropical colonies on Culebra, Puerto Rico. *Condor* 90:843–851.

———. 1991. Reproductive vulnerability: Parental attendance around hatching in roseate (*Sterna dougallii*) and common (*S. hirundo*) terns. *Condor* 93:125–129.

Gochfeld, M. 1983. The roseate tern: World distribution and status of a threatened species. *Biol. Cons.* 25:103–125.

Gochfeld, M., J. Burger, and I.C.T. Nisbet. 1998. Roseate tern (*Sterna dougallii*). In *The Birds of North America,* no. 370, ed. A. Poole and F. Gill. Philadelphia: Academy of Natural Sciences; Washington, D.C.: American Ornithologists' Union.

Kress, S.W., E.H. Weinstein, and I.C.T. Nisbet. 1983. The status of tern populations in northeastern United States and adjacent Canada. *Col. Wat.* 6:84–106.

Nisbet, I.C.T. 1984. Migration and winter quarters of North American roseate terns as shown by banding recoveries. *J. Field Ornithol.* 55:1–17.

———. 1990. The roseate tern. In *Audubon Wildlife Report 1989/1990,* ed. W.J. Chandler. San Diego: Academic Press.

Nisbet, I.C.T., and J.A. Spendelow. 1999. Contribution of research to management and recovery of the roseate tern: Review of a twelve-year project. *Waterbirds* 22:239–252.

Safina, C., J. Burger, M. Gochfeld, and R.H. Wagner. 1988. Evidence for prey limitation of common and roseate tern reproduction. *Condor* 90:852–859.

Least Tern

Atwood, J.L., and P.R. Kelly. 1984. Fish dropped on breeding colonies as indicators of Least Tern food habits. *Wilson Bull.* 96: 34–47.

Buckley, P.A., and F.C. Buckley. 1976. *Guidelines for Protection and Management of Colonially Nesting Waterbirds.* Boston: U.S. National Park Service.

Burger, J. 1984. Colony stability in Least Terns. *Condor* 86: 61–67.

———. 1988. Social attraction in nesting Least Terns: Effects of numbers, spacing, and pair bonds. *Condor* 90: 575–582.

———. 1989. Least Tern populations in coastal N.J.: Monitoring and management of a regionally endangered species. *J. Coastal Res.* 5: 801–811.

Burger, J., and M. Gochfeld. 1988. Defensive aggression in terns: Effect of species, density, and isolation. *Aggr. Behav.* 14: 169–178.

———. 1990. Nest site selection in Least Terns (*Sterna antillarum*) in N.J. and N.Y. *Col. Wat.* 13:31–40.

Carreker, R.G. 1985. Habitat suitability index models: Least Tern. *U.S. Fish Wildl. Serv. Biol. Rep.* 82(10.103).

Engstrom, T., G.S. Butcher, and J.D. Lowe. 1990. Population trends in the Least Tern (*Sterna antillarum*) from Maine to Virginia: 1975–1986. In *Survey Designs and Statistical Methods for the Estimation of Avian Population Trends,* ed. J.R. Sauer and S. Droege, 130–138. Biol. Report 90(1). Washington, D.C.: U.S. Fish and Wildlife Service.

Fisk, E.J. 1975. Least Tern, beleaguered, opportunistic, and roof-nesting. *Amer. Birds* 29: 15–16.

Goodrich, L.J. 1982. The effects of disturbance on reproductive success of the Least Tern (*Sterna albifrons*). M.S. thesis, Rutgers University, New Brunswick, N.J.

Jackson, J.A., and B.J.S. Jackon. 1985. Status dispersion, and population changes of the least tern in coastal Mississippi. *Col. Wat.* 8:84–62.

Kotliar, N.B., and J. Burger. 1984. The use of decoys to attract Least Terns (*Sterna antillarum*) to abandoned colony sites in N.J. *Col. Wat.* 7:134–138.

Moosely, L.J. 1979. Individual auditory recognition in the least tern (*Sterna albifrons*). *Auk* 96:31–39.

Sidle, J.G., J.J. Dinan, M.P. Dryer, J.P. Rumancik, Jr., and J.W. Smith. 1988. Distribution of the Least Tern in interior North America. *Amer. Birds* 42: 195–201.

Thompson, B.C., J.A. Jackson, J. Burger, L.A. Hill, E.M. Kirsch, and J.L. Atwood. 1997. Least tern (*Sterna antillarum*). In *The Birds of North America*, no. 290, ed. A. Poole and F. Gill. Philadelphia: Academy of Natural Sciences; Washington, D.C.: American Ornithologists' Union.

Tomkins, I.R. 1959. Life history notes on the least tern. *Wilson Bull.* 71:313–322

Black Skimmer

Blus, L.J., and C.J. Stafford. 1980. Breeding biology and relation of pollutants to black skimmers and gull-billed terns in South Carolina. Special Scientific Report—Wildlife, no. 230. Washington, D.C.: U.S. Department of the Interior, Fish and Wildlife Service.

Buckley, P.A., M. Gochfeld, and F.G. Buckley. 1977. Efficacy and timing of helicopter censuses of black skimmers and common terns on Long Island, New York: A preliminary analysis. *Proc. Colon. Waterbirds Group.* 1:48–61.

Burger, J. 1981a. Effects of human disturbance on colonial species, particularly gulls. *Col. Wat.* 4:28–36.

———. 1981b. Sexual differences in parental activities of breeding black skimmers. *Amer. Nat.* 117:975–984.

———. 1982a. Jamaica Bay studies: I. Environmental determinants of abundance and distribution of common terns (*Sterna hirundo*) and black skimmers (*Rynchops niger*) at an east coast estuary. *Col. Wat.* 5:148–160.

———. 1982b. The role of reproductive success in colony-site selection and abandonment in black skimmers (*Rynchops niger*). *Auk* 99:109–115.

Burger, J., and M. Gochfeld. 1990. *The Black Skimmer: Social Dynamics of a Colonial Species*. New York: Columbia University Press.

Erwin, R.M., J. Galli, and J. Burger. 1981. Colony site dynamics and habitat use in Atlantic Coast seabirds. *Auk* 98:550–561.

Gochfeld, M., and J. Burger. 1994. Black skimmer (*Rynchops niger*). In *The Birds of North America*, no. 108, ed. A. Poole and F. Gill. Philadelphia: Academy of Natural Sciences; Washington, D.C.: American Ornithologists' Union.

Quinn, J.S. 1989. Black skimmer parental defense against chick predation by gulls. *Anim. Behav.* 38:534–541.

Safina, C., and J. Burger. 1983. Effects of human disturbance on reproductive success in the black skimmer. *Condor* 85:164–171.

U.S. Fish and Wildlife Service and N.J. Division of Fish, Game, and Wildlife. 1996. *Endangered Beach Nesting Bird Management on N.J.'s Municipal Beaches*. Pleasantville, N.J.

Barred Owl

Allen, A.W. 1987. Habitat suitability index models: Barred owl. *U.S. Fish Wildl. Serv. Biol. Rep.* 82 (10.143).

Benzinger, J. 1994. Hemlock decline and breeding birds. II. Effects of habitat change. *Rec. N.J. Birds* 20:34–51.

Benzinger, J., and R. Speiser. 1982. Breeding birds of N.J.'s Ramapo Mountains. *Rec. N.J. Birds* 8:24–26.

Bosakowski, T. 1982. Status and habitat distribution of raptors in the Great Swamp Wilderness Area. *Rec. N.J. Birds* 8:63–67.

———. 1987. Census of barred owls and spotted owls. In *Proceedings on the Biology and Conservation of Northern Forest Owls*, 307–308. USDA Forest Service General Technical Report RM-142.

———. 1988. Barred owl. In *Proceedings of the Northeast Raptor Management Symposium and Workshop*, 114–120. Washington, D.C.: National Wildlife Federation.

———. 1994. Landsat reveals negative effect on forest fragmentation on barred owl distribution. *Rec. N.J. Birds* 20:66–70.

Bosakowski, T., R. Speiser, and J. Benzinger. 1987. Distribution, density, and habitat relationships of the barred owl in northern N.J. In *Proceedings on the Biology and Conservation of Northern Forest Owls*, 135–143. USDA Forest Service General Technical Report RM-142.

Bosakowski, T., J. Benzinger, and R. Speiser. 1989. Forest owl populations of the Pequannock Watershed. *Rec. N.J. Birds* 15:2–8.

Devereux, J.G., and J.A. Mosher. 1984. Breeding ecology of barred owls in the central Appalachians. *J. Raptor Res.* 18:49–58.

Earhart, C.M., and N.K. Johnson. 1970. Size dimorphism and food habits of North American owls. *Condor* 72:251–264.

Gutmore, D. 1977. Barred owl survey in the Pequannock Watershed. *N.J. Audubon* 3:184–185.

Johnson, D.H. 1987. Barred owls and nest boxes—results of a five-year study in Minnesota. In *Proceedings on the Biology and Conservation of Northern Forest Owls*, 129–134. USDA Forest Service General Technical Report RM-142.

Johnson, D.H., and D.G. Follen, Sr. Barred owls and nest boxes. *J. Raptor Res.* 18:34–35.

Kane, R., and M. Valent. 1986. 1986 north Jersey barred owl survey. *Rec. N.J. Birds* 12:69–70.

Laidig, K.J., and D.S. Dobkin. 1995. Spatial overlap and habitat associations of barred owls and great horned owls in southern N.J. *J. Raptor Res.* 29:151–157.

Mazur, K.M., and P.C. James. 2000. Barred Owl (*Strix varia*). In *The Birds of North America*, no. 508, ed. A. Poole and F. Gill. Philadelphia: Academy of Natural Sciences; Washington, D.C.: American Ornithologists' Union.

McGarigal, K., and J.D. Fraser. 1984. The effect of forest stand age on owl distribution in southwestern Virginia. *J. Wildl. Mgt.* 48:1393–1398.

Nicholls, T.H., and D.W. Warner. 1972. Barred owl habitat use as determined by radio-telemetry. *J. Wildl. Mgt.* 36:213–224.

Smith, C.F. 1978. Distributional ecology of barred and great horned owls in relation to human disturbance. M.S. thesis, University of Connecticut, Storrs.

Sutton, C. 1988. Barred owl survey of south Jersey, 1987. *Rec. N.J. Birds* 14:2–5.

Sutton, C., and P. Sutton. 1986. The status and distribution of barred owl and red-shouldered hawk in southern N.J. *Cassinia* 61:20–29.

Long-Eared Owl

Bosakowski, T. 1982. Food habits of wintering *Asio* owls in the Hackensack Meadowlands. *Rec. N.J. Birds* 8:40–42.

———. 1984. Roost selection and behavior of the long-eared owl (*Asio otus*) wintering in N.J. *J. Raptor Res.* 18:137–142.

Bosakowski, T., R. Kane, and D.G. Smith. 1989. Decline of the long-eared owl in N.J. *Wilson Bull.* 101:481–485.

———. 1989. Status and management of long-eared owl in N.J. *Rec. N.J. Birds* 15:42–46.

Duffy, K., and P. Kerlinger. 1992. Autumn owl migration at Cape May Point, N.J. *Wilson Bull.* 104:312–320.

Marks, J.S., D.L. Evans, and D.W. Holt. 1994. Long-eared owl (*Asio otus*). In *The Birds of North America*, no. 133, ed. A. Poole and F. Gill. Philadelphia: Academy of Natural Sciences; Washington, D.C.: American Ornithologists' Union.

Marti, C.D. 1976. A review of prey selection by the long-eared owl. *Condor* 78:331–336.

Moskowitz, D., T. Auffenorde, and M. Kovacs. 1997. Vegetation and surrounding landscape characteristics of long-eared owl (*Asio otus*) winter roosts in central N.J. *Rec. N.J. Birds* 23:2–6.

Russell, R.W., P. Dunne, C. Sutton, and P. Kerlinger. 1991. A visual study of migrating owls at Cape May Point, N.J. *Condor* 93:55–61.

Smith, D.G. 1981. Winter roost site fidelity by long-eared owls in central Pennsylvania. *Amer. Birds* 35:339.

Short-Eared Owl

Bosakowski, T. 1986. Short-eared owl winter roosting strategies. *Amer. Birds* 40:237–240.

Clark, R.J. 1975. A field study of the short-eared owl, *Asio flammeus* (*Pontoppidan*), in North America. *Wildl. Monogr.*, no. 47.

Earhart, C.M., and N.K. Johnson. 1970. Size dimorphism and food habits of North American owls. *Condor* 72:251–264.

Hanisek, G. 1978. Short-eared owls roosting in evergreen trees. *N.J. Audubon Res. Unit Suppl.* 4:40.

Holt, D.W. 1992. Notes on short-eared owl (*Asio flammeus*) nest sites, reproduction and territory sizes in coastal Massachusetts. *Can. Field-Naturalist* 106:352–356.

Holt, D.W., and S.M. Leasure. 1993. Short-eared owl (*Asio flammeus*). In *The Birds of North America*, no. 62, ed. A. Poole and F. Gill. Philadelphia: Academy of Natural Sciences; Washington, D.C.: American Ornithologists' Union.

Melvin, S.M., D.G. Smith, D.W. Holt, and G.R. Tate. 1989. Small owls. In *Proceedings of the Northeast Raptor Management Symposium and Workshop*, ed. B.G. Pendleton, 88–96. Washington, D.C.: National Wildlife Federation.

Sutton, P., and C. Sutton. 1995. Short-eared Owl. In *Living Resources of the Delaware Estuary*, ed. L.E. Dove and R.M. Nyman, 409–441. Philadelphia: Delaware Bay Estuary Program.

Urner, C.A. 1921. Short-eared owl nesting at Elizabeth, N.J. *Auk* 38:602–603.

———. 1923. Notes on the short-eared owl. *Auk* 40:30–36.

Red-Headed Woodpecker

Barnhart, R.K. 1986. *The American Heritage Dictionary of Science*. Boston: Houghton Mifflin.

Forbush, E.H. 1929. *Birds of Massachusetts and Other New England States*. Part II, *Land Birds from Bob-Whites to Grackles*. Boston: Massachusetts Department of Agriculture.

Ingold, D.J. 1989. Nesting phenology and competition for nest sites among red-headed and red-bellied woodpeckers and European starlings. *Auk* 106:209–217.

———. 1994. Influence of nest-site competition between European starlings and woodpeckers. *Wilson Bull.* 106:227–241.

Kilham, L. 1958a. Sealed-in winter stores of red-headed woodpeckers. *Wilson Bull.* 70:107–113.

———. 1958b. Territorial behavior of wintering red-headed woodpeckers. *Wilson Bull.* 70:347–358.

———. 1983. *Woodpeckers of Eastern North America*. New York: Dover.

Smith, K.G. 1986. Winter population dynamics of three species of mast-eating birds in the eastern United States. *Wilson Bull.* 98:407–418.

Smith, K.G., J.H. Withgott, and P.G. Rodewald. 2000. Red-headed woodpecker (*Melanerpes erythrocephalus*). In *The Birds of North America*, no. 518, ed. A. Poole and F. Gill. Philadelphia: Academy of Natural Sciences; Washington, D.C.: American Ornithologists' Union.

Wander, W., and S.A. Brady. 1980. Summer tanager and red-headed woodpecker in the pinelands. *Rec. N.J. Birds* 6:34–37.

Winkler, H., D.A. Christie, and D. Nurney. 1995. *Woodpeckers: A Guide to the Woodpeckers of the World*. Boston: Houghton Mifflin.

Sedge Wren

Benzinger, J., and S. Angus. 1992. Breeding birds of the northern N.J. highlands. *Rec. N.J. Birds* 14:22–41.

Burns, J.T. 1982. Nests, territories, and reproduction of sedge wrens (*Cistothorus platensis*). *Wilson Bull.* 94:338–349.

Dodson, S.I., T.F.H. Allen, S.R. Carpenter, A.R. Ives, R.L. Jeanne, J.F. Kitchell, N.E. Langston, and M.G. Turner. 1998. *Ecology*. New York: Oxford University Press.

Loggerhead Shrike

Anderson, W.L., and R.E. Duzan. 1978. DDE residues and eggshell thinning in loggerhead shrikes. *Wilson Bull.* 90:215–220.

Forbush, E.H. 1929. *Birds of Massachusetts and Other New England States*. Norwood, Mass.: Norwood Press.

Hanisek, G., and C. Club. 1977. The birdfinder's guide: Spruce Run Reservoir. *Rec. N.J. Birds* 3:35.

Morrison, M.L. 1981. Population trends of the loggerhead shrike in the United States. *Amer. Birds* 35:754–757.

Novak, P.G. 1989. Breeding ecology and status of the Loggerhead Shrike in New York state. Master's thesis, Cornell University, Ithaca, N.Y.

U.S. Fish and Wildlife Service. 1987. *Migratory Nongame Birds of Management Concern in the United States: The 1987 List*. Washington, D.C.: Office of Migratory Bird Management.

Yosef, Reuven. 1996. Loggerhead shrike: *Lanius ludovicianus*. In *The Birds of North America*, no. 231, ed. A. Poole and F. Gill. Philadelphia: Academy of Natural Sciences; Washington, D.C.: American Ornithologists' Union.

Bobolink

Bollinger, E.K., P.B. Bollinger, and T.A. Gavin. 1990. Effects of hay-cropping on eastern populations of the bobolink. *Wildl. Soc. Bull.* 18:142–150.

Bollinger, E.K., and T.A. Gavin. 1992. Eastern bobolink populations: Ecology and conservation in an agricultural landscape. In *Ecology and Conservation of Neotropical Migrant Landbirds*, ed. J.M. Hagan III and D.W. Johnston, 497–506. Washington, D.C.: Smithsonian Institution Press.

Cinquina, J. 1991. Breeding birds of Skylands Botanical Garden, Ringwood State Park, 1980–1990. *Rec. N.J. Birds* 17:46–50.

Gavin, T.A., and E.K. Bollinger. 1985. Multiple paternity in a territorial passerine: The bobolink. *Auk* 102:550–555.

Johnson, R.G., and S.A. Temple. 1990. Nest predation and brood parasitism of tallgrass prairie birds. *J. Wildl. Mgt.* 54:106–111.

Line, L. 1994. A summer without bobolinks. *Wildl. Cons.*, July–August, 35–43.

Martin, S.G., and T.A. Gavin. 1995. Bobolink (*Dolichonyx oryzivorus*). In *The Birds of North America*, no. 176, ed. A. Poole and F. Gill. Philadelphia: Academy of Natural Sciences; Washington, D.C.: American Ornithologists' Union.

Savannah Sparrow

Johnson, R.G., and S.A. Temple. 1990. Nest predation and brood parasitism of tallgrass prairie birds. *J. Wildl. Mgt.* 54:106–111.

Wheelright, N.T., and J.D. Rising. 1993. Savannah sparrow (*Passerculus sandwichensis*). In *The Birds of North America,* no. 45, ed. A. Poole and F. Gill. Philadelphia: Academy of Natural Sciences; Washington, D.C.: American Ornithologists' Union.

Grasshopper Sparrow

Johnson, R.G., and S.A. Temple. 1990. Nest predation and brood parasitism of tallgrass prairie birds. *J. Wildl. Mgt.* 54:106–111.

Vickery, P.D. 1996. Grasshopper sparrow (*Ammodramus savannarum*). In *The Birds of North America,* no. 239, ed. A. Poole and F. Gill. Philadelphia: Academy of Natural Sciences; Washington, D.C.: American Ornithologists' Union.

Windfelder, F. 1996. Taylor Wildlife Preserve. *Rec. N.J. Birds* 22:24–25.

Henslow's Sparrow

Barnhart, R.K. 1986. *The American Heritage Dictionary of Science.* Boston: Houghton Mifflin.

Burns, F.L. 1895. Notes from southern N.J.: Henslow's sparrow. *Auk* 12:189.

Dodson, S.I., T.F.H. Allen, S.R. Carpenter, A.R. Ives, R.L. Jeanne, J.F. Kitchell, N.E. Langston, and M.G. Turner. 1998. *Ecology.* New York: Oxford University Press.

Judd, S.D. 1897. Northern N.J. notes. *Auk* 14:326.

Rising, J.D. 1996. *A Guide to the Identification and Natural History of the Sparrows of the United States and Canada.* San Diego: Academic Press.

Samson, F.B. 1980. Island biogeography and the conservation of nongame birds. *Trans. North Amer. Wildl. Nat. Res. Conf.* 45:245–251.

Vesper Sparrow

Best, L.B., and N.L. Rodenhouse. 1984. Territory preference of vesper sparrows in cropland. *Wilson Bull.* 96:72–82.

Hausman, L. 1935. The sparrows of N.J. *N.J. Ag. Exp. Stat. Bull.* 553.

Rodenhouse, N.L., and L.B. Best. 1983. Breeding ecology of vesper sparrows in corn and soybean fields. *Amer. Midl. Nat.* 110:265–275.

Wray, T., and R.C. Whitmore. 1979. Effects of vegetation on nesting success of vesper sparrows. *Auk* 96:802–805.

REPTILES AND AMPHIBIANS

General References

Anderson, J.D., K.A. Hawthorne, J.M. Galandak, and M.J. Ryan. 1978. A report on the status of the endangered reptiles and amphibians of N.J. *Bull. N.J. Acad. Sci.* 23:26–33.

Bishop, S.C. 1994. *Handbook of Salamanders: The Salamanders of the United States, of Canada, and of Lower California.* Ithaca, N.Y.: Comstock Publishing Associates, Cornell University Press.

Carr, A. 1995. *Handbook of Turtles: The Turtles of the United States, Canada, and Baja California.* Ithaca, N.Y.: Comstock Publishing Associates, Cornell University Press.

Conant, R., and J.T. Collins. 1991. *A Field Guide to Reptiles and Amphibians of Eastern and Central North America.* 3rd ed. Peterson Field Guide Series. Boston: Houghton Mifflin.

Conservation and Environmental Studies Center, Inc. 1980. Reptiles and Amphibians of the N.J. Pinelands. Report prepared for the N.J. Pinelands Commission.

Cromartie, W.J., ed. 1982. New Jersey's endangered and threatened plants and animals. In *Proceedings of the Second Symposium on Endangered and Threatened Plants and Ani-*

mals of New Jersey. Pomona, N.J.: Stockton State College, Center for Environmental Research.

Martof, B.S., W.M. Palmer, J.R. Bailey, and J.R. Harrison III. 1980. *Amphibians and Reptiles of the Carolinas and Virginia.* Chapel Hill: University of North Carolina Press.

Office of Natural Lands Management. 1992. *Special Animals of N.J.* Trenton: Dept. of Environmental Protection and Energy.

Petranka, J.W. 1998. *Salamanders of the United States and Canada.* Washington, D.C.: Smithsonian Institution Press.

Tennant, A., and R.D. Bartlett. 2000. *Snakes of North America: Eastern and Central Regions.* Houston: Gulf Publishing.

Wright, A.H., and A.A. Wright. 1957. *Handbook of Snakes of the United States and Canada.* Vol. 1. Ithaca, N.Y.: Comstock Publishing Associates, Cornell University Press.

Wright, A.H., and A.A. Wright. 1994. *Handbook of Snakes of the United States and Canada.* Vol. 1. Ithaca, New York: Comstock Publishing Associates, Cornell University Press.

REPTILES

Bog Turtles

Arndt, R.G. 1977. Notes on the natural history of the bog turtle, *Clemmys muhlenbergi,* in Delaware. *Chesapeake Science* 18:67–76.

Arndt, R.G. 1986. Notes on the bog turtle, *Clemmys muhlenbergi,* in Warren County, N.J. *Bull. Md. Herp. Soc.* 22:56–61.

Barton, A.J., and J.W. Price. 1955. Our knowledge of the bog turtle, *Clemmys muhlenbergi,* surveyed and augmented. *Copeia* 1955(3):159–165.

Bury, R.B. 1979. *Review of the Ecology and Conservation of the Bog Turtle, Clemmys muhlenbergi.* Special Scientific Report—Wildlife No. 219. Washington, D.C.: U.S. Dept. of the Interior, Fish and Wildlife Service.

Ernst, C.H. 1977. Biological notes on the bog turtle, *Clemmys muhlenbergi. Herptelogica* 33:241–246.

Ernst, C., R.T. Zappalorti, and J.E. Lovich. 1989. Overwintering sites and thermal relations of hibernating bog turtles, *Clemmys muhlenbergi. Copeia* 1989(3):761–764.

Olohan, M.T. 1994. The minister's turtle. *N.J. Outdoors,* Fall 1994, 10–11.

Wood Turtle

Ernst, C.H. 1986. Environmental temperatures and activities in the wood turtle, *Clemmys insculpta. J. Herpetology* 20:222–229.

Farrell, R.F., and T.E. Graham. 1991. Ecological notes on the turtle *Clemmys insculpta* in northwestern N.J. *J. Herpetology* 25:1–9.

Rapp, M., and J.C. Sciascia. 1989. Wood turtle. *N.J. Outdoors,* September–October 1989, 40.

Strang, C.A. 1983. Spatial and temporal activity patterns in two terrestrial turtles. *J. Herpetology* 17:43–47.

U.S. Fish and Wildlife Service. 1995. Endangered and threatened wildlife and plants: 90-day finding for a petition to list the wood turtle (*Clemmys insculpta*) as threatened. *Federal Register* 60(102):27954–27955.

Marine Turtles

Burke, V.J., S.J. Morreale, and E.A. Standora. 1990. Comparisons of diet and growth of Kemp's Ridley and loggerhead turtles from the northeastern U.S. In *Proceedings of* the Tenth Annual Workshop on Sea Turtle Biology and Conservation. NOAA Tech. Mem. NMFS-SEFC-278.

Burke, V.J., S.J. Morreale, P. Logan, and E.A. Standora. 1992. Diet of green turtles (*Chelonia mydas*) in the waters of Long Island, N.Y. In *Proceedings of the Eleventh Annual Workshop on Sea Turtle Conservation and Biology*. NOAA Tech. Mem. NMFS-SEFSC-302.

Food and Agriculture Organization of the United Nations (FAO). 1990. *FAO Species Catalogue*, vol. 11: *Sea Turtles of the World: An Annotated and Illustrated Catalogue of Sea Turtle Species Known to Date*. Prepared by M.R. Marquez. FAO Fisheries Synopsis, no. 125. Rome: FAO.

Keinath, J.A., J.A. Musick, and R.A. Byles. 1987. Aspects of the biology of Virginia's sea turtles, 1979–1986. *Va. J. Sci.* 38:329–336.

Morreale, S.J., and E.A. Standora. 1998. *Early Life Stage Ecology of Sea Turtles in Northeastern U.S. Waters*. NOAA Tech. Mem. NMFS-SEFSC-413.

National Marine Fisheries Service. Green sea turtle. See *www.nmfs.noaa.gov/prot_res/species/turtles/green.html* (accessed Nov. 1, 2001).

———. Hawksbill sea turtle. See *www.nmfs.noaa.gov/prot_res/species/turtles/hawksbill.html* (accessed Nov. 1, 2001).

———. Loggerhead sea turtle. See *www.nmfs.noaa.gov/prot_res/species/turtles/loggerhead.html* (accessed Nov. 1, 2001).

Schoelkopf, R., and Stetzar, E. 1995. Marine turtles. In *Living Resources of the Delaware Estuary*. Philadelphia: Delaware Estuary Program.

U.S. Fish and Wildlife Service (USFWS). 1980a. Leatherback sea turtle. FWS/OBS-80/01.12.

———. 1980b. Green sea turtle. FWS/OBS-80/01.13.

———. 1980c. Hawksbill turtle. FWS/OBS-80/01.22.

———. 1980d. Kemp's (Atlantic) ridley sea turtle. FWS/OBS-80/1.30.

———. 1998. Sea turtles. Wildlife Fact Sheet. Available at *http://training.fws.library/pubs/turtle.pdf*.

Corn Snake

Davis, W.T. 1912. A corn snake from Lakehurst, N.J. *Proc. Staten Island Inst. Arts and Sci.* 89.

Zappalorti, R.T., and O. Heck. 1988. A captive breeding program of the corn snake, *Elaphe guttata*, with notes on a sampling program of released hatchlings in the N.J. Pine Barrens. In *Proceedings of the Twelfth International Herpetological Symposium on Captive Propagation and Husbandry*.

Northern Pine Snake

Burger, J., and R.T. Zappalorti. 1988. Habitat use in free-ranging pine snakes (*Pituophis melanoleucus*) in the N.J. Pine Barrens. *Herpetologica* 44:48–55.

———. 1989. Habitat use by pine snakes (*Pituophis melanoleucus*) in the N.J. Pine Barrens: Individual and sexual variation. *J. Herpetology* 23:68–73.

———. 1992. Philopatry and nesting phenology of pine snakes *Pituophis melanoleucus* in the N.J. Pine Barrens. *Behav. Ecol. Sociobiol.* 30:331–336.

Mitchell, J.C. 1994. *The Reptiles of Virginia*. Washington, D.C.: Smithsonian Institution Press.

Zappalorti, R.T., E.W. Johnson, and Z. Leszczynski. 1983. The ecology of the northern pine snake, *Pituophis melanoleucus melanoleucus* (Daudin) (Reptilia, Serpentes, Colubridae), in southern N.J., with special notes on habitat and nesting behavior. *Bull. Chicago Herpetol. Soc.* 18:57–72.

Queen Snake

See general reference list.

Timber Rattlesnake

Brown, W.S. 1992. Emergence, ingress, and seasonal captures at dens of northern timber rattlesnakes, *Crotalus horridus*. In *Biology of the Pitvipers*, ed. Jonathan A. Campbell and Edmund D. Brodie, Jr., 251–258. Tyler, Tex.: Selva.

———. 1993. Biology, Status, and Management of the Timber Rattlesnake (*Crotalus horridus*): A Guide for Conservation. Society for the Study of Amphibians and Reptiles, Herpetological Circular no. 22.

———. 1995. The female timber rattlesnake: A key to conservation. *Reptile and Amphib. Mag.* September–October, 12–19.

Galligan, J.H., and W.A. Dunson. 1979. Biology and status of timber rattlesnake (*Crotalus horridus*) populations in Pennsylvania. *Biol. Conserv.* 15:13–58.

Klauber, L.M. 1997. *Rattlesnakes: Their Habits, Life Histories, and Influence on Mankind.* Vol. 1. Berkeley and Los Angeles: University of California Press.

Martin, W.H. 1992. Phenology of the timber rattlesnake (*Crotalus horridus*) in an unglaciated section of the Appalachian Mountains. In *Biology of the Pitvipers*, ed. Jonathan A. Campbell and Edmund D. Brodie, Jr., 259–277. Tyler, Tex.: Selva.

Reinert, H. 1984a. Habitat variation within sympatric snake populations. *Ecology* 65:1673–1682.

———. 1984b. Foraging behavior of the timber rattlesnake, *Crotalus horridus*. *Copeia* 4:976–981.

Reinert, H.K., and R.T. Zappalorti. 1988. Timber rattlesnakes (*Crotalus horridus*) of the pine barrens: Their movement patterns and habitat preference. *Copeia* 4:964–978.

Rubio, M. 1998. Ensuring rattlesnake survival. In *Rattlesnake: Portrait of a Predator*, ed. Debbie K. Hardin and Deborah L. Sanders, 198–210. Washington and London: Smithsonian Institution Press.

AMPHIBIANS

Blue-Spotted Salamander

Anderson, J.D., and R.V. Giacosie. 1967. *Ambystoma laterale* in N.J. *Herpetologica* 23:108–111.

Bogart, J.P., and M.W. Klemens. 1997. Hybrids and genetic interactions of mole salamanders (*Ambystoma Jeffersonianum* and *A. laterale*) (Amphibia: Caudata) in New York and New England. *Amer. Mus. Novit.* (3218):1–78.

Chanda, D. 1993. The blue-spotted salamander. *N.J. Outdoors*, Spring 1993, 64.

DeMaynadier, P.G., and M.L. Hunter, Jr. 2000. Road effects on amphibian movements in a forested landscape. *Natural Areas J.* 20:56–65.

Hecnar, S.J., and R.T. M'Closkey. 1997. The effects of predatory fish on amphibian species richness and distribution. *Biol. Cons.* 79:123–131.

Hunter, M.L., J. Albright, and J. Arbuckle, eds. 1992. *The Amphibians and Reptiles of Maine.* Maine Agricultural Experiment Station, Bulletin 838.

Lowcock, L.A., L.E. Licht, and J.P. Bogart. 1987. Nomenclature in hybrid complexes of *Ambystoma* (Urodela: Ambystomatidae): No case for the erection of hybrid "species." *Syst. Zool.* 36:328–336.

Nyman, S., M.J. Ryan, and J.D. Anderson. 1988. The distribution of the *Ambystoma jeffersonianum* complex in N.J. *J. Herpetology* 22:224–228.

Uzzell, T.M. 1964. Relations of the diploid and triploid species of the *Ambystoma jeffersonianum* complex (Amphibia, Caudata). *Copeia* 1964(2):257–300.

Eastern Tiger Salamander

Anderson, J.D., D.D. Hassinger, and G.H. Dalrymple. 1971. Natural mortality of eggs and larvae of *Ambystoma t. tigrinum. Ecology* 52:1107–1112.

Arndt, R.G. 1989. Notes on the natural history and status of the tiger salamander, *Ambystoma tigrinum,* in Delaware. *Bull. Md. Herp. Soc.* 25:1–21.

Collins, J.T. 1997. Standard Common and Current Scientific Names for North American Amphibians and Reptiles. Society for the Study of Amphibians and Reptiles, Herpetological Circular no. 25.

Hassinger, D.D, J.D. Anderson, and G.H. Dalrymple. 1970. The early life history and ecology of *Ambystoma tigrinum* and *Ambystoma opacum* in N.J. *Amer. Midl. Nat.* 84: 474–495.

Semlitsch, R.D. 1983. Terrestrial movements of an eastern tiger salamander, *Ambystoma tigrinum. Herp. Review* 14:112–113.

———. 2000. Principles for management of aquatic-breeding amphibians. *J. Wildl. Mgt.* 64:615–631.

Zappalorti, R.T. 1995. Vernal pond breeders. In *Living Resources of the Delaware Estuary,* ed. L.E. Dove and R.M. Nyman, 321–330. Delaware Estuary Program.

Long-Tailed Salamander

Anderson, J.D., and P.J. Martino. 1966. The life history of *Eurycea l. longicauda* associated with ponds. *Amer. Midl. Nat.* 75:257–279.

———. 1967. Food habits of *Eurycea longicauda longicauda. Herpetologica* 23:105–108.

Bruce, R.C. 1982. Larval periods and metamorphosis in two species of salamanders of the genus *Eurycea. Copeia* 1982:117–127.

Eastern Mud Salamander

Bruce, R.C. 1974. Larval development of the salamanders *Pseudotriton montanus* and *P. ruber. Amer. Midl. Nat.* 92:173–190.

———. 1975. Reproductive biology of the mud salamander, *Pseudotriton montanus,* in western South Carolina. *Copeia* 1975:129–137.

Conant, R. 1957. The eastern mud salamander, *Pseudotriton montanus montanus:* A new state record for New Jersey. *Copeia* 1957:152–153.

Conservation and Environmental Studies Center, Inc. 1980. Reptiles and Amphibians of the New Jersey Pinelands. Report prepared for the N.J. Pinelands Commission.

Fowler, J.A. 1946. The eggs of *Pseudotriton montanus montanus. Copeia* 1946:105.

Petranka, James W. 1998. *Salamanders of the United States and Canada.* Washington, D.C.: Smithsonian Institution Press.

Pine Barrens Treefrog

Bunnell, J.F., and R.A. Zampella. 1999. Acid water anuran pond communities along a regional forest to agro-urban ecotone. *Copeia* 1999(3):614–627.

Freda, J., and P.J. Morin. 1984. Adult Home Range of the Pine Barrens Treefrog (*Hyla andersoni*) and the Physical, Chemical, and Ecological Characteristics of Its Preferred Breeding Ponds. Center for Coastal and Environmental Studies, Division of Pinelands Research, Rutgers University, New Brunswick, N.J.

Freda, J., and R.J. Gonzalez. 1986. Daily movements of the treefrog, *Hyla andersoni. J. Herpetology* 20:469–471.

Hulmes, D., P. Hulmes, and R.T. Zappalorti. 1981. Notes on the ecology and distribution of the Pine Barrens treefrog, *Hyla andersonii*, in N.J. *Bull. N.Y. Herp. Soc.* 17: 1–19.

Noble, G.K., and R.C. Noble. 1923. The Anderson tree frog (*Hyla andersonii*): Observations on its habits and life history. *Zoologica* 11:416–455.

Tiedemann, J.A. 1983. The occurrence of the Pine Barrens treefrog, *Hyla andersoni,* in Berkeley Township, Ocean County, N.J. *Bull. N.J. Acad. Sci.* 28:67–70.

Zampella, R.A., and J.F. Bunnell. 2000. The distribution of anurans in two river systems of a coastal plain watershed. *J. Herpetology* 34:210–221.

Southern Gray Treefrog

Grubb, J.C. 1972. Differential predation by *Gambusia affinis* on the eggs of seven species of anuran amphibians. *Amer. Midl. Nat.* 88:102–108.

Ritke, M.E., J.G. Babb, and M.K. Ritke. 1991. Breeding-site specificity in the gray treefrog (*Hyla chrysoscelis*). *J. Herpetology* 25:123–125.

FISH

Shortnose Sturgeon

Brundage, H.M. III, and R.E. Meadows. 1982. Occurrence of the endangered shortnose sturgeon, *Acipenser brevirostrum*, in the Delaware estuary. *Estuaries* 5(3):203–208.

Dadswell, M.J. 1979. Biology and population characteristics of the shortnose sturgeon (*Acipenser brevirostrum*) LeSueur 1818 (Osteichthyes: Acipenseridae) in the Saint John River Estuary, New Brunswick, Canada. *Can. J. Zool.* 57:2186–2210.

Dadswell, M.J., B.D. Taubert, T.S. Squiers, D. Marchette, and J. Buckley. 1984. Synopsis on biological data on shortnose sturgeon, *Acipenser brevirostrum* LeSueur 1818. NOAA Tech. Report, National Marine Fisheries Service 14, FAO Fisheries Synopsis no. 140.

Hastings, R.W., J.C. O'Herron II, K. Schick, and M.A. Lazzari. 1987. Occurrence and distribution of shortnose sturgeon, *Acipenser brevirostrum*, in the upper tidal Delaware River. *Estuaries* 10(4):337–341.

Meehan, W.E. 1910. Experiments in sturgeon culture. *Trans. Amer. Fish. Soc.* 39:85–91.

O'Herron, J.C. II, K.W. Able, and R.W. Hastings. 1993. Movements of shortnose sturgeon (*Acipenser brevirostrum*) in the Delaware River. *Estuaries* 16(2):235–240.

Taubert, B.D. 1980. Reproduction of the shortnose sturgeon (*Acipenser brevirostrum*) in Holyoke Pool, Connecticut River, Massachusetts. *Copeia* 1980:114–117.

INSECTS

Northeastern Beach Tiger Beetle

Cazier, M. 1954. A review of the Mexican tiger beetles of the genus *Cicindela* (Coleoptera: Cicindelidae). *Bull. Amer. Mus. Nat. Hist.* 103:227–310.

Hill, J.M., and C.B. Knisley. 1994. Current and Historic Status of the Tiger Beetles, *Cicindela d. dorsalis* and *Cicindela d. media* in N.J., with Site Evaluations and Procedures for Repatriation. Report to the U.S. Fish and Wildlife Service, Pleasantville, N.J.

Knisley, C.B., and J.M. Hill. 1992. Effects of habitat change from ecological succession and human impact on tiger beetles. *Va. J. Sci.* 43:133–142.

———. 1997. Experimental Methods for the Translocation of the Northeastern Beach Tiger Beetle, *Cicindela dorsalis dorsalis,* to Sandy Hook, N.J.—1995–1996 Study. Report to the U.S. Fish and Wildlife Service, Pleasantville, N.J.

———. 1998. Translocation of the Northeastern Beach Tiger Beetle, *Cicindela dorsalis*

dorsalis, to Sandy Hook, N.J.—1997. Report to the U.S. Fish and Wildlife Service, Pleasantville, N.J.

Knisley, C.B., J.I. Luebke, and D.R. Beatty. 1987. Natural history and population decline of the coastal tiger beetle, *Cicindela dorsalis dorsalis* Say (Coleoptera: Cicindelidae). *Va. J. Sci.* 38:293–303.

Stamatov, J. 1972. *Cicindela dorsalis* endangered on northern Atlantic coast. *Cicindela* 4:78.

U.S. Fish and Wildlife Service (USFWS). 1994. Northeastern Beach Tiger Beetle (*Cicindela dorsalis dorsalis* Say) Recovery Plan. Hadley, Mass.

American Burying Beetle

Amaral, M., and Prospero, M.L.N. 1999. One zoo, two islands, and a beetle. *Endangered Species Bull.* 24(3):10–11.

New York State Dept. of Environmental Conservation (NYDEC). 2001. American Burying Beetle Fact Sheet. See *http://www.dec.state.ny.us/website/dfwmr/wildlife/endspec/abbefs.html* (accessed May 1, 2001).

Raithel, C. 1991. American Burying Beetle Recovery Plan. U.S. Fish and Wildlife Service, Sept. 2, 1991.

Ratcliffe, B. 2001. The American burying beetle: An endangered species. See Nebraska Wildlife, *http://www.ngpc.state.ne.us/wildlife/beetle.html* (accessed May 1, 2001).

Wetzel, D. 2001. Captive reproduction and reintroduction of the American burying beetle. See Roger Williams Park Zoo, *http://www.cbsg.org/buryingb.htm* (accessed May 1, 2001).

LEPIDOPTERA

General References

Glassberg, J. 1999. *Butterflies through Binoculars: The East.* New York: Oxford University Press.

Gochfeld, M., and J. Burger. 1997. *Butterflies of New Jersey: A Guide to Their Status, Distribution, Conservation, and Appreciation.* New Brunswick: Rutgers University Press.

Iftner, D.C., J.A. Shuey, and J.V. Calhoun. 1992. Butterflies and Skippers of Ohio. Ohio Biological Survey Bulletin, new series, vol. 9, no. 1.

Opler, P.A., and V. Malikul. 1998. *A Guide to Eastern Butterflies.* New York: Houghton Mifflin.

Scott, James A. 1986. *The Butterflies of North America: A Natural History and Field Guide.* Stanford, Calif.: Stanford University Press.

Appalachian Grizzled Skipper

Allen, Thomas, 1998. *Butterflies of West Virginia and Their Caterpillars.* Pittsburgh: University of Pittsburgh Press.

Schweitzer, D.F. 1989a. A Review of Category 2 Insecta in USFWS Regions 3, 4, 5. Report prepared for the United States Fish and Wildlife Service.

———. 1989b. A Progress Report on the Identification and Prioritization of N.J.'s Rare Lepidoptera, 1981–1987. In *N.J.'s Rare and Endangered Plants and Animals,* ed. E.F. Karlin, 105–117, 235–237. Publ. of Institute for Environmental Studies, School of Theoretical and Applied Science, Ramapo College of N.J., Mahwah, N.J.

———. 1994. Element ecology and life history. In *The Comprehensive Report of Pyrgus wyandot.* NatureServe: An online encyclopedia of life [web application]. 2001. Version 1.5. Arlington, Virginia, USA: Association for Biodiversity Information. Available: http://www.natureserve.org (accessed Sept. 19, 2001).

Shapiro, A.M. 1974. Butterflies and skippers of New York State. *Search* 4:1–60.

Arogos Skipper

Schweitzer, D.F. 1992. Element ecology and life history. In *The Comprehensive Report of Atrytone arogos arogos*. NatureServe: An online encyclopedia of life [web application]. 2001. Version 1.5. Arlington, Virginia, USA: Association for Biodiversity Information. Available: *http://www.natureserve.org* (accessed Sept. 19, 2001).

Bronze Copper

See general references above.

Mitchell's Satyr

NatureServe: An online encyclopedia of life [web application]. 2001. Version 1.4. Arlington, Virginia, USA: Association for Biodiversity Information. Available: *http://www.natureserve.org* (accessed June 29, 2001).

Shuey, J., J.V. Calhoun, and D.C. Iftner. 1987. Butterflies that are endangered, threatened, and of special concern in Ohio. *Ohio J. Science* 87 (4):98–106.

U.S. Fish and Wildlife Service (USFWS). 1997. Recovery Plan for Mitchell's Satyr Butterfly (*Neonympha mitchelli mitchelli* French). Ft. Snelling, Minn.

Checkered White

Chew, F. 1977. The effects of introduced mustards (*Cruciferae*) on some native North American cabbage butterflies (*Lepidoptera: Pieridae*). *Atala* 5(2):13–19.

Schweitzer, D.F. 2001. *The Comprehensive Report of Pontia protodice*. NatureServe: An online encyclopedia of life [web application]. 2001. Version 1.5. Arlington, Virginia, USA: Association for Biodiversity Information. Available: *http://www.natureserve.org* (accessed Sept. 19, 2001).

Frosted Elfin

Schweitzer, D.F. 1994. Element ecology and life history. In *The Comprehensive Report of Callophrys irus*. NatureServe: An online encyclopedia of life [web application]. 2001. Version 1.5. Arlington, Virginia, USA: Association for Biodiversity Information. Available: *http://www.natureserve.org* (accessed Sept. 19, 2001).

Silver-Bordered Fritillary

See general references above.

BIVALVES: Freshwater Mussels

Anthony, J.L., and J.L. Downing. 1999. Extreme longevity in freshwater mussels (Family *Unionidae*) inferred from mark-recapture growth data. Abstract presented at the American Soc. of Limnology and Oceanography, Aquatic Sciences Meeting, Feb. 1–5, 1999.

Barfield, M.C., and G.T. Watters. 1998. Non-parasitic life cycle in the green floater (Conrad 1835). In Triannual Unionid Report no. 16, November. *http://ellipse.inhs.uiuc.edu/FMCS/TUR/TUR16.html*.

Bauer, G. 1992. Variation in the life span and size of the freshwater pearl mussel. *J. Anim. Ecol.* 61:425–436.

Bogan, A.E. 1993. Workshop on Freshwater Bivalves in Pennsylvania. Freshwater Molluscan Research, Inc.

Clarke, A.H. 1981. The Tribe *Alasmidontina* (*Unionidae: Anodontinae*), part 1: *Pegias, Alasmidonta,* and *Arciden*s. *Smithsonian Contrib. Zool.*

———. 1985. The Tribe *Alasmidontina* (*Unionidae: Anodontinae*), part 2: *Lasmigona* and *Simpsonaias*. *Smithsonian Contrib. Zool.* 399.

Fichtel, C. and D.G. Smith. 1995. *The Freshwater Mussels of Vermont.* Nongame and Natural Heritage Program, Vermont Fish and Wildlife Department, Technical Report 18.

Fuller, S.L. 1974. Clams and mussels (*Mollusca: Bivalvia*). In *Pollution Ecology of Freshwater Invertebrates,* ed. C.W. Hart, Jr., and S.L. Fuller. New York: Academic Press.

Goudreau, S.E., R.J. Neves, and R.J. Sheehan. 1993. Effects of wastewater treatment plant effluents on freshwater mollusks in the upper Clinch River, Virginia, USA. *Hydrobiologia* 252:211–230.

Helfrich, L.A., R.J. Neves, D.L. Weigmann, and R.M. Speenburgh. 1993. *Help Save America's Pearly Mussels.* Blacksburg, Va.: Virginia Polytechnic Institute and State University Press.

Hoggarth, M.A. 1992. An examination of the glochidia-host relationships reported in the literature for North American species of the *Unionacea* (*Mollusca: Bivalvia*). *Malacology Data Net,* 3(1–4):1–30.

Isom, B.G., and R.G. Hudson. 1984. Freshwater mussels and their hosts; physiological aspects. *J. of Parasitology* 70(2):318–319.

Kat, P.W. 1984. Parasitism and the *Unionacea* (*Bivalvia*). *Biol. Rev.* 59:189–207.

Layzer, J.B., M.E. Gorden, and R.M. Anderson. 1993. Mussels: The forgotten fauna of regulated rivers—a case study of the Caney Fork River. *Regul. Rivers Res. and Manage.* 8:63–71.

Lellis, W.A., and T.M. King. 1998. Release of metamorphosed juveniles by the green floater, *Lasmigona subviridis.* In Triannual Unionid Report no. 16, November. *http://ellipse.inhs.uiuc.edu/FMCS/TUR/TUR16.html.*

McMahon, R.F. 1983. Ecology of an invasive pest bivalve, *Corbicula.* In *The Mollusca,* vol. 6: *Ecology,* ed. W.D. Russel-Hunter. New York: Academic Press.

Michaelson, D.L., and R.J. Neves. 1995. Life history and habitat of the endangered dwarf wedgemussel, *Alasmidonta heterodon* (*Bivalvia: Unionidae*). *J. North Amer. Benthological Soc.* 14(2):324–340.

Miller, A., and D.A. Nelson. 1983. An Instruction Report on Freshwater Mussels. U.S. Army Corps of Engineers Instruction Report EL-83-2, Environmental Laboratory, U.S. Army Engineer Waterways Experiment Station, Vicksburg, Miss. 18 pp.

North Carolina Nongame and Endangered Wildlife Program. 2001. Atlas of North Carolina's Freshwater Mussels, *http://www.ncwildlife.org/pg07_WildlifeSpeciesCon/pg7b1a.htm* (accessed Nov. 1, 2001).

Ortmann, A.E. 1919. A monograph of the naiades of Pennsylvania, part 3: Systematic account of the genera and the species. *Memoirs of the Carnegie Museum* 8:1–384.

Sawhill, J. 1992. From the president. *Nature Conservancy,* November–December, 3.

Smith, D.G. 1986. Keys to the Freshwater Macroinvertebrates of Massachusetts (No. 1): *Mollusca Pelecypoda* (Clams, Mussels). Commonwealth of Massachusetts, publication no. 14, 676-56-300-12-86-CR.

Stolzenburg, W. 1992. The mussels' message. *Nature Conservancy,* November–December, 17–23.

Strayer, D. 1993. Macrohabitats of freshwater mussels (*Bivalvia: Unionacea*) in streams of the northern Atlantic slope. *J. North Amer. Benthological Soc.* 12(3):236–246.

U.S. Fish and Wildlife Service (USFWS). 1993. Dwarf Wedge Mussel (*Alasmidonta heterodon*) Recovery Plan. Hadley, Mass.

Watters, G.T. 1992. Unionids, fishes, and the species-area curve. *J. Biogeography* 19:481–490.

Williams, J.D., M.L. Warren, K.S. Cummings, J.L. Harris, and R.J. Neves. 1992. Conservation status of the freshwater mussels of the United States and Canada. *Fisheries* 18(9):6–22.

Index

Able, K. W., 233

accipiters, 57

airports, 104, 105, 108, 143, 165, 167, 251

American Museum of Natural History, NYC, 195, 222

amphibians, 210–231; salamander, blue spotted, 210–214; salamander, eastern mud, 222–224; salamander, eastern tiger, 214–218; salamander, long-tailed, 218–221; salamander, Trembley's, 210, 211; treefrog, pine barrens, 224–228; treefrog, southern grey, 228–231

Anitra tanker, 114

Arkansas, 238, 240

Assunpink Wildlife Management Area (WMA), 165

Atlantic City, 90, 104, 165

Atlantic County, 93, 194, 196, 222, 229

Atlantic Ocean, 19

Atlantic States Marine Fisheries Commission, 115

Audubon, John James, 170

Audubon Society Blue List of Imperiled Species, 33, 49, 60, 65, 106, 119, 141, 147, 150, 174

Audubon Watch, 114

Avalon/Stone Harbor (Seven Mile Beach), 81, 82, *83*

Baker, Allan, 113

Barnegat Bay, 190

bat: Indiana *(Myotis sodalis)*, 1–7; little brown *(Myotis lucifugus)*, 1–2; northern long-eared *(Myotis septentrionalis)*, 1–2

Beans, Bruce E., 1–7, 13–23, 185–193, 237–241

beetle: American burying *(Nicrophoorus americanus)*, 237–241

Bergen County, 11

birds, 30–175; bittern, American, 50–56; bobolink, 156–60; eagle, bald, 67–73; falcon, peregrine, 86–92; grebe, pied-billed, 30–35; harrier, northern, 73–79; hawk, Cooper's, 56–61; hawk, northern goshawk, 50–56; hawk, red-shouldered, 61–67; heron, black-crowned night-, 35–40; heron, yellow-crowned night-, 40–45; knot, red, 108, 116; osprey, 80–86; owl, barred, 129–133; owl, long-eared, 133–137; owl, short-eared, 137–143; plover, piping, 97–102; plover, upland, 102; rail, black, 92–97; sandpiper, upland, 102–108; shrike, loggerhead, 148–151; skimmer, black, 124–128; sparrow, grasshopper, 164–167; sparrow, Henslow's, 167–171; sparrow, Savannah, 160–164; sparrow, vesper, 171–175; tern, least, 120–124; tern, roseate, 116–120; woodpecker, red-headed, 143–148; wren, sedge, 148–151

birthrate, bat, 6

bittern, American *(Botaurus lentiginosus)*, 36, 45–50

bivalves, freshwater mussel, 257–266

bivalves, freshwater mussel: brook floater, 259–260; dwarf wedge, 258–259; green floater, 260–261; yellow lamp, 261–262

Block Island, Rhode Island, 238, 239, 240

Blue List of Imperiled Species. *See* Audubon Society

bobcat *(Felis refus)*, 23–29

bobolink *(Dolichonyx oryzivorus), 156*–160

Bowers-Altman, Jeanette, 232–237, 266

breeding biology of amphibians: salamander, 211–212, 213, 215–216, 220, 223; treefrog, *226–227,* 230

breeding biology of birds: bittern, 48–49; bobolink, 58; eagle, 69–70; falcon, 89; grebe, 32–33; harrier, 76; hawk, 54–55, 59, 64–65; heron, 38, 43; knot, 111; osprey, 82; owl, 131–32, 136, *140*–141; plover, *99*–100; rail, 94–95, 96, 97; sandpiper, 105; shrike, 153–154; skimmer, 126–127; sparrow, 162–163, 166, 169–170, 173–174; tern, 118, 122; woodpecker, 146; wren, 149–150

breeding biology of bivalves, 264

breeding biology of fish: sturgeon, 233

breeding biology of insects: beetle, 236, 239; lepidoptera, 242, 245, 247, 249, 251, 253, 255

breeding biology of mammals: bat, 3–4; bobcat, 25–27; whale, 20–21; woodrat, 9–10

breeding biology of reptiles: snake, 196, 199–200, 202, 206–207; turtle, 178–179, 182, 190

Breeding Bird Atlas, 55, 62

Breeding Bird Surveys, of: bittern, 49; bobolink, 159; harrier, 78; hawk, 55, 60; heron, 39; owl, 141; sandpiper, 106; shrike, 155; sparrow, 166, 170, 174; woodpecker, 147; wren, 150

Brigantine, 19,

Buckley, J., 233

bunting, bay-winged, 171

Bureau of Marine Fisheries, 23, 193

Burger, J., 40, 114, 200

Burlington County, 93, 105, 194, 222–223

butterfly. *See* lepidoptera

Canada, 254

Cape May, 17, 19, 231; birds at, 38, 81, 84, 88, 95, 106, 146, 157, 172

Carr, Archie, 186

cat, house, xv

Center for Remote Sensing and Spatial Analysis, Rutgers University, xvii

Champagne Island, 125

Chatsworth, Burlington County, 194

Chesapeake Bay, 190, 236

Chew, F., 252

Chile, South America, 114

Christmas Bird Counts, of: bittern, 49;

harrier, 78; hawk, 60, 66; owl, 139, 141; shrike, 155; sparrow, 163, 170, 174; woodpecker, 147; wren, 150

clam, Asian *(Corbicula fluminea),* 265

Clark, Kathleen, *xiii,* 67–73, 113, 214–218

Coastal Area Facility Review Act (CAFRA), 218, 230, 236

collecting: egg, 100, 123, 127, 132; feather, 119; snake, 196, 197–198, 200; turtle, 180, 184

Connecticut, 179, 207, 235; birds in, 34, 78, 95, 106, 142, 150, 166, 170, 174

contaminants, 72, 85, 147, 156, 214, 217, 221, 266; biocide, 249; DDE, 78, 84; DDT, ix, 38–39, 60, 78, 90, 91; herbicides, 151, 247; monitoring, 91; oil, 102, 114, 116; organochlorine, 85; PCBs, 38, 84, 85, 91; pesticide, 38–39

Convention on International Trade in Endangered Species (CITES), 184

cowbird, brown-headed *(Molothrus ater),* 158, 175

crab, horseshoe, 113–116

crayfish, as food source, 202, 203

crow, American *(Crovus brachyrhynchos),* 137

Cruickshank, 174

cultural history, xiv

Cumberland County, 95, 168

curlew, hudsonian *(Numeenius phaeopus),* 109

Dadswell, M. J., 233

DDE, 78, 84

DDT, 38–39, 60, 78, 90, 91, 155, ix. *See also* contaminants

death rate, bat, 6

Delaware, 17, 179

Delaware Bay, 85, 93, 94, 108–109, 110, 115

Delaware River, 142, 202, 233–234

DeMauro, M. M., 40

density, human population, ix, xiii

development, xiv–xvi, 60–61, 65, 106, 123, 166, 191, 192, 234,

diet of amphibians: salamander, 211, 215, 220, 223; treefrog, 226, 230

diet of birds: bittern, 47–48; bobolink, 157, 158; eagles, 69; falcon, 88; grebe, 32; harrier, 76; hawk, 53–54, 59, 64; heron, 37, 42–43; knot, 111; osprey, 81–82; owl, 131, 135–136, 140; plover, 98; rail, 94; sandpiper, 104; shrike, 153; skimmer, 126; sparrow,

162, 165, 169–170, 173; tern, 118,
121–122; woodpecker, 145; wren, 149
diet of bivalves, 264
diet of fish: sturgeon, 233
diet of insects: beetle, *236, 239;* lepidoptera, 242, 244, 247, 249, 251, 253,
255
diet of mammals: bat, 3; bobcat, 25;
whale, 19–20; woodrat, 9
diet of reptiles: snake, 195–196, 199,
202, 203, 206; turtle, 177, 182, 190
disease, 11, 12, 28, 192
distribution of amphibians: salamander,
211, 214–215, 218–219, 222; treefrog,
225, 229
distribution of birds: bittern, 47; bobolink, 157; eagle, *68;* falcon, *87–88;*
grebe, *31;* harrier, *74–75;* hawk, *51–
52, 57, 62–63;* heron, 36, *41–42;* knot,
109–110; osprey, *81;* owl, *130,* 135,
138–139; plover, *98;* rail, *93–94;* sandpiper, *103–104;* shrike, *152–153;* skimmer, *125;* sparrow, *161,* 164, *168–169,
172;* tern, *117, 121;* woodpecker, *144–
145;* wren, 148. *See also* migration
distribution of bivalves, 258–264
distribution of fish: sturgeon, *233*
distribution of insects: beetle, *235–236,
237–238;* lepidoptera, *242, 243–244,
246, 248, 251, 253,* 254
distribution of mammals: bat, 2; bobcat,
24; whale, 17–19; woodrat, 8
distribution of reptiles: snake, *194–195,
198–199, 202, 204;* turtle, *177, 181,
189–190*
Division of Fish and Wildlife, 11. *See also*
Endangered and Nongame Species
Dunne, Peter, 113

eagle, bald *(Haliaeetus leucocephalus),*
xvi–xvii, ix–xx, 67–73
Edwin B. Forsythe National Wildlife Refuge, Atlantic County, 90
eel, 115
Egg Harbor, 18
Endangered and Nongame Species Program (ENSP), DEP, xvi–xvii, ix–x, 11,
22–23, 28, 180, 193, 208; on birds, 42,
61, 72, 84, 86, 91, 124, 127–128; on
insects, 244, 249
endangered species: meaning of, xix;
role of, ix–x
endangered species acts, ix–x, 21–22,
22, 28, 71, 84, 184, 193, 234, 236, 243,
245
Essex whaling ship, 21

Fables, 93
falcon, peregrine *(Falco peregrinus),* ix,
xiii, xvi, xix, 78, 86–92
federal species status, xviii, xix, xx, 21.
See also status and conservation
fish, shortnose sturgeon, 232–234
Florida, 191, 192, 244
Freshwater Wetlands Protection Act, 6,
218, 221, 230

Garner, J. D. and J. E., 3–4
Gateway National Recreation Area,
Sandy Hook, 236, 237
Geographic Information System (GIS),
DEP, 266,
Geology Museum, Rutgers University,
18
Georgia, 179
Gochfeld, M., 40
Golden, David M., 198–203, 241–247,
243–245, 250–256
government. *See* New Jersey; status and
conservation; United States
Governor's Million-Acre Acquisition Pro-
gram, xvi
Great Lakes, 85, 266
Great Swamp, 145
grebe, pied-billed *(Podilymbus podiceps),*
30–31, 30–35, 33
Griscom, 174
gull: black-backed *(Larus marinus),* 115;
laughing *(Larus atrrricilla),* 115, 116

habitat: airport, 104–105, 108, 143, 165;
aquatic, 182, 219, 221, 246; Arctic,
110–111; bog, 180; cave/mine, 2–6;
cliff/ridge, 7–8, 88; desert, 24; ditch,
177; diversity of wildlife, xiv; freshwater, 257–259, 265–266; island, 42;
lake, 85; loss of, xvii; mapping of, 72,
208; marine, 190, 191; mountain, 8–
9, 24; ocean, 19, 233; protection from
invasive plants, 32; river, 233; suburban, 106, ; terrestrial, 182, 219–220,
221, 229, 231; thicket, 42; varied, 24–
25, 29, 37
habitat, agricultural/farm, 107–108, 137,
157–160, 163, 166–167, 170–171,
174; salt, 94, 95, 96
habitat, bay, 85, 93–94, 108–110, 114–
115, 142, 190, 233, 235–236
habitat, beach/coastal, 97–98, 101–102,
114, 119–121, 124–125, 128, 218,
230, 236, 259
habitat, forest, xvi, 195, 215, 218, 227,
244–245; birds in, 52, 55, 63–64, 66–

habitat, forest *(continued)*
67, 69–69, 130, 145, 147; pineland,
200, 201, 205–206, 225, 227, 228
habitat, grassland, 104–105, 106–108,
142–143, 158, 160, 166–167, 244
habitat, marsh, 32–33, 79, 86, 94, 96,
139–140, 142–143, 150–151
habitat, open, 75, 135–137, 153, 161–
162, 163–164, 172–173, 174, 175,
239, 242, 243, 251, 253, 254, 255,
256
habitat, pond, 211, 212, *213,* 215, 217,
218, 225, 227, *229, 231*
habitat, swamp, 24, 130–131, 145, 195–
196, 214, 216, 223, 225, *226,* 227
habitat, wetland, 6, 161, 163, 165, 177,
180, 227, 231, 247–248, 248, 249, 256;
birds in, 42, 47, 63–64, 67, 130–131,
133, 161, 163, 165
habitat of amphibians: salamander, 211,
215, 219–220, 223; treefrog, 225,
229
habitat of birds: bittern, 47; bobolink,
157; eagle, 68–69, 72; falcon, 88;
grebe, 32; harrier, 75; hawk, 52, 57–
59, 63–64, 75; heron, 37, 42; knot,
110–111; osprey, 81; owl, 130–131,
135, 139–140; plover, 98; rail, 94;
sandpiper, 104–105; shrike, 153; skimmer, 125; sparrow, 161–162, 165, 169,
172–173; tern, 118, 121; woodpecker,
145; wren, 149
habitat of bivalves, 257–266
habitat of fish: sturgeon, 233
habitat of insects: beetle, 236; lepidoptera, 242, 244, 246–247, 248, 251,
253, 255
habitat of mammals: bat, 2–3; bobcat,
24–25; whale, 19; woodrat, 8–9
habitat of reptiles: snake, 195, 199, 202,
205–206; turtle, 177, *182,* 190
Hall, Dr. John, 12
harrier, northern *(Circus cyaneus),* 73–79,
96
Harrington, Brian, 113
Hartmaier, Beth, 1–7
Hastings, R. W., 232, 233, 234
Hausman, L., 174
Hawaii, 192
hawk, 73–74; Cooper's *(Accipter cooperii),*
x, 56–61; fish, 81; marsh, 75; northern goshawk *(Accipter gentilis),* 50–56;
red-shouldered *(Buteo lineatus),* 61–67;
sharp-shinned *(Accipiter striatus),* 57
heron, x; black-crowned night- *(Nycticorax nycticorax),* 35–41, 46; yellow-

crowned night- *(Nyctanassa violacea),*
35, 40–45, 46
Hibernia Mine, Morris County, 2, 6
Hightstown, Mercer County, 238
Hill, J. M., 236
history, xiv
Hunterdon County, 77, 168
hunting, 200, 201; bird, 77, 100, 105–
106, 107, 123, 127, 158, 159; whale,
20–21, 22. *See also* collecting
hybrids, 212–13

ibis, glossy, x
identification of insects: lepidoptera,
bronze copper, *246*
identification of amphibians: salamander, *210, 212, 214, 216, 217,* 218–219,
222; treefrog, *224–25, 228–29*
identification of birds: bittern, 45–46,
48; bobolink, *156–157;* eagle, 67–68,
70, 71; grebe, *30–31, 33;* harrier, *73–*
74, *76;* hawk, 50–51, *53,* 56–57, *58,*
61–*62;* heron, *35–36, 40–41;* knot,
108–109; osprey, *80–81, 82, 83;* owl,
129–130, 133–135, 137–138, 140,
143–*144;* plover, *97–98;* rail, *92–93;*
sandpiper, 102–*103;* shrike, 151–*152,*
154; skimmer, 124–126; sparrow, *168,*
160–161, 164, 171–172; tern, 116–*117,*
120; woodpecker, 143–*144;* wren, *148*
identification of bivalves, 258–*264*
identification of fish: sturgeon, *232*
identification of insects: beetle, 235,
235, 237–238; lepidoptera, *241–242,*
243–244, 246, 248, 250, 252–253,
254, 255
identification of mammals: bat, 1–2;
bobcat, 23; whale, 13–17; woodrat,
7–8
identification of reptiles: snake, *193–*
194, 196, 198, 198, *199, 200, 201–202,*
203–204; turtle, *176–177, 178, 181,*
182, 185–186, 187–189
Illinois, 27
Indiana, 5, 6–7, 27, 207
Inman, Stephen, 18
insects, 235–56; beetle, American burying, 237–41; beetle, northern beach
tiger, 235–37; lepidoptera, 248–50;
lepidoptera, American burying, 237–
241; lepidoptera, Appalachian grizzled
skipper, 241–243; lepidoptera, arogos
skipper, 243–245; lepidoptera, bronze
copper, 246–247; lepidoptera, checkered white, 250–252; lepidoptera,
frosted elfin, 252–254; lepidoptera,

Mitchell's satyr, 248–50; lepidotera, silver-bordered fritillary, 254–256

International Piping Plover Census, 102

Iowa, 5, 27

Island Beach State Park, 19, 81, 82

Jenkins, Dave, 97–102, 120–124, 198–201

Kansas, 239

Kat, P. W., 265

Kearny Marsh, 33

Kentucky, 2, 4–5, 241

killdeer (*Charadrius vociferus*), 98

Knisley, C. B., 236

knot, red (*Calidris canutus*), 108–116

Lakehurst U.S. Naval Air Station, 169

Landscape Project, ENSP, xvii–xviii

Land Use Regulatory Program, xvi–xvii

Lazzari, M. A., 232, 233, 234

lepidoptera: Appalachian grizzled skipper (*Pyrus wyandot*), 241–243; argos skipper (*Atrytone arogos arogos*), 243–245; bronze copper (*Lycaena hyllus*), 246–247; checkered white (*Pontia protodice*), 250–252; Delaware skipper (*Anatrytone logan*), 243; frosted elfin (*Callophrys irus*), 252–254; Mitchell's satyr (*neonympha mitchelli mitchelli*), 248–250

license plate, Wildlife Conservation, xx

Liguori, Sherry: on amphibians, 210–231; on birds, 30–67, 73–108, 116–20, 124–175; on reptiles, 176–184, 193–198

limiting factors and threats to amphibians: frog, 227, 231; salamander, 213, 218, 221, 224

limiting factors and threats to birds: bittern, 49; bobolink, 159; eagle, 72; falcon, 91; grebe, 34; harrier, 78; hawk, 55–56, 60, 66; heron, 39, 44; knot, 114; osprey, 85–86; owl, 133, 137, 142; plover, 101; rail, 95–96; sandpiper, 106; shrike, 155–56; skimmer, 127; sparrow, 163, 167, 170, 174–175; tern, 119, 123; woodpecker, 147–148; wren, 150

limiting factors and threats to bivalves, 265

limiting factors and threats to fish: sturgeon, 234

limiting factors and threats to insects: beetle, 237, 240; lepidoptera, 243, 245, 247, 249, 251

limiting factors and threats to mammals: bat, 5–6; bobcat, 28; whale, 22; woodrat, 11–12

limiting factors and threats to reptiles: snake, 197–198, 200, 203, 208; turtle, 180, 184, 191

Maine, 28, 150, 166, 254

mammals, 1–29; bat, 1–7; bobcat, 23–29; whale, 13–23; woodrat, 7–12

Mammoth Cave, Kentucky, 2

mapping, 72, 208, 266

Marchette, D., 233

Marine Mammal Stranding Center, Brigantine, xx, 19, 189

Marlton, Burlington County, 222–223

Martha's Vineyard, MA, 235

Martin, W. H., 205

Maryland, 10, 179, 200, 201; birds in, 94, 95, 106, 142, 150, 155, 170

Massachusetts, 179, 207, 235, 236, 238, 240; birds in, 34, 78, 106, 142, 150, 155, 166, 170, 174

McDowell, Robert L., x

McGuire Air Force Base, 165

Melville, Herman, 21

Mercer County, 261

Mercer County Park, 165

Mexico, 191, 192

Middlesex County, 227

Migratory Bird Conservation Act of 1916, 106

Migratory Bird Treaty Act of 1918, 100, 119, 123, 127

Migratory Nongame Bird of Management Concern, xix

Missouri, 241

Moby Dick (Melville), 21

mockingbird, northern (*Mimus polyglottos*), 151

Moore's Beach, Delaware Bay, 114

Morreale, S. J., 189–190

Morris County, 2, 6, 11

mussel, 257–266; brook floater (*Alasimidonta varicosa*), 259–260; dwarf wedge (*Alasmidonta heterodon*), 258–259; eastern lamp (*Lampsillis radiata*), 262; eastern pond (*Ligumia nasuta*), 262–263; green floater (*Lasmigona subviridis*), 260–261; pocketbook (*Lampsilis spp.*), 265; tidewater mucket (*Leptodea ochracea*), 263; triangle floater (*Alasimidonta undulata*), 263–264; yellow lamp (*Lampsilis cariosa*), 261–262; zebra (*Dreissena polymorpha*), 265, 266

National Audubon Society. *See* Audubon
National Marine Fisheries Service (NMFS), 22–23, 193
National Shorebird Conservation Plan, 114
national. *See* United States
natural history, xiv
Nebraska, 239
Newark International Airport, 251
Newark Meadows, 139–141, 165
New Hampshire, 34, 78, 106, 150, 155, 170, 207
New Jersey: density of population in, ix, xiii; residents of, xviii, xx. *See also individual landmarks, cities, and counties*
New Jersey, species status in, xix. *See also* status and conservation
New Jersey Breeding Bird Atlas, 78, 93, 142, 163, 172
New Jersey Bureau of Marine Fisheries, 23, 193
New Jersey Department of Environmental Protection, xvi–xvii, 208. *See also* endangered and nongame species
New Jersey Division of Fish and Wildlife, x, 11, 27, 189
New Jersey Natural Heritage Program, xvii, xx; on amphibians, 212, 217, 220, 223–224, 227, 230; on hawk, 55, 60, 66; on heron, 39, 44; on owl, 132, 137, 141; on reptiles, 179, 183; on sparrow, 163, 166, 170, 174, 197; on other birds, 33, 49, 78, 85, 95, 101, 106, 127, 147, 150, 159
New Jersey Pinelands, 200, 201
New Jersey Sea Turtle Management Plan, 193
New York, 8, 10, 11, 179, 189–190, 195, 207, 235; birds in, 78, 95, 106, 142, 150, 153, 155, 166, 170, 174
Niles, Larry, *xviii*, 108–116
North Carolina, 179, 244
Northeast, 202–203

Ocean City, 18
Ocean County, 93, 229
odontoceti, order of, 13, 19, 20–21
Office of Natural Lands Management, 234
O'Herron, John C., II, *232, 233*, 234
Ohio, 10, 27, 207, 238
Oklahoma, 238, 240
Ontario, Canada, 254
osprey *(Pandion haliaetus)*, 78, *80*–86, ix–xx, xvi
owl, 91; barn *(Tyto alba)*, 130; barred

(Strix varia), x, xv, *129*–130; great horned *(Bubo virginianus)*, 66, 130, 135, 142, xv; long-eared *(Asio otus)*, 133–137; screech *(Otus asio)*, 135; short-eared *(Asio flammeus)*, 96, 137–143; swamp, 130
Oyster Creek Nuclear Generating Station, 189

Palisades, Bergen County, 11
Passaic County, 242
Passaic River, 213
Paturzo, Steve, 67–73
Pedricktown, 33
Penn, William, 17
Pennsylvania, 8, 11–12, 27, 178, 179, 207; birds in, 106, 142, 150, 155
pets, xv, 159, 184
Philadelphia, PA, 234
phragmites *(Phragmites australis)*, 95, 150, 151
Picatinny Arsenal, Morris County, 2, 11
Pine Barrens ecosystem, 225, 227, 228
Pinelands, 244, 245
Pinelands Commission, xvi
Pinelands National Reserve, 227
Pinelands Preserve, 55
Pinelands Protection Act, 197, 218
plants: invasive, 180
plover: Atlantic coast piping, 101; piping *(Charadrius melodus)*, 97–102, xvii; semipalmated *(Charadrius semipalmatus)*, 98; upland, 102
population, human, xviii, xx; density of, ix, xiii

raccoon *(Procyon lotor)*, 137
raccoon roundworm *(Baylisascaris procyonis)*, 11, 12
rail, black *(laterallus jamaicensis)*, *92*–97
raptor, ix–xx, 77–78, 80, 90
rat, Norway *(Rattus norvegicus)*, 7
recommendations for: beach replenishment, 102, 124; contaminants, 116, 151, 156, 214; contiguous/connected habitat, 29, 61, 175, 218; cooperation, 66, 72, 102, 107, 124, 128, 137, 156, 160, 171; genetic diversity, 231; grazing, 170, 177; replenishment of beaches, 124
recommendations for conservation and preservation: of breeding habitat, 151, 175; of farmland, 107, 160; of nesting habitat, 39, 44, 72, 79; of old growth forest, 133; of wetland, 231, 247, 256
recommendations for development and

human activity, 12, 61, 86, 92, 97, 198, 209; bird buffers, 34–35, 40, 45, 50, 56, 79, 96, 133, 143, 151; cooperative efforts, 66, 72, 102, 107, 124, 128, 137, 156, 160, 171; education, 102, 107, 128, 209; other buffers, 6, 184, 209, 230, 266

recommendations for information, monitoring, research and surveys, 7, 12, 23, 28, 192–93, 201, 203, 208, 209; on amphibians, 218, 220–221, 224, 230, 234; on birds, 50, 57–59, 86, 92–93, 97, 113, 123–124, 127, 132, 143, 151, 155; on insects, 237, 240, 241, 243, 245, 250, 254, 256

recommendations for management practices, xix, 137, 167, 175, 193, 203, 250; forest, 29, 147, 200–201; grassland, 107–108, 142–143, 170–171; incentive programs, 156, 167, 171; law enforcement, 49, 180, 192, 198; manmade habitats, 34, 79, 86, 91, 120, 198, 231; mapping, 72, 208, 266; marsh, 79, 142–43; nesting platforms, 88, 90, 91; predator control, 102, 116, 120, 124; protection guidelines, 266; public land acquisition and use, xvi–xvii, 133, 171; refuges, 151, 156; reintroducing species, 237, 241; warning system, 22–23, 228; water quality, 86, 184, 214, 221, 224, 228, 234, 266

recommendations for vegetative succession, 177, 180, 198, 256; for birds, 34, 107–108, 150–151, 156, 160, 163, 167, 170, 175

recommendations on amphibians: salamander, 213, 218, 221, 224; treefrog, 228, 231

recommendations on birds: bobolink, 160; eagle, 72–73; falcon, 91–92; grebe, 34–35; harrier, 79; hawk, 56, 61, 66–67; heron, 39–40, 44–45, 49–50; knot, 115–116; osprey, 86; owl, 133, 137, 142–143; plover, 102; rail, 96–97; sandpiper, 107–108; shrike, 156; skimmer, 128; sparrow, 163, 167, 170–171, 175; tern, 120, 123; woodpecker, 147–148; wren, 151

recommendations on bivalves, 266

recommendations on fish: sturgeon, 234

recommendations on insects: beetle, 237, 241; lepidoptera, 243, 245, 247, 250, 252, 254, 256

recommendations on mammals: bat, 6–7; bobcat, 29; whales, 22–23; woodrat, 12

recommendations on reptiles: snake, 198, 201, 203, 209; turtle, 180, 184, 192–93

refuges, wildlife, 151, 156, 167

reptiles, 176–209; snake, corn, 193–98; snake, northern pine, 198–201; snake, queen, 201–3; snake, timber rattle-, 203–209; turtle, bog, 176–180; turtle, marine, 185–193; turtle, wood, 181–184

residents, New Jersey, xviii, xx

Rhode Island, 78, 106, 166, 174, 235, 238, 239, 240

Rogers, J. A., 40

Roger Williams Park Zoo, Providence, RI, 240

rorquals, family of, 15–17, 20

Rutgers University, 18, 189, xvii

salamander: blue-spotted (Ambystoma laterale), 210–14; eastern mud (Pseudotriton montanus montanus), 222–224; eastern tiger (Ambystoma tigrinum tigrinum), 214–218, 231; Jefferson, 212; long-tailed (Eurycea longicauda longicauda), 218–221; Tremblay's (Ambystoma (2) laterale-jeffersonianum), 210, 211

Salem County, 85, 105

Salem Nuclear Power Plant, 189

sanderling (Charadrius alba), 98

sandpiper, upland (Bartramia longicauda), 102–108

Sandy Hook, 81

Schantz, Kris, 23–29, 203–209

Schick, K., 232, 233, 234

Schweitzer, D. F., 244, 245

scientist, Wildlife Conservation citizen, xx

Seven Mile Beach (Avalon/Stone Harbor), 81, 82, 83

Shapiro, A. M., 242

Sharpton, 165

shrike: loggerhead (Lanius ludovicianus migrans), 151–156; northern (Lanius excubitor), 151–152

Shriner, Charles, 113

skimmer, black (Rynchops niger), 124–128

Smith, H. T., 40

snake: corn (Elaphe g. guttata), 193–198; northern copperhead (Agkistrodon contortrix mokasen), 203–204; northern pine (Pituophis melanoleucus melanoleucus), 198–201; queen (Regina septemvittata), 201–203; red rat, 193; timber rattle (Crotalus horridus), 203–209

South America, 114
South Carolina, 179
South Dakota, 239
sparrow: grasshopper (Ammordramus savannarum), 164–167; Henslow's (Ammordramus henslowii), 167–171; Ipswich (Passerculus sandwichensis princeps), 161; savannah (Passerculus sandwichensis), 160–164; song (Melospiza melodia), 161, 171; vesper (Pooectes gramineus), 171–175
species: endangered or threatened, xix; exotic, 252, 265; of special concern, xix
species, entries on, xviii. See also breeding biology; diet; distribution; habitat; recommendations; status and conservation; and individual species
Squiers, T. S., 233
St. John River, Canada, 233
Standora, E. A., 189–190
status and conservation of amphibians: salamander, 212, 213, 217, 218, 220–221, 222; treefrog, 224, 227, 228, 230
status and conservation of birds: bittern, 45, 49; bobolink, 156, 158–159; eagle, 81; falcon, 86, 89–91; grebe, 30, 33–34; harrier, 73, 77–78; hawk, 50, 55, 56, 60, 61, 65–66; heron, 35, 38–40, 43–44; knot, 108, 113–114; osprey, 80, 83–85; owl, 129, 132, 133, 137, 141–142; plover, 97, 100–101; rail, 92, 95; sandpiper, 102, 105–106; shrike, 151, 154–155; skimmer, 124, 127; sparrow, 160, 163, 164, 166–167, 167, 170, 171, 174; tern, 116, 117, 119, 120, 123; woodpecker, 143, 146–147; wren, 148, 150
status and conservation of bivalves, 257, 265
status and conservation of fish: sturgeon, 232, 234
status and conservation of insects: beetle, 235, 236–37, 240; lepidoptera, 241, 242–243, 245, 246, 247, 248, 249, 250, 251, 253–254, 255–256
status and conservation of mammals: of bat, 1, 4–5; bobcats, 27–28; whale, 20–21; woodrat, 10–11
status and conservation of reptiles: snake, 198, 200, 201, 202, 203, 207–208; snake, corn, 193, 196–197; turtle, 176, 179–180, 181, 183–184; turtles, 185, 191
Stone, Witmer, 93, 106, 113, 146, 174

Stone Harbor (Avalon, Seven Mile Beach), 81, 82, 83
Stony Brook-Millstone Watershed, 168
sturgeon, shortnose (Acipenser brevirostrum), 232–234
Sussex County, 93, 249
swallow, cliff, x
swamp, 130–131

Taubert, B. D., 233
tern: common (Sterna hirundo), 99, 117; Forster's (Sterna forsteri), 117; least (Sterna antillarum), 99, 120–124; roseate (Sterna dougallii), 116–120
Tesauro, Jason, 176–180, 210–214, 243–245
Texas, 254
threatened species: meaning of, xix; role of, ix–x
treefrog: Cope's gray, 228; northern (Hyla versicolor), 229; Pine Barrens (Hyla andersonii), 224–228; southern gray (Hyla chrysoscelis), 228–231
Tsipoura, N., 114
Turnbull, 174
turnstone, ruddy (Arenaria itnerpres), 111
turtle, marine (sea), 185–193; Atlantic green (Chelonia mydas), 187–188, 189–193; Atlantic hawksbill (Eretmochelys imbricata), 188–189, 189–193; Atlantic leatherback (Dermochelys coriacea), 186–187, 189–193; Atlantic loggerhead (Caretta caretta), 185–186, 189–193; bog (Clemmys muhlenbergii), 176–180, xvii; Kemp's ridley (Lepidochelys kempi), 187, 189–193; wood (Clemmys insculpta), 181–184

U.S. Department of Environmental Protection (DEP): Geographic Information System (GIS) of, xvii; Land Use Regulation Program of, 208
U.S. Fish and Wildlife Service (USFWS), 5–6, 184, 237, 240, 244, 245; on birds, 49, 65, 78, 95, 102, 106, 114, 119, 141, 150
U.S. Geological Survey, xvii
United States government, on species status, xviii, xx. See also status and conservation
United States. See national; individual states

Valent, Michael, xv, 7–12, 23–29, 203–209

Vanderdonck, Dick, 17
Vermont, 106, 150, 155, 170, 207
Virginia, 42, 106, 150, 155, 170, 179, 237
volunteers, 72, 86, 208

Wallkill National Wildlife Refuge, Sussex County, 93
Warren County, 243, 249
West Virginia, 4–5, 200, 201
whale: baleen (Mysticeti), 13, 19, 20–21; baleen *(Mysticeti),* 13, 19, 20–21; black right, 17; blue *(Balaenoptera musculus), 14*–16, 18, 19, 20–21; fin *(Balaenoptera physalus), 14*–15, 18, 19, 20–21; humpback *(Megaptera novaeangliae), 16,* 18–19, 20–21; minke, 20; North Atlantic northern right whale *(Euba-* *laena glacialis), 17,* 18, 19, 20–23; *sei (Balaenoptera physalusborealis), 14*–15, 18, 19, 20–21; sperm *(Pyseter macro-cephalus), 13*–15, 18, 19, 20–21
whimbrel, 109
Wild Flora and Fauna Act, 184
wildlife. *See* identification; species
Wildlife Conservation Corps, xx
wildlife refuges, 151, 156, 167
woodpecker, red-headed *(Melanerpes ery-throcephalus),* 143–148
woodrat, Allegheny *(Neotoma magister),* xv, 7–12
wren, sedge *(Cistothorus platensis),* 148–151

Zappalorti, R. T., 200